FOUNDATIONS OF
CHILD AND YOUTH CARE

SECOND EDITION

CAROL
STUART
Vancouver Island University

Kendall Hunt
publishing company

Letters of Hope from www.lettersofhope.com with permission of Andree Cazebon.

Material retrieved from http://www.cyc-net.org used with permission.

"A Gender Sensitive Needs Assessment" from www.cyc.univ.ca used with permission.

Excerpts from *Journal of Child & Youth Care and Relational Child & Youth Care Practice* granted by Managing Editor, Vancouver Island University.

Cover image © Shutterstock, Inc.

Kendall Hunt
publishing company

www.kendallhunt.com
Send all inquiries to:
4050 Westmark Drive
Dubuque, IA 52004-1840

Printed in the United States of America
10 9 8 7 6 5 4 3 2

DEDICATION

To

Iain, my "life partner," and

"my girls,"

Kirstin,

Megan,

Shirol.

CONTENTS

PREFACE

This book is intended to introduce the field of child and youth care to people who are interested in becoming skilled and knowledgeable practitioners. Becoming a mature Child and Youth Care practitioner is a life-long process and my hope is that by reading this book, students will begin to master the reflective practice approach to learning and will develop the language that they need to undertake further learning. All the material is well referenced and instructors, students, and practitioners in the field are strongly encouraged to follow up the references to learn more about the concepts.

Child and youth care is a field in transition. The last 25–35 years of postsecondary education in Canada and the development of university-based programs is producing scholars who think, do, and live child and youth care. The second edition of this book aims to bridge the variety of approaches and definitions of child and youth care to the domains of practice grounded in history of the field. Readers will come to understand the original concepts of the field as it struggled to emerge as a distinct profession in the 1990s. They will also be introduced to critiques of these foundational ideas by scholars who challenge the traditions. These challenges are most evident in the way practitioners use theory on human development and theory on change to guide applied practice in the field.

I believe that child and youth care practice begins with the self and so all of the concepts and material discussed throughout the book are explored by considering various aspects of the self in relation to that material. Readers will encounter reflective exercises at the end of the chapters that will help them interact with the material. The reflective exercises will guide students and instructors through four aspects of learning (the format is introduced in Chapter 1):

1. An exercise with directions about what to focus on during the exercise in order to engage reflection-**in**-action/practice.
2. An exercise (or recalled experience) with specific questions to reflect on and learn from (reflection-**on**-action/practice).
3. An exercise that requires application to future practice with young people or families (reflection-**for**-action/practice).
4. A set of guided questions to apply theory (from the material in the book) to experience (theory-in-action).

Instructors may use or modify the exercises for classroom activities or assign them to students for additional work outside of class using a professional journal or portfolio. Some exercises address all four areas and others are limited to one or two.

In addition to the reflective exercises there are practice examples, case illustrations, personal reflections, tips, and resources throughout the book. These "boxes" provide concrete examples of some of the concepts discussed and enable readers to follow up for further information. There are many locations where students and instructors can download podcasts or videos to supplement the learning experiences. Rather than identifying relevant audio links in the text, the student and instructor are encouraged to review the following sites:

C2Y Podcasts: Discussions with, and for, young people, parents, and professionals who care about the youth social service system: http://c2ypodcast.podbean.com

The Learning Zone: www.learningzonenetwork.org/login/index.php

Many of the people who reviewed the book agreed that it seemed to cover "everything." The risk in trying to cover "everything" is that nothing is covered in depth and regional variations are lost. Individual readers and instructors will need to make decisions about where to follow a concept in more depth and what to leave out. Some concepts build the reader's understanding through several chapters and others are only captured briefly at a single point in time. My belief is, as novice practitioners learn more, the concepts introduced in this book can be understood with greater depth and clarity because the practitioner uses the reflective process to layer additional practice and theoretical knowledge onto their initial understanding.

The second edition includes some significant changes. Overall, I have made some changes to language, which is an attempt to follow the changing terminology within the field of practice/academia, as child and youth care is a rapidly developing discipline with multiple influences. This is a foundational text and students and new practitioners are in a phase of rapid professional growth and development. I have tried to both describe foundational concepts and at the same time offer a critical lens on some of those concepts so that readers and instructors can help students engage in praxis, reflecting on the underlying assumptions of those concepts in their own ways of being in the world. Language is reflective of culture and any attempt to neutralize the impact of culture makes communication convoluted. A simple example of this arose in the recommendation of one of the reviewers of the second edition. The suggestion was made that use of the terminology "parent" to refer to the primary caregiver within a young person's family was unfair and that "caregiver" would more fairly represent all young people, including those who had been raised by aunts, uncles, or grandparents. The problem with this solution is that "caregiver" is also used to refer to professionals who are early childhood educators and lay professionals who are foster parents, child and youth care assistants, and so on. For this reason "parent" has remained as the reference for the person in a unpaid relationship who has a responsibility in the eyes of North American society to raise a child. Resources and references have been updated to include a balance of Canadian and United States information reflecting a primarily North American perspective on the field.

From a practical perspective in the second edition, the following significant changes have been made:

- Chapter 1 has received minor updating and the referencing was enhanced to provide more resources for follow-up study.
- Chapters 2 and 3 from the first edition have been combined to address the historical perspectives on both childhood and the development of the profession.
- Chapter 3 has received minor updating and enhanced referencing.

- Chapter 4 has been refocused to a strength-based perspective with an increased emphasis on the social context as the "problem."
- Chapters 5–9 have been updated for language, references, and the inclusion of new and relevant research or theoretical thinking.
- Chapter 10 has been rewritten and reorganized to incorporate a critical perspective on theories and research in human development. This will facilitate students' critical thinking about theoretical perspectives that they learn in other coursework.
- Chapters 11 has been updated with material to facilitate critical thinking about the systems and structures that are representative of society.
- Chapter 12 has been updated to incorporate new thinking in the field of child and youth care that has redefined historical concepts of the therapeutic milieu, life-space intervention, and the therapeutic use of daily life events. Material reflecting the positive youth development movement has been added.

I often take inspiration from students and from the young people and families with whom I have worked, but none of the people's stories presented throughout the text are real, unless they are specifically attributed to the author. All the "case studies" are fictional representations of young people and families designed to illustrate the material in the text. The "Personal Reflections" throughout are "real" reflections from myself, practitioners, students, and young people who were willing to share parts of their learning journeys and therefore become a part of this learning journey.

Enjoy your journey!

ABOUT THE PHOTOGRAPHERS

In the first edition of this book all of the photographs were created by Jon Blak, who specializes in outdoor portraiture photography. He is also a former Crown Ward who continues to work with marginalized young people in Toronto and internationally. In the second edition, the photographic work of Laine Robertson has also been included. Laine makes an effort to explore photography that goes beyond traditional communication. She tries to express concepts through the simplicity of objects and people coupled with surreal photographic manipulation to change the viewer's perspective.

Images are powerful. Understand the history behind image-making so that they can be used responsibly.

ACKNOWLEDGMENTS

There are so many people who contributed to both editions of this book. It is impossible to thank them all. There are numerous people who influenced my thinking over the last 25 years and others who read chapters in their areas of expertise and gave vital feedback, helping make this a coherent whole.

The students of "Introduction to Child and Youth Care Practice" (CYC101) from 2006 to 2008 at Ryerson University were the guinea pigs for the early development of this material. Some of them are specifically acknowledged in the text because I used samples from their reflective journals. There was also a group of eight former students who read the first nine chapters of the first edition and offered helpful suggestions on everything from content to layout and design.

For the second edition I would like to acknowledge the instructors and coordinators of the child and youth care programs across Canada who have made use of the first edition of this text as well as the reviewers in Canada and the United States who provided valuable feedback that directed the revisions.

I would like to specifically acknowledge:

Dr. Thom Garfat, for his gentle and persuasive encouragement to find my voice and be less "academic."

Dr. Frances Ricks, a mentor who has inspired many things throughout my career and has always put aside her own thoughts and opinions to listen and reflect on what I need.

Dr. Kiaras Gharabaghi, a colleague with whom I have partnered on research and writing projects and is in his own right a "prolific writer."

Mr. Bill Carty and Ms. Mackenzie Dean were part of the research project "The Role of Competence in Outcomes for Children and Youth," which influenced the domains of practice that organize this work.

Ms. Caitlin McMillan was my research assistant for both the first and second editions. Twice now, she has read the entire text and commented. She summarized the comments of others, checked and found references, detailed glossary definitions, and generally did what needed to be done as we came down to the deadline.

Richard Ludlow, Charmayne McMurray, and Carla Kipper—the team at Kendall Hunt—who patiently kept me on track to complete the second edition and believed in the vision enough to keep the personal and relational examples of child and youth care as a field embedded in the text.

ABOUT THE AUTHOR

DR. CAROL STUART, B.A., B.P.H.E., M.ED., PH.D. (UVIC)

Dean, Health and Human Service Vancouver Island University Adjunct Professor, School of Child and Youth Care, Ryerson University, University of Victoria

Carol lives on the beautiful west coast of Canada on Vancouver Island with her husband and an assorted menagerie (domestic and wild). She was appointed at Vancouver Island University as the Dean of Health and Human Services in spring 2011.

Carol's career began in residential care in Ontario, Canada and she has 35 years of experience in the child and youth care field across three provinces. She has worked with in residential and community-based Child and Youth Care organizations and has been a faculty member at the Schools of Child and Youth Care with Grant MacEwan Community College (now University), University of Victoria and Ryerson University. Carol was the Director of the School of Child and Youth Care at Ryerson from 2003 to 2008 and was responsible for guiding the expansion of the School and the development of the full-time undergraduate degree program.

Carol's research interests include professional practice standards; integrated service delivery; the relationship between child and youth care competencies and outcomes for children and youth; participatory and qualitative approaches to research. She is the author of *"Foundations of Child and Youth Care"* and the co-author of *"Right Here, Right Now: Life-space Intervention for Children and Youth"* (2012-Pearson, Canada). Carol is the Managing Editor for *Relational Child and Youth Care Practice,* a Canadian journal for practitioners, educators, and researchers.

Carol has had a major role in developing the competencies and certification exams for child and youth care used in Alberta and in North America and is a certified CYC with Alberta, Ontario, and internationally with the Child and Youth Care Certification Board (CYCCB), Inc. She was a founding Board member and the chair of the Competency Review committee for CYCCB, Inc. Carol is the President of the Child and Youth Care Educational Accreditation in Board (CYCEAB) of Canada working towards accreditation of professional child and youth care education programs.

CHAPTER 1

DEFINING MOMENTS

Photo by Laine Robertson

CHAPTER OBJECTIVES

- To introduce the unique perspectives from which child and youth care practice emerged.
- To define the scope of child and youth care practice from multiple perspectives.
- To describe six core characteristics of child and youth care practice: passion, caring, the milieu, social competence, space and time, and experiential.
- To demonstrate the importance of personal reflection.

Child and youth care emerged as a new human services profession at the end of World War II. The profession has been defined by its history and the experiences of early leaders who worked with displaced young people. In the next few pages you will read about the essential characteristics of child and youth care, including its experiential nature. The stories, exercises, and pictures throughout this book are designed to help you to connect new ideas and concepts to your existing knowledge and experience, as well as to reflect on and learn from the experience of others.

DEFINING MOMENTS: MY EARLY STORIES

Stories are a wonderful way to learn and to share experiences with others. They are often used in practice to help children learn metaphorically. Michael Burns (1999, 2008) reminds us that storytelling, one of the oldest methods of teaching developed by humans, has been practiced since our early existence. Early in your professional career there will be moments that "define" your career and your understanding of child and youth care. Those moments and stories will stay with you throughout your career and each time that you reflect on them, you will learn something new. There are two defining moments that stand out from my early child and youth care practice that I will share as you begin your own journey of understanding this profession and the work that practitioners undertake.

PERSONAL REFLECTION

I spent most of my summers during adolescence and early adulthood working at summer camps. One of those camps had a transformational impact on my career choice and the rest of my life. I left university at the end of that summer and was hired by the agency to work as a child and youth care practitioner. That summer experience defined who I am as a practitioner, and as I learned more and developed my practice I have revisited these stories and others from that summer to understand their importance to me. The importance of meaningfulness is evident in this first reflection.

My summer job between third and fourth year in university, as I was completing my degree in psychology and physical education, was as a lifeguard and waterfront programmer at a summer camp for children with emotional problems. I was not yet a child and youth care practitioner. Prior to the start of camp in July, all the summer staff worked through the Northern Ontario blackfly season (May and June) to prepare the wilderness environment for the arrival of the children. The children lived in treatment homes in various towns throughout the province. Each "home" moved to a "campsite" in early July. The staff and children lived together, in the wilderness in tents on sites equipped with rough wooden kitchen shelters. As summer staff we helped to prepare tent sites and build shelters in the woods where nothing had previously existed except porcupines and bears. We were assisted by a "crew" of staff and young people who lived in the group homes operated by the agency in the town closest to the camp property.

On one of those hot, early summer days, I walked toward the next site location to be cleared with a young resident of one of the homes, whom I'd just met. He walked very close to me and talked about how he felt and about some of his personal history. While I'd just met him, I was comfortable with the distance between us–even though he was close enough to brush my arm occasionally. Even though we had just met, we seemed (to me) to be immersed in a very personal conversation about his family and his life. My experience to this point with young people was that there were certain social niceties that were expected before beginning to talk about more personal thoughts and feelings. I do not recall the specifics of the conversation, only the feeling that he was comfortable and that the conversation was meaningful.

Carol Stuart

Mark Krueger (2007a) says that the technique of "storying" is fundamental to our understanding of self and how we bring our self to child and youth care practice. That particular moment with that young person—a teenage client—represents for me the personal, intimate moments that occur with young people as we help them to develop, grow, and relate to the world around them. It was the ease with which people were open and personal throughout that summer camp experience that attracted me to the work. Some would suggest that the young man had no boundaries and revealed too much personal information to someone whom he didn't know and had just met. I was quite comfortable with him, and general social conversation—about the weather, for example—would have seemed difficult and awkward. I believe that we work with young people and families who are struggling to make their way in the world, and therefore we need personal information. We are paid for our time to help them, not for social conversations. However, as I have grown and matured in my practice, I have come to recognize that helping may also involve modeling social conversation in the day-to-day environment or being personal without revealing personal information. These beliefs are all part of my evolving worldview and I bring them to the relationships that I develop in my work with young people and with the practitioners that work with young people.

PERSONAL REFLECTION

When my father retired from teaching he asked that we all join him at the honourary retirement dinner and "roast." As with most fathers, he was proud of his children—although we didn't exactly follow his definition of a career path. His thinking about careers was rather traditional and he had not approved of me leaving university before I graduated to work at the group home. He wanted his coworkers to meet his (adult) children at this retirement event. I was introduced as "the Executive Director of a Residential Treatment Centre" for teenagers. I was surprised by the introduction. I didn't think he knew what I did. I'd been working as a child and youth worker for 7 years and had just recently taken over the management of an eight-bed treatment home after returning to finish my undergraduate degree and then completing my master's degree. Up to that point, he had never really asked about my work or seemed to understand what I did. With his introduction, I realized that he did understand my work. Upon reflection, I also believe that, because I had "status" as the manager or director, he was able to find the words to describe this to his colleagues, which perhaps he didn't have before.

Carol Stuart

Defining the field of child and youth care and describing it to other professionals, even those with similar backgrounds such as teachers, has been an ongoing dilemma throughout my career. It has posed both personal and professional challenges. Social conversation almost inevitably turns to "What do you do?" and answering the question with "I'm a child and youth care practitioner" has frequently required a follow-up explanation. Educators and professional associations have tried to help new practitioners with this task by creating definitions of the field. As you begin a career in child and youth care you need ways to describe what you do and to help others to understand your work and the value of working with young people and their families who may be cast off, actively disempowered, or simply ignored by adults in today's society.

Attempts to define child and youth care practice have been ongoing since the 1970s. These debates about what we do are part of our evolution. We are not unique in our struggle for identity; such debates are also found in other professions. Debates about how to define the child and youth care profession have helped to promote and develop the field of study and the field of practice, adding to its knowledge base.

The term "child care work" first emerged consistently in North American literature in the 1960s, around the same time that training and educational programs began to develop. Terminology eventually expanded to "child and *youth* care" work in recognition of the different ages and stages of childhood. Training and education for workers were necessary because the young people who were removed from the home and placed in mental health and juvenile justice institutions were challenging to work with and had significant needs beyond just care and supervision. Early training and writing in North America focused on residential treatment, even though practice subsequently expanded beyond the residential setting; "educateurs" were the European equivalent to child and youth care and were involved in residential care, streetwork, and community settings from the beginning of their development. The next section explores the occupational title and the varied definitions developed by leaders in the field as it emerged in North America.

DEFINING MOMENTS: NAMING A PROFESSION?

> I have deliberately abstained from calling them houseparents, since this title is a misnomer. . . . The title of child-care worker should not include the concept of parent substitute. Since in modern institutions most children have at least one living parent, nothing should permit the misinterpretation that institutional care is meant to be substitute family care. . . . This identification with a parent figure depends on the child's readiness for such a relationship. . . . Any administrative assignment to parenthood—even in title only—seems to me harmful rather than helpful to the child at the institution. I have chosen, therefore, the title of child-care worker . . . (Mayer, 1958, p. xii)

This opening quote captures how the early leaders in the field began to define the nature of the profession. An early book that still captures the imagination of new practitioners is *The Other 23 Hours: Child Care Work with Emotionally Disturbed Children in a Therapeutic Milieu* (Trieschman, Whittaker, & Brendtro, 1969). This classic defines child and youth care practice, in its title, as work with **emotionally disturbed**[1] children in residential settings. Definitions were not so important at that time because the field focused on residential care settings. The concerns of the

---

[1] This book includes a glossary, where terms such as this are explained in more detail. Glossary terms are **bolded** at first mention.

leaders centered on people who were already practicing and helping them learn about how to provide good care and treatment for children. Training and education was for people already working in the new field.

Later, as postsecondary educational institutions began to offer pre-service training for child and youth care practitioners, it was necessary to develop a way of explaining what it was that students would be learning and what type of work they would be prepared for, since the students were not

Tips and Resources

Books such as *Controls from Within: Techniques for the Treatment of the Aggressive Child* (Redl & Wineman, 1952); *Group Work in the Institution* (Konopka, 1954); *Group Work as Part of Residential Treatment* (Maier, 1965); *Cottage Six: The Social System of Delinquent Boys in Residential Treatment* (Polsky, 1966); and *When We Deal with Children* (Redl, 1966) formed the basis of training and professional development in the new field.

immersed in practice and were less familiar with the nature and intensity of the work. Thus the quest to define the scope of practice of child and youth care began to develop greater precision.

THINK ABOUT IT

I'm going to school to be a child and youth care practitioner, can you pay my tuition?

Perhaps you have already had this type of conversation. Recall, or imagine, choosing the college or university program that you want to enroll in. It's called child and youth care or Child and Youth Worker. Tell your parents, or another "sponsor," about your plan to enroll and ask if they will help with the tuition. The response is usually "I've never heard of child and youth care; what will you do when you graduate?"

Explain what child and youth care practice is and what you will be able to do when you graduate.

Compare your explanation to the following definitions:

The International Child and Youth Care Education Consortium is a group of educators primarily from North America who formed in 1990 to try and bring some consistency to educational preparation for the field. The 1992 meeting of the International Child and Youth Care Education Consortium adopted the following definition of child and youth care practice:

Professional Child and Youth Care practice focuses on the infant, child, and adolescent, both normal and with special needs, within the context of the family, the community, and the life span. The developmental-ecological perspective emphasizes the interaction between persons and the physical and social environments, including cultural and political settings.

Professional practitioners promote the optimal development of children, youth, and their families in a variety of settings, such as early care and education, community-based child and youth development programs, parent education and family support, school-based programs, community mental health, group homes, residential centers, rehabilitation programs, pediatric health care, and juvenile justice programs.

Child and Youth Care practice includes skills in assessing client and program needs, designing and implementing programs and planned environments, integrating developmental, preventive, and therapeutic requirements into the life space, contributing to the development of knowledge and professions, and participating in systems interventions through direct care, supervision, administration, teaching, research, consultation, and advocacy. (www.cyc-net.org/profession/pro-definitions.html)

The definition was subsequently adopted by the Association of Child and Youth Care Practice (ACYCP), a professional practice association based in North America.

The Canadian Council of Child and Youth Care Associations (CCCYCA) adopted the following definition of practice in 2008 to reflect the Canadian context:

Child and youth care practitioners work with children, youth and families with complex needs. They can be found in a variety of settings such as group homes and residential treatment centres, hospitals and community mental health clinics, community-based outreach and school-based programs, parent education and family support programs, as well as in private practice and juvenile justice programs. Child and youth care workers specialize in the development and implementation of therapeutic programs and planned environments and the utilization of daily life events to facilitate change. At the core of all effective child and youth care practice is a focus on the therapeutic relationship; the application of theory and research about human growth and development to promote the optimal physical, psycho-social, spiritual, cognitive, and emotional development of young people towards a healthy and productive adulthood; and a focus on strengths and assets rather than pathology. (www.cyccanada.ca)

Definitions of child and youth care have frequently been caught up in examining the roles and functions of the workers, the scope of practice, the settings in which the clients are located, and career progressions, as evidenced above. Each of these approaches to defining the field has a different purpose. Scope of practice, for example, is often used to succinctly differentiate the work of one regulated professional from another, or to define whether a professional is "authourized" to undertake a specific aspect of the work. Scope of practice is therefore often defined in legislation. The details of these various aspects of the work are explored throughout the chapters in this book. However, as descriptions that capture clearly and succinctly what child and youth care practice *is*, these definitions tend to be long, awkward, and difficult to use with laypersons.

Tips and Resources

FICE: www.fice-inter.org
ACYCP: www.acycp.org
CCCYCA: www.cyccanada.ca
South African NACCW: www.naccw.org.za

Many writers have struggled with defining the core of child and youth care practice, and through their writing we can see not just the early struggles for identity in the field but also the roots of the theoretical orientations to practice (reviewed in Chapters 2 and 5). Jerry Beker began defining the field in a series of editorials in *Child Care Quarterly* in 1976 (Beker, 1977). The first issue of the *Journal of Child Care* in 1982 focused on defining and professionalizing the field. Thom Garfat, in a series of editorials in the *Journal of Child and Youth Care* (1991), summarizes multiple perspectives, including voices of students and program workers, that explain what we do. Garfat and Fulcher (2011) described 25 characteristics of a relational child and youth care approach to practice. Child and youth care practitioners today are found in multiple settings with multiple roles, including less direct work with young people. In all of these settings and roles they take a child and youth care approach to their practice.

In the rest of this chapter the core characteristics of practice are described based on themes identified in a review of how practice has been defined and described by these authors and others. The following themes emerged and are discussed here in no particular order of importance:

- Passion
- Caring
- The milieu
- Social competence
- Space and time
- Experiential

The voices of practitioners and students are quoted in the following sections alongside the voices of experts in the field. As you read, consider which theme is closest to your first attempt at a definition.

Child and Youth Care Is a Passion

Historically, caring for young people was (and still is) done by families, mostly by women, though this varies from culture to culture and era to era. Christian-based orphanages operated in North America and Europe (Charles, McElwee, & Garfat, 2005; Charles & Garfat, 2009) providing care for young people orphaned by war or abandoned due to poverty. Members of religious orders cared for the children and believed it was their calling or their service to God to care for those less fortunate. Their reward was God's approval. The idea that people should be paid to care for young people is relatively new. Many modern-day child and youth care practitioners still feel "called" to the work that they do. They are passionate about, and devoted to, improving the lives of young people and families. They don't (initially) consider earning potential in the decision to enter the field, and it is their passion and devotion to young people that sustains them in later years.

> I am absolutely convinced that in 30 years I will be a Child and Youth Care worker because this career enters into my heart. I love it and I want to devote my next thirty years of my life to it. (Radostina Ivanova, student)

> It's my dream to form an organization to fight for children's rights [in my home country] and to make children a priority in all aspects of policymaking. (Nana Asiedu, student)

Being "called" to your work, as part of a religious tradition, can also require that the morals and ethics that form your belief system be transmitted to those you care for. While this religious calling was a part of the early work in orphanages and homes for abandoned children (see Chapter 2), such a singular vision of being called to the work of God is less applicable within the diversity of modern society. Instead, this more modern "calling" often reflects an affinity for and commitment to young people that draws us to help them find the path in life that is right for them without imposing our own beliefs about what that path should be. The passion that we bring to our work helps us to "hang in there" when times are tough and move at the pace of young people, rather than imposing our own pace of change (Garfat & Fulcher, 2011).

Austin and Halpin (1989) use the idea that child and youth care practice is a calling because "caring" is a calling, one that is devalued in general by society and community. They suggest that caring for children is not just a family activity; society needs to increase its value of caring and attempt to engender caring in all members of society. As Lorraine Fox wrote, "CYCW's have their primary credentials in their hearts—in addition to, or often instead of, credentials suitable for framing" (Garfat, 1991, p. 10). Most recently, Smith (2011) dares to connect the moral and ethical calling to care with the process of humanization, which "involves developing greater love for fellow humans curiosity for learning and greater awareness of our incompleteness as living beings" (p. 189). If you are called to the practice of child and youth care, it is more than something that you learn about and then *do*, it represents who you are, in every moment of your day. It is your *being*.

Child and Youth Care Is Caring

The caring connection is not a function of emotional attachment and its continuous hunger for reaffirming experiences of such attachment. Rather, it is manifested by the togetherness of the individuals and their affirmation of a common interest in and engagement of the space between them. In short, caring in child and youth care practice means to be present, fully and completely, throughout the life space. (Gharabaghi & Stuart, 2013, p. 60)

Gharabaghi and Stuart (2013) describe caring as an active set of elements in the work of child and youth care practitioners. These elements are composed of both the individual practitioner and the life-space or environment in which both child and practitioner are located. Life-space is both individual and collective as well as physical and symbolic. Children and practitioners carry with them a history that influences the caring relationship formed between them. This history comes into a physical location or **milieu**, and together with the symbolic aspects of emotional attachment creates a caring environment. Children come to the space with histories of abuse, neglect, trauma, and perhaps abandonment. In short, they need to be cared about. Practitioners bring the strength to care for young people and must value the act of caring.

[We] are there for the kids for the entire day. When the child is eating or sleeping or raising hell, the child care worker is there for the child. The child care worker gets the opportunity to help the child as their problems occur, not just talking about it afterwards. (Dennis Farn, cited in Garfat, 1991, p. 6)

Care though is often assumed to be a value-neutral intervention when in fact it carries with it many ideas of what the other person should be or not be, or do or not do (Dean, 2012), therefore practitioners ought to critically consider what caring means to them personally as well as to the young people they are working with. Ricks (1992) researched how child and youth care practitioners defined "caring" and discovered that caring required three elements: need, affect (or emotion), and action. She suggests that "what distinguishes the caring relationship in a caring profession from other caring relationships is the presence of three critical factors: (1) the condition of need, (2) an attitude of concern, and (3) intentional involvement in intervention. What distinguishes it further is that all factors are present for the care-giver *and* receiver and are *interactive*)" (p. 52). Basically, children care about practitioners too and bring to the relationship their own values about caring. The elements described by Ricks were found to be present in the Isibindi model (see *www.naccw.org.za/isibindi/*), a social franchise model for deploying community-based child and youth care workers to work with child-headed households in South Africa. Both the children and practitioners describe the importance of practical actions, such as cooking together, to the development of love, hopes, and dreams for the future amongst the young people (Thumbadoo, 2011). Supporting young people to develop **agency** is a critical component of the intentional involvement in the interventions that caregivers undertake (Langaard & Toverud, 2009), which takes them beyond simply identifying the condition of need and having an attitude of caring. Organizational culture encourages a caring culture founded on specific values such as love and charity, equity and concern, and strength and hope is critical to the provision of quality care (Rytterstrom, Cedersund, & Arman, 2009). The foundational values underlying the concept of care and the culture of caring have been part of child and youth care discourse for some time.

Tips and Resources

www.cyc-net.org
The International Child and Youth Care Network began as a vision of Thom Garfat (Canada) and Brain Gannon (South Africa) in 1999 and is currently the foremost source of child and youth care literature in the world. You can follow old discussion threads—see answers to the same questions that you have now, from 10 years ago—and read and interact with leaders, potential leaders, and elders in the field. Many of the articles cited in this book can be fully or partially retrieved as reprints from the site and you can search for the authors that interest you.

Caring in child and youth care practice has been described as "unconditional care" (Brown & Thompson, 1978), meaning that there is no expectation that the child will return the love that accompanies being cared about (Ranahan, 1999). There is a fine balance in child and youth care practice between caring for and loving a child. Ranahan (1999) distinguishes between the concrete acts of caring required in the relationships we have with the children we work with and the unconditional acceptance and empathy that represent an expression of love. Love is demonstrated when we bring our own "self" forward as the child's "self" is revealed to us. Similarly, Skott-Myhre and Skott-Myhre (2007) describe love as "the act of giving fully and completely of oneself without the worry that one would run out of oneself" (p. 55) and advocate this form of political love, free from domination and expectation, as a core component of the work of child and youth care practitioners.

Dean (2012) argues that care as a concept is deeply embedded within the "us and them" power structure present in the residential care system within child welfare and juvenile justice. The world of practice is divided into "those who can care, and those who need care" and it is this division that provides us with our work as child and youth care practitioners. This is not to say that we should abandon the work; rather, we must enter into the field of care with more than an expectation that "we care" and young people are "cared for," recognizing instead that humanity cares and young people care for and about us, as much as we care for and about them.

Smith (2006) argues forcefully that the reduction of care to a set of competencies and learning outcomes, as has been done in some attempts to define curriculum, has removed the humanistic and moral aspects of caring. He, too, refers to the idea of a religious calling or obligation that we have to care for others and the importance of incorporating that moral obligation into our practice. Smith (2011) points out that in our quest for professional status we have adopted the tenants of modern thinking and rationality, foregoing the importance of love and caring to the work we do. He suggests we adopt a moral stance that the expression of love is critical to the caring work that we do. While there is a set of skills and knowledge required to be a good child and youth care practitioner, there is also a set of morals and values that consistently underlie our practice. The obligation to care is not a uniquely associated with Christianity; it is found in other faiths and cultures and is a component of relational society.

> Africans have this thing called Ubuntu; it is about the essence of being human, it is part of the gift that Africa will give the world. It embraces hospitality, caring about others, being able to go the extra mile for the sake of others. We believe a person is a person through another person, that my humanity is caught up, bound up and inextricable in yours. (Desmond Tutu, cited in Smith, 2006, p. 8)

A core characteristic of child and youth care is caring—physically, emotionally, symbolically; individually, relationally, and collectively.

Child and Youth Care Is in the Milieu

> What we do, we don't do alone in an office; we do it by getting out there on the same level as the other person, and talking to them. We also know and believe we can make changes, with each other's help. Remember, E = MC² (Effectiveness = Me + Child/2). (Eric Skoglund, cited in Garfat, 1991, p. 1)

Child and youth care practice occurs in the daily environment of young people, including with their families, where they are living, learning, and relating to others. This environment is termed the **milieu**. Child and youth care practitioners are "experts in the art of living" (Mayer, 1958, p. xvi) and work with young people "on the spot" (Helmer & Griff, 1977, p. 145).

The concept of the **therapeutic** or **educative** milieu originally meant 24 hours a day and was first introduced in writing in North America[2] by Mayer (1958) and followed up by Trieschman, Whittaker, and Brendtro (1969) in *The Other 23 Hours*. The concept is based on the early writing of Redl and Wineman (1952) about the therapeutic use of the life-space of the child. The child and youth care practitioner is assigned the immediate responsibility for not just nurturing care and socialization, but also for the specific therapeutic requirements of the child (Maier, 1977) in group-life situations such as day care or residential care.

> Through residing with youth on a professional basis we have the opportunity to manage surface behaviors that other professionals do not observe during therapy sessions. We explore and work with not only a child's mental well-being but their physical, emotional and spiritual well-being. (Sheila Horvat, cited in Garfat, 1991, p. 7)

Child and youth care is "24/7" and while initially this meant that practitioners worked in residential settings, with varied shifts because they lived with the young people, or that the young person lived in the therapeutic milieu all the time, it now means that young people "live" in many environments and therefore child and youth care practice "occurs" in many milieus such as schools, residences, hospitals, detention centers, family homes, "on the street," and in after-school centres. These settings are explored in Chapter 4, but what they have in common is that the therapeutic work rarely occurs in an office and the techniques for creating change and enhancing development make use of the surrounding milieu and daily life events. Burns (2006) describes five elements of a therapeutic milieu that can be strategically influenced by child and youth care practitioners to provide for the needs of children. Briefly, he suggests that practitioners can manipulate the physical, emotional, social, cultural, and ideological elements of a milieu to ensure that the environment is conducive to the well-being of young people and families. Doing so ensures that the young person feels safe, loved, and valued and provides space for healing emotional scars. The work of child and youth care practice creates a therapeutic milieu.

---

[2] See Chapter 2 for a history of the concept of the milieu outside of North America.

There are many milieus that are comfortable, safe spaces where children are valued, but *therapeutic* milieus are consciously created and used to promote change. There are many aspects to assessing the therapeutic nature of a milieu. At the end of the chapter there is an exercise that gives you a taste of what to look for. For a comprehensive review of therapeutic milieus, see *Healing Spaces: The Therapeutic Milieu in Child and Youth Work* (Burns, 2006). This theory is followed up in Chapters 4 and 12 and you will come to understand it more fully at that time.

Child and Youth Care Focuses on Competence and Strengths

> Because they are flexible in their methods and beliefs with youths, I think that they are more willing to discover what combination of therapy works best for an individual child. Since children are unique, I believe that child/youth care workers recognize this quality and help the child benefit to realize his full potential to become his BEST SELF. (Shawn Shumlich)

> . . . Billy and I work with his positives and strengths to discover why he thinks and feels the way he does. I listen to him with an open mind. (L. Duboski, cited in Garfat, 1991, p. 6)

Developmental care is a central theme in child and youth care practice (Anglin, 1999, 2001, 2002; Ferguson & Anglin, 1985; Krueger, 1991b; Maier, 1979). Developmental care means that practitioners interact with young people and families and personalize the work that they do in consideration of the factors within us that change over time. Sometimes changes are predictable due to age, stage of family life, illness, even cultural background and at other times anticipating the trajectory of change for a young person is difficult. Still, the developmental care approach means that we consider the expected trajectory in the work that we do. Developmentally appropriate practice (DAP) underlies the youth development approach to prevention and intervention in which all young people, not just those "at risk," participate in developmentally appropriate programming that responds to personal needs within their ecological context (Meschke, Peter, & Bartholomae, 2012). Practitioners need a solid understanding of typical development while at the same time appreciating that culture, social environment, and personal attributes affect the judgement regarding what is typical. Indeed, young people who are "at risk" often exist on the margins of society or "on the edge" about to "fall off." Their resistance to complying with society's norms can actually be viewed as a strength (Gharabaghi, 2012). However, they are therefore difficult to find within the positive youth development movement.

Developmental care implies a focus on competence and strengths linked to the inherent value placed on young people. "Child and youth care practitioners want to be with young people; they value them, implying that children are competent simply for who they are" (Anglin, 2001, n.p.). Our goal is to help them develop further competence and effectively draw on the strengths that they have. Research has found that practitioners actively using a strength-based perspective identify strengths in seven different areas (McCammon, 2012):

1. Talents or athletic competencies
2. Resilience in the face of challenging circumstances
3. Goals or hopes for the future
4. Personal or social and community resources
5. Borrowed strengths based on the advice of another person
6. Strengths based on past accomplishments
7. Hidden strengths represented by behaviors that are currently "at risk"

Building on the strengths of young people means that the child and youth care practitioner uses a social competence perspective. The "initial expertise of the child care worker is in helping children develop emotional social competence in dealing with day-to-day problems" (Powell, 1977, p. 148). As with any approach, focusing on social competence may mean that the focus is on the deficit of social competence and therefore developing skills, or it may mean a belief that young people are competent and that we need to focus on strengths and minimize deficits, while at the same time addressing areas that prevent the young person from engaging successfully with the world around him or her. All too often professionals who are trained to help people change find it is easy to see the problem, focus on the "bad" behavior, identify and label the pathology, and create a treatment for that pathology (Taliaferro & Borowsky, 2012). Incorporating positive youth development into clinical treatment settings encourages practitioners to identify the many other positive, creative skills and knowledge held by young people and their families. When strengths are acknowledged and fostered, young people feel affirmed, self-esteem is enhanced, and growth and development increased (McCammon, 2012). This is the essence of developmental care.

Sometimes, practitioners forget that the problematic behavior is one that has helped the child survive in his or her family or has helped the family survive in a difficult world of poverty, unequal opportunity, or violence. As noted above, this should be viewed as a strength. Michael Ungar (Liebenberg & Ungar, 2008; Ungar, 2006) describes this as not just survival, but resilience. He reminds us that these are behaviours that make sense to the youth and have a purpose. Practitioners seek to understand that purpose and how it helps the child to be competent, to cope, and to be safe in their environments. One of the characteristics of resilient children is social competence and from this perspective, helping young people to develop social competence, to interact in a sociable manner, and to find support will help them to develop resilience. Resilience is the capacity to cope in the face of adversity. We all face adversity at various times in our lives. Young people rely on adults to help them deal with the adversities that they face and child and youth care practice helps them to discover their existing strengths for coping and to learn new skills.

Child and Youth Care Is in Children's Space and Time

The ultimate task of the child and youth care practitioner is to weave the elements of time and space together in a way that is meaningful to the children (Helmer & Griff, 1977; Vander Ven, 1991). Karen Vander Ven (1991) explains that we define child and youth care practice by the spaces that children are located in and that workers arrange those spaces to promote the development of the children. Space and time are adapted to meet the child's needs. The practitioner is present when the time is right and he or she responds to the needs of the child at that moment. It is the use of daily life events (Garfat & Fulcher, 2011) and the arrangement of space and time around those events that become the tools of intervention in child and youth care practice.

> What makes us different is our constant presence, our involvement in the little details of life, and our willingness to face and channel the lion of defiance in each child placed in care. . . . It is in these ways that we demonstrate our willingness to care, our ability to control, and our desire to help kids grow into responsible adults. We see ourselves as "doers" rather than "talkers." (Zygumnt Malowicki, cited in Garfat, 1991, p. 2)

The approach to practice is active, responsive to the moment in time, and engaged in creating and adapting the space to the needs of the people within. Practitioners consider a number of different factors related to time within the life-space. Routines structure the young person's life-space to provide stability and predictability. Helping young children to understand the concept of time is the core developmental task that evolves over several years. Routines and the structuring of time are part of the developmental path of a young person. "Two more sleeps, until school starts." "We'll do that after lunch." In child and youth care practice, these statements become strategies for intervention creating safety and predictability. Transition times involve moving from one activity to the next and are occasions where young people may need extra support. Practitioners are aware of these as times when they need to create supportive activities or conversation to support young people through these changes. Transition times may be as simple as moving from home to school on a daily basis. Alternatively, they could include the complexities of changing where you live or with whom you live, work, or go to school. Practitioners consider the timing of activities and difficult or emotional conversations and their impact on the young person so that they can exert some influence over the space and time for dealing with difficult issues. Practitioners work actively with the physical, emotional, and spiritual aspects of the space that young people exist within. The most obvious examples of the use of space as a strategy for intervention include the physical arrangement of space in ways that are aesthetically pleasing, culturally appropriate, and safe. Practitioners develop an understanding of the emotional space that is unique to each young person, thereby responding to personal needs in the process of caring for young people. "The core of 'child and youth care work' models the most needed human service of the future because of its focus on the life space, use of relationships and activity, and its fluid boundaries can resonate with a rapidly changing world" (Vander Ven, 2006, p. 234).

> The key thing we do as Child and Youth Care Workers is work directly with children on a full time basis . . . and by being around a child for forty hours a week it is helpful in building a relationship. Once a child has a relationship with a child and youth care worker, many other things grow strong, such as trust, honesty and love. (Darin Perpar, cited in Garfat, 1991, p. 6)

Milieu work is not restricted just to children or youth. Experienced practitioners evolve into more advanced forms of practice, working with families in the family space(s); with youth in community spaces such as streetscapes (Griffin, 2009); with new practitioners in supervisory and educational roles; and influencing policy and creating political change (Anglin, 2002; Vander Ven, 1990, 2006). The use of space and time is a characteristic of practice that moves beyond direct care to indirect care as child and youth care practitioners become supervisors, managers, trainers, and consultants (Ferguson, Pence, & Denholm, 1993; Maier, 1977; Powell, 1977). They take with them this core way of working into other roles and functions.

Child and Youth Care Is Experiential

> Child and youth care is a process of human interaction and, as such, is enriched and fraught with all the emotions, challenges, struggles, and discoveries that are part of being human. Workers try their best and learn from their successes and failures. As they interact, they form relationships with youth, learn, develop skills, change their stories, and grow together. (Krueger, 2007b, p. 235)

There are two defining characteristics of the field that are frequently described separately. Child and youth care is **relational** and involves the use of the **self** as a vehicle for growth and development. These characteristics are combined in the concept of experiential learning. Gerry Fewster (1990b) has written extensively about the relational and the self-development aspects of child and youth care practice. The core of child and youth care from his perspective is the experiential focus that embodies both the relational and the self. "In taking the courage to share their own experience in working with young people, they have an opportunity to generate a body of knowledge that promotes understanding, caring and respect" (Fewster, 1991, p. 62). Practitioners bring their experiences to the work, young people and families bring their experiences to the work and through experience they learn more, in a cyclical process of experience, reflection, learning, and application.

You have already begun some aspects of experiential learning in this chapter. Exercises at the end of the chapter ask you to remember experiences, reflect on them, and learn from them by linking them with the new ideas presented in the chapter. Reflections by other practitioners demonstrate their learning, based on experiences in their practice. In Chapter 3 you will learn more about how to embed experiential learning in your professional development. This is part of the ongoing process of child and youth care practice. In his study of the "interventive moment" Garfat (1998) attempts to capture the experiential nature of the moment during which a child is open to change and the practitioner is ready, present, and engaged in facilitating that change. The "interventive moment" is that perfect moment in time when theory and practice merge together, as in the following example. Too much focus on theory can lead to inaction. Too much focus on practice leaves us without a theoretical understanding of what young people need at any given moment in time.

> Hearing a disturbance at the nearby main entrance to our centre, I hurried from my desk to see what was happening. Jack, a 14-year-old recent arrival, was directing a high-pressure hose onto the glass front doors and window panels, and there were puddles from water that had sprayed through before the doors had been locked.
>
> A small group of office and program staff had gathered out of Jack's sight in a hallway, discussing the situation. "He's just looking for attention," said one, while another ventured that he was trying to set up a confrontation. A caseworker pointed out that his father had recently died and his mother had rejected him, so he was probably very angry. Someone else speculated that if a firm response was not forthcoming he would soon turn to damage the nearby cars.
>
> I joined in the diagnostic exercise as the tension grew. Jack, staring impassively, moved to sit on a bench by the entrance, still holding the hose. Every now and again he would glance furtively towards the door to see what we were going to do, preparing, it seemed, to put up strong resistance when the confrontation came.
>
> While we were still planning a response, someone else decided to act. Julie, the residential care director, emerged from the side door with a piece of cake and a cool drink. "Would you like a snack?" she asked and placed the plate beside him, sitting down a few feet away. He did not answer and was clearly nonplussed. Julie did not press him or mention his behaviour. She suggested that he seemed to be upset and that a snack might make him feel better. "I'd like to chat with you when you've finished it," she said. "When you are ready we could go around the back where there are no people around." Jack placed the hose in her outstretched hand. He sat for a few minutes after she had left, then ate the cake and shuffled off. (Bath, 1995, cited in www.cyc-net.org/quote3/quote-1310.html)

The experiences of child and youth care practitioners are brought to their relationships through knowledge and understanding of the self. The learning that comes from self-reflection is engaged and transmitted through the relationships developed in practice. These same relationships also provide experiences for reflection and learning. Young people learn and change through the experiences that we construct for them. Similarly, we learn through those experiences, and the other past and present experiences of our lives. We bring this learning to the daily work that we do with young people. The effective development of experiential learning requires that we attend to all the different aspects of the experience and the learning process. Self-reflection, making sense of the experience, exploring emotions, thoughts and actions, identifying what could be done differently, and implementing the change are all aspects of an experiential learning cycle used by practitioners in their work.

> The only "fancy jargon" we have found most effective is PATIENCE, TIME, and our wealth of past experiences. (Chris Bieszczadcsw, cited in Garfat, 1991, p. 2)

Stating that personal experience is forefront in the work that we do with young people ignites a debate about objectivity, consistency, and professionalism. One of the initial debates in the professionalization of child and youth care was the craft versus profession debate. Eisikovits and Beker (1983) suggested we should conceive of child and youth care as a craft. In a craft, each product is a little different and we cannot standardize our work because it depends on the uniqueness of the parts and how they come together, forming a unique whole that is greater than the sum of its parts. Maier (1983) suggested that all professions arise as crafts and move along a continuum toward professionalism. "While the answer may be a decade away, we may wish to ask the following question: Can we identify the point of the craft–professional continuum where, in general, child/youth workers now find themselves?" (Maier, 1983, p. 117). Others argue that what is required is a framework for thinking about the field as a value-based as well as a skill- and knowledge-based profession. Only when we begin to graduate practitioners who are equipped with the values and the language to describe their craft (McDermott, 1994; Phelan, 2000) will they be equipped to demand the recognition that is deserved of professionals. The domains of practice, described in later chapters, use a framework that summarizes competence in practice as a set of attitudes, skills, and knowledge guided by the self as a central domain of practice.

DEFINING CHILD AND YOUTH CARE: THIS MOMENT-IN-TIME

One of the struggles with definitions is that what you say depends a little on the audience and purpose for the definition. In a developing professional field any definition is also time-sensitive. Some definitions were written to help educational and training programs develop the curriculum. There are also definitions to help professional associations prepare for legislation and regulation of the scope of practice. (See Appendix A.) Definitions of child and youth care frequently state that child and youth care extends beyond direct practice. The following summaries may be useful to you in situations that address the direct practice of child and youth care and those that address the "field" of child and youth care, including the parameters of study and indirect work such as consulting, research, supervision, and management.

CYC Practice Defined for Other Professionals

Child and youth care practitioners care for and about young people and families while working with them in their own milieu. We use the characteristics of the space that clients are located in and carefully adjust our timing to maximize the opportunities for change that are present within that milieu. Children are naturally competent, and by believing in them and valuing them as competent people we help our clients learn how to resolve problems as they come up, building on their skills and helping them to be ready to address the next problem. We bring our own experiences to the work and therefore we must be very clear about how our experience might be helpful or *not* for clients. Caring *for* young people addresses a broad spectrum of developmental needs to ensure that healthy growth and development are maximized. Caring *about* young people focuses on social competence and places value on young people as competent members of society. Our techniques and strategies for change are unique to the moment and to the individual because in our practice, timing, location, and relationship allow us to support change in young people's life-space.

CYC Practice Defined for Friends and Family

Being a child and youth care practitioner is not something that I "do"; it is what I "am." I feel compelled to work with young people and families in their own milieu. I care for them and I care about them. I use the events, relationships, and experiences of everyday life to help them learn about and manage problems, as well as discover the strengths they need to continue to grow and develop. All my previous experiences come together with the experiences of the young people I'm working with, and together we focus on changing their approach to life just at the moment that they are struggling.

CYC Practice Defined for the Field of Child and Youth Care

The child and youth care field focuses on the developmental needs of young people and families within the space and time of their daily lives. People who work in the field are dedicated to improving the lives of young people and families through an active and engaged recognition of the competence and value of the people with whom they work. This translates to involving your **self** directly in the work you do, whether that work includes direct care, supervision of care workers, consulting, research, advocacy, or teaching. It is this equitable, active, and engaged relationship between two individuals, and the recognition of the importance of this experience to both lives, that is a distinguishing feature of the field.

WHAT'S NEXT?

Now that you have a (momentarily) clear definition of practice in the field of child and youth care, the rest of the book will explore the details surrounding these defining moments. We will expand the language and conceptual frameworks that novice, experienced, and mature practitioners bring to understanding their work.

- Chapter 2 introduces you to young people in a very general way. You will learn about the abuse of children, education of children, and care and supervision of children throughout history. It also introduces the modern voices of young people and families that are cared for by child and youth care practitioners. The chapter includes a brief overview of the development of child and youth care since World War II. The influences of psychology, education, social work, and politics are addressed, in light of how they have affected the settings where child and youth care practitioners are located and the approaches to practice.

- Chapter 3 describes a framework for practitioner development through several stages of competence: novice, experienced, and mature practice. The emphasis is on life-long learning and the role and importance of supervision. Terms like **maturity** or **mature practitioner** and **wisdom** focus on the field's basis in experiential learning, self, meaning-making, and context.

- Chapter 4 describes the settings in which direct care practitioners work and the "type" of clients with which they work. It also describes how the jurisdictions, such as health/mental health, education, social services, and justice, influence policy, programs, and practice with children, youth, and families.

- The concept of "theory" is introduced in Chapter 5 along with an overview of the seven domains of practice that organize our work with young people. The conceptual framework for understanding practice and the definitions of each domain are presented. The chapter ends with an overview of how to integrate all the domains of practice and to apply them in multiple contexts and identifies three important contexts for application: the practice milieu, the organizational system, and culture.

- The domain of **self** is explored in Chapter 6, and students are introduced to strategies for reflective practice, setting boundaries, self-care, and the use of self in interventions with young people and families.

- Chapter 7 addresses the domain of **professionalism**. The emphasis in this chapter is on how the skills and knowledge of being a professional put a professional "face" on the values and beliefs of the self, engaging the self in a different way in the domain of professional practice.

- Chapter 8 describes the domain of **communication**, which provides the forum for translating self and professionalism into day-to-day work with children, youth, and families. The art of conversation is introduced; basic ideas about the influence of information technology on communication are discussed; and the importance of a child and youth care language within interprofessional communication are reviewed.

- Chapters 9–12 address the four domains of practice that focus on supportive change with young people and families. There is a discussion of relational work and the **relationship** domain as it is expressed in child and youth care practice in Chapter 9. The concepts in the domain of **applied human development** are introduced in Chapter 10 and students are prepared for a critical thinking approach to reviewing developmental theory and understanding patterns of growth and development. Child and youth care developmental approaches, consistent with a social competence perspective, are introduced. Chapter 11 introduces the domain of **systemic context**. The unique approaches to change used by child and youth care practitioners are addressed in Chapter Twelve on the domain of **intervention**.

- Finally, the appendices provide the reader with a variety of definitions of the Scope of Practice; the current internationally adopted Code of Ethics for child and youth care practitioners; and an identification of the detailed competencies and the elements of performance that might be expected of a novice practitioner within the seven domains of practice. The 5 domains addressed by the certification competencies for practitioners in some jurisdictions in North America are also included in the appendices.

Photo by Laine Robertson

CHAPTER EXERCISES

DEFINING MOMENTS

Experience

The author describes two defining moments early in her child and youth care career. Consider your own experiences with young people. Recall a "**defining moment**" that influenced your choice to become a child and youth care practitioner. Write or sketch out the moment.

Reflection-for-Practice

What meaning does it hold for you now?

CARING AND MORALITY

Reflection-on-Action

One of the characteristics of child and youth care, as described by the author, is the concept of passion, reflected in the calling that we feel to the work that we do. What calls you to your work with young people?

Does that voice (the one calling you) obligate you to ensure that the people that you care for are taught to recognize the morals and ethics of a higher power? Who is that higher power? What if those young people follow a different higher power?

CARING

Theory-in-Action

Define what **caring** means to you, consider how love fits in the caring work you do with young people. Look up what Frances Ricks (*www.cyc-net.org/features/ft-ricks-fem.html*) and Mark Smith (*www.cyc-net.org/cyc-online/cycol-0612-smith.html*) have to say on CYC-Net.org, the International Child and Youth Care Network.

IS IT A THERAPEUTIC MILIEU?

Experience

This exercise involves recalling and visualizing an experience and you will need to take a few moments to sit, close your eyes, and be relaxed. Ideally someone should read the rest of this exercise out loud to you.

Sit in a relaxed position. Close your eyes and take three deep breaths. Inhale counting to five, hold for one count, and exhale counting to four. Keep your eyes closed and visualize a space where children spend a lot of time, one where perhaps you have spent a lot of time. I want you to look at it differently now than you did in the past.

Reflection-in-Practice

We're going to do a "brief" assessment of each of the five elements of therapeutic milieu.

Physical. Look around. What do you see that represents the children's work or ideas? What do you see that poses a risk of injury to children? What does the physical environment "say" to you?

Emotional. Now picture the children busy in the environment. What feelings and emotions do you see being expressed? How do the adults feel? How are these feelings being communicated?

Social. Continue to watch the children and focus on how they interact. What are the rules for play and social communication? How are the adults encouraging social interaction? Who is left out?

Cultural. Observe the diversity among the children and the adults. Consider differences based on culture, race, ethnicity, gender, religion, disability, sexual orientation. Can you see and describe a majority group? A minority group? Is social interaction restricted by group?

Ideological. What are the beliefs about children that are held by the group and the organization that owns this space? How are children's rights respected?

Reflection-on-Practice

Reviewing what you have observed, make note of what the adults do and the elements of the milieu that seem to be specifically designed to promote change, growth, and development for children.

Reflection-for-Practice

Take three more deep breaths—open your eyes and record three things that you believe are consciously therapeutic or three things that you would change to make the environment consciously therapeutic.

COMPETENCE

Reflection-on-Action

Remember something that you did in your early teenage years that you constantly got into trouble for. What purpose did that behavior serve for you at that time? What benefit did you get out of doing it? How did the adults around you respond? How has this skill transformed into something useful today?

YOUR DEFINING MOMENT

Reflection-for-Practice

CYC Practice Is . . .

You will shape your practice and your definition of practice continuously throughout your career. Now is a good time to begin to clearly and succinctly describe what child and youth care means to you. Perhaps you are one of those people who uses a yellow highlighter to highlight important points in books. What did you highlight above? Review your highlights and try to summarize how you would define child and youth care. Compare it to your earlier attempt to explain the field to your tuition sponsor.

FINAL CHAPTER REFLECTION

My friend Marilyn once said: "You like children, you really like them. Not everyone does, you know, even their parents." Prior to her comment it had never occurred to me that someone would not like children. What about you—do you like children? Do they make you smile?

Carol Stuart

HISTORICAL PERSPECTIVES ON CHILDHOOD AND PROFESSIONAL CAREGIVING

Photo by John Campbell

CHAPTER OBJECTIVES

- To identify social and psychological constructions of childhood.
- To explore how children were treated throughout history in a variety of societies.
- To be exposed to the ideas of some of the leaders who recognized the need for more humane methods of educating and caring for the most vulnerable members of society.
- To understand how European and North American societies began to address the abuse of children and the education of those with special needs.

- To describe the development of the profession of child and youth care since World War II.
- To describe the influences of the justice, health, education, and social welfare service orientations.
- To introduce theoretical orientations from psychology, medicine, sociology, education, and social work that influenced today's practice.

Child and youth care practitioners listen to the voices of the young people both as a way of working with their concerns and as a forum for understanding the experience of young people and families within the services and systems that affect them. The images and voices of young people throughout this book represent a modern view of childhood in a North America context. Caring for young people in other societies occurs in a different context. The individualistic and materialistic emphasis of our modern North American society differs from the collectivist and spiritual emphasis in other parts of the world. The profession, occupation, or craft of child and youth care developed largely in modern European and North American societies and within a set of societal conditions that valued a distinct stage of life called childhood that included various ideologies, government structures, and jurisdictions, and numerous theoretical orientations.

This chapter begins with an introduction to the concept of childhood and the historical influences on childhood. The eras within the development of the profession are examined while considering the influences of culture, jurisdiction, and theory for each era. The chapter ends by discussing the current issues that the profession is addressing. By necessity, this is a very brief overview and readers are encouraged to do an in-depth analysis of various authors to deconstruct how ideology and societal trends influenced the thinking of these historical leaders, and how they might have influenced our professional values and treatment of young people today.

STAGES OF LIFE: CONSTRUCTING CHILDHOOD AND ADOLESCENCE

Childhood is of course an abstraction, referring to a particular stage of life. (Heywood, 2001, p. 10)

Historians, sociologists, and cultural psychologists have proposed that childhood is a **social construction.** Simply put, this means that we have collectively defined (or constructed) the meaning of childhood. How we understand and treat children is based on societal norms and philosophy. In medieval times children were thought of as **sinful** and parents worked to eradicate evil from the child. The idea that children are a **tabula rasa,** proposed by John Locke in the 17th century, reflects the image of society at the time that children were malleable by both the good and the evil forces that confront us in this world. Locke believed that all humans began as a "blank slate" and everything they interacted with shaped them as either a good or an evil person. In the 18th century, philosopher Jean Jacques Rousseau stressed that children were inherently good and, if permitted to grow naturally, without constraints, this goodness would emerge. Viewing childhood as a social construction implies that biological immaturity is only meaningful within the culture of a particular society. Societal differences in socioeconomic class, race, gender, religion, and so on, influence how a particular subgroup treats children (Heywood, 2001).

Sociologists and anthropologists believe that it is culture and society that determine our concept of childhood. Biologists focus on the physical maturity that marks adulthood and is most often characterized by the ability to reproduce. Psychologists also focus on childhood as a real scientific concept. They believe that childhood can be defined and described by studying the relationship between parents and children and that childhood is identified by the changes in neurobiology of the brain as we mature through adolescence. While sociologists and anthropologists tend to work with the idea of childhood as a social construction, biologists and psychologists focus on childhood as a **psychological construct,** a real scientific concept that can be defined and described. It is thought to involve a sequence of developmental stages leading to adulthood. In this conception of childhood, parents are thought to respond to the (universal) biological and psychological needs of children across cultures and societies; therefore, childhood is the same in all societies. When universal ideas about childhood are thought of as "truths" in child development, they are applied to all cultures and societies. The emphasis on science, research, and knowledge about child development, however, is primarily a Western emphasis (Montgomery, 2009) and other societies do not necessarily hold the same truth.

The view that childhood is either a social construction or a psychological construct has influenced the way historians described the nature of childhood and therefore the development of services to protect children and promote their development. There are many detailed histories of childhood, children's education, child labour, and the treatment of poor and orphaned children over time. Any one of these provides a fascinating historical analysis of childhood embedded in the cultural views of North American and European society. A brief summary of these historical analyses is provided here.

RAISING CHILDREN THROUGH THE AGES

Some historians of Western society note that until the 18th century children were simply treated as imperfect adults whose well-being was not that important.[1] Others argue that the indicators of this lack of interest in childhood have been misinterpreted (Colón & Colón, 2001; Rahikainen, 2004; Stearns, 2005). Because historians rely on artifacts (writings, drawings, objects) from earlier times to describe the way of life in those societies, and children did not leave evidence of their lives behind, historians largely ignored children or thought that the concept of childhood did not exist in historical societies. In early civilizations the protection of children was less important than the protection of family wealth, and there were few cultures that emphasized the rights of children; therefore, seeing childhood through the eyes of children was difficult to impossible (Colón & Colón, 2001; Stearns, 2005) until very recent times when young people began to "publish" and digital records became more public.

While all cultures and civilizations ensured that infants were fed, kept clean, and made safe, childhood was, and is, radically different from one cultural location and era to the next. A combination of history, cultural tradition, and social/environmental pressures influenced how children were treated throughout the ages (Montgomery, 2009).

---

[1] Philippe Aries is generally credited with proposing the idea that "premodern western society lacked a concept of childhood, tending to view children as small adults with no special emotional or legal allowances" (Stearns, 2005, p. 4).

Tips and Resources

A Different Childhood

Democratic Republic of Congo: "When they came to my village, they asked my older brother whether he was ready to join the militia. He was just 17 and he said no; they shot him in the head. Then they asked me if I was ready to sign, so what could I do—I didn't want to die." —A former child soldier taken when he was 13 (BBC report)

> Child Soldiers International: www.child-soldiers.org/about_the_issues.php
>
> Amnesty USA: www.amnestyusa.org/our-work/issues/children-s-rights/child-soldiers/stories-from-children-associated-with-fighting-forces
>
> Coalition to Stop the Use of Child Soldiers (webpage for the Global Report 2008): www.childsoldiersglobalreport.org/content/voices-child-soldiers

There are many examples of variation and contradiction in the way childhood is defined from society to society. For example, child soldiers are actively used in 20 different countries by state armies, 17 of which have formally recruited children between January 2010 and June 2012 (Child Soldiers International, 2012). Most of these countries are located in Africa and Southeast Asia but the list of countries is surprising. In North American history, recall that many participants in the American Revolution were 14 or 15 years of age (Stearns, 2005).

Children in Japan or China are pressed to succeed academically. They study long hours, go to school on Saturday, and, in urban centres, sometimes ride the train to school for over an hour. While Japan adopted Western educational practices in the 19th century, shaming and strict obedience, group cohesion, and respect remained a hallmark of their society (Stearns, 2005). In rural Mexico, children are carried in robozos[2] for several years, going everywhere with their mothers. In Australia, 6-year-olds are out surfing with their families before going to school for the day. Swaddling children and using wet nurses have both long been practiced as warm and nurturing parental responses in many societies (Colón & Colón, 2001) but have been rejected in North America and Europe. These differences indicate the high degree of variation in how childhood was, and still is, socially constructed.

Judgements about childhood, the appropriate activities for children, and the practices of adult caregivers are based on our societal and cultural views of what childhood is, or should be, that is, our social construction of childhood. And yet, "despite the enormous variations in the ways in which childhood is understood, there is no society that does not acknowledge that children (however they are defined) are very different from adults, have different needs, and have different roles and expectations placed on them" (Montgomery, 2009, p. 9).

Historians distinguish broad eras in time that correspond roughly to economic production within that society. The time of the hunting-and-gathering society was followed by the time of the agricultural society. Agricultural societies gave way to industrial societies as we entered the modern age. The modern age is characterized by manufacturing and technological innovation. Most recently we seem to be experiencing a global society where technology makes information available worldwide. In the year 2006, for example, young women in an isolated Russian village and an urban slum in rural Madagascar hold Britney Spears in high esteem (Stearns, 2005), something they have in common with my own teenage daughter in Canada. Young people play video games online with invisible friends around the world. Technology is eradicating some

---

[2] A shoulder sling formed from a shawl with the baby hung on the mother's chest.

aspects of cultural boundaries; however, others remain strongly present and knowledge about childhood requires some consideration of the context of the knowledge provider.

Early Societies

In hunting and gathering societies the birth rate was low. Children could not contribute to the work of the family and life was difficult so the survival rate of children was low. There is evidence, however, that they were present, cared for, and loved. Reaching adulthood was marked by ceremony and ritual, represented in artifacts from that time (Stearns, 2005).

Historians who focus on childhood in the early societies note that in agricultural societies the birth rate increased as families remained in one location and children became useful for the production of food. Families balanced the influences of property ownership and their need for labour with the time and cost related to the care and feeding of children. In multigenerational families older children contributed to the heavy labour in the fields and younger children contributed to caring for both infants and grandparents. There was a balance to be achieved between mouths to feed and hands to help. Schooling was available to upper-class families who did not need their children to work in the fields because they had slaves (who were often children).

There were some differences between civilizations documented by historians (Montgomery, 2009; Stearns, 2005) at this point in history. Chinese mothers, for example, demonstrated an intense focus on their children, with a strong emotional connection not in evidence in Mediterranean (Greek and Roman) societies, which were more focused on the beauty of youth. Religion influenced some of these differences. Hinduism took a more individualistic view of the child and thus Indian society was more indulgent with young children and had a great aversion to physical discipline not found in China or the Mediterranean at the time. Overall, historians report that agrarian societies had similar views of children and that the considerations given to raising children were relatively common across different societies.

Industrial Societies

Historians of Western culture tell us that in medieval times (up to the 15th century) children were thought of as sinful creatures (Heywood, 2001). They were expected to earn an income as soon as possible, and were often trained in the parent's trade or handed over to the church or to a master as an apprentice (Rahikainen, 2004). The rights and protections that they might have enjoyed in earlier civilizations were lost; children were regarded as property and thus there were laws that required children to work or that specified rules that permitted child sacrifice (murder), prostitution, slavery, and abandonment (Colón & Colón, 2001; Rahikainen, 2004).

The elite viewed their own children as a source of amusement and sweetness, and some historians argue that childhood was rediscovered as a distinct stage of life during this era (Heywood, 2001). However, the practical realities of the poor and working class were very different. Laws enacted in the 1500s ("Elizabethan Poor Laws") placed the responsibility for orphaned children on tax-supported churches and on governments, which created almshouses for people of all ages, including children. Orphaned children or those from destitute families were given to whomever would take them, or sold as apprentices to become servants and work as farmers, householders, and business helpers (Askeland, 2006). Working-class families saw education and schooling as a means of upward mobility. Uneducated children laboured in factories or on farms or became part of the household staff for the elite (Rahikainen, 2004).

Children were likely to be horsewhipped or caned with a stick as punishment for wrongdoing. As the idea of childhood innocence took hold, such punishment would be reported as an assault and the adult offender dealt with by the courts. These were early indications of protecting children from abuse. The social class of the family made a difference in determining whether adult behaviours that we would now consider abusive toward children were accepted or reported (Warner & Griller, 2003).

Most historical descriptions of childhood have a Eurocentric focus and are thought to apply universally; however, cultural traditions present in North America in the 17th and 18th centuries serve as a reminder of the importance of cultural differences, which may be unseen by historians. The Iroquois Nation had formal rituals providing for adoption into family or clan, as well as for the adoption of entire groups to protect them from extinction (Askeland, 2006). On the other hand, slavery in the United States posed a serious threat to family kinship in the African nations. Family ties were denied any kind of legal status and the (European) masters determined if children were sold; the child's lineage was tied to the master not to the family or clan. Children who could not work in the fields as slaves were cared for by elderly women. Those separated from kin would negotiate their way into new families by offering extra labour for protection. Establishment in a new family was not quick or guaranteed, but was equal to a blood tie once achieved (Askeland, 2006).

MODERN TIMES: RESTRICTING CHILDREN'S LABOUR IN THE TECHNOLOGICAL REVOLUTION

Tips and Resources

History of Childhood in Canada in the Canadian Encyclopedia:

www.thecanadianencyclopedia.com/index.cfm?PgNm=TCE&Params=A1ARTA0001579

During the transition from the age of industry to the age of technology, working-class families still required children's wages to support the family. Laws against labour for children under the age of 8 were enacted in the United States in 1836 (CLPEP, 2009) and in France in 1841 (Rahikainen, 2004). The age at which children were permitted to leave school and work was gradually increased as their labour in factories was no longer required.

Laws restricting child labour were closely tied to laws regarding compulsory schooling. Primary schooling became compulsory in Canada (Ontario) in 1871 (Oreopoulos, 2006) and in France in 1882 (Rahikainen, 2004). Schooling in Japan was already the main task of children in the late 1800s, with government support for universality. At the same time, Russian society also adopted schooling as the primary focus for children and youth groups as a mechanism for transmitting key values and beliefs of the communist philosophy of equality (Stearns, 2005).

In the 20th century, children in Western culture needed to be trained into "mature, rational, competent, social and autonomous adults" (Heywood, 2001, p. 3). Children were economically worthless when assembly-line technology replaced the need for manual labour and therefore school replaced work as the daily occupation of children. Cultural psychologists say that modern North American society is focused on independence and autonomy at a very early age (Mattingly, 1995a). Parents have been encouraged to separate children into their own bedrooms and have discouraged gender-specific toys or play, do not use physical punishment, and place their children in daycare while they both go to work. This is in contrast to other societies and cultures where more than one generation lives in the same small household, grandparents care for children, girls and boys have distinct roles and expectations, and physical punishment is acceptable (Montgomery, 2009). Most of the historical descriptions refer to children because adolescence was first conceptualized as a distinct stage of life by G. Stanley Hall, a psychologist and researcher interested in child development, in the early 1900s. He recognized biological and psychological differences in this stage of life (Montgomery, 2009). As these ideas about the distinct nature of childhood and adolescence have taken hold, laws regarding child labour, criminal behaviour, and mandatory schooling have changed to recognize that children are ready to take on adult responsibility at a later age. Modern childhood and adolescence in Western society is currently defined by school, an increased lifespan of childhood into adulthood, and a lower birth rate.

Tips and Resources

Child Labor Education Project (CLPEP):

www.continuetolearn.uiowa.edu/laborctr/child_labor/about/

THE REFORMERS: TAKING CARE OF THE HOMELESS AND EDUCATING THOSE WITH SPECIAL NEEDS

The previous section reviewed how childhood was constructed through various historical eras and the implications for how children were thought of and treated when they followed what was socially constructed as a normal developmental path. As medical and psychological knowledge advanced, the "normal" or average path of development has been psychologically constructed through scientific research and modern social structures have been created to help the many children who do not fit the "norm." All societies have had to deal with children who are different in some manner. Children with physical disabilities and those that have chronic or life-threatening illnesses are the most visibly different. However, there are many children with "invisible" disabilities or challenges that are not visibly identifiable. For example, children may be unable to learn and retain information, or perhaps see letters and numbers in reverse or cannot process information that is visual or auditory. Children may not understand emotions or they might see and hear things that other people do not.

In the history of childhood, children who did not fit society's construction of normal were often reviled and abandoned as deviant or deficient. Other children, having lost their parents through war or other circumstances, were sent to orphanages or left to fend for themselves in the almshouses (Askeland, 2006). Large institutions were often the holding places for the children that nobody wanted.

Throughout European and North American history there were many leaders who wrote about the need to care for and educate these children. They created and led educative communities. These philosophers, early educators, and child advocates led the efforts to create a caring and humane world for all children to grow up in and formed the basis for the development of the profession of child and youth care. They had a significant impact on changing how young people were raised by their families and the nature of the social structures that support them.

Sporadic attempts to help children with special needs can be traced back to the Middle Ages, but the first systematic educational provisions began to appear in the 18th century. In 1749, Pereire, a native of Spain, demonstrated before the Academy of Science in Paris his success in teaching a congenital deaf-mute to speak and read. . . . Itard published a study of his famous attempt to teach the "wild boy of Aveyron," and in the process he developed educational methods and materials. . . . In Switzerland, Pestalozzi established the first home and school for war orphans and began to evolve an educational philosophy and principles of teaching which have had an enduring impact on both regular and special education. (Juul, 1990, p. 92)

The leaders who changed the thinking about how to care for and educate young people over the last 200 years in Europe and North America were professionals from varied backgrounds with a special interest in the well-being of young people and the humane treatment of those who were different and/or abandoned by their caregivers.

Library of Congress, Prints & Photographs Division, [LC-USZ62-84527]

Jean Jacque Rousseau was an 18th-century Swiss/French philosopher who wrote on many topics, including the origins of inequality and the political economy. He is well known for his philosophy of education called *Emile OR On Education*,[3] a semi-fictional work on methods of education that put forward the idea that children are basically good (not evil) and will naturally develop with a healthy sense of self and good morality if placed in a natural environment. He argued against the punishing methods of the Christian religions of the time. His educational ideas were controversial but were adopted by the bourgeoisie and working class, leading to reforms in the way children were treated (Rahikainen, 2004).

Jean Marc Itard was a physician who specialized in hearing impairment and is known for developing methods for teaching deaf-mute children. He is most well known for his work with Victor, the wild boy of Aveyron, who was not deaf, but likely autistic or cognitively impaired. Itard believed that language was key to learning and that together with empathy, language distinguished humans from animals. Victor lived with Itard beginning around the age of 12 in 1800 and, while he did not learn to speak, he learned to respond to language and could say some basic words. Itard was successful to the extent that Victor demonstrated emotion and empathy for his caregivers ("Jean Marc Gaspard Itard," 2008). Itard's methods were revolutionary for their humanity and his belief that all children could learn. (See Itard, 1962.)

J. J. Kelso was a reporter with the *Globe and Mail* in Toronto when he founded the Toronto Humane Society in 1887 and the first Canadian Children's Aid Society in 1891. The early work of the Toronto Children's Aid Society (TCAS) focused on protecting children from cruel treatment and dealing with the moral and social problems of neglect, which were closely related to the juvenile justice system. Supervision and caring for delinquents brought in by the police was necessary and thought to be essential to the future of society (Chen, 2005). In 1893, with the creation of the first legislation for child protection, Kelso was appointed as the Children's Superintendent responsible for ensuring that neglected and dependent children were treated humanely. He established a network of children's aid societies across the province, which continues today.

---

[3] Rousseau (1979).

Kelso believed that the "habitat, habits, and heart" of the child were important objectives for parenting and child-saving. Habits were learned and could therefore be changed with vigilance in all aspects of the child's life. Once changed, the child would be able to self-regulate in adulthood. Kelso argued that instead of using hands to scold, one should use head and heart to shape a child. Workers should have compassion and Christian love and "the ability to reform parents and children through this kind of calculated compassion was precisely the 'special ability' that was called for in the child savers" (Chen, 2005, p. 58).

THE LATE CHARLES L. BRACE, OF NEW YORK.
From a Photograph.

The first "children's aid" in the United States was founded in New York City in 1853 by Mr. Charles L. Brace and other reformers. Incorporated in 1856, the Children's Aid Society ran the first boys' lodging house and industrial school for Newsboys beginning in 1854 and developed a girls' lodging and training school in 1862. By 1893 there were 21 Industrial Schools, and they were sending "orphan trains" to rural farms across the United States where young people could live with families and work the fields. The "fresh air fund" developed a summer retreat for children in 1874 and continued to provide lodging for young people, particularly those with longer-term illnesses that could not be cared for within their families.

Tips and Resources

Children's Aid Society (United States): www.children saidsociety.org/about/history

> The case of Mary Ellen Wilson in 1874 spurred the movement for formalized child protection in the United States, through the American Society for the Prevention of Cruelty to Animals (ASPCA).
> www.americanhumane.org/about-us/who-we-are/history/mary-ellen-wilson.html

> Engage in some historical research of your own and review this story of a young Quebec girl who died in circumstances suspiciously like child abuse. Original documents, newspaper articles, court documents, and community reaction describe the societal attitudes of the time.
> www.canadianmysteries.ca/sites/gagnon/accueil/indexen.html

Johann Henreich Pestalozzi followed the ideals of Jean Jacque Rousseau from the late 1700s and implemented a series of boarding schools or **educative communities** in castles and country estates around Switzerland. He created a self-sufficient community farm, implementing the principle that basic household work contributed to a sense of community and self-worth. He attempted to teach the ideals of social justice, freedom, and self-sacrifice. He believed that using methods of love and relationship rather than punishment would help children to learn the ways of society and would prepare them for life (Brendtro, 1990). Pestalozzi's ideals are found among the methods of American leaders in residential care who refused to implement behaviourism in residential institutions in the mid to late 20th century, and in the work of Janus Korzak during the world wars. In more recent times, therapeutic communities following similar principles provide services for adults with mental health disorders, addictions, and/or developmental disabilities.

Janus Korczak, a physician, ran an orphanage for Jewish children in Poland during the world wars. His children's community was operated as a just and self-governed community where both staff and children could be called before a tribunal to be judged for right or wrong. Lesser offences were forgiven, and more serious offences were punished through formal apologies and public statements. Korczak believed that children were oppressed, and thus he listened and respected their opinions on par with those of adults. He hosted a children's radio programme, founded a newspaper run by and for children, defended street kids in juvenile courts and won literary fame with his classic children's story "King Matt The First" that has been translated into 20 languages.[4] After the Nazis occupied Poland, his Jewish orphanage was moved into the Warsaw Ghetto. Refusing all offers for his own rescue, he accompanied the 200 children on the train that took them to Treblinka. (Brendtro, 1990; Brendtro, Brokenleg, & Bockern, 1990; Brendtro & Hinders, 1990). His orphanages operated for many years before the famous march to the train of death. Joseph Aaron, a graduate of one of Korczak's communities, commented that life was difficult after leaving the orphanage because he was educated to believe in a "life of justice and truth," which didn't exist (Aaron, 1983, cited in Brendtro & Hinders, 1990). Korczak has been honoured by UNESCO-United Nations Educational, Scientific, and Cultural Organization and is remembered in the work on the United Nations Convention on the Rights of the Child (UNCRC).

Library of Congress, Prints & Photographs Division, [LC-DIG-ggbain-14964]

The Montessori method of education, still popular today, is based on the methods of Maria Montessori in the early 20th century. She achieved success working with developmentally delayed and physically disabled children using sensory stimulation and self-corrected methods of interacting with learning apparatus. Montessori applied her methods, designed to promote cognitive development, to study the intellectual development of all children. She promoted self-corrected, discovery-based learning using materials that were age-appropriate. Her methods have been labeled controversial and research demonstrating effectiveness of the Montessori method over traditional approaches is inconclusive; however, the movement persists. What she offered at the time was evidence that children with developmental delays could learn and she introduced the idea that learning and cognitive processing were different for children and that traditional methods of teaching were not the only avenue; rather, children could learn through play.

[4] Korezak (1983).

THE EMERGENCE OF A PROFESSION

Whether called a profession, occupation, or craft, child and youth care is a modern discipline that developed largely in the European and North American cultural contexts. While occasionally a different view is presented, the focus in this chapter is European and North America historical perspectives. Caring for young people in other continents looks different. Youth work in "divided and contested societies" (Magnuson & Baizerman, 2007) contrasts markedly with the history of child and youth care in Europe and North America.

The profession of child and youth care developed within a set of societal conditions that included various political ideologies, government structures, and jurisdictions and numerous theoretical orientations that are based in the values and beliefs of those societies. To understand the complexity of these important influences on professional services, the concepts and the impact of culture, government jurisdictions, theory, and research are introduced.

These brief introductions are followed by a review of different eras in the development of the profession. The influences of culture, politics, jurisdiction, and theory vary depending on the era and are described in more detail as each era is reviewed. This is followed by a discussion of the current issues the profession is addressing. You are encouraged to read the more in-depth analyses offered by the various authors referenced here in order to better understand how ideology and societal trends influenced the history of the profession.

CULTURE

Culture today is often associated with racial or ethnic background. More broadly, culture is represented by the way of life in a society and includes the norms, rules of social interaction, values, beliefs, artistic traditions and objects, legal and social institutions, and religious and political belief systems. Child and youth care as a profession began within post–World War II society and culture in Europe and North America. Its cultural origins subsume theories, ideas, and social norms such as:

- Individualism
- Focus on rationale and scientific thought
- Industrialization
- Equality and democracy
- Christian biblical tradition
- Separation of church and state

It has been common practice in the "Western" world to view global cultures in a dichotomous manner (e.g., Western vs. non-Western), which fails to recognize the diversity within a single society. Cultural diversity transcends the borders between continents, states, and even major cities. The terminology "Western world" developed after World War II and refers to the primary disagreements in ideology that lead to the world wars. Since the end of World War II in 1945, war has continued in many parts of the world and is often related to the assertion of cultural and spiritual identity over masses of people. Countries with ideologies that are different from the Western world are actually the "majority world," not the minority, and their cultures are very different from ours (Pence & Marfo, 2008); yet the theory and philosophy of Western culture is often used to understand the needs of young people in these countries and societies. Youth work in the majority world is largely undertaken by either the youth themselves or people who travel there and assist those youth.

People who have emigrated to North America from such a country may recognize the limited view of the child and youth care profession as a result of our historical and cultural influences. Alternatively, it may all be so familiar that it is difficult to understand how there could be any other way of working. In today's global world practitioners need to develop openness to the differences in other contexts and modify their work with young people who have come to North America from the "majority world." Being paid to care for young people began within specific historical and social-political contexts that emphasized social control and education for con-formity (e.g., Kelso's ideas about habitats, habit, heart). Political ideals vary in their approaches to power and equality, the economy, and management of wealth, state-defined ethics (i.e., laws that reflect moral ideas), and their orientation to assisting those in need (for social, health, or economic reasons).

These political ideals influenced the funding of services, laws for child protection, laws for criminal acts by or against children, and children's rights in Europe and North America. The emergence of Social Care[5] programs in Europe occurred because it was possible for professional caring to come to the fore, since the responsibility for those in need was shared across several different systems: the church, the government, and private industry (Hallstedt & Hogstrom, 2005). It became possible for people to "make money" by caring for children. Within this type of ideology there was a differentiation between the **service** or volunteer orientation and the **professional** orientation. The ethnocentric, Anglo-Saxon orientation within which services in North America initially developed promoted this differentiation. That is, those who were not within the elite of society (the poor and disadvantaged) were "inferior" and in need of assist-ance (Charles et al., 2005) and the elite in society were obligated to provide for them. Within the conservative climate a private industry of children's services developed where the profit was accrued to the owner and the wages were low.

GOVERNMENT JURISDICTIONS

There are many branches of government responsible for services and programs for young peo-ple and families. Each branch carries a different orientation toward the problems and needs of young people. Most of modern professional child and youth care practice occurs within the jurisdictions of social service, health, criminal justice, and education. As described by Fulcher and Ainsworth (2006) in **Figure 2.1**, there are overlaps in the responsibility and the core phi-losophy of the systems.

The central purpose underlying each of these systems is different: education of children, response to criminal behaviour, management and cure of health problems, or the protection of children from neglect and abuse. These systems evolved at different times in the political histories of both North America and Europe and were influenced by theory and politics of

---

[5] Social care, social pedagogue, and educateur specialise are common terms used in relation to child and youth care practice in Western European countries. They are used interchangeably to describe professional development in those countries.

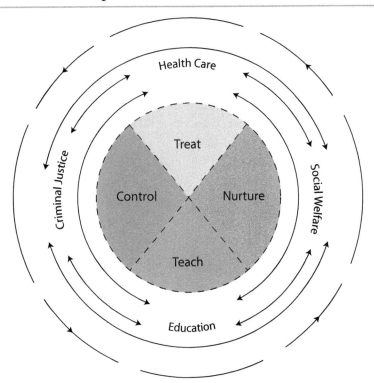

Figure 2.1 Resource Systems, Underlying Purpose, and Areas of Overlap (Fulcher & Ainsworth, 2006, p. 6)

the day. For example, conservative politics takes a harsh view of criminal activity and expects both individual and family responsibility for children's criminal activity. Offenders must be removed from society (institutionalized) and punished. Social democratic politics, with its focus on social justice and equality, heavily influenced the development of rights for the disabled and for children, moving away from institutional care and toward universal education and community living. The profession of child and youth care grew primarily from the social welfare, and secondarily from the educational systems that dealt with young people, particularly those who could not conform to the mainstream systems.

Child and youth care roots are in residential institutions for young people who were delinquent, mentally ill, or in need of housing due to poverty or abuse. There were also moral philosophies associated with Christianity and Judaism in North America. Residential institutions were also used for educational purposes and in Canada, for example, Aboriginal young people were sent to residential schools run by religious orders to be assimilated into society. Movements such as the YMCA or Boys and Girls Clubs were developed to provide for the young people from immigrant families who were poor (Charles et al., 2005; Charles & Garfat, 2009). These religious orders had strong and very specific moral and ethical values based on religious teachings. Youth who were "at risk" because of poverty, delinquency, or lack of family were thought to need good moral education to set them on the right path and to integrate them into society. Their care providers worked for Christian or Jewish child welfare organizations designed to provide that moral education.

Tips and Resources

Child and Youth Care in South Africa

Veeran (2011) provides an excellent analysis of the effects of culture, political ideals, and government policy on the empowerment of young people in South Africa. During the apartheid era institutionalized racism legitimized the violation of basic human rights for all black people. The Soweto riots in June 1976 saw between 400 and 600 schoolchildren killed in the streets during a peaceful protest against the policies of the apartheid government, which affected their education. The National Association of Child Care Workers was formed in 1975 in South Africa, through the merging of provincial associations. Child and youth care in South Africa was significantly affected by apartheid policies, which limited the number of residential homes for black and colored children. Standards of care were different, access to education for caregivers was different, and the national association began to advocate for change. Detailed history on child welfare in South Africa can be found at www.cyc-net.org/reference/refs-history%20-%20beukesgannon.html (Beukes & Gannon, 1996). More recently, with the impact of AIDS, child and youth care work has focused on family support in child led families devastated by the AIDS epidemic.

National Association of Child Care Workers (South Africa): www.naccw.org.za

THE INFLUENCE OF THEORY AND RESEARCH

In the context of human services, professions have a unique, specialized knowledge base that begins with theory and is advanced through research. Theories are idealized explanations for the development of troubling behaviour among young people—behaviour that is out of line with society's expectations. The theoretical explanations for human behaviour that are the foundations for professional child and youth care are closely tied to both the ancient philosophers as well as modern political ideals of democracy and individual freedom (post–World War II). The primary influence on the profession is **psychoanalytic** theory, with some moderation by **humanist** theory, **symbolic interactionism,** and **behaviourism**.

Early North American work on children with troubling behaviours, such as *Controls from Within: Techniques for the Treatment of the Aggressive Child* (Redl & Wineman, 1952), focused on techniques for developing the ego, thought to be responsible for regulating behaviour, a core concept in psychoanalytic theory. Behaviourists theorized that all behaviour was externally controlled by reinforcement, not internally controlled, and developed point and level systems as reinforcers for developing socially appropriate behavior. Humanists focused on offering unconditional care so that young people could grow to their full potential. Symbolic interactionism was founded on the premise that our actions and behaviors are part of symbolic communication embedded in societal norms and that all behavior must be understood in the context of its purpose in interaction with others. These varied theoretical explanations for behaviour continue to create tension in child and youth care practice today (VanderVen, 1995).

The child welfare system grew out of a welfare system that was designed to support those in poverty. The initial reforms in this system developed large orphanages as alternatives to the street or the almshouses of the 18th century. By the mid-19th century in the United States, foster care programs began to develop, run largely by Christian organizations as a means of rescuing children from immoral environments where parents were lazy, did not work, and could not provide for their children. It was around this time that the philosophical and scientific arguments about whether institutional care or foster care was superior began. A 1930 study directly comparing the outcomes of children in foster care with those in institutional care concluded that both types of care did good work and were needed (Lindsey, 2004). Similar arguments began to focus on family preservation in comparison to the child-saving movement (which removed children from their families) represented by J. J. Kelso. As the system evolved, the focus in the child-savers movement shifted from children who had no family to children whose family was immoral, to children whose family was abusive. The overall approach retained the philosophy that state intervention was a measure of last resort when no other family or kinship networks were available (Lindsey, 2004).

Work with young people in North America was heavily influenced by the objective, scientific paradigm that equated knowledge with power. Research in child welfare, as it evolved over these time periods, looked at two issues consistently. First, what were the reasons that children were not living at home? Over time, the reasons that children were taken into care shifted from children who were orphans or whose families lived in poverty, to neglect and abuse, and about in 1960 began to include the child's behaviour as a reason for placement. The influences of medicine and psychology and research on child development and children's psychopathology shaped the health care and education systems. "Battered child syndrome" was first discovered by Kempe in 1962 (Lindsey, 2004) and represented a scientific, medical approach with the expectation that the syndrome could be cured through protection interventions.

Second, research examined whether young people need protection or attachment. From the beginning of reported research studies around 1950, one-third or more of the children were noted to have spent 4 or more years in foster care (Lindsey, 2004), often in multiple placements. This is consistent with today's research. The influence of sociology (protect young people from the difficult social conditions) began to compete with the influence of psychology (children need to be attached to a primary caregiver and not drift aimlessly in foster care), locking the system into a child-saving versus family-preservation debate that continues today. Child and youth care has positioned itself as a field and as a profession to work with both sides of this debate. Practitioners are found in the young person's milieu; thus we are able to support young people in their families and communities or to care for them separately from their families in residential environments, hospitals, and schools.

With this brief description of the various societal influences on our professional development as background, how the profession of child and youth care developed through several modern eras and was influenced by culture, political ideologies/government jurisdictions, and major theoreticians of the time is considered.

POST–WORLD WAR II: THE CHILDREN NOBODY WANTED—1940 TO 1960

After World War II the number of children needing a safe place to live increased, and childhood and adolescence emerged as distinct stages of life. Foster families recruited by the child-savers could not afford to take children. Postwar economic depression left families in difficult circumstances; children were often unaffordable and could be sent to detention institutions or orphanages when families struggled financially. Work previously available to young people was now being taken by adults (as "war work" disappeared), and the age of mandatory education increased as the modern education system developed.

Tips and Resources

The Dictionary of Informal Education (Social Pedagogy)

www.infed.org/index.htm

Postwar Western European countries struggled with how to house large numbers of young people whose parents were killed in the wars. Today these young people would be diagnosed with "posttraumatic stress disorder"; however, in the late 1940s they were seen as being in need of care, education, and training for employment. The challenges of meeting their needs were significant. In 1942 France began an association of "Educateur Specialise." These professionals worked with children and were total life specialists responsible for pulling the potential *out* of troubled youth (Ness & Mitchell, 1990). They were not "educators," who are responsible for teaching or putting information *in*. Educateur Specialise[6] in Europe play a central role on the treatment team and have high professional status (Juul, 1990).

The influence of socialist politics was evident as communities of care were created for children. The International Federation of Educative Communities/Fédération Internationale des Communautés Educatives (FICE) formed in 1948 with the express purpose of creating and supporting children's communities, following the traditions of Pestalozzi in Switzerland (Lasson, Nobs, & Anglin, 1990). FICE continues as an association today with a focus on residential care and treatment.

Freud's psychoanalytic traditions were strong in Europe, particularly following his escape from Nazi Germany in 1938 and his death the following year. Psychoanalytic theory, with a focus on child development and the importance of the preadolescent and adolescent years, strengthened the relationship-based orientation adopted by the profession and permeated the work and the early curriculum developed for Educateurs. "Child care, while consolidating its identity, opened itself to intermediate structures: children's villages, communities of youth . . . and the 'milieu ouvert' (streetwork)" (Traber, 1990, p. 126).

In North America, where capitalism and industrial development predominated, the field of child care work (Mayer, 1958) was taking a different track. Large correctional institutions developed to house juvenile delinquents, taking a punitive focus consistent with the justice orientation. Hospital-type facilities focused on housing children with physical and medical disabilities, and were similarly large and institutional in nature.

At the same time the large orphanages of the religious orders began to be dismantled and replaced by specialized "smaller" treatment programs (Charles et al., 2005) influenced by the social welfare system, which provided for basic needs, and the education system, which hoped to socialize children and prepare them for adulthood. Fritz Redl and David Wineman, in their opening to *Children Who Hate: A Sensitive Analysis of the Anti-social Behaviour of Children in Their Response to the Adult World*, summarized the problem presented at that time:

> No matter how their specific pathology of "hatred" looks in the beginning, or which part of their personality has been most severely affected by it, the children who hate become an insoluble problem for the communities in which they live. The result is an enormous and unfortunate amount of human waste. . . . They are literally, the children nobody wants. (1951, pp. 23–24)

Early writers in the therapeutic use of the life space such as Redl and Wineman and Bruno Bettleheim immigrated to the United States during the period of the world wars and followed the

---

[6] "In Norway the title for an educateur is 'barnevernpedagog.' In Russia, they are known as 'defectologists.' In Belgium their title is 'educateur sociale,' and in Sweden and Denmark it is 'socio-pedagogue'" (Ness & Mitchell, 1990, p. 200).

work of Western European psychoanalysts such as August Aichhorn and Anna Freud. Their published works were research, following the psychoanalytic tradition. Research methods in this tradition do *not* include measurement and statistics as a method of inferring effectiveness; rather, they use a case-study approach. They worked in an environment where the wealthy foundations (and individuals behind them) felt obligated to provide for the less fortunate, as well as to be recognized for their contribution to knowledge production. The authors were "studying" the disturbance of the behavioural control functions of "children who hate" both to help the children and to learn about the development of these functions in "normal" children. These early works guided the design of child and youth care curricula and the design of residential programs for young people.

Psychoanalysts were also battling the rise of behaviourism in the United States (VanderVen, 1995). Behaviourism focused on children as passive beings in the learning and development process. The belief was that they simply responded to stimuli. Parents and educators were therefore responsible for teaching them correct behaviour and early writings attempted to provide guidelines for healthy environments in order to prevent institutionalization (Burns, 2006; Charles & Gabor, 2006).

Marie Rodgers was placed in a Belfast orphanage immediately after her birth in 1950.

> The entire building was surrounded by a huge wall with barbed wire and pieces of broken glass on top of it. I spent 17 years there and endured a life devoid of caring and love. We were bathed in Jeyes Fluid. Each day, after washing ourselves, we had to call out our orphanage number to be inspected by the nun in charge. My number was 51. . . . I felt ostracised by the rest of the world and intimidated by those charged with caring for me. I was afraid to question their authority or ask for their guidance or help. It would be many years before I would be able to break free from the pattern set in my childhood. (Rodgers, 1998, p. 211)

In 1952 the development of the profession in Western Europe (France and Germany) converged briefly with development in the United States, when the School of Social Work at New York University developed and delivered an educational curriculum for Educateur Specialise from France and Germany (Ness & Mitchell, 1990). In Europe training became a requirement, and the profession grew in France, Germany, Norway, and Denmark. The pioneers of child and youth care in North America had progressive approaches but did not have the same success in growing the profession. In a time of highly authoritarian and punitive approaches, they treated children with respect and saw them as young people "in development" (Brendtro & Shahbazian, 2004) who needed educational guidance to reach their full potential (Stevens & Furnivall, 2008), but the North American profession did not take the next steps to professionalization by developing an association or creating postsecondary training until nearly 20 years later. Most of Europe forged ahead with professionalizing the *Educateur Specialize* or the *Social Pedagogue.*

1960 TO MID-1970S: SPECIALIZED INTERVENTION

Children's services in the 1960s in Europe featured competing philosophies of residential care and different streams of treatment. **Therapeutic communities** developed in Great Britain and Europe that were based on a philosophy consistent with socialism. In the educational sector, alternative schools such as Summerhill (Stevens & Furnivall, 2008) were founded, where lessons were not compulsory and rules were decided at weekly meetings where children and adults held equal power. The child and youth care worker in France and other locations in Europe followed these traditions of equality and democracy, and work became "more and more horizontal—workers were less formal, wore unisex clothing, and engaged with the children in sports and leisure activities" (Traber, 1990, p. 127). At the same time, in the health care and justice systems and in some sectors of the educational system in Europe, an approach that involved labeling the problems of young people[7] and heavily structuring the milieu to deal with them evolved (Peters, 2008). Labeling children allowed them to move from one system to the next with a one- or two-word history (the label) that determined how they would be treated in the next system. Structure within the organization became increasingly rigid, and groups of young people could be controlled through rules, consequences, and punishment rather than democratic negotiation.

In North America, in spite of the early writings that influenced the development of the profession toward psychoanalytic traditions, behaviourism began to influence many residential institutions, and **token and level systems** were developed as methods of treatment. These methods also provided control and structure that were easy to follow. "In Europe, behaviorism has nowhere acquired the popularity that it has in the United States. It has however, been the subject of intense philosophical and political controversy, and it has been described both as an expression of a Marxist view of the individual and society and as symptomatic of capitalistic mentality" (Juul, 1990, pp. 97–98). Children were viewed more holistically by the Social Pedagogue, who understood problem behaviours to include social, emotional, medical, and educational rationale.

This period of time saw professional child and youth care service orientations in the United States diverge further from those in Europe. Socialist influences in Europe continued to support the development of educative collectives for the treatment of delinquent and substance-addicted youth. Deinstitutionalization of those in mental health institutions in the health system and integrated education began in Italy and spread to other areas in Europe. Deinstitutionalization was resisted in the United States where segregated institutional care and special education systems continued (Juul, 1990). The European model was actively rejected and attempts to bring the Educateur model to United States were unsuccessful (Ness & Mitchell, 1990). It was during this period in history that the next step in professionalization of child and youth care occurred in North America; formal post-secondary education began. In Canada, the Program for Educateur Specialise developed at the University of Montreal in 1973 under the leadership of Jeannine Guidon. The 4-year curriculum with a strong European influence subsequently developed into a network of college programs in the province (Nicolaou & McCauley, 1991). At the University of Victoria in Canada, the program began in 1973, following on the initiatives of Ontario (in 1969) and Alberta (in 1972), who implemented programs variously called Child Care Work or Youth Development at local community colleges (OACYC, 2006; Phelan, 1988). The names of these programs reflected the continued influence of the psychoanalytic traditions by focusing on child development and internal controls.

---

[7] For example, labels such as emotionally and behaviorally disturbed or mentally retarded were broad categories of diagnosis based on emotional labiality or cognitive deficit.

Locating programs in universities and colleges in Canada was a very different approach from that of the United States, where training was provided by the employer with only a few postsecondary programs, which were placed in education or psychology departments (Jones & Vander Ven, 1990). The State University of New York had a program from 1974 to 1978.

The first professional associations began in the 1960s. Oregon formed an association in 1961 (Krueger, 1991a) and Ontario was incorporated in 1969 (OACYC, 2006), but it wasn't until the 1970s that they began to work toward regulating the profession. The Child and Youth Care Learning Centre at University of Wisconsin under the leadership of Mark Krueger was formed in the 1970s as a partnership with the Wisconsin Child and Youth Care Association, and began publishing material in 1982 to facilitate the training, growth, and development of child and youth care practitioners (Krueger, 1982); however, most training programs in the United States remained within the large residential organizations or developed as specialized graduate programs in partnership with those organizations (Nicolaou & McCauley, 1991). Educational programs at this time focused on practitioners in the residential sector, and it wasn't until the **normalization** principle, **mainstreaming,** and the early intervention/prevention movements began to emerge that professional child and youth care education began to broaden its scope (Ferguson et al., 1993), following the lead of the European educateurs.

PERSONAL REFLECTION

My brother Hugh was born in 1968, 11 years before I began working in the field. He was (in the words of that time) "mentally retarded." He benefited somewhat from the normalization movement that was emerging at the time and from the fact that my parents did not want him institutionalized. He lived at home until he was 14 and, after an agonizing period of decision making, went to live in a small cottage at a local institution. The societal forces that I have been describing up to now are perhaps best represented in the letters from his grandmothers, written to my parents at the time that he was "diagnosed." My father, a scientist who liked to keep the original data rather than construct history, kept them for 40 years.

"I like your attitude to keep working with him and trying to help him all you can. Your hearts are heavy with disappointment, but the good Book says, cast thy burden upon the Lord and he will sustain thee. Give Hughie lots of love and attention and I am sure it will help all the way around. Love, Mother."

"One thing you may be happy about is that he is not repellent to look at and also he is not aware of what he is missing, which sometimes is almost a blessing, and lately there is a great effort being made to enable retarded children to make the most of what they have. . . . If you can manage to teach the little fellow some coordination, toilet habits, and ability to communicate, I believe he could then be happier in a school or institution where his associates are of similar mental ability. Whatever you do, don't let his trouble warp the lives of your little girls. With very much love Mother." . . .

Hugh's grandmothers demonstrate the attitudes of society in 1968. Strong religious traditions obligated you to care for and love these children, but accept God's will. Children who were deficient were to be isolated and had nothing to offer to enrich other lives. Parenting was a role for mothers. Indeed, as the revolution of the following years demonstrated, many mothers became "accidental activists," fighting to have their "deficient" children enrolled in regular schools in their local communities or to house them locally in small, comfortable, homelike atmospheres (Panitch, 2008). There was a difference between young people who were developmentally delayed (the unfortunate) and those that did not conform to the norms of society (the misbehaving). The movements of normalization and deinstitutionalization emerged in different ways based on the "special needs" of different groups of children and the jurisdiction responsible for those needs.

Hugh went to a day nursery for the mental retarded when he was 3. He started kindergarten at the local "school" for the mentally retarded and by the time he got to high school he was attending TMR (trainable mentally retarded) classes at the high school where his father was the vice-principal; he was bussed there from the cottage where he lived and they had lunch together every day. I'm not sure what they talked about, since Hugh never learned to talk. He graduated high school at 21, a year before he died of cancer. His life in the 1970s and 1980s included playing on the street where we lived, swimming every summer at the local pool, shopping with his parents, going to camp, coming home on the weekends. He had a profound effect on many young people because he touched the lives of our friends and neighbors through his integration into society.

Carol Stuart

MID-1970S TO 1990: NORMALIZATION AND THE HALLMARKS OF PROFESSIONALIZATION

The normalization principle originated with Wolfensburger, who became its leading proponent within the health sector, which was charged with caring for the developmentally and physically disabled at that time. The policy initiative originated in Denmark and moved through Europe in the 1960s (Fulcher & Ainsworth, 2006). At the same time in the educational sector, the mainstreaming movement brought education for the disabled, physically or cognitively impaired, into regular schools. Sometimes it brought them into the regular classroom as well, though this movement did not occur until the next era (Rasmussen, Haggith, & Roberts, 2012). With normalization came deinstitutionalization, meaning less need for child and youth care practitioners in staffed residential settings and practitioners were needed to support the children in the school environment with their social, emotional, and at times physical needs. The influence of normalization also lead to an associated movement toward deinstitutionalization (Fulcher & Ainsworth, 2006) in child welfare and justice jurisdictions, resulting in "small-scale provision" (Colton & Helljnckx, 1994, p. 564) of service for residential care, which continued to be popular in Europe. Large institutions were split into smaller "homes" but were still located in rural areas far from family. The practitioners in the field of child and youth care had the skills and theoretical knowledge to work with young people in the smaller homes and in nonresidential settings.

Attempts to define professional competence and delineate the boundaries of the profession continued throughout this era. The educational model of the social pedagogue in France was blended with the "scientific and observable" orientation of the time and researchers and educational programs began to try and define the **competencies,** or skill base, required of practitioners.

An important development in the professionalization of child and youth care during this era was the beginning of professional regulation, which "certified" that practitioners were competent to practice. A strong professional association was important to this progression. In 1979 the Alberta government implemented a Child Care Counsellor Training and Certification Program (Phelan, 1988) and in 1984 the certification part of the program became available to nonprofit agencies when it was taken over by the Child and Youth Care Association of Alberta (CYCAA). The administration of a program certifying competence by the professional association was another significant step in the development of the field as a profession and is generally recognized as one of the first formal programs to regulate the field through required testing of knowledge and skill.

The Child Care Workers Association of Ontario (CCWAO) petitioned in 1974 for a regulatory college, which would require legislation to define the qualifications for practice as a child and youth care worker. The regulatory college was rejected by government, but in 1976 the Ministry of Education established a standardized curriculum for Child Care Worker (CCW) Programs in Ontario Colleges of Applied Arts and Technology. In 1979 the CCWAO set criteria (a CCW diploma from an Ontario college) for certification of its membership.

In the United States, where training occurred primarily within individual organizations, the Wisconsin Association for Child and Youth Care Professionals finalized a partnership with the University of Wisconsin–Milwaukee Division of Outreach and Continuing Education in 1979, forming the Child and Youth Care Learning Center. The educational courses at the Center are held in conjunction with the professional association and formed the certification process for that state. The Certification Board of Review has been approving and certifying applications since 1981 based on training in this partnership. The CYC Certification Institute in Texas offers training and certification (requiring previous postsecondary education in a related field) for multiple practice settings from early childhood through to juvenile justice. The Texas system is linked to training and is unique in that it recognizes a wide variety of training programs as long as they cover the domain areas required. The Ohio Association of Child and Youth Care Professionals formed in 1979, started certifying practitioners around 1989, and currently requires that all certified members have completed Tier I and II of the Core Competencies for Child and Youth Care Professionals (Ohio Association of Child and Youth Care Practitioners, 2011). Without government regulation, certification developed in small pockets where state or provincial associations were strong.

In 1981 the first Canadian national conference was held at the University of Victoria followed quickly in 1985 by the first International Child and Youth Care conference hosted by a fledgling collective of state and provincial professional associations called NOCCWA; the National Organization of Child Care Worker Associations. The conferences signaled a number of important developments in defining the profession. Co-incident with this time, two North American journals emerged to join the existing *Child and Youth Care Quarterly* (initiated in 1972): the *Journal of Child and Youth Care Work,* published annually by NOCCWA in the United States, and the *Journal of Child and Youth Care (now Relational Child and Youth Care Practice)* published in Canada.

A review of the literature (Small & Dodge, 1988) examined published documents that focused on the tasks and functions of the work and extended as far back as 1930. The authors were interested in describing the tasks and functions of child and youth care work in the United States as a preliminary taxonomy that could then be validated with front-line workers. The material focused on residential care for the "emotionally disturbed," "mentally retarded," or "delinquents."

Three important trends were identified that represented turning points for child and youth care around this time. First, professional child and youth care was no longer defined according to the setting (residential) or the characteristics of the client population, but rather according to generic functions and competencies that were stable across different programs. Second, "practice models stressed the clinical exploitation of life events throughout the environment and . . . identified the childcare worker as potentially the most important therapeutic agent in the program" (Small & Dodge, 1988, p. 9). This shift moved the focus from just nurturance and daily care to practice that included planned interventions and treatment planning conferences and focused on interventions in the daily milieu. Finally, child and youth care began to emerge outside of the residential setting in areas involving family intervention, school settings, youth centers, and streetwork.

Throughout the 1970s and 1980s the profession struggled to articulate a definition of the work and tried to reach agreement about the content and the level of education required (Krueger, 1991a). In some provinces and states, progress was significant; employers required certified workers, and postsecondary education flourished. Those with appropriate credentials were paid more. In Canada, specialized programs expanded at colleges and universities across the country. In the United States education was located as a subspecialty in departments of psychology and education. The University of Pittsburgh, for example, created a specialization for child and youth care within their Masters program in Applied Developmental Psychology. Nova South Eastern University had a specialization in child and youth care administration in their Masters of Science in Human Services; however, these programs did not achieve status independent of the host psychology or education departments like the college and undergraduate programs in Canada.

The requirement for a practice-based component to formal education for the profession, which was included in the education of Social Pedagogues in Europe, was incorporated into postsecondary education in Canada, both through practical work for which students received credit and with part-time coursework that encouraged existing practitioners to return for further education. However, in both the United States and Canada, academic institutions resisted the need to provide education to people already working in the field, and set entrance standards that limited minorities from accessing the courses (Krueger, 1991a). This was particularly concerning in urban centers, where minorities were often significantly affected by poverty and social conditions and qualified practitioners were needed in the communities.

In Europe the theoretical influences of neo-Marxist, feminist thought and symbolic interactionism caused those working in residential institutions to reconsider what they were doing. The child was no longer thought to be separate from the influences of family, and it became important to involve the family in the work (Colton & Helljnckx, 1994). Increased flexibility, despecialization, and the importance of continuity and relationship in the professional work required more professional discretion and therefore in France, Germany, and the Netherlands the requirements for working with young people in residential settings increased to a degree level in the 1970s and 1980s (Peters, 2008). The development of the profession was uneven throughout Europe and in some areas there was no unification of the profession (Colton & Helljnckx, 1994).

Things changed radically in Europe when a public outcry occurred as some children were severely injured or killed by untrained and inexperienced workers. The government moved to legislate and control access to the profession, attempting to set minimum standards for entering the profession. The same issues arose in the United States and in Canada, spurring the impetuses, at least by the profession, for self-regulation and the authority to oversee a basic standard of practice and care. The government support for self-regulation in North America was limited and focused only on residential settings where the risks of injury were greater. In Nova Scotia, for example, standards for residential care, implemented in 1998, require a diploma in Youth Work or a general undergraduate degree for front-line workers in residential care.

1990 TO THE PRESENT: THE MEANING OF QUALITY OF CARE AND SERVICE

Throughout the 1990s and into the 21st century, efforts continued in North America to solidify child and youth care as a profession. Most of the efforts toward professionalizing the field were based on the belief that "becoming" a profession and achieving those hallmarks (education, knowledge, ethics, and self-regulation) would result in improved quality of care and service for children (Krueger, 2002). This section considers three distinct aspects of recent efforts toward professionalization and describes how these are affecting child and youth care as a profession in Canada, the United States, and Western Europe. The **development of education and training** programs, the **certification** of practitioners, and the demands for **evidence-based practice** are each considered in turn.

Development of Training and Education

The educators and professionals in the United States and Canada focused on developing curricula for the new profession. While in Western Europe degree-level credentials were required by employers and governments in several countries, the enhancements in education in North America are largely the result of the educators themselves. In 1990 the North American Consortium of Child and Youth Care Education Programs was formed to explore accreditation standards for child and youth care education programs. The group decided that the time was not right for accreditation, and worked instead on defining core content for the education programs. They published, in 1995, "four basic assumptions for an interactional/interpersonal perspective to child and youth care and four segments of core content for educating Child and Youth Care workers: **carework** as an interpersonal process; **contextual** interactions in the milieu; **therapeutic interventions**; and **indirect elements** in carework practice" (Krueger, 2002, p. 17). The consortium has met regularly during preconference meetings at national and international conferences in North America since that time.

In 1993 the Ontario Government, through the Ministry of Advanced Education, developed the *Vocational Learning Outcomes for Child and Youth Worker Programs,* which were intended as a tool to evaluate the college programs. The vocational outcomes are followed by the college programs in Ontario (Ontario Ministry of Training, 2002) and linked to their curriculum. College diplomas in child and youth care began in Nova Scotia and New Brunswick in the public community colleges in the late 1990s and were followed by private college programs.

In Canada, preparation of child and youth care practitioners has evolved as preservice education in colleges and universities. By 2009 every province had implemented at least a college-level diploma, and in several provinces undergraduate degrees integrated with the diploma system are widely available. Practitioner demands and support from educators has led to graduate-level programming in some institutions. The initiative to accredit educational programs in Canada was revitalized in 2006 with the support of the Canadian Council of Child and Youth Care Associations. The Child and Youth Care Educational Accreditation Board was incorporated in 2012 to implement an educational accreditation process and standards. In the United States preservice postsecondary education is incorporated into other disciplines as a specialty, while private training institutes, largely attached to specific social service organizations, follow independent and unregulated curricula.

Certification

In 1992 the International Leadership Coalition for Professional Child and Youth Care began several initiatives that would create a North American definition of practice, ethical stance, and ultimately a certification process that would reach beyond the state and provincial programs that existed at the time.

While the individual professional associations had created and adopted ethical codes of practice as part of the self-regulation movement, these statements were hard to find, diverse, and tended to be rule-bound rather than value-based. Child and youth care was clearly a value-based field, requiring principled ethics rather than codified ethics to guide the work of practitioners (Mattingly, 1995a). The process of developing an international code of ethics was open-ended, consultative, and continuous. Even the final published code (see Appendix B) is labeled as a draft and includes questions for discussion. The code is gradually being officially adopted at local and national levels. Wisconsin adopted the code immediately; Ohio adopted the code in 2000. The Canadian Council of Child and Youth Care Associations adopted it in 2008, as did Alberta. Other states and professional associations have also opted to use the international code of ethics rather than develop their own.

The North American Certification Project (NACP) published a set of competencies for first-level "professional" child and youth care practice in 2003 (Mattingly et al., 2003). The competencies took 8 years to develop and were based on a review of over 100 published and unpublished documents, including early versions of the Alberta, Ontario, Texas, and Ohio certification programs noted above. The five NACP domains and their competencies were subsequently developed into an exam and an on-the-job evaluation tool, which established a national certification program for the United States in 2007. The certification program is administered through the independent Child and Youth Care Certification Board, Inc. (CYCCB) associated with the Association of Child and Youth Care Practice (ACYCP), which defines the competencies. Certification by the CYCCB is a means by which organizations can demonstrate the quality of care and service they offer.

In 2008, Maryland became the first state to require certification for residential child and youth care practitioners (see *http://dhmh.state.md.us/crccp/*). The existing Maryland certification board, formed in 2004 to certify managers of residential homes, was required to process and examine 10,000 residential workers in the state by 2015. Registered child and youth care practitioners are individuals who are assigned to perform the direct responsibilities related to activities of daily living, self-help, and socialization skills in a residential child care program under the direction of a certified manager. The mission of the state certification board is to improve the quality of care in residential homes. There is no formal connection between this initiative and the CYCCB certification process.

In Canada, certification is voluntary and is administered through the professional association in each province. Professional associations in Alberta and Ontario have certification standards and are advocating for legislated regulation of the profession. The evolution of child and youth care in Quebec has followed the European tradition of the psycho-educateur, and practitioners are called educateurs in most work settings. In 2003 a National Charter of Competencies was drafted for Quebec, based on the psycho-educateur model of reeducation. Provinces in eastern Canada are exploring the CYCCCB certification process.

Research and Evidence-based Practice

Currently, most services for young people are funded through the government with the expectation that the organizations will engage in research and use scientific procedures to demonstrate that interventions work with the young people referred to them. Evidence-based treatments or interventions are those that are proven to create change when procedures are specifically followed. The need for such specificity of procedures has been challenged and research has now demonstrated that the integration of clinical expertise and critical thinking that acknowledges each client as unique is essential in evidence-based practice (Gibbs & Gambrill, 2002).

Child and youth care practitioners continue to adopt an independent professional stance toward their practice but are working in organizations that are required to respond to the demands for evidence-based practice. Some authors claim that evidence-based practice is not possible because success requires the cooperation of the client, which (paradoxically) requires individual response on the part of the practitioner to the client encouraging the client to interact and co-produce the result (Peters, 2008). This co-production approach necessitates that professional child and youth care practitioners have a collaborative approach to practice. Evidence-based practice is about demonstrating that what you do is effective, which could mean using a scientific approach, or it might mean good observation and documentation using the case-study approach. There is a tension between the integration of practice knowledge and formal knowledge or scientific findings when making practice decisions. Bates (2006) demonstrated that school-based social workers were able to adopt and implement the beneficial aspects of evidence-based practice and to creatively adapt them to benefit their clients. "The diversity of practice problems and their unique presentations, and the notable gaps in the research literature ensures that practice expertise will always be required to integrate available evidence with informed practitioner judgment and service consumers' wishes. Evidence and practitioner judgment inform one another" (Howard, McMillen, & Pollio, 2003, p. 255). The process and the refinement of a practitioner's knowledge and skills is the subject of the next chapter, which posits that learning is a continual process. Practitioners must review the emerging research relevant to the special needs of young people and their circumstances in order to determine how it applies to a particular concern. They must integrate available evidence with informed judgment and the stated needs of young people such that each informs the other. Then, they must make the best choice for interacting with and supporting the young person to meet their needs.

SUMMARY

The European philosophers and educators, and their North American counterparts, who adopted a humanistic and children's rights–based perspective promoted a just and equitable society. These ideas remain at the heart of child and youth care. Whether in professional capacities in hospitals, schools, residential centers, or homeless shelters in North America, or functioning as youth workers in war zones in Northern Ireland, Africa, or the Middle East, the core philosophies of child and youth care begin with what young people want and are based on developing relationships. Equity, tolerance, justness, nonviolence, service to the community, working with and within the children's community all characterize a particular way of being with young people. This is the "way" that forms the basis for modern child and youth care work. It holds a particular set of values and attitudes and, most importantly, implements those in day-to-day work with young people in their own environments. How the field of child and youth care will respond to the social, political, and historical trends of the next 50 years, we don't know. Our emergence in modern history has roots in socialist politics, psychoanalytic theoretical traditions, and the government-operated social welfare systems. Practitioners expanded their perspective to include symbolic interactionism and to respond to the needs of young people as deinstitutionalization occurred. Practitioners are challenged to consistently uphold a standard of practice across diverse provinces and states.

In the next two chapters the issues related to professional development as a practitioner and the career options that are available are described. Chapter 3 discusses the stages of professional development and Chapter 4 considers more specifically the settings that child and youth care practitioners work in and the "type" of clients with which they work. These chapters review in more detail how the jurisdictions such as health/mental health, education, social services, and justice influence service provision. The client groups and specializations in child and youth care practice, which include young people with developmental disability; physical disability; youth at risk; youth with mental illness; child protection; young offenders; and children in or from war-torn or third-world countries are also reviewed.

> Professional Child and Youth Care is committed to promoting the well-being of children, youth, and families in a context of respect and collaboration. (Mattingly, 1995b, p. 372)

Photo by Laine Robertson

CHAPTER EXERCISES

THE SOCIAL CONSTRUCTION OF CHILDHOOD

Theory-in-Action

What are your socially constructed ideas about childhood?

Choose one of the following statements and describe what you think it represents about childhood today. Give some examples of children's activities that demonstrate the truth of the statement.

- Childhood is becoming longer and longer.
- Children are innocent beings.
- Children are born with a distinct nature that will emerge within the environment in which they are raised.
- Childhood ends when the child becomes independent from his or her parents.
- Children need stimulating activities in preparation for independence.
- Children today grow up too quickly.
- Children have no sexuality.
- Children need to be occupied in order to stay out of trouble.

VARIATIONS IN MODERN CHILDREARING TRADITIONS

Theory-in-Action

As you read the following list, try to identify variations in how these issues are addressed today, according to culture, religion, or socioeconomic class. Make note of how your family dealt with this issue. Find someone from a different cultural background and inquire about his or her experience. The issues present in childrearing in various societies over time include such things as:

Birth Control, Fertility, Family Size. How is the expense and time required to care for children managed? Preventative birth control? Infanticide?

Birth. Who births the child? Midwife or physician? Until the 19th or 20th century, Western physicians rarely attended births—in the majority of the world today women are attended by midwives.

Toilet Training. In homes with earthen floors, before sanitation and cleanliness were understood as methods of disease prevention, small children wore gowns and little else.

Baptism and Naming. Religious ceremonies for celebrating the child's birth and naming ceremonies have many practical as well as celebratory functions.

Wet Nurses—Daycare. Care arrangements for children that require the child to leave the family and depend on another caregiver for nurturance are common across the centuries. Swaddling, a robozo, to wrap up young children?

Wives Tales versus the Science of Child Development. How to treat children and to care for them and raise them are things that new parents need to learn. Who teaches these things? The method by which the knowledge is developed varies by culture.

Education and Socialization. Formal and informal education in the necessary tools for functioning in society has occurred in a variety of ways.

Discipline. Are children taught or controlled?

Affection. How and for how long are children shown affection?

Fathers. What role do fathers play in raising their children? How involved are they?

Family Members. What role do family members, siblings, grandparents, nieces, nephews, even neighbors, play in raising a child? When, if ever, are parents no longer responsible for ensuring that a child is safe, secure, and healthy?

YOUR CHILDHOOD STORY

Personal Reflection

Identify an incident from your childhood and develop it into a story that gives voice to your experience as a child. Perhaps as you read this chapter you recalled a story told by your parents, or you identified an experience that you had in interaction with your parents that was similar to something described in the text. Make some "factual" notes about the experience. Construct a story. Describe what this story might mean to you within your child and youth care practice. Revisit and rewrite the story as you grow in your practice.

BUT I JUST WANTED TO WORK WITH KIDS . . .

Personal Reflection

Take a moment to record your answers to these questions. Don't think deeply, just quickly.

- Why are young people violent?
- Why do we put young people in jail for aggression and violence?
- Why do we hospitalize young people when they are "out of control"?
- Why do we protect young children from violent or neglectful parents by taking them away and putting them in foster care?

Pause to make sure you've quickly answered them all.

These questions all imply a different explanation for the same phenomena. Societies and governments have preferred certain answers to the above questions over others at different points in our history. These government preferences and societal attitudes have influenced services for children and youth as well as the nature of our work.

WHAT ARE MY BELIEFS?

Theory-in-Action

Which one of the following statements do you most believe?

- Everyone should have a guaranteed income.
- If someone can demonstrate need for income, they should get it.
- Business, religious orders, and charitable groups should help the state by providing income or housing for those in need.
- Individuals should not profit; all profit should go to the government to assist those without economic means.

Have a discussion with a friend or classmate about the role of government funding for:

- Universal daycare
- Universal health care
- Disabled children who want to live at home and have parents willing to care for them, but have needs that are beyond the parents' capacity.

Try to identify your social or theoretical orientation and read further about the values and beliefs that accompany it.

What is the meaning of social justice?

WHERE DID THE DEFINITIONS COME FROM?

Theory-in-Action

As noted in Chapter 1, this is a profession that **meets the developmental needs of children, youth, and families within the space and time of their daily lives within an equitable, active, and engaged relationship that recognizes the importance of this experience to both lives.**

Focusing on the bolded aspects of the above definition, identify some of the philosophical, political, and theoretical orientations that might create a foundation for this definition? Underline keywords in the definition that match keywords in the definitions (see Glossary) of the various political and theoretical orientations.

THE LEARNING JOURNEY: STAGES OF PROFESSIONAL DEVELOPMENT AND TRANSFORMATIVE LEARNING

© Kiselev Andrey Valerevich, 2013. Under license from Shutterstock, Inc.

CHAPTER OBJECTIVES

- To describe the developmental phases of the professional practitioner from novice to mature practice.
- To describe the experiential learning process and its contribution to transformative development as a practitioner.
- To consider the role of self in transformative learning.
- To consider the role of relationships in transformative learning.
- To introduce the concept of praxis as an essential component of professional development.

This chapter describes the nature of the journey undertaken by a child and youth care practitioner through several developmental phases of learning about practice. The development of practice skills and a knowledge base are a life-long process marked by the general phases of **novice, experienced,** and **mature practice**. Terms like "experience," "maturity," and "wisdom" acknowledge that there is both an experiential and a reflective component to being proficient that only comes with time. The ideas of maturity and wisdom also recognize that the adult view of the world will change and practitioner's values and beliefs may be challenged and perhaps changed as a result of the work they do. Experiential learning, self, relationship, and context are humanist concepts explored in this chapter because they affect practitioner development.

In a simple world the professional development journey should begin as a student, with the learning of new knowledge and skills and the consolidation of a set of professional values and ethics. When practitioners graduate and begin to practice the craft, they learn to apply the knowledge and deepen their skills. Experience through a series of stages is marked by increasingly competent interactions with young people and families until they arrive at expertise. The world of practice is not simple. In reality, the development of skill and knowledge is not linear, with a clear beginning and a clear end. It is not defined by evenly divided stages, with clear transition points. Practitioners may never feel that they have reached a level of competence termed "expertise." Since child and youth care is a field of practice that is both experiential and relational, competence as a practitioner is set in the context of the relationships they have with young people and families and the conditions of the settings where they work. The nature of these settings and how they might affect practice are discussed in the next chapter.

STAGES OF THE JOURNEY

I began by saying that there are three phases to professional development: **novice, experienced,** and **mature**. Several authors have struggled with how to define the stages of practitioner development, and their ideas are informative for understanding what these phases might look like.

Phelan (2003) developed a three-stage model of practitioner development, which he applied to new practitioners in the field as well as to new supervisors and new managers. As frontline practitioners move up the career ladder, Phelan says they return to an earlier stage of development where they learn to apply their skills in the new career context. In the first level, practitioners are focused on safety and make use of skills that help to create external structure for young people and establish their authority as an adult (or, after a promotion, authority as the supervisor). In the second level, the practitioner focuses on the young person or family and is able to apply theory and be creative in his or her practice. In the third level the practitioner becomes **relational** and is fully aware of and makes use of the **self** in interaction with children and youth. Phelan describes what practitioners might expect as they transition through various stages of professional development, but he does not describe the process that promotes the transition from one level to the next, or how they cycle back through the levels or stages of development as conditions change or they are promoted to a more responsible position.

STAGES OF PROFESSIONAL DEVELOPMENT

Level 1

The practitioner focuses on personal safety. The focus of skill development is implementing external controls, routines, and reinforcement related to client behaviours. The practitioner values expertise and looks for correct answers.

Level 2

The practitioner focuses on supporting clients to take control of themselves. Skills related to implementing internal controls, applying theory and creative intervention techniques are developed. The practitioner values individualized approaches.

Level 3

The practitioner focuses on observing self and self in interaction with clients. Skills related to the conscious use of self are developing, although to others the interactions appear intuitive. The practitioner values self in relationship.

(Phelan, 1990, 2003)

In *Developmental Stages of Child and Youth Care Workers: An Interactional Perspective* (2001), Garfat explains that as we learn to become practitioners, we develop through a series of stages that are both initiated by and characterized by **transformative experiences.** A transformative experience is an event that becomes such an intense learning experience that our thinking, our behaviour, and our perspective are dramatically changed. It is characterized by a nonlinear progression whereby the person is transformed from one state to the next. This transformation is also characteristic of the type of change, called a second-order developmental change, that we hope to achieve with young people (Maier, 1987, 2002). Thus you will experience transformations in your own professional learning that will be similar to what you hope young people and families will experience as a result of your interventions.

Growing up is marked by many **transformative events.** Such events stand out because they carry us forward to the next stage of development. Transformative events, and the transformational learning that occurs as a result, are characterized by changes in how we understand ourselves, what our beliefs and values are, and how we behave (Mezirow, 2000; Taylor, Mezirow, & Associates, 2009). Transformative events are associated with reflective moments that help define the learning. Transformative learning is also characterized by a social context and reflective interaction, which positions the learner in a particular sociocultural orientation. Transformative moments go forward with us, influence our thinking about practice, and are often remembered as defining moments in practice.

On the other hand, learning and development in practice can also occur through focusing on experiences and reflecting on self and relationships as a conscious part of the learning process. This is what Garfat (2001) refers to as the **interactional perspective.** Your professional development evolves in interaction with others and is not dependent (except by coincidence) on the amount of time you spend in the field. In other words, as Maier (2002) reminds us, **first-order developmental change,** which is the incremental and gradual change that occurs through the application of specific interventions, can lead, over time, to **second-order developmental change**.

A Few of Life's Transformative Events

- A baby's first step, opening a new world for exploration, no longer controlled by the parental hand
- The first day of school
- The first kiss; first love; first breakup
- Peer teasing or bullying
- Winning a sports event
- Graduation

Before exploring the tools of this interactional perspective, let's consider what it's like for a **novice** practitioner in a student role.

"Growing up" in child and youth care practice is not much different from growing up in life. Chris Beneteau, in *My Developmental Stages as a Child and Youth Care Student* (1993), describes four transformative events in his first field placement that helped him through the nervousness and helped him to feel confident in his work.

Beneteau's (1993) "stages" are illustrated with events that parallel Phelan's (2003) description of the stages of practitioner development. Beneteau begins by feeling accepted by the children, as their friend, and his fear gradually dissipates. He is confronted by a worker, and his beliefs about being a "friend" to youth are challenged. The worker does not believe that friendship is an appropriate approach, and Beneteau must defend his beliefs. In the third event, Beneteau is faced with a decision about imposing external controls on a child who is misbehaving, and instead presents the child with two choices about his behaviour and a short amount of time to make the decision; he has applied a classic theoretical premise in an Adlerian approach, as adapted by Rudolph Dreikurs in *Children: The Challenge* (Dreikurs & Soltz, 1964). Providing children with choices and outlining the logical consequences to the choices will lead to the child making a good choice and a change in behaviour. Finally, Beneteau takes a young child out into the community and is confident enough to join him in a swimming pool, relaxing and having fun, creating a successful outing even when he needed to "cue" the child during misbehaviour. These events, described by Beneteau, illustrate transformative shifts in his practice from the use of external controls, application of theory, and the use of self as a mechanism for helping the child exert internal controls. Beneteau seems to have arrived at level three of Phelan's stages of professional development. However, he concludes, "I felt I had 'come of age' as a Child and Youth Care worker with a variety of skills. I know I have a lot more to learn, but passing through these developmental stages makes me feel confident about the future stages" (p. 40). What future stages? Has he not arrived? Let's consider how and why practitioners cycle through the stages of development, engaging in second-order developmental change and learning more to top off their previous experiences.

Tips and Resources

Read Beneteau's full article at

www.cyc-net.org/cyc-online/cyconline-june2008-beneteau.html.

Perhaps these stages of development are multidimensional: Beneteau will now reenter a similar phase of development to level one, as suggested by Phelan (2003), but within a different dimension when he enters a different program or setting. Indeed, Phelan describes the same stages in supervisors and managers, suggesting that the levels are multidimensional and we move through cycles of development as we change settings or move up the career ladder. This is consistent with the principles of lifespan developmental psychology—we never stop developing throughout our lives and so you should never stop developing through your professional career. **Figure 3.1** illustrates the ongoing growth process from the perspective of a new practitioner. While Phelan has explored the stages of professional development, the next section explores Garfat's (2001) concepts related to the multidimensionality of the stages of practitioner development.

DIMENSIONS OF THE JOURNEY: SELF AND RELATIONSHIP

What are the dimensions of practitioner development? Garfat (2001) says that stages of practitioner development are defined by the nature of the **relationship** and the interaction between the youth and the worker, as well as the role of **self.** It is therefore possible to return to stage one or two at any time as practitioners start a new relationship with a different young person. Garfat focuses on the nature of the relationship and the interactions that practitioners have with young people to describe the various stages of development, and does not

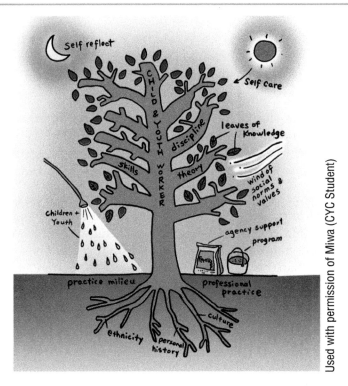

Figure 3.1 The Growth and Development of a Child and Youth Worker

believe that professional development is logical or linear. Self-awareness and reflection on self are critical to these stages, and the processes of awareness and reflection are managed differently in each stage. The practitioner implements various degrees of self-awareness, self-observation, self-consciousness, and self-inquiry. These are all concepts explored in more detail in the next section, which examines the role of self in transformational learning. The self, sometimes called your "**being,**" clearly has a strong influence on your development as a practitioner.

> In conceptualizing the worker's development according to how the worker positions self in relation to the contextualized interaction with the youth, . . . we become more focused on the characteristics of that interaction. . . . The worker, in essence, experiences a transformation of perspective. Being and doing are modified as a result of this transformation of perspective. (Garfat, 2001, n.p.)

Garfat (2001) explores four stages of practitioner development, with a focus on the relational interactions that practitioners have with young people:

Stage One: Doing For
Characterized by insecurity but deep caring, this stage can lead to confusion about roles and boundaries. The worker helps the youths to feel good about themselves and arranges experiences for success.

Stage Two: Doing To
Characterized by a more directive role, the worker begins to identify what the youth "needs" and to construct experiences that will provide for those needs, or attempts to stop the youth from engaging in dangerous or risky behaviour.

Stage Three: Doing With

Characterized by a facilitative role, the worker involves the youth in decisions about interventions, personal goals, and future outcomes. Boundaries between the workers and the youth exist with greater clarity.

Stage Four: Doing Together

Characterized by highly individualized interventions the worker's awareness of the surrounding contexts of the young person, and their mutual relationship brings greater clarity and interactions to the work that they do together. Interventions are highly creative, and the worker has a role in creating the context. Learning is a mutual experience. (Garfat, 2001)

The process of learning and professional development requires interaction with both self and other to progress through the phases of development. To be explicit, professional learning in child and youth care is more than learning about theory, absorbing facts, and practicing specific and discrete skills. By virtue of the involvement of self and relationships with others, it is much more than this. The next section considers the transformative nature of learning and explains the cycle of **experiential learning,** following which the tools of **reflective practice** are introduced.

NATURE OF LEARNING THROUGHOUT THE JOURNEY OF PROFESSIONAL DEVELOPMENT

The nature of the learning journey in child and youth care practice is transformative. Transformation of a person and any resultant change in practice may occur through small incremental changes (first-order developmental change), as well as large and sudden shifts in understanding or ways of being (second-order developmental change). Both of these types of transformation are facilitated through the nature of experiential learning and reflective practice, which provide practitioners, teachers, and supervisors the tools for conceptualizing and facilitating the learning process through the stages or phases of professional development.

Experiential Learning

Practice evolves and changes, and early in a practitioner's career learning is consciously applied, almost in a one-dimensional manner. This process of conscious application, reflection, integration, and development of new knowledge, and reapplication of that knowledge, is also known as the experiential learning cycle (Kolb, 1984). Experiential learning is not about simple knowledge transmission or simple application of theory and knowledge to practice. Teachers and supervisors who support experiential learning and reflective practice do not "tell" people what to do. They help them to engage in a learning cycle that includes active and concrete experiences, observation and self-reflection on those experiences, the distilling of an abstract knowledge that is linked to experience and reflection, and then the application of that newly formed knowledge to a new experience (Kolb & Kolb, 2005) (see **Figure 3.2**). Sometimes the experiences that people have are transformative events that are sudden and sometimes they are a sequence of events, but each event includes a process of observing and reflecting on the event and distilling new learning through integrating theory and knowledge.

The nature of this process is embedded in the early stages of practitioner development and indeed is based on some of the fundamental ideas of the educative communities for children and youth that form part of the history of the field. The classroom and/or the practice experience

The Experiential Learning Cycle

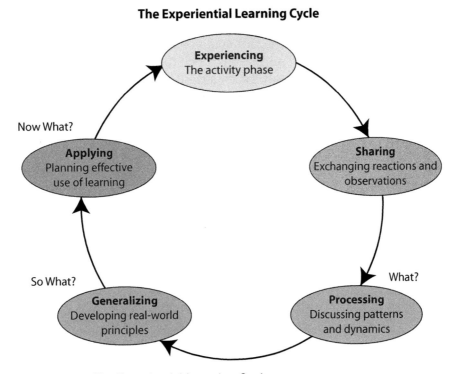

Figure 3.2 The Experiential Learning Cycle

becomes the life-space of the practitioner and the forum for learning and developing. The nature of practitioner learning is consistent with one of the core characteristics of the field, the experiential nature of self and relationship as a forum for learning (Fewster, 1991). As practice evolves, you continue to follow the experiential learning cycle, but it becomes more intuitive and built into your way of being as a professional.

Reflective Practice

Experiential learning requires that we recognize a learning experience, reflect on it, and learn something from it, refining our skills or adapting our behavior as a result. The creative and highly individualized interventions required in practice demand that we are constantly monitoring and reflecting on experiences in the moment, in order to remain focused on the young person's learning, growth, and development.

The idea of reflective practice was best developed by Donald Schon in *Educating the Reflective Practitioner* (1987). His ideas extended previous work on experiential learning and focused on the role of observation and reflection in the learning process. Schon introduced the ideas of **reflection-in-action** and **reflection-on-action.** In a time when technical knowledge, rational thought, and formal theory were seen as critical to being professional, Schon introduced the idea that experiential knowledge and practice knowledge are valid forms of knowledge and demonstrated that reflective practice was essential to furthering this knowledge and integrating it with formal knowledge. Schon's work continues to be used in human services fields, where the importance of reflective practice is emphasized (Burns, 2012; Dewane, 2006; Stokes, 2011).

Reflection-in-action is the more difficult form of reflection because it occurs in the moment of interaction and often involves mental pictures of what you are doing, identifying options and choices that are made as the interaction is occurring. Reflection-on-action occurs at a later point in time, often with a supervisor or peer, and involves describing what happened and trying to articulate what the choices were and the rationale for making those choices in order to better understand what you did and how it might have been different. The first exercise at the end of this chapter will help you to understand the experiential learning cycle and its importance in reflective practice.

PRAXIS

To take learning beyond reflection in the professional journey, formal knowledge and theory must be integrated with practice-based knowledge. This is sometimes known as **praxis.** Praxis is a well-known concept in the educational and professional practice literature that is "drawn from the traditions of social pedagogy meaning theory-into-action . . . applied learning and daily uses of knowledge to inform more responsive daily encounters with children or young people" (Fulcher, 2004, p. 34).

White (2007) defines "praxis as ethical, self-aware, responsive, and accountable action. In other words, praxis involves knowing, doing, and being" (p. 226). Praxis is at the centre of knowing, doing, and being and is the active integration of these three things. Praxis determines what action to take in a particular situation with a child, youth, family member, or coworker. Active awareness and use of the experiential learning cycle and reflective practice will enhance praxis. The exercises at the end of each chapter in this book are built around these foundational elements to help practitioners and anyone facilitating their professional development to be conscious about the integration of these concepts surrounding any experience with which they engage. In this chapter, each exercise attempts to fully address all aspects of the experiential learning cycle, with a focus on being a reflective practitioner and the active development of praxis.

Reflection-in-practice exercises focus on the experience or the "doing" of practice and ask practitioners to undertake Schon's reflection-in-action by focusing in the moment on their awareness of the action or the mental processes that are unfolding. These are the action/experience moments of learning, and are useful for concrete illustrations of the concepts.

Reflection-on-practice exercises follow Schon's concept of reflection-on-action to help review and explore an event that has happened in light of the new concepts presented in the chapter. Sometimes new practitioners lack experience to do this, and therefore an experience is used as part of this reflection. This helps to distill new knowledge and new aspects of "knowing" in praxis.

The reflection-for-practice exercises consider how to apply the concepts to practice scenarios and will prepare practitioners for their own practice. Conscious preparation and practice for "doing" encourages practitioners to reach for authentic "being" in practice.

The "think about it" exercises are theory-in-action questions to reinforce the theoretical and conceptual ideas by asking practitioners to look for theory explicitly in practice. Using the exercises and designing new ones in the same structure will help practitioners fully understand how theory and practice relate and how we can use one to understand the other.

It is the nature of praxis (knowing, doing, and being) that makes our development as practitioners multidimensional and cyclical. Each situation presents a new problem and results in new learning. The notions of self, self-awareness, use of self, and observation of self are all critical dimensions to the practitioner's developmental process. The concept and context of relationship is also critical to the developmental process. Learning and development rarely occurs without those with whom we have a relationship. The role of **self** and the role of **relationship** in learning and in praxis are introduced in the next two sections and developed further in Chapters 6 and 9.

THE ROLE OF SELF IN EXPERIENTIAL LEARNING AND PRAXIS

What Is Self?

As they develop professionally the ability of practitioners to be authentic, or

"Be Your . . . Self"

is critical. There is a constant cycle and layering to practitioner development that requires understanding, exploring, and recognizing the influence of self on development. Burns (2012) reminds us that it is not *your* life, happiness, or mental health that is at risk when you practice the art of child and youth care; rather, young people and families who come to engage in healing could stand to lose everything. This "places an awesome responsibility on the child and youth worker . . . [to] . . . uncover all the prejudices, biases, barriers, and impediments that prevent you from assisting children, youth, and families" (p. 9). So what is self and how do we become "aware" of it?

PRACTICE EXAMPLE

Jane grew up as a foster child as a result of her mother's physical abuse toward her. In her early training as a child and youth care student she came to understand that she was still angry at her mother, not only for the abuse but for abandoning her to the child welfare system. This anger manifested when she rejected offers of help for various tasks. When working with her residential care team she constantly monitors herself to make sure she is not simply automatically rejecting offers of help. Accepting their help is not only functional (things get done faster) but it makes her feel better about herself, as she knows she is leaving old patterns behind.

Jane feels emotionally drawn toward Susie, who has just been admitted to the home. During the weekly clean-up Jane is startled when Susie yells, "Get out of my room; you are doing it all wrong!" when Jane enters with the dusting rags.

She hastily leaves, putting the rags on the bed and telling Susie, "No need to yell, I didn't know that you had a special way of doing things; perhaps you can show me sometime." She contemplates the interaction later, checks Susie's file, and recognizes a similar personal history to her own. (1)

She has not told any of her clients to this point about her family history and decides to maintain that personal/professional boundary. However, the next week during clean-up when Susie responds in a similar manner, Jane stays in the room, sitting and chatting while Susie does her cleaning. (2)

She comments, "You know, most of the other kids would jump at the chance to have help; you are very independent and particular." To which Susie responds, "Yeah, well I've never gotten any help in the past, why should I start now?" Jane hears the opening and responds, "Sometimes it's just a nice way to get to know each other and the work goes much faster. I feel a little lazy just sitting here watching you." (3)

Susie throws the dust rag at her. "Here, make sure you take everything off first; don't just shuffle them around." "Sure," says Jane. (4)

In child and youth care, self is a mediator of knowledge and skills as they are incorporated into the roles and functions of practice. That is, everything that is learned as a practitioner is influenced by the self as learning is translated into practice. This is the essence of praxis—"being" is intimately related to "knowing" and "doing." The self is the sum of "your experiences, your genetics, your mind and your body, everything conscious and unconscious you. You are an amazingly gifted and competent being but unless you make an effort to realize that fact, you will be much less" (Burns, 2012, p. 11).

Practitioners must understand the factors that affected their own development as a young person and the influence of those factors on their practice interventions. They must care for the self in all aspects of its being because it is the instrument for praxis. As they take this **self-awareness** into relationships with young people, there is a tension between who they are and the demands of those professional relationships. This tension influences how they express themselves within their relationships.

Self-awareness also requires that practitioners understand their culture and its impact on day-to-day practice. Practitioners have a sense of identity as a person and as a professional. The use of self, more extensively discussed in Chapter 6, is foundational to child and youth care. To make effective use of self in practice, practitioners must first be aware of and able to articulate the nature of whom they are. The use of self in practice goes beyond awareness to conscious and later intuitive use of self during practice interactions. Self is also a forum for learning in the experiential learning cycle.

In the practice example, Jane took some time to consciously use reflection-on-practice, both on her own actions and on the nature of Susie's response. She was already able to monitor herself in relation to her coworkers (reflection-in-practice) but when confronted with a youth who had a response similar to her own, she was not able to be reflective-in-practice. The incident required her to be more conscious about her reflection, an earlier phase of practitioner development. She was initially confused and withdrew from Susie. Investigation and reflection allowed her to be more open to the next incident and to maintain her personal boundaries with Susie (she did not share her own background) but to creatively adapt in the moment and express her own desire to get to know Susie and at the same time use that interest as a means of helping Susie to accept her help, this developed a new behaviour on Susie's part (incremental first-order developmental change).

Self is at the core of child and youth care practice and is involved in a particularly unique way in the work that we do with young people and families, yet it has not always been acknowledged in this way, so defining it is difficult (Garfat, McElwee, & Charles, 2005). Self is the core of our experience (Fewster, 2001), the essence of who we are and also the lens through which we interpret our experiences (Ricks, 1989). Or, as Garfat et al. (2005) conclude, "In the quiet of the night, in the bustle of the day, in the intimacy of life, self is who we are. Self is the answer to the question 'Who am I?'" (p. 110). Self is separate and distinct, in the sense that it can be examined and reflected on, and yet it is not separate, and sometimes it is difficult to separate from our own perception of self and to see ourselves as we are, or as others see us. And yet, learning how to engage in this process is fundamental to practitioner development. Another key aspect of working with self is your ability to choose what, when, and where to share various aspects of your self. The next section provides you with a conceptual framework for self-inquiry.

Opening the Window: Revealing Self to Self and Revealing Self to Other

In the late 1950s two psychologists, Joseph Luft and Harold Ingham, needed a way to help people understand the interpersonal nature of self-awareness, the importance of communication about it, and its role in group dynamics. They developed something called the "Johari Window" (Luft, 1970). As you develop your practice there are two dimensions to your developmental work with self that are critical. First, you will progressively become more aware of who you are, developing your self-awareness. Second, you will develop skill and awareness about how to communicate who you are to other people, clients, and coworkers in a professional manner. A modification of the Johari Window, as illustrated in **Figure 3.3**, captures these ideas.

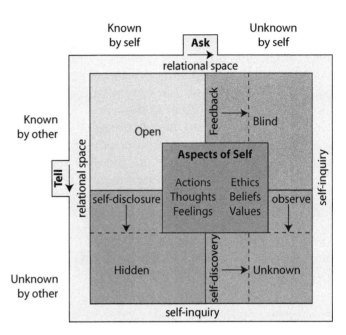

Figure 3.3   The Johari Window and the Processes of Practitioner Development

In the centre of the window is yourself, represented in the figure by **aspects of self.** The window is **open** when these aspects of self are known to both yourself and another person. The open area of the window changes with different people with whom you develop relationships. Throughout your journey as a practitioner the **blind spots** will gradually reduce and you will become clearer on the central aspects of self when supervisors, coworkers, and clients point out things that you do not know (but are obvious to them). As you develop a relationship you will make choices about the **hidden aspects** of self and when to reveal them to the other person. Over time, the **unknown aspects** of self become smaller as you learn about self and as you learn how to share aspects of self with others through self-disclosure. The process of self-inquiry and relationship inquiry advance you through the stages of practitioner development, and depend on self-inquiry and on being present in a relational space with coworkers and with children, youth, and families.

Discovering or revealing to yourself the nature of your **being** (Lundy, 2008; White, 2007), another term for self and how you present self, is a significant part of development as a student and as an early practitioner. In fact, revealing the nature of your being is an ongoing process of development as a practitioner, although there is a greater emphasis on it early in your career. Opening the hidden areas and exploring the blind areas of the window are a developmental process. Your emotions and thoughts, your values and beliefs, your actions will be uncovered and in some cases will surprise you. You will gradually reveal to yourself your being. Understanding being is complex and requires a constant cycling back to reflect on self as you learn more knowledge and engage more in practice-based action; these are the knowing and doing that are essential to praxis, the integrated learning process at the heart of being an ethical, self-aware, and accountable practitioner (White, 2007).

Being is largely subjective and is roughly composed of external (actions, statements, physical characteristics) and internal (emotions, values, beliefs, ethics) aspects of self that are rooted in our relational experiences (Lundy, 2008). The external aspects of being include your personal style (dress, hair, posture) and your actions, including statements. These are the obvious things that others see and experience. Your being is much more than the self that shows up when you walk down the street or into a room; however, these are only the visible or open aspects of self that you choose to present to the world. Your being includes internal aspects of self that are hidden until you reveal them to others. It takes courage to reveal these aspects of your self in the initial stages of practice. Self-doubt, thoughts, emotions, and value-laden judgments about self and others can override your theoretical knowledge and personal knowledge as you enter an unfamiliar situation. Novice practitioners may therefore, quite naturally, become focused on control instead of applying theory-in-action (Phelan, 2003). Active reflection-on-practice is required to stay focused on the needs of the moment, instead of self-doubt.

The Johari Window is surrounded by self-inquiry and relational space. **Self-inquiry** gives you the tools to explore the hidden quadrants of your being, as well as those blind and unknown aspects of self, and draw them into the open.

> A few questions I might ask of my self [to engage in self-inquiry] are these: What's in my awareness, right now? What am I feeling, right now? What's important to me? What do I need? What are my values, my assumptions, my sense of what is right? These questions are at the subjective heart of me, the heart of my self. (Lundy, 2008, p. 210)

Posing these questions is part of the process of reflection-in-practice as well as reflection-on-practice. The questions help you to articulate your worldview, based on your life experience. If you are 14 years old and all your life you've seen and heard adults abusing teenagers and/or other adults, then you likely believe that all adults are (or could be) abusive. You might value safety and security and anything that protects you from that adult abuse. This combination of a value and a belief could lead you to a teenage street gang that offers safety and protection from adults. As a novice practitioner on a street outreach team, you may need to explore your own feelings about the dangers posed by gangs and your sense of justice as it relates to the concept of justice within the gang.

One way of developing and understanding your being is to explore the self-awareness model developed by Ricks (1989), which is illustrated in the aspects of self that are in the center of the Johari Window. On one side our values, beliefs, and ethics represent our worldview, including the things we hold as important (values), our ideas about what is true (beliefs), and our rules for behaviour (ethics). Our worldview develops in the context of the messages that we receive from the world around us and interacts with our feelings, thoughts, and actions—the momentary and personal aspects of our being, which are more noticeable during reflection-in-practice. In future chapters the dominant discourse which influences the worldview of practitioners in North America is examined more closely.

As we develop professionally, the self dimension engages in reflection and self-inquiry, expanding our understanding of our being and its role in our practice. Ricks (2003) describes these aspects of self-awareness as **conscience** and **self-consciousness.**

> Conscience is the inner compass for right and wrong and plays a critical role in providing the focus for noticing. . . . Any principles of right and wrong, good and bad, or values that I "hold dear," are the foundation for what I will bother to observe, sense, or take in when I am engaged in relationships. (p. 71)

Conscience determines the clarity and openness of the window we have on the world, and affects how we ask our own self, and others, for feedback, and how honestly we engage in self-inquiry. In the previous example, there is a potential clash between valuing safety and believing that all adults are abusive. This could lead to a rule (or ethic) that adults are not to be trusted and prevent the young person from seeking safe adult relationships.

> Self-consciousness is the capacity to reflect on what I experience . . . a kind of preoccupation with cognitive awareness or mindfulness about self-reflection and introspection. . . . I make the observations and make meaning of my observations. (Ricks, 2003, p. 72)

Learning self-consciousness is the focus of early development as a practitioner. Self-consciousness is what has new practitioners focused on their fears and their personal safety. Until we become comfortable with self-consciousness, there exists a strong fear that we will "do it" wrong. This fear will resurface as we enter new positions and new organizations because of uncertainty about self and other. But we are at the beginning of the professional development journey, the early stages of practice, we need to open the window on the values and beliefs that guide our ethics and our conscience—our principles about what is right and wrong. Our attitudes about troubled young people and their families are formed by our life experiences to date. Take a few moments to complete the "I've Got Attitude" exercise at the end of the chapter.

There is an interaction between your worldview (values, beliefs, and ethics) and the momentary and personal aspects of your being such as emotions, thoughts, and actions. Another part of self-inquiry is reflection-in-practice (self-observation) on the swirl of emotional reactions and thoughts that form the immediate consciousness. When in practice with young people this swirl is intense and chaotic and requires constant attention to reflection-in-practice as demonstrated by the earlier example of Jane's work with Susie. Self-observation, the ability to step both inside and outside of your self and observe through our five senses what is going on, is an important self-inquiry process illustrated in the exercise on self-observation at the end of the chapter.

Making the connection between these two sides of the aspects of self is part of the reflection-on-action learning process, which will promote a deeper understanding and a change in the way you interact with people in your practice. Reflection-on-practice can enhance your ability to engage in reflection-in-practice. I have tried to capture this in the exercise on self-observation at the end of the chapter.

Self-Disclosure: Sharing of Self

Of course self-observation also requires **self-disclosure** in order to learn more from that observation. This self-disclosure, in the context of learning about practice and professional development, occurs within our relationships, initially with coworkers and supervisors and later (much later) with the young people and families that we work with.

The self, though, does not exist in isolation. In fact, it is impossible for it to be in isolation as the Johari Window illustrates—another person is always present because humans are relational beings. **Other,** or being in relationship, is critical to transformative learning and professional development. It is through the reflective process of self-consciousness focused on the interactions and relationships that we have with others that we learn and develop our capacity as a practitioner.

Tips and Resources

Self-Disclosure

- Self-disclosure is reciprocal; provide time and space for the other person to share thoughts or feelings with you as well.
- Self-disclosure involves risk and therefore requires trust. Consider whether you trust the person to receive the information and be prepared to risk in order to learn.
- Self-disclosure moves from less personal to more personal information in increments. Begin with basic biographical information, then attitudes and values (the left side of aspects of self), then thoughts and feelings. In the professional context this may be all that is necessary; you will only share deeply personal aspects of self with long-time colleagues or friends.

THE ROLE OF RELATIONSHIP IN TRANSFORMATIVE LEARNING AND PRAXIS

Child and youth care practice focuses on the form and nature of interpersonal relationships, not just with young people but with other practitioners. Indeed, relationship is a domain of practice with a highly specific knowledge and skill base. From the point of view of your development as a practitioner, though, relationship is the "space" in which you learn about yourself, apply your skills and theory, and integrate new experiences in a process of continuous growth as a practitioner. To reveal more of the blind and unknown aspects of your being you must engage in **relational inquiry** by asking for feedback, you must tell others about your internal being and reflect on their responses. These activities are done within a **relational space.**

What Is Relational Space?

Relationship is a context within which we develop our practice. Our relationship histories, both with the person we are relating to and with those that go before, profoundly influence what we bring to each new relationship. Our history influences how we engage with each other in the process. The meaning of relationship for work with young people and families will be explored in a later chapter; however, for now we need to consider the meaning of relationship for your development as a practitioner.

New relationships, particularly in the context of work, are consciously developed by child and youth care practitioners. In the earlier practice example, since Susie didn't want Jane's assistance, Jane simply sat on the bed and shared the time with her in a different manner. Jane got to this point by reflecting on a previous interaction that she had with Susie; she reflected within their relational space and learned from it. She shared briefly with Susie her reflection. She may also have talked with a coworker or supervisor and used that relational space to reflect and learn, thus transforming her practice.

Mature child and youth care "practitioners actively develop relationships with others through communication and shared activities. They are conscious of the process of relationship development and actively consider how the psycho-social developmental status and culture of the other person and their own developmental history and culture influence the nature of any particular relationship. They are clear about the nature of personal and professional boundaries with clients and co-workers and respectful of the professional needs of others" (Mattingly, Stuart, & Vander Ven, 2003, p. 48). How does one get to a stage of mature practice? Relationship is key. It is both a method of working and a context for learning.

Relationship is "about being in a state of co-created connected experiencing with other" (Garfat, 2008, p. 14). The relational space is the "bubble" that surrounds the relationship and the people. Of course, we have multiple relationships, and in the process of developing as a practitioner we learn from all those relationships and from reflecting on the nature of the connected experience that we have. However, the bubble of relational space is not limited to the present. People who enter a relationship carry aspects of previous connections and relationships into the bubble. They also bring in all those aspects of self that have been influenced and developed in previous relationships. While everyone is different, as you enter into a relationship with a new teacher, a new supervisor, or a new coworker, you will have expectations for the nature of that relationship, as will they. Learning will occur for both of you, if you engage in a process of awareness and communication about the expectations and the nature of your relationship, in short when you make explicit your conscience and your self-consciousness (Ricks, 2003). The learning process is enhanced through relational inquiry, an active process of asking and telling that is focused on aspects of self as well as practice experience and the integration of theory and knowledge. The Theory-in-Action exercise on relationship at the end of the chapter will help you to observe yourself and your relationships with others.

What Is Relational Inquiry?

As the Johari Window shows us, there is a role for other as well as self in reflective practice. "When your self and my self come together in any form of relationship, a we-space is created. This we-space is an intersubjective space in which communication between conscious beings generates shared experience, shared meaning, shared values, and shared beliefs . . . [it] is the inter-relational space in which Child and Youth Care is practiced" (Lundy, 2008, p. 210).

The relational space becomes an interrelational space as the people in the space become active through communication and relational inquiry. The other person in the relationship provides feedback upon which you can reflect. You learn how they see you and you learn how you affect them. You reflect on how to do things differently. You might share aspects of your inner being that you have not previously shared: values, beliefs, ethics, emotions, or thoughts. You are told about knowledge and theory of which you were previously unaware, and you might share some of your own "book" or "practice" knowledge. The process of telling, reflecting on that telling, and receiving the response of the other person is a process of shared reflection that contributes to your development as a practitioner. The experiential learning cycles of both people come together to create additional learning for each person when we engage in relational inquiry. The relationship context is multidirectional (you affect them and they affect you) as well as developmental; your relationships and your being change and evolve over time. You engaged in some of this relational inquiry and reflection-on-practice in the self-observation exercise that you did previously to identify and understand the aspects of self.

Self-observation, the ability to step both inside and outside of your self and observe through your five senses, is a critical self-inquiry process. Giving and receiving feedback is an important aspect of the relational inquiry process, especially when you engage in exchanging feedback with a more experienced practitioner. Learning is most comfortable when you are ready to receive feedback, but it can also be transformative when you receive unexpected feedback and are able to reflect on the feedback and the moment of receiving it. Relational inquiry should be active, meaning that you ask for observations and feedback from others. Giving feedback to a coworker should be guided by the characteristics and values of child and youth care practice. Receiving feedback requires that you prepare yourself to listen and that you engage in reflection-in-action as well as reflection-on-action as you receive that feedback. Notice what types of emotions are elicited and in relation to what feedback. The following boxes provide some concrete "tips" for giving and receiving feedback.

Tips for Receiving Feedback

- Be sure to ask regularly for feedback and specify what you want feedback on: an incident, a pattern of behaviour that you have become aware of, a specific aspect of yourself.

- Be aware of your body language and tone of voice—remain open and neutral.

- Ask questions about their observations and their interpretations.

- Acknowledge and appreciate the feedback.

- Ask permission to clarify your intentions or describe what was going on for you.

- Ask for advice—if you really want it. Ask for details on how to learn more about a new idea or interpretation (theory).

- Listen carefully, identify for the other person what you will do differently, and commit to change, then follow up by asking for feedback on your implementation.

- Listen and wait. Listening to feedback doesn't mean you have to agree with it. If it seems critical, take the criticism in; don't take the criticism on.

- Agree with any part of it that's true. Open the space for an honest discussion and be honest in your personal reflection.

- It's hard to receive feedback and it's an ongoing process of relational inquiry. You don't have to do it perfectly. You can always go back to the person later and revisit the issue.

Tips for Giving Feedback

- Consider the space and time of the feedback. Ask permission. Choose a time when there is enough time to discuss, but be immediate, don't wait. Choose a private space.

- Be caring. Include the positive in the message— "Here's what I thought you did well . . . And here's what I thought could use some improvement . . ."

- Be personal and reflect on your own experience in relation to the other person and the event. Give information, not advice, as people will often resist advice (e.g., "I was confused when you sent all the children to the table to sit, when it was only Rajit and Jana that were involved in the fight. I thought I had the others under control and they were having fun" is better than "You shouldn't punish the other children when they weren't involved"). Let the other person comment on their rationale or reflect on what could have been different.

- Be descriptive; focus on the behaviour; don't make inferences.

- Don't judge or blame; inquire about their thoughts, feelings, and actions, and listen to their logic.

- Paraphrase back what you hear as their values and beliefs—the aspects of self that you hear them describing.

- Provide information or theory that might inform other choices—but only after inquiring and listening to their reflections on the event.

- It's hard to give feedback and it's an ongoing process of relational inquiry. You don't have to do it perfectly. You can always go back to the person later and revisit the issue.

ABSTRACT KNOWLEDGE AND THEORY IN EXPERIENTIAL LEARNING

There is an important role for theory and abstract knowledge in the process of relational inquiry and learning. As noted earlier, praxis is at the centre of being, doing, and knowing and enables us to integrate these three aspects of practice. There are "big" theories and "little" theories, or theory developed by academics and researchers and the theory of the everyday. This idea is best illustrated by combining Kurt Lewin's ideas that:

- there is nothing quite so practical and useful as a good theory, and
- there is nothing quite so theoretical as good practice (Anglin, 2002).

The theory of the everyday is our experienced knowledge (Hunt, 1992) and the more experience we have, the more knowledge we have. These theories of the everyday are what novice practitioners integrate into their learning as they build their own experienced knowledge and personal theory. Equally as valid, novice practitioners and experienced practitioners will rely on formal theory to understand and explain the work that they do. Revisiting this formal theory and knowledge is also an important part of transformative learning. New practitioners are wise to return to "the books" or draw on the formal knowledge of coworkers in the relational space to better understand their practice experiences and to learn and change what they "know" and "do." Mature practitioners are constantly returning to previously learned theory and knowledge to reconsider their previous learning and integrate praxis. We return to these ideas about theory, knowledge, and experiential learning in Chapter 6 when you are introduced to the domains of knowledge and practice in the field.

SUMMARY: THE CYCLICAL NATURE OF LEARNING AND DEVELOPMENT IN PRACTICE

The processes of learning described previously, the experiential learning cycle, including the events, reflections, integration of theory, and application of theory-in-action, are ongoing throughout our lives. It requires self-observation and awareness of all aspects of self, including both our worldview and our internal and external reactions to events as well as an ongoing inquiry into the nature of self made up of reflection-in-practice and reflection-on-practice as well as reflection-for-practice. Within a relational space ongoing inquiry is required as is self-disclosure, requests for feedback, seeking of new knowledge, and integration of theory. The journey of professional development is complex and life-long.

> I must be able to observe, know that I am observing, know what I am observing, and know that I am reflecting on and making meaning of what I am observing. This is a complex process and one that becomes more complex in the larger contexts of work, school, and community: in other words when I am engaged in relatedness. (Ricks, 2003, p. 72)

As you experience transformative events in your practice and follow the experiential learning cycle, you will move through phases of being a novice, becoming experienced, and developing maturity and wisdom in your practice. Your maturity and wisdom will deepen with each new practice setting and role that you take within those settings. But you will never "arrive" at an end point and you will often cycle back to feeling and acting like a novice, particularly in the context of a new relationship (Garfat, 2001; Maier, 2002) or a new setting, system, or community of practice (Lundy, 2008).

The next chapter examines the practice settings and systems within which child and youth care practitioners work and the nature of the clientele that might be found there. In the next chapter less discussion will occur about how the settings influence the journey of professional development; however, an awareness of this influence is essential because the context for practitioner's relationships with young people is the institutional values and beliefs embedded within the settings in which they work. The learning cycle and professional development are heavily influenced by the settings in which practitioners work and the issues and problems of the young people and families with which they work.

CHAPTER EXERCISES

THE EXPERIENTIAL LEARNING CYCLE AND THE REFLECTIVE PRACTITIONER

The Experience: Practice Knowledge versus Formal Knowledge

> Much of good practice exhibited by child and youth care workers is the result of tacit knowing. It is well known that skilled craftspeople and athletes often cannot articulate precisely how they do what they do. It sometimes takes a less skilled but highly observant and experienced teacher or coach to be able to articulate with some precision the elements and dynamics of an expert activity or performance (Anglin, 2002, p. 25).

Think of something that you are very, very good at: Walking? Wheelchair balance (i.e., balancing on the back wheels of your wheelchair and moving forward)? Making friends? A sport? A creative activity such as drawing or writing?

Reflection-in-Action

Imagine yourself doing it; put yourself into that situation. Now, can you provide a metaphor or a visual image for *how* you do it?

Reflection-on-Action

Imagine that you just finished doing that "thing," now describe how you do what you do so well, step by step in detail so that someone else could to it. What did you learn by describing what you do this way?

Linking to Formal Knowledge or Theory-in-Action

Now, go to Google Scholar (*http://scholar.google.ca/schhp?hl=en&lr=*).

Do a search simply using the keyword for the activity or skill that you identified. Read one of the articles that you find in the search. What did you learn? How is it different from what you already knew? What you found in Google Scholar is a representation of formal knowledge.

Reflection-for-Action

What have you learned in this exercise that you will take into practice with young people and families?

DEVELOPING SELF-CONSCIOUSNESS

Experience: I've Got Attitude

Complete the following sentences quickly with the first thing that comes to mind. As you work on the sentence completion, note the images and thoughts that parade through your mind's stage, dancing and swirling. No need to record them or hold on to them, just try to notice. This noticing is reflection-in-action.

Young people are . . .

Troubled young people are . . .

Troubled young people believe . . .

Families are . . .

The families of troubled young people are . . .

Caring is shown by . . .

Helping involves . . .

Reflection-on-Practice

Choose one of your responses to discuss with a fellow colleague. Share your response and listen carefully to the other person's response. Try to explain how you came to this belief and any nuances that might affect the belief or change it. Note how others are different from you. Actively identify the differences that each of you have in your beliefs. What is your social/cultural context that frames your beliefs? Are your influences cultural, ethnic, religious, gender-based? Be honest—be your . . . self. (Exercise modified from Garfat et al., 2005, p. 119)

Reflection-for-Practice

What is the implication of your thinking for working with young people?

Theory-in-Action

Go to *www.cyc-net.org* and search self-consciousness to find additional theoretical and conceptual writing about the importance of self-consciousness in practice.

SELF-OBSERVATION

Experience

For this exercise you will create an experience and reflect while it is occurring. Creating an experience is highly recommended because retrospective memory can be influenced by the reflection-on-action that happens after an experience. You'll need a "friend" to complete the exercise. An automatic timer is also beneficial.

Collect your friend and sit with your backs touching. Don't tell your friend what you are doing. Sit there for at least 2 minutes. Don't say anything.

Reflection-in-Practice

Pay attention to how you feel. Do the feelings change? Are there physical or emotional feelings (e.g., Is your skin crawling?)?

What are you thinking? (Besides "this is a stupid exercise, when will it end!")

What do you find yourself doing? Pay attention to your actions and behaviours, your breathing.

Sharing and Reflection-on-Practice

After 2 minutes turn to your friend and tell them what you noticed as feelings, thoughts, and actions (which they couldn't see because you were back to back). Ask about their feelings, thoughts, and actions, and compare. Reflect a little more (with or without your friend) about the differences and whether they might be explained by different values and beliefs about personal space, silence, or other characteristics of the exercise.

Reflection-for-Practice

Set some concrete goals for enhancing your self-observation in the midst of busy conversations with young people.

Theory-in-Action

Self-observation is an important strategy for change in Cognitive Behavioral Therapy. Find more information on developing this strategy by looking up this therapeutic intervention.

EXERCISE: RELATIONSHIP JUDGMENTS

Theory-in-Action

Consider the following questions:

- What is a relationship?
- What is a learning relationship?
- What is a "good" relationship?
- What is your experience of previous relationships with coworkers?
- With supervisors?
- How do you form relationships?

Now sort your answers to these questions into the various aspects of self in the centre of the Johari Window (values, beliefs, ethics, emotions, thoughts, and actions).

TAKING SELF TO PRACTICE

Reflection-for-Practice

What Would YOU Do Differently?

Choose one of the four numbered points noted in the scenario between Jane and Susie and rewrite the scenario from that point as if you were Jane. Use the first person and describe what you would do. Ideally, you could role-play this scenario with someone else. Be honest. Remember, you are not actually in the scenario, so go with your "gut reaction." Susie is not a real child and this is a learning exercise. Take it to a natural conclusion trying to imagine your process.

Now find a peer, a coworker, or your supervisor/mentor and talk with them about your choices. Ask for feedback. Reveal to them aspects of your self as they relate to this scenario, using the Johari Window framework. Reflect on the feedback and identify what quadrant of knowledge about self the feedback fits into.

CHAPTER 4

UNDERSTANDING THE MILIEU

Photo by Laine Robertson

CHAPTER OBJECTIVES

- To identify the typical characteristics of the young people and families that practitioners work with that lead them to seek help.
- To further describe how government jurisdictions influence programs and policy within the health/ mental health, education, social services, and justice sectors.
- To describe the settings or practice milieus where child and youth care practitioners work.
- To describe the basic roles and functions of front-line practitioners in a variety of settings and the options for career development.

YOUNG PEOPLE AND FAMILIES

Like many other human services professionals, child and youth care practitioners work with young people and, in most cases, their families. What distinguishes child and youth care is the "where, when and how" of the work, which is within the milieu. The remainder of the book introduces the "how" of the work; this chapter is mostly about the "where" and the "when."

Let's first consider "who" practitioners work with. Not all young people and families have a child and youth care practitioner involved with them. Chapter 2 introduced the history of childhood and child and youth care practitioners' work with young people, but the specific characteristics of the young people and families, and the labels used to describe them, will vary. Most programs have a specific mandate that determines the type of young people that they service; these young people have some common needs and common circumstances that make them more vulnerable and in need of support.

Most child and youth care practice is with young people between the ages of 5 and the legal age of adulthood (age 18, 19, or 21, depending on the jurisdiction). Specialized work with younger children with special needs and their families is a possibility and in some circumstances (e.g., homelessness services) youth up to 25 years of age are included. Many program(s) specialize in both a particular age range and a particular set of needs or circumstances for the young person. In this section the special needs and special circumstances of the young people that practitioners most typically work with are described.[1]

Child and youth care practice, with roots in residential care, orphanages, and educative communities, began as work with young people who were emotionally disturbed, aggressive, delinquent, or orphaned. Thirty years ago, Chantelle and Gino (see Practice Example) lived together in a five-bed treatment home on a corner lot in a residential neighbourhood, across from a community school, which they never attended. Social and family circumstances related to abuse and neglect, a learning disability, and mental illness brought them together in the same home. Today, the chances that they would live together are remote because few residential programs deal with such a wide range of ages and most programs have funding related to a single mandate such as child welfare, mental health, or justice.

Gino would not likely be apprehended or placed in group care today; instead, a child and youth care practitioner would work with his family at home to help them learn how to cope with parenting four children under the age of 8, and to help a child with a learning disability. A school-based practitioner would help Gino with his frustration and anger during school hours. Chantelle might encounter a child and youth care practitioner in an intensive psychiatric program while in a hospital to deal with her own suicide attempt, and then again in a supported independent-living program. If either of them encountered a brush with the law,

---

[1] Whenever words such as *special, vulnerable, at risk, disadvantaged*, and so on, are used, they imply a dichotomy whereby there is a group of young people who are *not* special, vulnerable, disadvantaged, and that the first group should aspire to lives and circumstances more like the second. I continue to use these terms because they are common in the field of practice, however, I will attempt to draw attention to the assumptions that underlie some of the terminology. Readers may want to engage in reflective practice and inquire into these assumptions a little further.

PRACTICE EXAMPLE

Chantelle is 17½. Her single mother is diagnosed with schizophrenia and her slightly older sister is pregnant for the third time. Chantelle arrives at the group home angry to be there—she thinks she could live with her mother—but she is glad to have left the institution she lived in, and frequently ran away from, for the last 2 years. She has made frequent suicide attempts and in 6 months will be living on her own.

Gino is 8. He's the oldest child in his family and his parents and three younger siblings live in a two-bedroom townhouse. When Gino got to first grade he had trouble learning to read, and he started getting angry and frustrated at home. His father got angry back, and the child protection worker came and took Gino away to a program that had small treatment homes and a school that Gino could attend with specialized classes for children with learning disabilities.

---

they might meet a child and youth care practitioner doing restorative justice in the community or staffing a young offender center. They, and their family circumstances, would remain much the same but the services they each receive would be determined largely by the system and organization that first made contact with them, and by how the **presenting problems** were described.

The young people encountered during child and youth care practice are first and foremost young people, growing and developing as members of society. Since they are receiving care and attention from a practitioner, they have special needs (personal) and/or special circumstances (interpersonal or societal) that require assistance. The assistance of the practitioner will enable them to cope and/or change themselves and/or those circumstances. The contributions of social factors such as poverty, socioeconomic class, geography, and immigration, as well as the impact of unalterable differences such as race, religion, gender, and disability, cannot be underestimated. These factors, which are often beyond the control of a young person, can have a detrimental effect on their developmental trajectory.

Special Needs

All children are special, but some have needs that are beyond the ability of their parents or family caregivers to help them as they grow. The term "special needs" is most common in education, but is also used in child welfare, health, and justice settings to identify young people who have problems relating to physical, emotional, or mental health; unusual behaviours; or unusual or delayed development. The terminology used in practice often assumes that there is bifurcation between the "usual" or "normal" in comparison to the "unusual" or "abnormal" (Pence & White, 2011). Problems related to emotional or mental health in children are often, but not always, associated with unacceptable and/or unusual behaviour. Young people who are identified because of difficult behaviour are often referred to child welfare or mental health services where they may be labeled as **emotionally and behaviourally disturbed** and diagnosed with a variety of childhood mental illnesses or mental health disorders. Distinguishing between the concepts of "illness" and "health" is important because child and youth care takes a social competence approach that focuses on health. There is a continuum from health to illness and we are not one *or* the other, just as we are not "normal" or "abnormal."

Illness can be temporary or chronic, and illness is often defined in relation to physical or cognitive functioning only. Deficits in creativity, emotional stress, or spiritual crisis are not typically thought of as an illness, though they are recognized as components of wellness. In the health system a diagnosis that identifies or names a cluster of symptoms is undertaken by a health professional, often a physician, and leads to the appropriate treatment. The broad term "health" includes overall functioning in the physical, mental, emotional, or social domains. While a young person might have a specific illness, disability, or disorder and be treated by physicians or other health care practitioners, overall well-being and the ability to cope with personal needs, as associated with that illness or disability, may not require professional assistance. The young person may have an image of themselves as healthy, an image that a child and youth care practitioner would support.

Health and illness are concepts that are juxtaposed within the medical field, but the definition of health in particular has been expanded and adopted in other fields. The World Health Organization defines health as a state of complete physical, mental, and social well-being and not merely the absence of disease or illness. The inclusion of mental well-being and social well-being as components of health means that child and youth care practitioners should be dealing with issues of **mental health**, social health,

Tips and Resources

World Health Organization

www.who.int/en/

and well-being in their work. According to Ungar (2004), health is a process of finding the resources to create an image of oneself as healthy. This image makes a person resilient and able to cope with difficult social circumstances as well as illness or disability. Special needs in young people are often related to social circumstances, considered later in the chapter, but for the moment let's just consider the types of needs that young people might have as a result of their individual developmental progress and how those needs are described by the services that they receive. Child and youth care practitioners work with children who have special needs in the realms of emotional, behavioural, cognitive, physical, and social development.

Child and youth care practitioners may be working with young people who have diagnosed and undiagnosed mental health disorders. Estimates on the prevalence of childhood psychiatric disorders range from 0.6 to 60.7%, prompting researchers in Canada to conclude an overall prevalence rate of 14%. In the United States, similar reviews conclude a prevalence rate of 17% for mental, emotional, and behavioural disorders among youth up to age 25. Reviewing studies that have attempted to estimate the prevalence of psychiatric disorders in both Canada and the United States, researchers have concluded that the research results are highly variable and are not representative of immigrant or Aboriginal populations. The difficulty with determining an estimate or even making comparisons among studies is related to wide variation in the populations sampled, methods, and definitions of what constitutes a disorder (Richardson, 2011). Common mental health disorders diagnosed in childhood and adolescence include:

- Attention-deficit/hyperactivity disorder, which is thought to exist in 3–5% of the population in North America
- Eating disorders such as bulimia or anorexia nervosa
- Anxiety disorder
- Mood disorders such as depression
- Pervasive developmental disorders (autism spectrum disorder) including autism and Asperger disorder
- Attachment disorder
- Substance abuse

Once a young person has been identified as suffering with a mental health disorder, obtaining help is often difficult. An analysis of the 2007 Canadian National Survey of Children's Health estimates that nearly 8% of children aged 6–17 years have been diagnosed with depression or anxiety and 5.4% have been diagnosed with behavioral or conduct problems. Only 53% of those diagnosed had received help within the last year (Ghandour, Kogan, Blumberg, Jones, & Perrin, 2012). Disorders that appear first in childhood or adolescence are ranked highest in the World Health Organization's estimates of the global burden of disease (Costello, Mustillo, Erkanli, Keeler, & Angold, 2005). The Ontario Student Drug Use and Health Survey(s) reported that in the previous year 15% of students in grades 7–12 had visited a mental health professional, although 34% identified symptoms of elevated psychological distress. The survey also found that while 13% of students may have a drug use problem, only 1% had sought treatment for alcohol and/or drug use (Paglia-Boak, Adlaf, & Mann, 2011; Paglia-Boak et al., 2012). The annual Ontario survey has indicated an increase in mental health symptoms but a decrease in visiting a mental health professional between 2007 and 2012.

Tips and Resources

Website for the Chief Public Health Officer's Report on the State of Public Health in Canada, 2011 (see Chapter 3, "Mental Health"): www.phac-aspc.gc.ca/cphorsphc-respcacsp/2011/index-eng.php#toc

A review of the literature and available data sources on mental health. Washington, DC: Urban Institute. www.urban.org/url.cfm?ID=412207

Access & Wait Times in Child and Youth Mental Health: A Background Paper: www.cihr-irsc.gc.ca/e/43055.html#s1

Ontario Student Drug Use and Health Survey(s) are available at: www.camh.ca/en/research/news_and_publications/ontario-student-drug-use-and-health-survey/Pages/default.aspx

McCreary Centre Adolescent Health Survey: www.mcs.bc.ca/ahs

E-mental health. A searchable Canada-wide community resources listing: www.ementalhealth.ca

A support site for youth and young adults: http://mindyourmind.ca

Teen mental health resources: www.teenmentalhealth.org

Young people with chronic physical health problems may also have difficulties with social integration or emotional or mental health. The practitioner's primary concern is the social, emotional, or behavioural difficulties the young person is having and an awareness of the perceptions and bias regarding young people with physical disabilities. Similar to the earlier discussion about health and illness, *disability* is a relative concept and young people may not view themselves as "unhealthy" or disabled. A disability may occur in the realms of physical, cognitive, or social attributes. Disability is relative to a set of standards or norms for a similar population, and there is some disagreement about the best model for approaching issues related to disability. A detailed discussion is beyond the scope of this chapter, but a brief definition of the two approaches to helping a child with a disability is important.

In a medical model of disability the disabled person is compared to a standard for average or normal functioning by an individual of similar age. In the medical model, the focus is on "fixing" the person or helping the person adapt to the disability and become more like the standard. In the social model of disability, the focus is on modifying the social environment or adapting it to include all people regardless of ability or disability. The "problem" to be fixed in the second model is society and the actions and ideology of people whom the young person encounters.

PRACTICE EXAMPLE

Hui took Leila shopping to buy new jeans on their weekly visit. The case plan included the goal that Leila would be more independent in the community as well as the goal that she would manage her own clothing allowance. Both goals are appropriate for a 15-year-old. The family was struggling with money and living on a single income so Hui took Leila to Mike's Jeanwear, a local discount store that specialized in jeans and work clothes. The wheelchair ramp had been cleared of snow, but when they got in the door they discovered that Leila's chair wouldn't fit down any of the aisles, which were crowded with clothing racks. Hui helped Leila to approach the manager about the issue and educate him about accessibility. The manager apologized and assigned a salesperson to move racks and clear aisles so that they could complete their trip. A few weeks later they returned because Leila wanted to price winter boots. They were pleased to discover that the entire store had been rearranged and they had no trouble moving through the aisles.

For young people who have physical disabilities, the practitioner's work will focus on supporting the young person within the environment and helping others to modify the environment to accommodate the young person's needs. In North America today it would be unheard of (and a violation of human rights) for a school or recreation centre to refuse entry to a child in a wheelchair, but challenges remain in many other locations and aspects of life. Physical and social accommodations within the environment are part of recognizing the diversity of young people and very often it is not the young people that are the **presenting problem**.

It is also necessary to accommodate children who are blind or visually impaired or deaf or hard-of-hearing in regular or mainstream classrooms, although there is more controversy about this approach within the Deaf and Blind communities. Sensory disabilities affect the young person's capacity to communicate. Since children with these sensory disabilities were educated in segregated schools for the deaf and/or blind for many years, some members of the Deaf and Blind communities have fought to have this separation continue. Because school is a strong socializing agent for children, it is thought that young people become part of the Blind or Deaf culture through learning in a separate environment. Deaf culture includes a separate language (sign language) and a distinct set of values, norms, and social rules for people who are part of the Deaf community. In working with young people who are blind or deaf, practitioners need to be informed about the nature of their communities and the role of the community in the lives of the young people and families with which they are working.

In additional to visible or obvious conditions that present challenges for young people, many young people whom practitioners encounter in their work will have "invisible" disabilities such as learning disabilities, which affect not only learning but also influence socialization. The *Canadian National Longitudinal Study of Children and Youth* (NLSCY) reported that in 2002/03 about 4% of 8- to 11-year-olds were identified as learning disabled and that these children had lower scores on the altruism/prosocial behaviour scale than did other children (Milan, Hou, & Wong, 2006). Many young people with learning disabilities have cooccurring mental health disorders.

Tips and Resources

Alliance for Equality of Blind Canadians: http://blindcanadians.ca/publications/?id=64

Canadian Association of the Deaf: www.cad.ca/youth.php

American Society for Deaf Children: www.deafchildren.org

National Association of the Deaf: www.nad.org

American Association of the Deaf-Blind: www.aadb.org

Tips and Resources

Putting a Canadian Face on Learning Disabilities is a study that makes use of Statistics Canada data to better understand the impact of learning disabilities on the lives of Canadian children and adults. www.pacfold.ca

National Center for Learning Disabilities: www.ncld.org

Learning Disabilities Association of America: www.ldanatl.org/index.cfm

Council for Exceptional Children (international): www.cec.sped.org/am/template.cfm?section=Home

National Dissemination Centre for Children with Disabilities: http://nichcy.org

---

"Learning Disabilities" refer to a number of disorders which may affect the acquisition, organization, retention, understanding or use of verbal or nonverbal information. These disorders affect learning in individuals who otherwise demonstrate at least average abilities essential for thinking and/or reasoning. As such, learning disabilities are distinct from global intellectual deficiency. (Learning Disabilities Association of Canada, 2002)

The Individuals with Disabilities Education Act (IDEA) uses the term **specific learning disability (SLD)**. According to the IDEA, SLD is "a disorder in one or more of the basic psychological processes involved in understanding or in using language, spoken or written, which disorder may manifest itself in the imperfect ability to listen, think, speak, read, write, spell, or do mathematical calculations. Such term includes such conditions as perceptual disabilities, brain injury, minimal brain dysfunction, dyslexia, and developmental aphasia. Such term does not include a learning problem that is primarily the result of visual, hearing, or motor disabilities, of mental retardation, of emotional disturbance, or of environmental, cultural, or economic disadvantage." (20 U.S.C. § 1401 (30)) (Cortiella, 2011, p. 3).

Young people with learning disabilities are overrepresented in the juvenile corrections institutions, with 33.4% in correctional facilities receiving special education services, a figure approximately four times higher than those in regular public schools during a comparable time period (Quinn, Rutherford, & Leonoe, 2005). Child and youth care practitioners therefore frequently encounter young people with learning disabilities. Sometimes the work involves helping them to adapt personally or helping the environment around them adapt to manage their learning needs, though adaptations to facilitate learning in school are most often the work of the teacher. More frequently the child and youth care practitioner will focus on how the learning disability affects a young person's social and emotional functioning. Working within the social model of disability practitioners helps the system and community to fully include all young people, regardless of ability.

Young people with developmental delays have delays in multiple areas of development or more global delays that are due to genetic or neurological diseases. Developmental delays are diagnosed when children do not meet **developmental milestones**, which are the ages at which they are expected to accomplish certain tasks such as smiling, recognizing faces, crawling, sitting, talking, playing cooperatively, and so on. Research on child development has defined approximate ages for speech, understanding language, fine and gross motor skills, and much more. There are many underlying reasons for the neurological damage that is the cause of a developmental delay, but rarely can the damage be reversed; therefore, young people with developmental delays and their families benefit from ongoing support to maximize developmental progress. It is generally thought that early intervention between the ages of 0 and 5 is the best time to improve the child's chances of optimal development and this is one of the times when child and youth care practitioners are likely to be working with children in the younger age range or working with early childhood educators as part of a team approach to supporting families with young children. Children who are deaf or hard-of-hearing and children with **pervasive developmental disorder (PDD)** may also be developmentally delayed, but, once diagnosed, are often referred to programs that are more specialized. Changes to the *Diagnostic and Statistical Manual of Mental Disorders* (DSM) in 2013 eliminated PDD and subsumed it into the category of autistic disorder, leading to significant controversy when many young people were no longer eligible for funding or services that would support their development. In this example the social context interacts with the diverse abilities and characteristics of young people and disadvantages a particular subgroup. The changes in diagnostic protocols and reductions in government-supported programs have significantly impacted many young people and families and created a potentially inequitable educational system.

In the foregoing review of the special needs of young people, the focus has been on the needs and developmental abilities of the individual. This is only one approach to describing the nature of the issues that practitioners will face when working with young people. The social model of disability focuses on society as the problem or source of the difficulties of people with disabilities. Similarly, a social justice approach to working with young people and families focuses on the social issues and circumstances surrounding families and communities as the explanation of emotional and behavioural struggles of young people and these influences are examined further in the next section.

Circumstances of Family and Community: The Social Determinants of Health

Young people may experience many of the previously discussed special needs as a result of environmental and social circumstances. Conditions in the social environment or the physical environment can be strongly correlated with difficult behaviours. Therefore, the family or the community might be the focus of the changes required. This section focuses on describing the social determinants of health most commonly found among the young people and families that child and youth care practitioners are involved with. The ecological framework is introduced here as a way of understanding the circumstances of young people and families and examining the social determinants of health.

ELEMENTS OF THE ECOLOGICAL PERSPECTIVE

Microsystem(s): The immediate systems the child is located in and the people, activities, and space (e.g., family, peers, school).

Mesosystem: Relationships between two or more microsystems. The young person's developmental trajectory is enhanced by the quality of connections between the microsystems.

Exosystem: The outside systems that indirectly involve the young person, but influence him or her, such as the parent's workplace or current media trends.

Macrosystem: Beliefs, values, and rules of society and culture.

Chronosystem: Timing of changes in individual and social ecology.

Urie Bronfennbrenner (1979) challenged researchers in child development to get out of the "laboratory" and consider the ecology in which young people live and how it influences their development. He proposed that children's development—particularly the etiology of difficult behaviour and the application of effective methods for dealing with disease, disorder, disability, and illness, and promoting optimal health—could only be understood if the environmental context within which the young person was living and growing up was considered. His framework for understanding the environment included concepts related to the macrosystem, exosystems, microsystems, and the mesosystem, which connects the microsystems. **Figure 4.1** introduces these concepts within the young person's environment. Factors within these various systems may pose risks to the young person and lead to behaviours that must be dealt with by parents and by child and youth care practitioners.

Bronfennbrenner included the concept of the **chronosystem**, or time, to reinforce that the nature of these systems changes over time, and their influence on development also changes over time. Chapter 11 describes these concepts further; however, the ecological framework is introduced in the following sections to describe some of the special circumstances of young people that bring them into contact with child and youth care practitioners. The ecological framework is used extensively in the social services jurisdiction because it describes the various social systems that young people experience and the relationships between those systems, and therefore helps to understand the work of practitioners in social service programs.

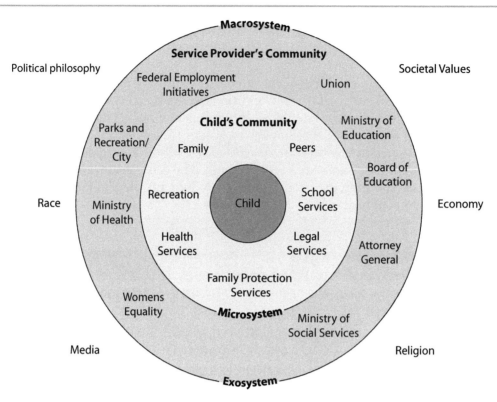

Figure 4.1 An Ecological Description of Influences on Young People, Families, and Service Providers

At the macrosystem level (outside the outer circle in Figure 4.1), young people who require assistance are more likely to be living in poverty. Poverty is a primary social determinant of health and living in poverty influences education, employment, recreation, and so on, all of which are additional social determinants of health. Campaign 2000, in an effort to create an awareness of the influence of poverty on families and children, completes an annual report card of progress toward the elimination of poverty. The 2011 report card states that in Canada "nearly 1 in 10 persons, including 1 in 10 children still live in poverty. . . . In 2009, the first full year following the recession of 2008, 639,000 children still lived in poverty. The rate of child and family poverty in Canada, though slightly higher than in 2008, decreased to 9.5% in 2009 from 11.9% in 1989. This change of 20% over 20 years is strikingly small when compared to the unprecedented period of growth since 1998" (Campaign 2000, 2011, p. 2). Poverty rates in the United States are double those in Canada. "According to the American Community Survey, the overall child poverty rate for the United States rose slightly from 21.6 in 2010 to 22.5 percent in 2011, resulting in an estimated 16.4 million children living in poverty. Of these children, 6.1 million are young (under age 6)" (Mattingly, Bean, & Schaefer, 2012, p. 1).

Young people who grow up in poverty are at a greater risk for health problems, disability, and death, and they are more likely to drop out of school, have emotional and mental health problems, get in trouble with the law, and engage in risk-taking behaviour. Children in poverty also have the greatest exposure to the effects of environmental pollution because of the locations and standards of their housing (Health Canada, 1999). Young people who participate in risk-taking behaviours and those who have disabilities or emotional or mental health concerns, are more likely to be involved in school-based prevention and intervention programs with child and youth care practitioners. They are more likely to come from poor families, have parents with lower educational levels who experience greater unemployment, and are more likely to be members of racialized, visible minorities and other marginalized groups of Canadian and American society who experience discrimination and social exclusion.

Tips and Resources

Social Determinants of Health

World Health Organization: www.who.int/social_determinants/thecommission/finalreport/key_concepts/en/index.html

Canada: http://cbpp-pcpe.phac-aspc.gc.ca/public-health-topics/social-determinants-of-health/

United States: www.cdc.gov/socialdeterminants/

DEFINING POVERTY IN CANADA

Measures of poverty and low income vary, therefore it's important to identify how the statistics are calculated. The definitions of poverty and low income provided by these Canadian and American analyses are quite different. Keep in mind that there are also hidden costs such as health care that vary between countries as well.

Campaign 2000–The 2011 Report Card: www.campaign2000.ca

Poverty, Low-income = A single parent with one child earning less than $27,098 (after tax)

- 48% of children (0–14 years) living in a family that recently immigrated to Canada live in poverty.
- 36% of children (0–14) who identify as Aboriginal live in a low-income family.
- 1 in 4 children in First Nations communities is growing up in poverty.
- More than half (52.1%) of female lone mothers with children under six live in poverty.

DEFINING POVERTY IN THE UNITED STATES

Child Trends: www.childtrends.org/index.cfm

Poverty = A family of 4 earning less than $22,113

Low-income = A family of 4 earning less than $44.226

Deep Poverty = A family of 4 earning less than $11,057

- In 2010, the poverty rate among single-mother families with children under age 6 was 54.0%, while the poverty rate among all single-mother families with children under age 18 was 40.7%.
- Overall, poverty levels have increased slightly among single-mother families and decreased slightly among dual-parent families.
- More than one in 10 children are living in deep poverty, more than one in five is living in poverty, and more than two in five are low income.
- In 2010, poverty levels among African American and Hispanic children (39.1 and 35.0%, respectively) were higher than those for white (12.4%) and Asian (14.4%).

Young people are strongly influenced by their **microsystems** (inner ring of Figure 4.1). The social membership and geographic location of school, peers, and neighbourhood overlap. The social connections between school, peers, and neighbourhood represent the strength of the social support that young people have within the **mesosystem**. The conditions of the school and the neighbourhood are known to influence the development and the coping skills of young people. The *Adolescent Health Survey* reported that young people in British Columbia who felt connected and safe at home, at school, and in the community consistently had better health, took fewer risks, and had higher educational aspirations (Saewyc & Tonkin, 2008). When young people are not well integrated socially, they are more likely to manifest physical and mental health problems. Young people with good relationships with their parents were better adjusted, more satisfied with school and peer relationships, and avoided health-risk behaviours. There is a direct relationship between emotional well-being and how easy it is for young people to talk with their parent(s) (Freeman, King, & Picket, 2011). Having friends and talking with them about concerns is seen by young people to be a safeguard against negative life experiences. Girls tend to be more comfortable than boys talking about personal issues with close friends, but between grades 6 and 10, 80–90% of young people report having at least three close friends and 80% of boys and 90% of girls confide in a "best friend" (Freeman et al., 2011).

Completing school significantly affects future earning potential and overall health and well-being of Canadian youth. Before young people drop out they may be found in specialized educational programs and after they drop out they may be found in street outreach programs with child and youth care practitioners. When Canada's Labour Force Survey first started collecting data in 1990, one out of every six (16.6%) young people aged 20 to 24 had not obtained a high school diploma and were not enrolled in school. Since that time, dropout rates have been falling and by 2000 one in nine (11.1%) young people had dropped out of high school. By 2009/2010, one in 12 or 8.5% of 20- to 24-year-olds had not obtained their high school diploma. In comparison to the whole population, young men are more likely to drop out (10.3%) than young women (6.6%) and immigrant youth are less likely to drop out (7%). The dropout rate among First Nations people living off-reserve, Métis and Inuit, age 20–24 was 22.6% compared to 8.5% for non-Aboriginal people in 2007/2008. The unemployment rate of dropouts is almost double that of those who have completed high school, and they are more significantly impacted during economic downturns. When they are employed they earn less money than high school graduates and are more likely to be working in the private sector in trades, business, and sales positions (Gilmore, 2010).

Similar trends for high school completion are present in the United States. According to the American Psychological Association (APA; 2012) summary and review of available data, "the fact that so many students never complete high school has a deep and wide-ranging impact on the U.S.'s long-term economic outlook." Data reviewed by APA drawn from U.S. Department of Education, National Center for Education Statistics in 2011 indicates that the median income of those who have not completed high school was roughly $25,000 in 2009. Estimated dropout rates are higher for African Americans and Latinos and students from low-income families are five times as likely to drop out of high school than those from high-income families (APA, 2012).

The degree of violence and fear that one has been exposed to has a significant influence on a young person's well-being. Exposure to violence happens in families, schools, and communities. Based on 2009 police-reported data, 85% of the 55,000 incidents where children and youth under the age of 18 were sexually victimized or physically assaulted involved someone they knew and 3 in 10 were perpetrated by a family member. While rates of physical assault were similar for boys and girls, the rate of family-related sexual offences was four times higher for girls than for boys (Statistics Canada, 2011). Young people can be directly impacted by family violence and they may also be significantly affected as a witness to domestic violence. According to Statistics Canada self-reported data in 2009, victims of spousal violence are unlikely to report the incident to police, implying that many young people affected by domestic violence may not come to the attention of authorities. Just under one-quarter (22%) of spousal violence victims stated that the incident came to the attention of the police. While not all spousal violence involves young people, it appears to remain a hidden issue that affects many young people directly and indirectly.

The *Canadian Incidence Study of Reported Abuse and Neglect* (Public Health Agency of Canada, 2010) found that in 2008, 14.19 children per 1,000 were the subject of a substantiated maltreatment investigation in Canada.[2] There are five types of abuse and neglect considered in this ongoing examination of reported abuse and neglect. Exposure to family violence represented 34% of the investigations and neglect was the primary concern in another 34% of the investigations. In 20% of substantiated investigations, the concern was physical abuse and emotional maltreatment was identified in 9% of the cases. Sexual abuse was identified as the primary concern in 3% of substantiated investigations. The study found that 22% of these investigations involved Aboriginal families, while approximately 4.4% of the Canadian population reports some Aboriginal ancestry.

In a comparable study of child abuse investigations in the United States (U.S. Department of Health and Human Services, 2011), 9.2 children per 1,000 were the subject of a substantiated maltreatment investigation. Of these children, 81.3% were victimized by a parent. The children were victims of a variety of abuse. Four-fifths (78.3%) of them were neglected, 17.6% were physically abused, 9.2% were sexually abused, 8.1% were psychologically maltreated, and 2.4% were medically neglected. The highest rates of victimization were among young people of African American, American Indian or Alaska Natives, and multiple racial descents.

Violence against young people may result in an apprehension, which removes young people from their homes and places them in care settings supported by child and youth care practitioners or foster parents. While every effort is made to prevent apprehension by working with the family, young people are more likely to be removed if the presence of emotional or physical harm is clear, they are older, the caregiver has clear risk indicators, or housing is unstable or unsafe (Tonmyr, Ouimet, & Ugnat, 2012). Practitioners may enter the young person's home

---

[2] Investigations are not always substantiated, but are an initial measure of rates. Similarly, not all incidents of abuse are discovered or reported.

and work with the family to prevent the apprehension and support the parents in dealing with poverty, learning needs, or their own anger and frustration.

Young people who have experienced life challenges, such as a health condition, a family history of suicide, or physical or sexual abuse, often start drinking or using marijuana earlier. Youth who waited until age 15 or older to start drinking or using marijuana were more likely to feel cared about by their families and connected to school, to have friends with healthy attitudes about risk behaviours, and to feel that they were listened to and engaged in the activities they took part in (Smith et al., 2009).

In 2011 in the United States, 9% of eighth-graders, 19% of 10th-graders, and 25% of 12th-graders reported the use of illicit drugs in the previous 30 days. Among high school seniors, nonmedical use of prescription pain relievers has remained steady for the past 5 years, with 3.6% of high school seniors reporting use in 2011 (Federal Interagency Forum on Child and Family Statistics, 2012).

In Ontario, 12% of youth surveyed in the *Ontario Student Drug Use and Health Survey* (OSDUHS) worried about being threatened or harmed at school (Adlar, Paglia-Boak, Beitchman, & Wolfe, 2007). Twenty-three to 27% of youth experienced verbal victimization; 4% were bullied physically and 1–3% experienced theft and/or vandalism.

In Ontario, 11% indicated they had assaulted someone in the last year and 9% carried a weapon (Adlar et al., 2007). According to the Federal Interagency Forum on Child and Family Statistics (2012), in 2010, the rate at which young people (ages 12–17) in the United States were victims of serious violent crimes was 7 crimes per 1,000, down from 11 per 1,000 in 2009. Serious violent victimization rates of male youth declined and serious violent victimization rates of female youth remained relatively stable between 2009 and 2010. The rate of youth crime victimization has declined sharply from the early 1990s (42 per 1,000 in 1990) through the early 2000s, and has declined more slowly since then. Violence, substance use, and bullying are issues that young people experience and will bring to practitioners.

Exosystems are those systems where young people are the passive recipients of stress or information from a system in which they do not participate directly. Examples include the employment settings of parents and all types of media, which passively or actively affect our lives. Young people are presented on a daily basis with idealized images from the media, which influence their self-image and personal esteem. The changes to methods of social contact have evolved significantly in the last 20 years. "New communication technologies support constant contact with peers and the formation of new and geographically dispersed contacts. For adolescents to be part of a peer group today, they must engage in perpetual communication online after school hours. Perpetual communication, however, raises the risk of their becoming involved in negative social ties as well. This need will certainly lead to greater demands on social skills as the size, heterogeneity, and intensity of involvement in social realms increase" (Mesch, 2012, p. 100). Internet safety is an emerging issue, especially for girls. Almost one in four girls has been in contact with a stranger on the Internet who made her feel unsafe (May, Katzenstein, & Tonkin, 2004). Child and youth care practitioners create prevention programs for cyber-bullying, and help young people cope with the pressure of societal ideals related to body image and sexuality that are perpetuated by the media.

Programs in which practitioners work are designed to help young people and families cope with the special needs of individual young people as well as the disadvantages within their environment and to develop resilience in the face of the combined adversities that they experience.

> The developmental-ecological perspective emphasizes the interaction between persons and the physical and social environments, including cultural and political settings. Professional practitioners promote the optimal development of children, youth, and their families in a variety of settings. (www.cyc-net.org/profession/pro-definitions.html)

Having briefly introduced the nature of the special needs of young people that practitioners work with and reviewed the social determinants of health that may impact young people and families, the next section describes the milieus or settings in which practitioners work.

PRACTICE MILIEUS

The concept of the **therapeutic milieu** and working within the milieu is common to all settings where child and youth care practitioners are located. Therefore, the five elements of the milieu described by Burns in *Healing Spaces: The Therapeutic Milieu in Child and Youth Work* (2006) are used in this section as a conceptual framework to describe the locations where practitioners are found. A novice practitioner has many options when deciding which milieu to work in and the nature of those milieus can be quite different. In Chapter 12 the theory and interventions within the therapeutic milieu are considered in more detail. The five elements described by Burns are the physical, emotional, social, cultural, and ideological aspects of the milieu.

People working with young people and families are found in many, many settings, but they do not necessarily adopt the characteristic child and youth care approach described in previous chapters. There are distinctive provincial and state differences in how the field is defined and therefore the settings that are thought to be "representative" of child and youth care practice vary according to the state or provincial jurisdiction. The occupational titles of people working in these settings may also vary. The milieus described here are organized around the various **microsystems** in which young people participate, and are generally described according to the character of the five elements of the milieu within that setting (Burns, 2006).

FIVE ELEMENTS OF THE MILIEU

Physical: The nature of the physical environment (building, room, etc.).

Emotional: The emotional makeup of each individual and how it contributes to the emotional environment.

Social: The social relationships and interactions within the milieu.

Cultural: The level of acceptance and celebration of difference, both cultural difference and human difference.

Ideological: The individual (and collective) values, beliefs, and ethics held by the people in the milieu.

Family

> Working in family settings requires the practitioner to enter a family home and work with both the child and the family towards change. What does it look like to work with a family using a youth care approach? "Simply put, it means being with them while they are doing what they do. . . . It means folding laundry, weeding the garden, tucking children into bed, peeling potatoes, fights about curfew. It means being with families and struggling with them as they change and learn more effective ways of being in relationship with each other. These are the details that make family work, the child and youth care way, unique. . . . We are in relationship with individual family members in such a way that it encourages others in the family to be different in relationship with each other. We are intimately a part of the therapeutic process. From "From Frontline to Family Home: A Youth Care Approach to Working with Families" by Kelly Shaw and Thom Garfat. In Child & Youth Services, 25(1–2). Copyright © 2004 by Hayworth Press, Inc. Reprinted by permission of Taylor & Francis Ltd, http://www.tandf.co.uk/journals.

The physical elements of the milieu in a family setting will be largely outside of the practitioner's control, as it is the family's home and they are the ones that design the environment. There may be wide variation in the nature of the physical environment based on the family's socioeconomic status, their cultural background, and the community in which they live. The practitioner enters the home and works with those elements, inquires about them, and works with the family to assess and change, as necessary, those parts of the physical environment that need to be different. Ultimately, the family must decide on how safety, culture, religion, aesthetics, etc., will be represented within their home and local neighbourhood.

The emotional elements of the family milieu will almost certainly reflect a certain tension as the practitioner enters the home. Asking for and receiving help is difficult and having a stranger enter your home is also difficult. The family may have been "ordered" to work with the practitioner due to a child protection concern. The emotional climate of the family home will include both the emotions that are typical of the family's day-to-day functioning and the emotions that are related to the reason for practitioner involvement. Child and youth care practitioners may be working in family homes for a variety of reasons:

- To work with parents and infants to enhance developmental progress when there are developmental delays or disabilities (Brynelson, Cummings, & Gonzales, 1993).
- To reintegrate the young person into the home after a period of hospital or residential care (Ainsworth, 2006; Shaw & Garfat, 2003).
- To work with the family, encourage parenting skills, and prevent the child from being removed due to neglect or abuse (Dolan, Canavan, & Brady, 2006).
- To include the family within a group care program where the child is located temporarily (Ainsworth, 2006).
- To work with a foster family and support them to keep a foster child who has difficult and troubling behaviours in a family setting or to provide additional training in child-centred techniques for caring for young people.

The reason for visiting the family home and the length and strength of the relationship that a practitioner has with the family will all affect the emotional climate of the milieu, as will events that happened just before a visit. Practitioners must be skilled at quickly assessing the emotional climate in the family as they begin their work for that visit.

The social climate of the family milieu is also dependent upon the members of the family and the nature of their relationship. Sibling rivalry, marital tension, relationships with extended family members (who may or may not be present on your visit), family traditions, and power structures are all social elements of the milieu that will affect the nature of the work done by the practitioner within the family home. Of course, these elements affect work done in other practice milieus but when practitioners step into the family home they walk into the family's social climate rather than the family walking into the program workspace and its social climate.

The cultural element of the family milieu is also largely defined by the members of the family. Practitioners should not assume a relatively consistent ethnic-racial, cultural background for the family, with a set of traditions, celebrations, religious practices, values, and beliefs about right and wrong. With the increasing diversity of the North American population, the family may be struggling to integrate two different sets of cultural expectations. The practitioner's background may also be very different from that of the family, or in the case of a foster family, the child may come from a different cultural background and the family may find themselves struggling with acknowledging and appreciating differences. The family-focused programs in which practitioners work will also have a unique culture made up of the individuals who are part of the program, "their perception of diversity, and their cultural backgrounds" (Burns, 2006, p. 3) and will support the work of practitioners within the family.

The ideology of the milieu in family work includes the family values, but more important is how the program places value on the importance of the family to the young person's development. Programs that work within the family milieu are supporting the family and therefore hold a set of basic principles (an ideology) common to family-centred work (Dolan et al., 2006; Garfat & Charles, 2010), which includes:

- Working in partnership with young people, families, professionals, and communities.
- Interventions that are led by the needs of the family and strive for the minimum intervention required but remain with a clear focus on the well-being of young people.
- A focus on strengths and resilience in young people and families.
- Interventions that find and strengthen informal support networks.
- Flexibility in services that incorporate changes in location, timing, or setting and address changing needs. Service provision could include child protection and, if necessary, out-of-home care.
- Multi-access referral paths and self-referral.
- Families are highly involved in the planning, delivery, and evaluation of family support services.
- Social inclusion approaches require addressing issues around ethnicity, disability, and rural/urban communities.

Schools

The way was opened for child and youth care practice to enter the school milieu when the normalization and mainstreaming movements required schools to integrate young people with special needs into their settings rather than isolating them in separate institutions and separate programs. Young people with diagnosed mental health disorders as well as cognitive delays and physical disabilities require additional support to integrate socially and emotionally and to achieve their educational goals.

Since most people have attended school, we think we are familiar with the physical elements of the school environment in North America.[3] These elements are relatively the same in most school buildings. Classrooms have desks or chairs and tables for each young person, usually a large writing surface is present (blackboard, whiteboard, projection screen, or electronic board) that can be used to present information during a lesson, and contain resource materials appropriate for the subject or the grade. Children's work or learning materials are probably displayed on the walls. Hallways between classrooms are often decorated with the work of students and awards for students and/or school teams, as well as teachers' pictures and graduating classes. There are usually resource rooms for young people with special needs, which have tables and chairs where teacher and student can sit together to go over work. Resource rooms have fewer pictures and are often quieter and smaller than regular classrooms. The office space will include chairs for students who need to wait because they are in trouble, sick, or late for class. A reception area and offices for the administrators are contained in the office. Larger schools, particularly at the secondary level, will also have a separate counselling and/or resource area where guidance counsellors, social workers, and child and youth care practitioners may be found. There may also be specialized learning rooms for art, cooking, automotive or carpentry work, drama, and so on, and all schools will likely have a gymnasium or similar area for physical activity. Both elementary schools and secondary schools will probably have a library and computer labs, which are accessible to classes and to individual students as needed. Outside, there will be a playground, probably with asphalt and grassy areas and equipment suitable for the age of the children, perhaps an area for track and field, soccer, or baseball depending on the interests of the community. The extent of specialization and the amount of available equipment are a function of many factors including the size of the school and school population, the grade levels included in the school, the wealth of the school district and the surrounding community, and the educational priorities and policies both at the time the school was built and in the current day. Variations in the physical elements, as well as emotional, social, cultural, and ideological elements, of the school milieu in which a child and youth care practitioner works are also affected by the program model used to define the school-based services.

The following description of school-based program models is adapted from Denholm and Watkins (1993). Program funding and lines of accountability vary among school districts, provinces, and states, so this adaptation focuses on the nature of the program model as it might be experienced by the young person or family. In all school-based program models the practitioner works with other professionals, including teachers, social workers (in and out of school), nurses, and (depending on the program) there may also be community development workers, nutritionists, recreationists, and health care professionals involved. These models are intended to describe programs found in publicly funded schools.

- **Prevention/Intervention Focused on Community Risks—School Focused.** The child and youth care practitioner is an independent professional attached to a specific school (usually identified as a "high-needs" school) and is responsible for basic prevention as well as targeted interventions with individuals and groups of students. The program is confined to the school as a milieu and the practitioner works primarily with the young people. There is little contact with parents beyond information sharing. Some of the programming would involve after-school hours, such as homework clubs or recreation activities.

---

[3] Schools in other countries and indeed even in remote areas of Canada and the United States are very different from this description.

- **Prevention/Intervention Focused on Community Risks—Neighborhood Focused.** The practitioner works as described previously; however, there is an additional emphasis on family outreach and community involvement and there may also be a family resource center located within the school. A variation of this model involves a practitioner who is assigned to several schools within the community rather than just one. Usually the single school model indicates an extremely high-risk community or neighborhood and is most viable with a large school population. When funding is limited or school populations are smaller, practitioners will work in several schools.

- **Special Assistance for Integration.** The practitioner is specifically assigned to one or more young people who are attending a single school. The intent is to help a child with special needs to integrate socially and behaviourally into the classroom, and perhaps to provide additional physical assistance or specific educational assistance for difficulties associated with physical or learning disabilities. The young people are primarily located in, and supported in, regular classrooms. These positions are often called educational assistants.

- **Specialized Classrooms.** The practitioner is assigned to a single classroom within a regular school. The intent is to help young people with special needs integrate into the school as a stepping-stone to full classroom integration or allow the child to remain in a local community school where friendships with neighborhood children can be maintained outside of school. The practitioner works in partnership with the teacher assigned to the class (who has specialized training in the children's educational needs), and class size is often much smaller than in regular classrooms.

- **Alternative Schools.** Alternative school programs vary widely, but the basic models would have one or more classrooms at a single site, often physically separate from a "parent" school. Occasionally an alternative school will be independent, with its own school administration. There are often several child and youth care practitioners working on a team with several teachers to offer an educational program that has less structure and more individuality, so that the emotional or behavioural issues of the students are the priority. Attendance is typically voluntary and students are referred from the other schools in a larger neighborhood catchment area, or may travel quite a distance to attend. Alternative schools tend to have a different educational philosophy from the regular school system and some may be associated with a residential treatment centre. They will likely also have very different physical elements from the regular school, leaning more toward comfortable chairs and couches, lots of space for personal conversations, and few, if any, rows, or large writing surfaces (e.g., blackboards). They will not have the same type of specialized educational resources and may even lack basic resources like gymnasiums or libraries, relying on the public library and public space to serve these functions.

- **Temporary Stay Programs.** The greatest variation in programming and staffing would be found in this school-based model. When children and youth are hospitalized, incarcerated, placed in residential treatment programs, or otherwise unable to attend a regular school because health or safety needs require them to be constantly monitored, those other milieus must also ensure that the educational needs of the child are met. In North America legislation dictates compulsory schooling up to a specific age. Similar to the previous two models, practitioners work on a team with teachers, either with young people individually or collectively in a small "classroom." The primary focus in these programs is emotional and/or behavioural needs. Educational activities are often simply to keep the young person engaged in the school routine, so that when they leave, the "school habit" is still present. Young people attend these programs for very short periods of time, 8–12 weeks in most cases, and assessment of educational progress, as well as knowing where to start, is difficult. The classrooms are often "contained" in a larger institution such as a hospital or corrections center and attendance is a requirement of the institution. In some cases the program is a "day treatment" program whereby specific issues such as substance abuse or eating disorders can be treated on an intensive basis, since they interfere with the youth's ability to complete educational tasks. Young people in day treatment programs could live at home or they may be in a residential care program and attend the day treatment program from the residence rather than attend school.

The emotional milieu of a school-based program will vary greatly. In the more traditional schools the emotional climate will reflect the population of young people who attend the school combined with the emotional climate of the school staff. In a small rural school where everyone knows everyone else, the emotional climate may be friendly and supportive with little conflict. Occasionally high emotional response to a crisis such as the death of a young person or a fire or natural disaster in the community will engulf everyone. In a neighborhood where there are many immigrants who do not speak English and teachers struggle to keep up with curriculum, stress will be high and teachers' comprehension of the children's emotional experience may be low. The children themselves may have fled conflict and, since they have been torn from a familiar community in a different country and thrust into an unfamiliar community, there is an emotional climate of stress, grief, and uncertainty most of the time. Similar feelings and strong emotions are likely also present in alternative schools and in temporary-stay programs as a function of the social and emotional needs of the children and youth.

The social element of a school-based program involves not just the young people and child and youth care practitioners, but also the teachers and administrative personnel, as well as other children who are not directly involved in the specific program. In program models where the practitioner is responsible for prevention and intervention due to the risk factors of neighbourhood or community, there may be gang rivalries or racial tensions that are part of the social element of the milieu. In a mainstream school where young people who have special needs are integrated into classrooms or into social events the social climate may be one of acceptance or simply one of tolerance. The young people may be active in all school activities, with appropriate accommodations, or they could be targeted by other children for bullying and teasing and therefore need to be protected. Do children with special needs (of any kind) have friendships and who are they friends with? Is attending the resource room an option for all children who need some assistance, or is it known that only the "dumb" kids go there? The social climate of an alternative school or a temporary-stay program will achieve some stability from the professionals who are regularly working at the school, but the group membership of the young people changes quickly so the social relationships may be more superficial and characterized by the tensions involved in integrating newcomers into the group.

The cultural element of the school milieu should represent both the ethnic-racial backgrounds and cultural practices of the professionals, young people, and families as well as the culture of childhood. Schools should be playful environments, where children are readily forgiven and are taught to forgive. Childhood is a time of learning and development as well as freedom. Art and festivities that celebrate young people and their activities should be part of the culture of the school. Mainstream school curricula, at least in large urban centres, teach children about the meaning of major religious festivals and encourage opportunities for culturally based food and celebration in the school. Modern secondary schools have student-initiated antiracism and gay pride groups that promote acceptance and celebrate difference. Child and youth care practitioners play a major role in school-based milieus by helping to promote values related to acceptance of difference and by supporting student initiatives that address these issues. Practitioners also address these issues during individual work with young people to resolve conflicts and enhance self-esteem.

The ideologies of school-based milieus and programs vary greatly. Mainstream schools draw from the thinking behind the early development of the school system. School was a place for young people to go during the "work day" because they were no longer needed for labour. It then developed into the location where society shaped the minds of young people to prepare them for contributing to society. Most schools focus on knowledge transmission with specific curriculum requirements that are defined by the government. Information is conveyed by the teacher, and tests assess how much the children remember. Young people are believed to be a "blank slate" upon which adults should convey knowledge. Private schools and alternative schools frequently develop with different educational philosophies linked to different learning styles and methods. Montessori schools, for example, are based on the educational philosophies of Maria Montessori, who believed that children's environments should be adapted to maximize their ability to learn and that children would naturally seek to learn about the world. In some locations child and youth care practitioners are having significant influences on the ideologies of the school overall. Restorative justice programs, for example, begin with a small subset of children and then expand to the entire school (Ashworth et al., 2008; Kelly, 2009), providing an alternative to suspension or punishment associated with conflict and violence between children. These types of conflict-resolution approaches can change the ideology of the school regarding violence and punishment, and paradoxically can increase academic performance by making the children more attached to the school (Heydenberk & Heydenberk, 2006).

Community

The diversity of communities and the people within them pose a challenge to describing the "typical" elements of a community milieu. Instead, some things to consider and an example will explain what the community-based practice milieu is like. The programs where child and youth care practitioners work within communities include recreation programs, adventure programs, drop-in centres, after-school programs, neighbourhood houses, community centers, parenting centres, and many more. Street outreach programs are described specifically in a separate section, but all others will be generally addressed in this discussion of the community as a practice milieu. Some community-based programs operate from well-known North America organizations, such as the YMCA, Boys and Girls Clubs, 4H clubs, and the Scout and Guide movements. These organizations focus on youth development in the community very broadly. They work within the community, often hiring a variety of professionals from different disciplines, including child and youth care, and see their broad mandate is one that develops leadership skills and socializes youth to fit with societal expectations[4] and become confident leaders as adults.

---

[4] Considering the earlier discussion on special needs, this might suggest that, in these youth development organizations, the disorder is "youth" and the cure is teaching them how to be leaders. Youth development workers would argue that they take an asset-based approach rather than a pathology-based approach.

Youth development and positive youth development are community-based approaches to providing opportunities for youth to enhance their leadership skills and optimize the development of youth toward healthy contributing adults in today's society. Positive youth development is closely linked to the prevention of risky behaviors amongst youth and recognizes the multiple contexts in which youth exist; therefore, programs are always community-based.

Other programs reach out and use the community as a base for intervention, making use of local parks and facilities to engage young people and families in activities and use of community resources that they might not otherwise reach. A community centre in Vancouver, British Columbia, will be used to illustrate the elements of the community-based practice milieu. The story of this centre is provided in the series of boxes beside descriptions of the five elements of the community milieu.

PHYSICAL

Community Centres are an essential part of neighbourhood life in the Metro Vancouver area; funded largely by municipalities, community centres run programs for all ages. Each community centre has its own unique features but all have gymnasiums, exercise rooms, meeting rooms, and regular programming of a broad range of activities (arts, sports, fitness, leadership, hobbies, culture, cooking, and . . .) for all ages. Community Centres have a neighbourhood Board of Directors. (Martin & Tennant, 2008, p. 21)

The physical elements of communities include geography, municipal boundaries, and the more general characteristics of urban, suburban, rural, and small-town communities. Most programs will operate out of a building (or more than one) and in community-based practice this building may well be used for other purposes and may be owned by a municipality, school board, or community association. The program is then one of several that pay for space in the building. Schools sometimes receive extra funding to be a "community school" and thereby provide space and custodial services to community groups or programs to use the gymnasium or theatre. Physical elements of the community itself can have an impact on programming for the young people that are served in community-based programs. To describe the physical elements of the community milieu, consider the following questions that affect the work that practitioners do and are determined by the community in which they work:

- How far apart do members of the community live?
- Is there a central location where community members "hang out"?
- What are the transportation arteries and methods to a common location?
- What are the things that contribute to safety in the community? Traffic is a threat in large urban communities; bears or cougars may be a threat in rural areas. Sidewalks, bike paths,

open green space for recreation, and lakes and rivers and what they are used for are all physical elements of the community milieu.

- Where is "home" for the program(s), and how are young people or families able to access the space?

These are just some of the questions that begin to describe the physical space of community work.

EMOTIONAL

We have, for example, had times at Ray-Cam when one of the youth has had a death in her/his family. Our role was to be supportive to this youth and their family. We also helped the youth find the words to talk about the sadness and to think of ways to talk with their friends about how they were feeling. We helped the friends of the youth understand what was happening for their sad friend and provided the space and time for the grieving process to occur. Over time the youth and friends developed closer ties with each other and the youth was able to develop a deeper understanding of their own ability to cope with one of the saddest events in life. (Martin & Tennant, 2008, p. 22)

Like all practice milieus, the **emotional** environment of the community is reflective of the members of the community. Community leadership and public/private events affect the community milieu on a regular basis. Close-knit communities, for example in urban subsidized housing complexes or in small towns associated with largely rural communities, may find the entire teen population emotionally affected by a peer's death through suicide, accident, or violence. The practitioner will assist in youth to deal with the emotions and understand the impact of the event. A practitioner operating an after-school program in a large urban location, in contrast, may simply notice that certain young people are absent and upon inquiry discover that a family or neighbourhood has had a crisis.

SOCIAL

[CYCs] are in the unique position of having connections not just with the youth but also their parents, school officials, and many other service providers including police, probation officers, social workers, health workers, etc. They are usually among the first to know that a new drug is circulating amongst the youth, that a gang is actively recruiting kids, or that a new youth to the neighbourhood is stealing cars. They often know these things before the police or the youth's parents do. The CYC worker will follow up on these issues that often involve many hours of one-to-one contact with the youth, contact with parents, health officials, police, etc. This follow-up builds rapport and increases their connectedness in the community. Typically parents or other community members will come to them with concerns about problems families are having with social service agencies, housing management, etc. (Martin & Tennant, 2008, p. 24)

The **social elements** of the community-based milieu place practitioners in the centre of a busy social environment. They are immersed in the milieu and connected to many, many professionals and community members as well as strongly connected to youth, who at this time in their development may be less connected to the other adults in the community. Practitioners are more likely in the community milieu to be social members of the community as well as professional members of the community, raising many questions about how to govern boundaries between their personal and professional lives.

CULTURE

At Ray-Cam, the north doors open onto busy East Hastings Street and the south doors open to the 480 units of social housing. Members of the community walk through the center on a daily basis on their way to and from a major bus stop. The comings and goings of the whole community helps to create a community living-room feeling. This inter-generational reality and familiarity of the members helps to create a "safe" space where everyone has some responsibility for setting the "tone" in the community center. The CYC worker helps to shape the environment so that it is inclusive of new youth, open to all youth of whatever cultural background and free from bullying, racism or exploitation. (Martin & Tennant, 2008, p. 22)

It is essential that the **cultural** elements of the community milieu reflect the diversity of the community members, including the practitioners who are working in the community. Issues of oppression, prejudice, and stigma are likely to be issues that the community will struggle with and may want to take on. The stereotype that low-income housing communities are transient and filled with fear and violence, for example, may be perpetuated by the media and outside members, just as rural communities may battle a stereotype that farmers are uneducated. In fact, many low-income communities have families who have lived there for several generations, and modern farms are highly sophisticated technological business enterprises.

IDEOLOGY

. . . relationships with youth support their individual development, create feelings of connectedness and foster new program development. Experience at Ray Cam has taught us that youth programs work best when the youth initiate and develop the programs. This finding is at the heart of community CYC work-community is about relationships. (Martin & Tennant, 2008, p. 21)

The **ideology** of community-based practice holds engagement of community members as a core value. Teen councils and other forms of youth engagement are a fundamental part of practice in the community. Youth learn the skills they need for future leadership, and at the same time their voices are heard in relation to their needs and those of their peers. When youth are viewed as resources rather than problems that need to be controlled, they make a significant contribution to the community and have the potential in high-risk neighbourhoods to reduce crime and increase safety (Maloney, 2007).

Community-based programs have the greatest variability, but at the same time are most effective at taking into account the social and cultural contexts in which young people grow up. They do not isolate them in distinct milieus and practitioners tend to move fluidly between family, neighborhood, schools, churches, and recreation centers working where the young people are located. Community-based practitioners must work to truly understand the fullness of a young person's life-space (Gharabaghi & Stuart, 2013) in a multiplicity of locations and relationships.

Hospital

The development of special pediatric wards, and later children's hospitals, in the late 1800s recognized that children's needs are different from adults. The focus in hospitals is on the medical needs of the young person and on the nature of illness and treatment for disorder and disease. In most cases this means either chronic or acute physical illness. Young people's social and emotional needs and development can be neglected when a medical crisis interferes with physical health. Child-life programs began to develop in North American hospitals in the 1920s and rapid expansion and professionalization of child life specialists occurred through the 1980s and 1990s. The development of the child life specialist does not seem to have occurred in the same way in Great Britain, Europe, or other countries (Yates, Payne, & Dyson, 2009). The role of the child life specialist is to assist young people and families with the social and emotional aspects of illness. They are sometimes referred to as the "play ladies" in recognition of the important role of play in children's development.

> Child life specialists are experts in child development, who promote effective coping through play, preparation, education, and self-expression activities. They provide emotional support for families, and encourage optimum development of children facing a broad range of challenging experiences, particularly those related to healthcare and hospitalization. (www.childlife.org)

The creation of specialized in-patient mental health programs for young people was a natural next step in the recognition of their specialized needs. Programs have developed to deal with eating disorders, substance abuse and addictions, and a range of mental illnesses that require involuntary commitment to the hospital because of concerns about self-harm or harm to others. These types of in-patient (and out-patient support) programs may be staffed by child and youth care practitioners rather than child life specialists and, depending on the size of the hospital, the "patients" may be part of the regular pediatric ward or on a specialized unit. While the roles of child life specialist and child and youth care pracitioner in the hospital milieu are slightly different, they have similar education and a common focus on the young person's social and emotional needs within the hospital setting.

The basic **physical elements** of a hospital setting are designed to minimize the transmission of disease and to ensure quick response when the patient goes into crisis. There is a primary focus on disease prevention and on safety for all patients. Surfaces such as plastic or tiles allow for the frequent cleaning that is required to maintain health. Equipment such as blood pressure monitors and portable electro-encephalogram machines are found in the hallways. Beds fold in the middle, have wheels, and with the push of a button a practitioner can move the head or the foot up and down. Bedside tables with drawers (also on wheels), metal lockers for cupboards, and washrooms in each room are basic to the hospital milieu. The nurse's station in the centre of the unit houses all the record-keeping functions and provides a central visual space to see all the rooms in case of emergency. For safety, specialized mental health units for young people are locked. Children's hospitals and pediatric units recognize the developmental needs of young people by including playrooms with televisions and toys and a separate schoolroom. There are meeting rooms for family to visit and/or meet privately with physicians, psychiatrists, or other medical personnel. In pediatric units there may be children's artwork and varied colours of paint or murals that provide additional visual stimulation.

The **emotional elements** of the hospital milieu often involve dealing with fear and anxiety over unknown and unfamiliar medical procedures, worry about serious medical conditions, or frustration that life has been interrupted. When young people are admitted for mental illness, often under an involuntary commitment, or because anxiety, obsessions, eating habits, or substance use is interfering with other aspects of average childhood activity (such as school, friendships, recreation), these same emotions are present along with anger, depression, or confusion. The challenge for staff in the hospital setting is maintaining a calm and stable group climate with only occasional outbursts of emotion.

The **social elements** of the hospital milieu are constantly in flux. Patients come and go; staff work shifts to cover the 24-hour setting. Relationships must be developed quickly with patients and the relationship is focused on short-term goals related to the reason that the young person has been admitted. The family is often present in the social life of the hospital and practitioners may develop deep relationships with parents as they help them manage the young person's illness. During inpatient programs for young people with mental health concerns, therapy groups may promote relationships between the patients, but otherwise socializing between peers in a hospital milieu is limited. These are all typical aspects of the social life in hospitals that child and youth care practitioners can influence. Group work facilitated by the youth worker, for example, can play a role in reducing the isolation that young people feel while in the hospital (Yates et al., 2009). Life for young people outside of the hospital may include bullying, stigma, or isolation from peers as a daily reality (Heeney & Watters, 2009; Yates et al., 2009), and practitioners can help young people cope by visiting classrooms to educate peers about specific conditions or reduce the stigma associated with mental illness or chronic physical conditions.

The **cultural element** of the hospital milieu will in part be reflective of the community where the hospital is located. Racial and ethnic differences in a community will influence the culture of its hospital when the employees reflect the diversity of the local community. Hospitals have many different professionals—physicians, nurses, dieticians, social workers, and so on—as well as many different support positions—administrators, lab technicians, respiratory technologists, x-ray technicians, custodians, and volunteers. The potential for oppression and prejudice is increased by the structure of power within the organization and the medical professions.

> . . . recognition of the differential forms of power that characterise the situation surrounding young people in hospitals, and takes the role of challenging this where necessary. This can involve enabling young people to exercise more control over their treatment options, and advocating support for young people's needs or the needs of specific groups of patients at a policy level. (Yates et al., 2009, p. 86)

The dominant **ideology** in the hospital milieu is known as "the medical model," whereby there is a focus on diagnosing and curing the cause of a disorder or managing and eliminating the symptoms. This ideology implies that there is an ideal standard or norm that people should strive for and that they must comply with the directions of those that hold the "answer" through diagnosis or cure. Physicians, and the nurses who carry out their orders, are the more powerful and there may be an expectation that one should follow their direction without question. The approach of child and youth care practitioners, which focuses on caring and on youth engagement, can help youth to follow essential medical procedures and at the same time support them and advocate for them with practitioners who expect compliance.

Residential

Even though child and youth care practice originated in residential settings, residential milieus have just as much variation as the other milieus described here. Residential milieus are those where young people are living, generally in 24-hour care, with a home-like atmosphere, but with practitioners who do not live within the residence. (This eliminates foster care models, which have been alluded to in the description of family-based settings.) Residential models can range from small homes with two to six young people in them to large campuses with several "cottages," each having 10–20 or more young people. Literature indicates that the size of a residential program (by itself) has limited influence on the outcomes of young people who reside in the program, but that smaller units are more beneficial to the experiences of the young people and the staff (Chipenda-Dansokho, n.d.). Size of the program is largely determined by economic and ideological factors, though theory is beginning to play a role in defining the ideal size of a program. Residential settings within the justice sector may be "open-custody" group home settings or large institutional settings housing hundreds of youth in "jail." The focus in this section is on less institutional settings with open access rather than those programs with locked doors, though many of the characteristics described here will apply to locked settings, with the added feature of security and a stronger focus on control that is present in those settings.

The **physical elements** of the residential setting are meant to resemble a home-like atmosphere. Of course, the elements that make a house a home are highly dependent on culture, community, and family. Additionally, in a residential setting the physical environment is most often arranged with considerations for safety and control as the top priorities. The difference between a house and a home is that a home is one where the people within it have control over the space and make it their own (Bailey, 2002). In a residential setting the young people are often perceived to be in need of external controls and therefore thought to be without the capacity for internal control that would be required for them to control the physical space and make it "home-like." The house or cottage will have a kitchen and common living space as well as bedrooms, which may be shared with other residents. Bailey (2002) reviewed published literature on the physical environment and states that while the culture of the milieu is the most important aspect in young people's response, the physical environment is an expression of that culture. His review identified that attention to the following areas is important:

- Creating private spaces for quiet reflection.
- Including art and music.
- Varied lighting and colour throughout.
- Use of wall hangings and other sound-absorbing, but artful objects to reduce noise levels.
- Comfortable but high-quality furniture.
- Use of personal objects for decoration, particularly in bedrooms where personal style and space can reflect personality and engender a sense of control and "home-likeness."
- Kitchens should be functional, comfortable, and, above all, well stocked.
- Bathrooms must offer privacy and comfort as well as be well stocked with essential items, which for teenagers include personalized hair products, cleansing creams, and medications for skin conditions.
- Access to the outdoors is essential, with play areas that are safe, fun, and protected.

The **emotional elements** of the residential milieu are volatile, just as they are in a hospital setting, though the young people in residential care are often there for a longer time and will become attached to peers and staff within the setting. The volatility comes from the internal and external manifestations of pain that young people experience. "What staff variously called 'outbursts,' 'explosions,' or 'acting out' on the part of residents would occur in the homes, and while it appeared to an observer that the reaction evidenced inner turmoil and pain, seldom did careworkers acknowledge or respond sensitively to the inner world of the child" (Anglin, 2002, p. 108). Volatility can be reduced by acknowledging the emotional climate of the residents and recognizing that, as young people accept their emotions and learn to cope with them, the other aspects of their lives improve.

The **social elements** of the residential setting are affected by the emotional climate of pain but vary greatly depending on the age of the young people and the purpose and length of their stay in the program. The social climate in most residential settings is focused on acts of day-to-day living: get up, eat, get to school, do homework, play, get to sleep. The direction of these routines is a primary social task for practitioners (Anglin, 2002). Young people do not choose their peers in residential settings. Some settings encourage family age groups to approximate sibling relationships. Other settings deal with narrow age ranges such as adolescence or pre-adolescence to facilitate similar interests and social programming based on those interests. Social relationships are a primary method of working with young people in residential care. "The most appropriate and therapeutic culture that promotes healing, wholeness, and hope for children in residential care is one that focuses on relationships and understanding rather than mere control of behaviour" (Bailey, 2002, p. 25). The young people, however, may need to learn how to engage in basic conversations, make friends, or even to play, so these social aspects of day-to-day life are a consciously taught part of life in a residence.

The **cultural elements** of the residential setting should appreciate difference and recognize diversity among the young people in care. Realistically, how difference is acknowledged depends on the staff and young people present. With only a few exceptions, there is little research that identifies how young people's identities as lesbian, gay, bisexual, queer, transgender, two-spirited (LGBQT2S), Aboriginal, Mexican American, black Caribbean, African American, and so on are developed and appreciated in residential settings.[5] Young people with cognitive and physical disabilities are rarely integrated into a typical residential setting. Instead, they are often placed in programs for "dual-diagnosed" or "multiply challenged" young people.

The **ideology** of a residential setting should be determined by its theoretical orientation. There are a diverse range of approaches to residential programming, ranging from therapeutic communities that are invested in a psychodynamic approach to purposeful life-space work to cognitive-behavioural approaches with roots in behavioural psychology (Stevens & Furnivall, 2008; Gharabaghi & Stuart, 2013). In a study of group home life and work, Anglin found that the core of group home ideology could be expressed as "congruence in the service of children's best interests" (2002, p. 52). The young people are at the centre of the programming in residential work and there is a drive toward creating a sense of "normal" for them within the familial living environment. Ideals and values about what is normal and how to create "normalcy" for young people in residential care are determined by the experiences of the staff and the theoretical orientation of the program.

---

[5] For an analysis of the multiple identities of young women and their place as a "minority" in child and youth care practice, see Definney, Loiselle, and Dean (2011).

Streetwork

The homeless youth population in major urban centres is large in comparison to smaller centres because young people from outlying centres are attracted to the city. It is this population that is served by outreach workers and shelters for homeless youth. Most shelters include an outreach program because to move young people off the street, into a shelter, and on to living in an apartment or other alternative, workers must first develop a trusting relationship with them. Overall in Canada, it is estimated that 65,000 young people are homeless or living in a shelter at some point throughout the year (Evenson & Barr, 2009). Recent research notes that on any given night in Toronto there are 1,700–2,000 homeless young people, but over the course of a year the actual number is much larger (O'Grady, Gaetz, & Buccieri, 2011). In Ottawa in 2011, 401 youth used homeless shelters, staying an average of 37 days (Alliance to End Homelessness, 2012).

Streetwork programs are found in large cities and in small towns and streetwork is a large part of the European social pedagogy where child and youth care practice originated (Traber, 1990). Are the streets a therapeutic milieu? What are their characteristics as such (Griffin, 2009)? The physical elements of the streetwork landscape seem pretty common, including the street itself, with vehicles and pedestrians, sidewalks, stores, office buildings, perhaps underground subways, parks and green spaces, and/or bright lights and neon signs. However, as Griffin reminds us, these aspects of the physical space can only be understood as a therapeutic milieu when they are considered as a "socio-spatial environment consist[ing] of physical, social, cultural, and imagined environments" (2009, p. 17). Space and place are intimately related through the perceptions of the people involved in the environment.

Tips and Resources

The Homeless Hub, a web-based research library and information center: www.homelesshub.ca

Raising the Roof: www.raisingtheroof.org

National Alliance to End Homelessness: www.endhomelessness.org

Young people may be living on the streets and/or using the streets to earn income. Street-involved youth are a social community. If they live on the streets their peers are their family and the street is their home, with all the expected social relationships. The idea introduced previously under residential milieus, that "home" is defined by the degree of control one has over the environment, is relevant here. Street-involved youth perceive this to be their place of employment, their living room, and their family. It provides a sense of safety, belonging, and attachment. Street-involved youth create **social** networks in relation to the locations in which they feel comfortable (Griffin, 2009, 2011).

Street culture, like other cultures, is unique, and it is this unique cultural aspect of the street that gives it a therapeutic potential. The street shapes the identities of youth who live there and street workers accept the choices of the youth, working to minimize the harm that might come to them. Between 15 and 40% of the street youth population identifies as LGBTQ2S, although only 5–10% of the general population identifies as such (Ray, 2006; National Alliance to End Homelessness, 2008). Therefore, acceptance of the LGBTQ2S lifestyle by practitioners is critical and the associated safety issues must be addressed in working with young people on the street. To connect with young people on the street, the worker needs to listen, value the person, not judge, offer respect, and actually "like" young people who themselves have experienced very little, if any, of these things. "Trust is built on these connections, and the youths are drawn to that rare experience of trust, which serves as a platform for effective work. As one worker put it, they must be a 'mind boggling' figure in the kid's life. Practitioners must adjust their understanding of the helping process to reflect the realities of homeless clients, including changing how they define change and who is responsible for that change, there must be an underlying belief that these kids deserve to be helped and can benefit from help to have better and healthier lives" (Kidd, Miner, Walker, & Davidson, 2007, p. 29).

The **ideology** of streetwork demands an understanding of oppression and a commitment to advocacy both for and with street-involved young people. "At the agency policy level, there was a general condemnation of agencies with inflexible policies that do not reflect the realities of working with homeless youth. . . . The social stigma associated with homeless youth means both limited resources, which can hamper and undo the best efforts at engaging the clients, and having to address and work with the youth's reactions to their occupying a dehumanized position in society" (Kidd et al., 2007, p. 29). These values and beliefs are firm elements of programs that work with street-involved youth.

SUMMARY

This chapter has explained the characteristics and special needs of the young people that are encountered in child and youth care practice. Those needs have also been described using an ecological framework to help explain how the social determinants of health found within the circumstances of family, neighbourhood, school, and community as well as culture and society can affect the social and emotional development of young people. A core characteristic of child and youth care practice is work in the therapeutic milieu. While the nature of this work will be detailed in subsequent chapters, this chapter has explained how various settings in which practitioners work can be described in terms of five elements of a therapeutic milieu. The variation in those milieus and how they differ in social, cultural, and ideological ways was described, and the influence of government jurisdictions, funding, and policy on both the therapeutic milieu and the young people within it was examined.

Chapters 1–4 have considered how practitioners work with young people and families and introduced knowledge and skills that will be expanded on throughout a practitioner's career. Chapter 5 provides an overview of seven domains of practice. Each subsequent chapter expands on one of these domains, introduces new concepts, and revisits some of the concepts introduced in the first five chapters to add more detail and expand upon the work of the child and youth care practitioner.

CHAPTER EXERCISES

Photo by Laine Robertson

SCATEGORIES

Remembered Experience

Recall a period of time in your life when you felt that someone did not understand who you were or what you could do. When you felt that your identity has been placed into a box, by this person. What was the label or category that the person used to describe you? Take a blank piece of paper make a box in the middle of the paper and write the label in the middle of the box.

Reflection-in-Action

As you are writing the label down on a piece of paper, pay attention to the feelings that are evoked as you put that label into the middle of the box. Flip the paper over and write these feelings on the back. Additionally, consider:

- What are the feelings, memories, and thoughts that occur as you reflect on that label?
- What other identities or self-labels did you hold at the time? Write these on the front side of the paper, placing them wherever they set in relation to the label that was assigned to you.

- If you were to pick opposing labels to those that were assigned to you, what would they be? Cross out the original labels and write the opposing label in their place.
- What are these feelings and thoughts associated with the opposing labels? Flip the paper over and write these feelings on the back.

Reflection-on-Practice

Talk with a learning partner or a friend about the two-sided labels that you can identify on the paper. To what extent are these labels, discrete and opposing? To what extent are they inside the continuum with many other descriptors that should be included? What is the reference point for the labels? What characteristics that you had at the time you are thinking of did you not consider in choosing those labels?

Reflection-for-Practice

What have you learned? How will this influence the way in which you describe the needs of young people?

Theory-in-Practice

A critical approach to child and youth care practice involves questioning the assumptions behind theory and practice in order to reveal different ways of being with young people. Try to identify some of the assumptions that are revealed in this exercise. Which assumptions would you like to challenge? What would be the outcome of that challenge for your practice and the practice of others?

IDENTIFYING LOCAL INFLUENCES

Theory-in-Practice

Review the description of Bronfenbrenner's ecological perspective. Consider Figure 4.1 and choose a community of reference that you know well. You might choose the community that you grew up in and place yourself as the child in the centre. Alternatively, you might choose a child that you know well and place them in the centre. Identify the community groups (microsystems), service providers and government departments (exosystems), and the community values and orientations (macrosystem) that surround the young person. Identify the essential characteristics and describe the influence they have had on the development of the young person that you have in mind. The further you move out from the centre circle, the more you will likely have to stretch to identify the influence on development of an individual. For example, a union would appear to have very little to do with child development, except to ensure fair wages for the family. However, it is possible that during a contentious strike a young person may not be allowed to play with their friend because of opposing views. Apparent choices made by families to cross a picket line in order to provide food for their children can have multiple impacts on the young person's development. These are things you should try and explore in this exercise.

PROGRAM TOUR

Experience

Choose one of the milieus in which child and youth care practitioners work and arrange a tour of the facility. You will of course introduce yourself as a novice practitioner in trying to understand the different types of young people and settings with which you might engage for your new career.

From the moment you contact the setting until you finish the tour, engage in a reflection-in-practice exercise and pay attention to the following:

- What are the feelings, memories, and thoughts that occur each time you contact the program?
- What is the very first thing that you notice as you walk through the door of the building?
- How do your personal values align with the values of the program? What is important to them? Look for and listen for explicit and implicit values.
- How is caring expressed to the young people in the program?
- How do staff members learn? How do young people learn? Do they learn together?
- When and how are youth involved in decision making?

Reflection-on-Practice: Sharing

After the tour, try to describe the setting to a friend who is not a child and youth care practitioner. What is his or her reaction? What is your reaction to the reaction?

Reflection-for-Practice

What have you learned? How will this influence your professional choices about the setting in which you work?

CHAPTER 5

AN INTRODUCTION TO THEORY AND THE DOMAINS OF PRACTICE

Photo by John Campbell

CHAPTER OBJECTIVES

- To describe the nature and role of theory in child and youth care practice.
- To introduced seven domains of practice.
- To describe how core characteristics of practice and theoretical frameworks are organized into the seven domains and expressed in skill and knowledge competencies.
- To describe how the domains of practice are integrated within the milieu, organizational system, and culture as practitioners become more experienced and mature in their practice.

You have been reading about the history and the settings that child and youth care practitioners are located in and you have begun to learn about the theoretical orientations that are part of the field. In this chapter you are introduced to seven domains of child and youth care practice. You will begin to understand how the core characteristics of child and youth care and the theoretical frameworks described in previous chapters are organized, for professional purposes, into skill and knowledge competencies.

A "domain" is the **sphere of influence** or professional territory within which you acquire expertise and therefore are able to exert an influence on the lives of young people and families. The **domains of practice** described here, and in the rest of this book, are a system of categorizing and describing the aspects of self, the skills, and the knowledge base that is required for effective practice. As described in Chapter 3, expertise in practice is based on an integrated application of **praxis** and you will now be introduced to the theory, knowledge, and skills within each domain and will begin to apply them at a novice level. The seven domains of practice described here are self, professionalism, communication, relationships, critically applied human development, systems context, and interventions.[1]

Professional bodies, educators, and trainers who develop curriculum are particularly interested in describing practice using domains because it provides them with a logical method of defining, organizing, and teaching what practitioners do and therefore need to know. The domains described here are based on a review of numerous documents that describe the competencies required for certification as a child and youth care practitioner in North America (Stuart & Carty, 2006). The domains are therefore relevant to the geographic and social environments of North America and may not resonate with those working in other locations such as Europe, Asia, and Africa. Some attempt will be made to address international differences, but this will be superficial at best. Prior to introducing the domains of practice, it is useful to consider the relationship between theory and practice within the field of child and youth care.

THEORY-IN-PRACTICE

Child and youth care is an evolving practice-based discipline. A discipline is a branch of knowledge with a specific focus and orientation to the world in a specific subject area. In the recent past, people have come to the practice of child and youth care from the disciplines of psychology, sociology, medicine, social work, and education.

> Disciplines are "collectives that include a large number and proportion of persons holding degrees with the same specialization name". . . . Disciplines represent some collective interests that correspond to a common intellectual interest and instructional tasks of a group of academics. Each discipline has its own body of knowledge and preferred ways of training and educating its members. Each discipline develops its own pedagogy and curriculum that is accredited by its respective professional organization. (Ricks & Charlesworth, 2003, p. 1)

---

[1] The appendix contains two documents that outline domains of practice. This text is based on competencies identified by Stuart and Carty (2006). The Stuart and Carty review included competencies developed by Mattingly, Stuart, and Vander Ven (2003). There are a variety of other documents that identify competencies for child and youth care practice; however, these two documents are likely the most comprehensive and most widely used in education and practice in North America.

Practice, on the other hand, is the application of knowledge and theory. You prepare for practice early in your adult life by going to college or university and undertaking training in your chosen field. Professional practice is based on the theory and knowledge generated by the discipline, and disciplines evolve and develop in response to the needs in society as a whole. The discussion about whether child and youth care is a profession has also expanded to whether it is a discipline. Little (2011) takes up the question of discipline as she reflects upon and articulates her professional identity. She notes that disciplines are intended to "discipline" the novice practitioner by educating them in the truths of the discipline. As I have noted elsewhere:

> We not only lack a specific knowledge but we also lack a way of creating that knowledge from within the field. We have no unique theory base from which we can test hypotheses and generate knowledge. Thus, we cannot define for other professional disciplines who we are, nor can we generate sufficient interest within our professional associations to have a dynamic impact in the political arena. (Stuart, 2001, p. 265)

One could argue that child and youth care's multidisciplinary history leaves it open to challenge as both a profession and a discipline. Perhaps because it is an emerging profession without a strong single discipline history, the field is more open to questioning itself and others regarding "the underlying assumptions and beliefs about knowledge, power, and standardized approaches to practice" (Pence & White, 2011, p. xvi). It is therefore poised to move beyond the relational and into the political realm of practice (Bellefeuille, McGrath, and Jamieson, 2008). This struggle between the political and the practical is a day-to-day reality for practitioners educated in the discipline as they confront practices that are in sharp contrast to what they have learned in their discipline, a discipline that has drawn on theory from multiple areas and is beginning to actively and critically question the stances that theory presents. Indeed, the focus of the discipline discussion seems to relate to whether child and youth care has a unique theory base and may rest on the question of "What is theory?"

> There are multiple levels of theory. . . . First, there are the implicit or tacit theoretical notions that various workers and others hold about the meaning of their work. Second, there are explicit formulations that guide the residential homes and that may be written down in program descriptions. . . . Third, there are many types of formal theories about such phenomena as child development, child rearing, and behaviour management that abound in the literature on the care and socialization of children. (Anglin, 2002, p. 26)

Theory offers varied points of view and generates debate about explanations for behaviour and development that guide interventions to promote the development of children and youth. Critical perspectives emerging from child and youth care scholars (see Pence & White, 2011) question theoretical explanations from other disciplines and begin to open up new ways of understanding our practice. As the practice of child and youth care evolves into a discipline, it is making unique theoretical contributions to work with children and youth that other disciplines have not previously considered. The contribution is primarily in the area of the milieus surrounding children and youth, and how elements of context and environment are part of the developmental change process.

The notion of theory is one that is often resisted in child and youth care (Anglin, 2002); however, this reaction seems to be related to the notion that theory determines practice and is removed from or irrelevant for practice. Another perspective is that theory is simply an articulated and systematic way of thinking and is grounded in actual experience (Anglin, 2002; Hunt, 1987; Schon, 1987). Once theory is viewed as grounded in experience, the theoretical orientations that have emerged from child and youth care practice can be described and it is possible to identify how they have subsequently shaped our understanding of what practice is.

Theory is most often generated by "traditional" experts: academics and researchers who have devoted their life to looking in on the world of young people and families. Through these observations and their own worldviews, theorists have developed explanations for behaviour and from those explanations, techniques for intervention. As Fulcher (2006) notes, the "traditional expert model that assumes an inability on the part of children, young people, and their families to participate fully in care and treatment" (p. 29) has no place in responsive child and youth care practice. Responsive practice, policy development, and theory development listens to the voices of young people; listens to the families who are struggling within the service system; listens to the front-line practitioners; and is grounded in all these voices, not just in the voices of experts.

THEORY? WHAT'S MY THEORY?

Take a few moments before reading on and do the following exercise:

Consider your experience thus far with children and youth, either as a practitioner or with those children that you have come in contact with. Record your answers to the following questions.

- What do you believe are four important influences that change a child's behaviour and/or emotional orientation to the world? (Keep in mind that change can be for "the good" or for "the bad")
- What specific environmental conditions would a child need to develop into an adult who could function adequately in society? (Be sure to define what you mean by "function adequately," as this is an individual judgment.)
- How do these conditions and influences relate to each other (do they combine, correct for each other, lead one to the next, etc.)?

What you described in the previous exercise is a basic theory. We all carry implicit and informal theories with us and we add to these as we study formal theoretical explanations of behavior and development.

In child and youth care practice, competence includes more than just the theory, knowledge, and skills required to perform a particular job, it also demands a particular worldview (way of being), which is drawn from the core characteristics of child and youth care practice. When **being** is integrated with theory and the "more personal and intuitive response based on a mixture of common sense and pooled practice wisdom" (McMahon & Ward, 1998, p. 28), it leads to praxis as described in Chapter 3. The domains of practice are an attempt to describe the basic aspects of praxis in child and youth care. The domains are not discrete; the aspects of self, skills, and knowledge required for practice overlap across domains, making the domains and praxis interdependent.

ASK: ASPECTS OF SELF, SKILLS, AND KNOWLEDGE

Doing good work with young people and families is challenging and requires a sophisticated integration of the domains of practice as well as the application of praxis. This section helps you understand the various components of praxis that are represented in the descriptions of each domain and subdomain of practice. Initially you will assess your **self** and your skills, and develop your knowledge base so that you can work toward integration of these aspects of competence within and across the seven domains. The framework for developing curriculum and assessing field-based competence through professional certification in child and youth care typically addresses three components, represented by the acronym ASK for the **aspects of self,** the **skills,** and the **knowledge** that are part of knowing, doing, and being.

Aspects of Self

Aspects of self were explained in Chapter 3, and represent the mindset of the practitioner in relation to the environment or milieu that you work in as well as your own feelings and emotions. Aspects of self include the values, beliefs, and ways of being that form your worldview. It is the being part of "knowing, doing, being" described by White (2008). Praxis requires a self-reflective, inquiry-based approach to learning. Praxis examines aspects of self, integrates them with knowledge and theory, and then takes that learning and moves it into action—moment to moment, with young people and families.

Your way of being will change as you are exposed to different philosophies and programs and as societal norms and values shift. Initially, your ways of being are determined largely by your personal history. Your culture, as influenced by your ethnicity, religious beliefs, family practices, country of origin, and membership in particular communities, whether they are geographic or identity-specific (sexual orientation, ability, gender, etc.), strongly influences your being. As you develop your practice you will adopt the worldview of child and youth care professionalism. For example, contemporary practice has an underlying orientation toward growth and development and a focus on abilities and strengths. This orientation is founded in the social pedagogue and psycho-educateur movements in Europe and adopted within the child and youth care field in North America. However, in settings where the multidisciplinary team is influenced heavily by medical professionals, there may be a strong influence from the psychopathology approach to development.

Values and beliefs are important enough to child and youth care learning and development that professional certification requirements for practitioners address core beliefs (CYCAA, 2000; Mattingly et al., 2003).

The seven domains of practice described in this chapter assume that practitioner's beliefs and values are congruent with the core of care outlined in Chapter 1. These fundamental orientations to world view, beliefs and values within the field of child and youth care should be integrated with a personal world view and guide day-to-day actions, thoughts, and feelings as well as the development of professional skills and knowledge. Ricks and Charlesworth describe this as an evolving theory-in-action and note that:

> A closely watched practice can reveal how your "theory-in-use" is evolving. You may see your strengths and limitations reflected in the use of certain theoretical orientations and methodologies, or you may discover how you engage with others in seeking and giving support in relationships. (2003, p. 19)

Skill

Skill involves the hands-on practices that are demonstrated by competent practitioners. Some individuals seem to have "innate" or intuitive skills or abilities but in reality are simply combining an ability to assess minimal cues from the other person with the ability to process and interpret these cues, which helps them to make an informed decision about how best to respond. "The young person's and the worker's inner worlds come into contact with each other" (McMahon & Ward, 1998, p. 30). Generally speaking, skill is acquired through informed, guided experience in the field; however, as identified by White (2007), "doing" also requires the skills of critical thinking and reflection.

Critical thinking and reflection are part of the development and application of the skills in all of the other domains of practice. The domain of self includes a subdomain of **reflective practice**, which identifies the skills of reflective practice, and because the domain of self surrounds all of the other domains; reflective practice is integrated with all of the competencies in the other domains. Aspects of self, skill, and knowledge or being, doing, and knowing (White, 2007) come together within the skills and knowledge of competent reflective practice. Experiential learning is applied to all other domains of practice and encourages practitioners to challenge the congruence between the self and the knowledge and skills developed in their work with young people. Practitioners' skill set and knowledge base should therefore be consistent with their stated worldview as well as with the core of care in child and youth care practice.

Knowledge

A body of knowledge is theoretical, factual, and experiential. Knowing represents the various mechanisms by which we absorb that knowledge. Aristotle described three "forms of knowledge: **episteme** (theoretical, contemplative knowledge), **techne** (action-oriented, pragmatic, and productive knowledge) and **phronesis** (practical and context-dependent deliberation about values or 'wise judgment'" (White, 2007, p. 119). Such conceptualizations make a simple identification of the content of the knowledge base for child and youth care practice difficult because they include intuition and wisdom as well as theory and fact. This is further complicated by the idea that knowledge and knowing are contextual, social, and set within a particular cultural way of being. Modern, published knowledge about child development, for example, was developed by Western European and North American scholars, and therefore has some inherent bias when applied to other social climates and cultures.

Through praxis, knowledge is applied in a manner that integrates theory and fact with experiential knowing and aspects of self. This integration with time and experience results in **mature,** high-quality practice as knowledge deepens and is applied to many and varied problems. Mature practitioners recognize that theories and facts have multiple applications. Developmental theory explains not just the behaviour of a child or youth but also the behaviour of a coworker or the way coworkers relate to each other. Theory and knowledge is applicable across the field of child and youth care irrespective of the practice milieu, specific program, or jurisdiction in which practice occurs. This capacity to transition across contexts is related to the practitioners' experiential knowing, which encourages adaptation and modification.

Knowledge, in the form of theories and facts, often receives the most attention in educational settings because it lends itself to detailed analysis and evaluation by means of written and oral examinations. In short, it can be judged as "correct." There is a growing realization in the post-modern world that factual and theoretical knowledge might not be appropriate in a different social context from whence it was developed. While knowledge is important, it is what one does with knowledge that is critical for the quality of child and youth care practice.

At the end of this chapter we return to considering how to integrate aspects of self, skill, and knowledge within different contexts. The next section of the chapter considers the seven domains of child and youth care practice. The summaries below broadly describe each domain and identify the subdomains that form the core of the knowledge and skills essential to practice. The following chapters look in greater detail at the subdomains and the nature of skills and knowledge within those subdomains. To help the reader understand the domains from a practice orientation, a case study is provided throughout the chapter and the exercises at the end of the chapter address various aspects of the case study within each of the domains of practice.

OVERVIEW OF THE DOMAINS

There are seven interrelated domains of practice in child and youth care, as illustrated in **Figure 5.1**. When the central focus of practice is the young person, then the quality of care and service provided to assist him or her with optimal development is directly influenced by the work of the practitioner. In these circumstances child and youth care practice occurs in multiple programs[2] and with clientele that come to those programs for varied reasons.[3] Practitioners are concerned about the presenting problems from the young person's perspective and work to optimize physical and mental health for the young person (Stuart & Carty, 2006) within a holistic health perspective that also addresses a range of social-political influences on health and well-being.

An alternative practice focus is emerging that addresses the work of practitioners of who focus on young people through the lenses of education, policy, or programming. Through "comprehensive and critically conscious perspectives, . . . [they] ask a number of challenging and provocative questions" (Pence & White, 2011, p. vii) that expand the possibilities for intervention. Some of these possibilities are addressed in the domain of interventions. For these practitioners, young people are still at the heart of their work.

---

[2] For example, youth justice; child welfare; residential; family support; recreation; youth employment; schools; shelters; and addictions.

[3] For example, abuse; criminal activity; physical or cognitive delays; symptoms of mental illness; homelessness; and financial need.

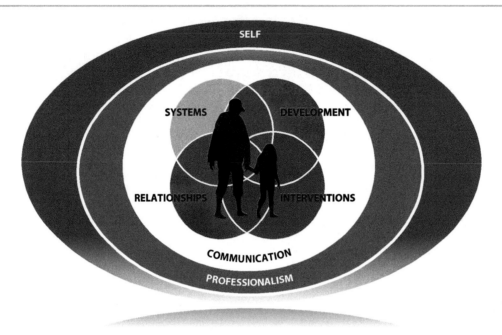

Figure 5.1 The Domains of Child and Youth Care Practice

The foundation of effective practice is the domain of self. Practitioners use awareness of self to guide their interactions with all young people and families as well as with other professionals on the team. A lifelong commitment to developing and utilizing the self in practice ensures that self-care and reflective practice surround all the other domains of practice. For example, practitioners have clear personal values so that in the domain of **professionalism,** they are easily able to tell the difference between ethical dilemmas and conflicts of professional opinion with the multidisciplinary team. Clarity and strength of self allows even the novice practitioner to differentiate those interprofessional conflicts that are based on different values from those where the domain of expertise, scope of practice, and/or theoretical orientation are different.

The domain of professionalism includes professional presentation and professional identity during interpersonal interactions in the context of work. Personal identity should readily translate to the professional identity of a practitioner. The worldview that draws practitioners to the field should be consistent with the professional way of being and the values of the field. Practitioners should have congruence between their personal and professional worldviews, including values, beliefs, and ethics, because these are all aspects of the self.

Communication is the domain through which the self and professionalism are expressed to young people, families, coworkers, and multidisciplinary team members. The self and professional identity are demonstrated in the verbal, nonverbal, written, and electronic communication of the practitioner with young people, families, and team members in multiple contexts.

These three domains surround and therefore "contain" the four domains that describe the specific competence required for direct practice with young people and families (see Figure 5.1). The four domains that focus on the needs of young people and families overlap and it is difficult to define whether a particular skill or knowledge base is specific to one domain or the other.

While the skills and knowledge are described separately within each domain, integration is essential to good practice. The four centre domains must be simultaneously combined and applied for effective work with young people. An integration of skills and knowledge across multiple domains within the practice context is required. The four central domains that delineate the scope and the focus of practice for child and youth care as a field are:

- Relationships
- Critically applied human development
- Systems context
- Interventions

The practitioner applies knowledge, skills, and aspects of self from all four domains in an integrated manner in day-to-day work. For example, traditionally the practitioner assesses the status of a child's **development** (holistically) and identifies areas of strength and areas of developmental delay. The criteria for assessing development must be considered through the lens of theories that were developed in a particular cultural context and adjusted through both a professional understanding of human diversity and the unique systemic conditions of the young person's life. Critical application of knowledge about history, culture, and developmental theory begin to inform the work. Development occurs within the **systemic context** of the young person's life and the multiple systems that both young person and practitioner are involved in affect their interactions. This assessment and critical understanding forms the basis for the **interventions** that are implemented. **Relationships** are essential to the implementation of

interventions as well as the interpersonal inquiry that is necessary for a developmental assessment. Young people as well as their families must trust and feel safe in their interpersonal interactions with child and youth care practitioners; safety and trust develops through relationship.

The integration of the domains is illustrated in the practice example of Autry. When working with Autry, a practitioner who cannot integrate developmental assessment with systemic context might focus only on providing Autry with self-talk techniques for depression without considering the difficult nature of his family, community, and peer systems, which also require some intervention. A practitioner who was an immigrant might identify how his or her own experience would influence a relationship with Autry and adjust his or her communication to connect with Autry without imposing his or her own experience. The case study of Autry provides a variety of questions designed to elicit components of the practitioner's worldview and current knowledge. For a novice practitioner, these questions will be difficult. Later chapters provide a better understanding of the relevant knowledge domains for the case study, but for the moment the questions are simply assessing current experiential knowledge.

PRACTICE EXAMPLE: AUTRY

What are your first reactions to this story? Respond to the questions within each section to explore components of your worldview— consider how your values, beliefs, and ways of being might influence your interaction with Autry and where you would seek additional knowledge.

Photo by John Campbell

My name is Autry and this is my life story. I was born in Jamaica and spent the first 6 years of my life living there. Now that I'm 18, I don't remember much about my home country except what my parents have told me. They say it was not a very good life for us there but it's difficult for me to believe them because I have memories of playing football with my cousins and chasing dragonflies around our yard. I recall feeling very happy most of the time. However, my parents believed that life in Canada would provide us with better opportunities, so we moved to Toronto.

What attracts families to immigrate to Canada?

Because of my race and immigrant status, I was taunted by my classmates and called terrible names. I could not understand what was happening to me and why I was feeling like such an outcast all of a sudden, especially considering that there were other people of colour in my school. They made fun of my accent and the fact that my parents worked at a fast-food restaurant. The children would say: "All the dumb immigrants work in fast food because they are not smart enough to do anything else." This was not the case: My dad had a medical laboratory technology diploma but wasn't allowed to practice in Canada because of the "differences" between the two countries' medical systems.

How are children affected by teasing and what do you think moderates the effects?

Fact: The Longitudinal Survey of Immigrants to Canada (LSIC) shows us that within 2 years 80% of immigrants find full-time work but only 42% in their field (Doiron, 2006). Fuller & Martin (2012) explains that new immigrants follow multiple trajectories toward employment, including full-time employment; part-time employment; self-employment (full or part time); family care; study or upgrading without employment, including job search, preparations for self-employment, language courses; and other nonemployment activities. These different trajectories over a 4-year period lead to varied capacities for future employment as well as varied states of economic dependency on others. The trajectories can lead to different end states, including low-paying but stable employment in a different field. The data available about employment patterns is therefore difficult to interpret and does not account for how immigrants might be disadvantaged.

Why is the medical system closed to foreign-trained (internationally educated) personnel? What options are available to Autry's father and what would be the issues involved in proceeding with those different options?

Through my teen years I struggled with depression and anxiety. My parents wanted me to get good grades, especially my father who is quite an educated man himself. My family faced discrimination and had to work for minimum wage in order to support me and my three younger sisters. We could only eat what my parents would bring home from the restaurant because they had four kids to support and we also needed money for clothes and to pay the bills. It was impossible for them to get ahead. They didn't have the right education for Canadian jobs, which meant they could only get low-paying work, and so we had to live in subsidized housing or in places owned by slum landlords.

What is the cause of depression, anxiety, and other mental health disorders during the teenage years?

During my early teens I was often taken to the doctor because I felt tired and was apathetic. Part of my mood was my life circumstance and the other part was that I couldn't get enough to eat and I wasn't very healthy. I would give food to my younger sisters who would whine a lot because they were hungry. I did not want to stress my mother out further by making her listen to her children complain.

What are the needs of the children and how could Autry's mother have better met those needs, particularly for Autry?

I am 18 years old now and I feel quite lost. I was told by some of my more supportive teachers that I was smart enough to understand the concepts and I should do better in school. I want to get a degree in sociology and study crime at university. This is of particular interest to me because I was temporarily kicked out of high school in grade 11 for punching a classmate in gym class. We were playing a game of basketball when he tripped me and called me the "n word." He was not suspended at all. I feel pretty badly about myself, and I know that there are a lot of people out there who want me to fail. I think that a lot of my peers that get caught up in gang activity or selling drugs are set up because there is no other way to get ahead.

What should the school have done to help?

I am still living with my parents and little sisters and have a part-time job at Tim Horton's. I don't know what to do. I can't get a lot of money from the student loan program because I live at home and both my parents work so they are expected to help with tuition. The government rules don't seem to work for people with very little money. They don't think about things like how my sister Hyacinth needs to go to the doctor so often and one of us has to drive her.

She has bad asthma, which the doctor claims is caused by the dust mites in our two-bedroom apartment. Our living conditions don't offer any privacy. I'm feeling low because I don't have very many friends and I hang out with my sisters on weekends. My father doesn't want me getting into drugs or getting into trouble "again." I just hope I can save enough money to go to university but I'll have to give up the time and the fun I'm supposed to have at my age.

What advice would you give Autry to improve his life?

The following section is an overview of the seven domains with a general description of each sphere of influence and a description of how the domains are related to each other. Each domain has several subdomains that describe more precisely the nature of the skills and knowledge that need to be integrated together to work with children and youth. Each domain and its subdomains are examined in more detail in Chapters 6–12.

THE SELF

Practitioners are insightful about their personal and professional development. They understand how the self influences the work that they do with young people and families. You may recall that a core characteristic of child and youth care practice is its experiential nature. As described in Chapter 3, experience and reflection on the learning that comes from experience develops your self-awareness and self-understanding. Aspects of self mediate the knowledge and skills in the six other domains of practice. Reflective practitioners take responsibility for developing self-awareness and must have a life-long commitment to utilizing the self to ensure best practices with young people and families.

> You only have one tool and that's you! *(H. Skott-Myhre, personal communication, May 2008)*

There are four subdomains that help to organize the competencies of the self domain:

- **Reflective practice:** Practitioners actively reflect on professional experiences and personal history to identify how their emotions, feelings, and attitudes guide their interactions with young people. Reflective practice leads to enhanced competence when the learning is applied to new practice scenarios.
- **Boundaries:** Practitioners determine clear personal and professional limits and boundaries that facilitate the safe and effective delivery of service to young people and families.
- **Self-care:** Caring for yourself physically, emotionally, and spiritually ensures that practitioners have the capacity to respond to the needs of young people and families.
- **Use of the self in interventions:** The practitioner is interactive, immediate, authentic, and child-centered when intervening to help young people.

In the domain of self the foundational knowledge requirements include:

- Self-awareness models
- Burnout and stress theory
- Vicarious stress theory and critical response theory
- Community resources for personal and professional needs

PROFESSIONALISM

Professionalism includes your professional demeanor or professional "self" and your interpersonal interactions with young people, families, community members, and other professionals. You bring forward all aspects of your personal self into the sphere of professionalism and interpret who you are as a person through the requirements of your work milieu and the professional training you have received. The focus of a professional relationship is the work that you engage in with young people and families to assist them with challenges to their development and difficult life circumstances. The focus of a professional relationship is not social or personal. In child and youth care practice, professional, interpersonal interactions sometimes appear to be social or personal because the work occurs within the milieu or daily life-space of the young people; therefore, casual conversation about the weather and hockey game last night may actually be professional interactions. The intent of the interaction and the understanding that the young person and the practitioner have about their relationship determine the nature and meaning of the interaction.

There are four subdomains in the domain of professionalism that more clearly define the competencies required to translate the self into professional practice. These are described further in Chapter 7.

- **Ethics:** Practitioners follow codes of personal and professional behaviour in the day-to-day performance of their work. They also follow an ethical decision-making process that enables them to make the best possible decisions under difficult circumstances when beliefs and values conflict with each other.
- **Professional development:** Practitioners have a commitment to life-long learning through ongoing training, education, and self-directed learning as well as critical reflection on practice and experiential learning.
- **Supervision:** Practitioners provide high-quality care by discussing their practice with experienced colleagues and supervisors and they take responsibility for applying new learning in practice.
- **Diversity:** Practitioners respect and understand differences related to cultural and human diversity in the process of creating change for young people and families.

The foundational knowledge for the domain of professionalism constantly evolves as the field grows and professionalizes and the legal and societal context of the profession changes. The central knowledge areas include:

- The history of the profession and the evolution of social service systems;
- Legal rights, responsibilities and laws affecting young people and families in multiple service systems;
- Professional boundaries and ethical codes;
- Models of understanding diversity.

COMMUNICATION

Communication is the domain where relationships with people are established and the quality of service is enhanced through the ability to communicate effectively. This domain surrounds the four domains of practice focused on the work with young people. Through communication practitioners express aspects of the self and professionalism to young people and families. Communication is a two-way process, which means it is also the mechanism for gathering information and creating interventions for the young people and families with which they work. The communication domain influences competence in the central four domains. Practitioners must have the skill to analyze their audience, identify what is required, and match the needs of the recipient(s) with the most appropriate means of communication in written, spoken, and visual messages. Communication is a mediating domain that brings the outer two domains together with the inner four as illustrated in **Figure 5.2**.

The Communication domain has four sub-domains, which are discussed further in Chapter 8:

- **Verbal and nonverbal communication:** Practitioners make effective use of both verbal and nonverbal avenues of communication to enhance the quality of service and promote understanding and trust.
- **Written communication:** Practitioners keep accurate written records of interactions and organizational issues that are fundamental to planning and to integrated service delivery for young people and families.
- **Information technology and communication:** Practitioners use information technology for communication, information access, and decision making with careful consideration for personal privacy.
- **Professionals and the community:** Practitioners make use of effective communication skills with allied professionals and the community, including investigating and understanding the language and concepts used by other professionals in relevant settings.

The knowledge requirements for the domain of communication are:

- Communication theory
- Communication and cultural diversity
- Family communication patterns
- Communication and human development
- Principles of electronic communication
- Legislated and legal requirements related to documentation

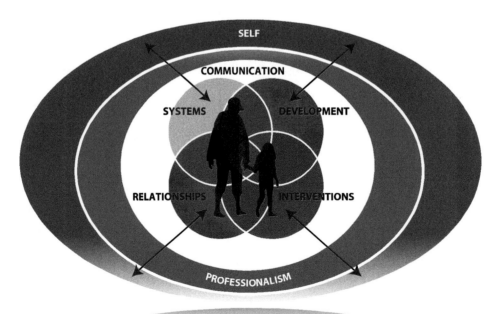

Figure 5.2 The Mediating Influence of Communication

RELATIONSHIPS

Genuine relationships based on empathy and positive regard for young people and families are critical for optimal development. Forming and maintaining relationships is a central strategy for change in practice. According to Garfat and Charles (2010), the relational process of intervention involves noticing, reflection, preparation, and intervention in the context of relationships with young people and families. The self comes to every relationship through noticing and reflecting on the elements of the interaction. Your relationship with a young person very often *is* the intervention. It is the context within which the young person learns and practices new ways of relating to people and thereby experiences a different self within a healing relationship (Garfat & Charles, 2010). Relationships are the foundation upon which groups of people become "systems" and help you to truly understand what young people experience in their developmental path toward adulthood.

PRACTICE EXAMPLE: RELATIONSHIP AND ACTIVITY

Karen Vander Ven[4] is a basketball player. She's not WNBA material, but she loves basketball. She is consulting with a local agency about the use of activities to engage youth and promote their development. As she leaves the building she notices a basketball game on the agency court. She doesn't know the youth playing, so she stands at the fence surrounding the court with her nose pressed against the wire watching. Her right hand bounces a bit imitating the dribbling action of a youth who is clearly a star on the court. There is a short break in the play and he turns around to notice her. "Hey, do you play ball?" he asks. "Sure," says Karen. "Wow, I've never met a lady with white hair like yours that plays. Come show me what you've got!" Karen steps on the court and plays a little one-on-one with him. Every time she goes for a lay-up he steals the ball away and every time she tries to steal it back he deeks around her and puts it in. After just a few points he stops the game and shows her how to break her step and control the dribble to get around his attempt to steal the ball. He has her practice the 'step, step, lift' to get up and lay the ball on the backboard. When they go back to one-and-one and she successfully ties the score, she says she has to go. They shake hands and agree that they'll have another game next week when she returns again for a training session.

Within the relationship domain there are four subdomains that represent the uniqueness of the child and youth care approach:

- **Caring:** The practitioner values caring for others as an essential component for emotional growth, developing social competence, and promoting healthy development.

- **Engagement:** Practitioners actively and genuinely develop therapeutic relationships and an empathetic understanding of the perspective of another, be it young person, family member, coworker, community member, or fellow professional. To be "engaged" with young people or families means that the person is meaningfully involved in and directs the nature of the relationship.

- **Use of activities:** The practitioner selects recreational activities and day-to-day life experiences for young people with a view to opportunities for developing relationships, engaging the young person in social learning and developing competence in new areas.

---

[4] Karen is a colleague of mine and variations of this story have been told many times. See *www.cyc-net.org/cyc-online/cycol-0703-karen.html* and *www.cyc-net.org/cyc-online/cycol-0604-karen.html* I developed this version of the story.

- **Teamwork:** The practitioner works with interprofessional and program teams. Working effectively in a team requires a relationship with coworkers as well as the relationships that one has with young people and families.
- **Professional relationships:** The practitioner understands integrated service delivery and works in partnership with other professionals and community organizations. The practitioner values the linkages between services and programs and actively works to develop professional relationships in other services and programs.

The domain of **relationship** requires foundational knowledge in the following areas:

- Characteristics of interpersonal relationships and helping relationships
- Characteristics of team development
- Principles of therapeutic programming

CRITICALLY APPLIED HUMAN DEVELOPMENT

This is the domain of practice where theory and research are examined and applied to understanding the current developmental status of a young person. Judgments about behaviour and development require an understanding of young people's social history, cultural and ethnic diversity and history, and the immediate situational variables. The focus is on optimizing children's development and social competence that recognizes the strengths that the young person has. These strengths will encourage him or her to cope with environmental or physiological circumstances that pose risks to developmental outcomes. A practitioner's influence on a young person's developmental progress today is set in the larger framework of what that young person needs through the ages and stages of life. Developmental theory is applied to understand behaviour which is placed in the larger context of the totality of development. Since developmental theory and research generally use language and ideas generated by the minority (Western) world (Pence & Marfo, 2008) and theory and research by the majority world, indigenous communities are just becoming public and available to the English-speaking community, all aspects of skill and knowledge in applied human development must be merged with an understanding of diversity from professionalism in order for the practitioner to meet the young person's needs. Chapter 10 offers more detail on how critically applied human development is integrated and applied in the diversity subdomain of the professionalism domain.

There are four subdomains:

- **Developmental theory:** The practitioner knows, understands, and can critically reflect on current research and theory on human development with an emphasis on synthesizing several theoretical perspectives and applying them to practice.
- **Patterns of growth and development:** The practitioner applies recent research in patterns and trajectories of child and adolescent development to observation and assessment of young people while recognizing that patterns of growth and development are culturally and socially based.
- **Linking developmental theory to risk and resilience:** The practitioner applies developmental theory to assist in understanding difficult and risky behaviours in young people. In some jurisdictions (health) these behaviours may be described as pathology; however, the

goals is to develop strength-based interventions that promote change for young people and to maximize developmental outcomes.

- **Psychotropic medication:** The practitioner is familiar with psychotropic medications commonly prescribed for treatment and understands the role of medication and its place in the management of children's psychiatric disorders within a strength-based and developmental approach.

The background knowledge for the domain of development evolves through research, critical examination of concepts and theories, and new theoretical perspectives. Regular professional development to understand new theory and research evidence that influences practice is essential. The foundational areas include:

- Lifespan development research
- Child development theory
- Exceptionality and special needs
- Social learning theory
- Risk and resilience

SYSTEMS CONTEXT

The systems surrounding young people and families provide the lens through which assessment and intervention occurs. The practitioner must incorporate the environmental conditions for young people and families into his or her work by considering:

- The historical and cultural environment of the child
- The political, community, and family environment
- The systems within which the young person, family, and practitioner interact such as school, peer group, church, or group care setting

Understanding the systems context will orient you to the complexity within young people's life-space. Thinking systemically allows you and the young person to identify realistic goals. It helps you identify individuals and programs that will contribute to success for the young person. Central to the systems orientation is the idea that all the components of a system are interrelated. Thus, changes to one part of the system influence all the other parts, affecting the possibilities for growth, change, and successful outcomes.

There are four subdomains to **systems context**, which are described in more detail in Chapter 11:

- **Systems theory:** The practitioner understands systems theory as a conceptual framework for practice. Systems theory emphasizes the relationships between the individual, family, service, and community and describes how these groups work together.
- **Ecological perspective:** The practitioner is familiar with the ecological perspective that emphasizes the interaction between persons and their physical and social environments, including cultural and political settings. The practitioner understands how institutional systems such as justice, health, child welfare, and education can help or restrict the growth and development of young people.

- **Family systems:** The practitioner knows that optimal development occurs within the family and surrounding social environment. Practitioners have a sound knowledge of family systems theory and value the family's input, ensuring that cultural values and beliefs held by young people and families are respected.

- **Legal guidelines and practice:** The practitioner understands how his or her practice is guided by a set of rules governed by provincial, state, and federal legislation governing children and families. These laws and guidelines are understood and applied in everyday practice.

The foundational knowledge for systems context includes:

- Systems theory
- Ecological theory
- Family theory
- Current societal trends

INTERVENTIONS

Intervention is the heart of change in child and youth care practice, but it cannot be accomplished without a dynamic interaction with the other three domains just described. **Interventions** include the practitioner's ability to integrate and apply current knowledge of **human development** with the skill, expertise, and self-awareness essential for developing, implementing, and evaluating effective intervention programs for young people. The goal of any intervention is to further the young person's development, to encourage socially appropriate behaviour, and to teach alternatives. Interventions require relationships with young people and families; interventions are enacted within the systems context of the practitioner and the young person or family. There are five subdomains in interventions that represent both the unique characteristics of child and youth care practice interventions and the systematic or planned approach to practice. While there is an individual uniqueness to working in the milieu with young people and families, it is critically important to document progress and review that progress individually and collectively to identify effective interventions and create an evidence base for future work. The five subdomains are:

- **Life-space intervention:** Effective use of the environment and daily life experiences shared with a young person creates opportunities for growth and development. The practitioner understands that every interaction with the young person is a momentary opportunity and this understanding is integrated into the relationships, communication, and activities developed with and for the young person. Through the planned arrangement of the physical environment and the activities of daily living, including eating, grooming, hygiene, sleep, and rest, opportunities for learning and change are created. The practitioner designs and implements individual and group activity plans that reflect the significance of play and recreational programming to young people.

- **Advocacy:** The practitioner understands the inherent potential of the young person and family and their capacity for growth and change. Practitioners have basic advocacy skills that ensure young people and families have their views heard and considered during the decision-making processes that directly affect them.

- **Group work:** The group is a powerful socialization agent and group work provides opportunities for members to experience social development and to build on their existing strengths and competencies. Practitioners adapt their behaviour management and communication skills to function within the group context.

- **Planned intervention:** Planned interventions arise from the selection of individual goals or objectives based on treatment, educational, and developmental plans. Practitioners design activities, interactions and behaviour management methods that support these goals and objectives. Intervention strategies are continuously adapted, anticipating the steps and measures required to meet the young person's objectives. Together with the following subdomain the planning and evaluation process forms what is typically called case management.

- **Intervention plans:** The practitioner has strong, objective observation and assessment skills. These skills are used to assess and evaluate the daily processes of living in a group environment and observe events in relation to intervention plan(s) in order to create developmentally appropriate opportunities in which children can experience success. Practitioners understand that when outcomes are evaluated there is a theoretical basis to the expected outcomes and regular reviews are necessary to identify both outcomes and additional areas of developmental need. Evaluating progress is critical to ensure successful outcomes for young people and families as well as to gather evidence for improved practice and service delivery.

The foundational knowledge for the domain of interventions is constantly evolving and requires updating through professional development with a focus on evidence-based practice and program evaluation. The central areas of knowledge include:

- Therapeutic milieu and environmental design
- Principles of psychoeducational interventions
- Principles of life-space intervention
- Crisis theory
- Principles of conflict resolution
- Theories of personal change
- Group theory
- Principles of (current) therapeutic approaches (e.g., narrative, solution-focused, play, and/or art therapy)
- Nutrition and first aid

BECOMING A MATURE PRACTITIONER: INTEGRATING THE DOMAINS

Becoming competent in practice requires the integration of aspects of self, skill, and knowledge that are learned through education and experience, into the milieus in which practice occurs. Competence also requires a commitment to reflective practice through relational inquiry and self-inquiry, as outlined in Chapter 3. In Chapter 4 the various milieus where child and youth care practitioners work were described according to the five elements of a therapeutic milieu. The milieu is the first layer within the context where practice occurs. The domains of practice have a three-dimensional nature when they are viewed in the practice context. The layers in the practice context are (1) practice milieu, (2) organizational system, and (3) culture.

This section explains each of these layers and describes how aspects of self, skill, and knowledge are integrated and applied across the layers of the practice context.

PRACTICE MILIEU

The milieu is the primary location within which practice occurs and includes a variety of environments where young people are found. The practice milieu is structured to enhance the developmental trajectories of young people and families. In this layer, practitioners must integrate all the domains of practice, responding to multiple possibilities for relational interaction and intervention activities. There are many possible settings in which a novice practitioner can work (Chapter 4) and one of these will be the primary location within which a practitioner is first challenged to develop and integrate the domains of practice.

Practice in this layer is focused primarily on the person(s). Quality practice includes work that is spontaneous, challenging, proactive, and planned. Program activities are designed to therapeutically structure the environment, but other activities are spontaneous, drawing on practitioner skills with activities but considering the immediate needs of the child and any group or environmental needs at that point in time. Change is facilitated in the practice milieu through the interventions chosen by the practitioner. The self is constantly drawn in so that interventions shift when a practitioner reflects on the knowledge and skill that was successfully or unsuccessfully applied in the day-to-day work with young people and families. The focus in the practice milieu is on communication within and the development of relationships in the immediate environment. Mature practitioners structure the milieu to be inclusive. They build a group culture that includes activities and norms based on the diversity of members of the group integrating the elements of practice from the diversity subdomain in professionalism with their skills and knowledge in critically applied human development and the interventions they have learned. They also work to modify as necessary the organizational system to be more inclusive, assisting young people and families to have influence on program policies that are discriminatory or oppressive.

THE ORGANIZATIONAL SYSTEM

Child and youth care practice also occurs within the context of multiple programs and milieus, representing an organizational system that is more than the milieu where the young person or family is located. While the organizational system will define the culture and ideology of the milieu, the system extends beyond the therapeutic milieu and can be a context in which experienced practitioners use their knowledge of systems theory and skills in systemic assessment to understand the nature of the organization they work in and how this influences their practice. They also work to influence the system so that it offers quality service to all young people and families. They interpret policy, procedures, and legislation according to the nature of the developmental status of the young people they work with. Professional communication is congruent with but is not limited by the system rules and requirements as it might be with a novice practitioner. The planning and implementation of practice methods take into consideration the nature of the system and its philosophical standpoint. Mature practitioners integrate the culture of the organization, their own culture, that of the young person, and their coworkers by respecting difference and negotiating a common understanding of right and wrong within the organizational context.

Experienced practitioners assess young people in multiple milieus (e.g., school, peer groups, family, neighbourhood, etc.) and the relationships among various systems and subsystems are accounted for in the person's development. The effects of organizational policies on the young person's development are considered. Experienced practitioners are familiar with and consistently follow the agency standards regarding intervention plans. They engage in regular reviews of progress. Quality practice requires fluency with the systemic approach using the concepts and language of a systems orientation. Mature practitioners who integrate the domains and apply them in the organizational context go beyond the quality work of an experienced practitioner and are able to strategize and mobilize the community, identify needs, know and support the community resources, facilitate community capacity building, and cultivate community relations. These elements of practice go beyond the art of practice with individuals and families but make use of the same basic aspects of self, skills, and knowledge developed by the novice practitioner.

Just as mature practitioners account for factors in the immediate milieu, they are aware of, mindful of, and attempt to influence factors beyond the immediate milieu. They use communication skills to advocate for people. They develop relationships with individuals in organizational roles that can wield a positive influence on the lives of young people. Quality practice requires sensitivity to cultural, spiritual, and socioeconomic factors and how they influence children and their environments. Mature practitioners pay attention to the symbiotic interaction between society's culture(s) and the institutions and systems that represent society.

CULTURE

As a layer within the practice context, culture includes multiple aspects of race or ethnicity, as well as the social and political norms, values, morals, faith, language, and socioeconomic status of groups of people with a common history. Mature practitioners bridge differences through communication and respect for individuals and groups. They actively seek an understanding of how cultures influence the developmental history of young people and their families and reflect on how those histories may diverge from their own referential framework. Experienced practitioners recognize and adopt a professional culture, without forsaking their own personal culture.

Mature practitioners advocate for the rights of young people, represent them and their views, and participate in procedures advocating for the appropriate resources both individually and as a group. They work (alongside young people) to affect the values of their society relative to the healthy development of young people and families. They assess the mutual influence of culture on the individual and the individual on culture. They work with the institutions of society so as to change them and promote positive development that benefits young people. Families are better able to fulfill their functions and help children grow up when practitioners work to influence issues related to transportation, health care, housing, mass media, employment, religion, recreation, legislation, and education. They participate in strategic planning and visioning of services for the future and offer leadership. Practitioners promote an understanding of diversity and culture within the broader culture in which they exist.

Novice practitioners are often one-dimensional and consciously work to integrate theory with practice across the domains within their specific practice milieu. Experienced practitioners are comfortable and integrated in their application of the domains of practice within a single context and recognize the different layers of their context for practice, consciously applying skills and knowledge in different layers. Mature practitioners engaged in praxis (knowing, doing, and being) have fully integrated the aspects of self, the skill and knowledge components of each domain of practice into any action they engage in and they adjust their practice according to the primary context of the moment. This integration and contextual application of practice brings the domains into a three-dimensional framework, making them "spheres" of influence rather than "circles of influence."

The application of the knowledge, theory, and skills within the various layers in which practice occurs requires a fluid integration of the contexts for practice. Skills are applied within a specific context in a manner that demonstrates your awareness of the unique meaning, atmosphere, and nature of the activities in that context (Krueger & Stuart, 1999). The values and beliefs that form your worldview should also form a solid base for all your work with young people and families across multiple contexts. An example of how skills and knowledge within one of the subdomains can be used in these different layers will illustrate how mature practitioners evolve and transfer knowledge and skills into different contexts.

An ethical decision-making process (in the **ethics** subdomain within the professional domain) is applied when a practitioner is faced with a decision about whether to report evidence of neglect during a visit with a family. In the practice milieu of family support, or supervised access, the practitioner must consider the meaning of making a report, the number of people involved, and the effect of the report in comparison to a different intervention that might mitigate the neglect and assist the family. The activities and responsibilities of the practitioner are specific to one or two children and the parents. The child protection legislation and the policies of the program are clear and specific. There is less information to observe and the processing of information has a smaller circumference. A novice practitioner has the skills and knowledge required to make the decision and uses a reflective process as well as consultation with his or her supervisor to make a decision about reporting.

The same ethical decision-making process would be applied when a practitioner is faced with a decision about whether to report licensing violations observed in a foster home or after-school care setting while visiting a person in that setting. In the context of the **organizational system** the meaning of making a report, the number of people, and the nature of the effects on those people are much broader. Consideration is given to the families and children whom you do not work directly with and who may have limited options if the program is closed. Decision makers have many more components to observe and reflect upon. However, it is still an application of the skills of ethical decision making. A mature practitioner at an advanced level of practice brings a more integrated application of knowledge and attitudes to the skill of ethical decision making, accounts for more variables in the process, and may well arrive at a decision faster and with greater clarity. These are two examples of applying the same ethical decision-making process in different layers of the contexts in which practitioners work.

Similarly, developing a relationship with and communicating with a supervisor is different from communication with a young person, yet the basic skills are described in the subdomain of verbal and nonverbal communication within the domain of communication and in the subdomain of teamwork with the domain of relationship. It is the layer within which the action occurs (practice milieu vs. organizational system or culture) and the integration of the appropriate attitudes and knowledge that differentiate the application of these skills by a novice, experienced, or mature practitioner.

SUMMARY

This chapter introduced the seven domains of child and youth care practice and described their relationships to each other. The domains of practice are applied within multiple layers of the practice context. Understanding the interaction of context and domain is a life-long developmental task for the practitioner undertaken through praxis: "knowing, doing, and being." The following chapters focus more specifically on the domains of practice and each chapter introduces how those domains are applied in various settings as well as how the use of theory informs practice. The exercises in the following chapters help to develop praxis and apply the theory.

Tips and Resources

Praxis: The application of self coupled with the integration of theory and knowledge and skill to practice with young people and families.

The theory, knowledge, and skills required for child and youth care practice must be developed through ongoing coursework and application of skills in the field. The aspects of self that make up your being will be revealed through self-inquiry and through relationships with coworkers and with young people and families. In other words, you will not learn **everything** by reading this book (though I hope you will learn **something**). Indeed, you will find that some of the subdomains identified above are covered in more depth than others. As alluded to in previous chapters, much of the knowledge base of child and youth care practice comes from other disciplines. In the following chapters you will read, understand, and begin to apply the child and youth care perspective so that when you learn more theory and knowledge that is drawn from other disciplines you will understand and interpret it as a child and youth care practitioner.

Photo by Laine Robertson

CHAPTER EXERCISES

VALUES AND BELIEFS

Reflection-on-Practice

The following exercise is drawn from the professional certification program in Alberta to help you reflect on some of the core values of the field and demonstrate their importance to the domains of practice.

Child and youth care practitioners should agree with and demonstrate the following attitudes in their practice (CYCAA, 2000). Review each of these statements. Which of these do you agree with or disagree with? Provide an example from your practice or a semi-professional interaction with a young person or family that illustrates how you express that worldview in your behaviour.

- **"Respect** for the child and family" is expressed in ethical practice that includes respect for confidentiality and privacy as well as respect for the diversity of cultural values and beliefs.
- **"Empowerment** of individuals, families and communities" is expressed in the actions that practitioners take to assist families to promote optimal development for their children.

- "**Collaboration** with children, families, and allied professionals and community members" means that service plans are developed with the active involvement of children, their families, and their community service providers.

- "**Respect** for difference" is a core value that is represented in all domains of practice. Human beings cannot be thought of in isolation from their social environment or their individual identity and the complex nature of the interaction between the two.

- "**Deinstitutionalisation** and community-based service" is reflected in the increased role of child and youth care practitioners in community services, youth development programs such as Boys and Girls Clubs, and family-based intervention programs.

- "**Growth and development** is life-long" and therefore the practitioner understands problem behaviours as an indicator of developmental lags in specific areas.

SELF: VALUES, BELIEFS, ETHICS

Reflection-on-Practice

The exercise of identifying your worldview in relation to Autry and his family is fundamental to effective practice within the Self domain. You are less likely to act unconsciously on your values and beliefs if you are aware of what they are. You need to identify the boundaries around what personal information to share and how to use your values and beliefs effectively in developing interventions with Autry. As you become experienced within this domain you will recognize how to respond to your emotional reactions to Autry's scenario.

Review your responses to the questions about Autry and his circumstances. Choose one response and try to identify some of the aspects of self as they are described in Chapter 3. Use the chart and the examples below to assist your exploration of your values, beliefs, and ethics. You will do more work on these concepts in Chapter 6.

DEFINING ASPECTS OF SELF	EXAMPLES	YOUR STATEMENTS FROM THE AUTRY CASE STUDY
Values: The positive or negative evaluations of importance that you attach to someone or something based on your experience.	Normal childhood experiences are good. Teasing is bad.	
Beliefs: True statements about your experience of reality.	Children are cruel but teasing is a normal part of growing up.	
Ethics: A "rule" for behaviour that is connected to your values and beliefs.	Bullies should have their behaviour corrected by being punished.	
Can you find a "factual" statement that relates to your response? How do you know it is a "fact"?		

PROFESSIONALISM—SUPERVISION

Reflection-for-Practice

"Your front-line supervisor is your translator. Your job is to bring to them the raw materials that you cannot understand and they will help you learn the language and put your experience into a context that is understandable." (K. Gharabaghi, personal communication, May 2008)

When you work with Autry you bring your self to the relationship, including your cultural background and your own personal identity. These are translated in your professional identity but you also have an obligation as a professional to learn about his culture and identity. You also need to know the policies and laws that might apply to the situation that he finds himself in. You will use your supervisor, a practitioner with more experience and knowledge, to direct you into areas that you need to learn about. Your obligation as a professional is to identify the areas where you need help and discuss them with your supervisor. You will talk with your supervisor about your attitudes and reactions to the family sharing your responses to questions like: "What are the needs of the children and how could Autry's mother have better met those needs, particularly for Autry"? Your supervisor may challenge your responses and help you examine the sources of bias in those beliefs.

Review your responses to Autry and the questions in the case study and identify two things that you might put on a "supervision agenda" for discussion.

E-COMMUNICATION

Reflection-for-Practice

Given Autry's age and his isolation from others, your first contact with him might be through an e-counselling service like the one provided by "Kids Help Phone" (*http://org.kidshelpphone.ca* or *www.yourlifeyourvoice.org*). You will need to have some skill in how to use the technology of the e-counselling service for effective communication. You will also need to consider the ethics and boundaries of your interactions (professional domain) and how to communicate those to Autry.

How would you respond to the following posting from Autry? What are the critical communication issues to consider both in receiving and sending a message?

I have to go to the doctor because I feel tired and I'm not interested in doing anything. Part of my mood is my life circumstance and the other part is that I can't get enough to eat. I give food to my younger sisters who whine a lot because they are hungry. I don't want to stress my mother out further by making her listen to her children complain.

RELATIONSHIPS—USE OF ACTIVITIES

Reflection-for-Practice

Autry has had some supportive adult relationships in school but overall he reports that he knows few people, has few friends, and doesn't really know how to approach adults. His ability to create relationships seems compromised. Relationships are about a shared history with which you build further your relationship with the young person. Doing an activity with a youth creates a set of moments that you can share. As a child and youth care practitioner you may start by creating relationship through activity as Karen does in the story above.

Based on Autry's story, what activities would you engage in with him to begin developing a shared history that you can build on?

DEVELOPMENT AND DIVERSITY—CRITICAL REFLECTION

Theory-in-Practice

At age 18 Autry is leaving adolescence and entering adulthood. He feels pressured to go to the university and establish a vocation. He also feels pulled to look after his younger siblings. His adolescence was filled with incidents of discrimination based on his ethnic background, and these have influenced his developmental path. Eric Erikson's theory of social-emotional development indicates that Autry is transitioning from the stage of identity formation to intimacy. Erikson states that the struggle for a unique ethnic identity within a dominant culture is common throughout the world for ethnic minorities (Santrock, MacKenzie-Rivers, Leung, & Malcomson, 2011). Autry also faces subtle systemic discrimination because of poverty and lifestyle. Theory about human development must be combined with both research knowledge and experiential knowledge about the uniqueness of Autry's ethnic and cultural background as well as other aspects of diversity in order to successfully navigate this domain of practice.

Discrimination and oppression are what inspire groups such as the Jamaican Canadian Association (*www.jcaontario.org*) in their work to promote and organize youth development events. Explore one or more of the following websites and identify how the development of young people might be influenced by immigration, poverty, and racial origin.

http://immigrantyouth.org

www.iyjl.org/about-2/

SYSTEMS CONTEXT—ECOLOGICAL PERSPECTIVE

Theory-in-Practice

In the previous example of applying developmental theory to Autry's circumstances and considering points for intervention, you may have begun to understand the cultural and ethnic influences on Autry's development. There are multiple systems that affect Autry. His family, school, peer group, and church are all groups of people with norms, rules, and structure that guide how Autry relates to the group and what his membership and role is within the group. The practitioner who thinks systemically recognizes that Autry's family is likely a strong support for him, providing practical and material support, as well as some emotional support and guidance. At the same time, Autry returns this support to his family and worries about them, caring for his sisters above himself. The social trend of increasing enrollment in university has likely affected his goals for the future while at the same time the economic circumstances of the family and the restrictive rules about student loans limit his ability to meet those goals. These are all points of intervention for the practitioner that thinks systemically.

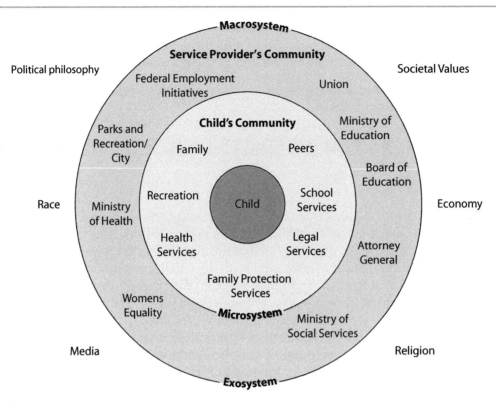

Figure 5.3 Mapping Your Community

Using your own state or province as a point of reference, put Autry in the middle of the following diagram and make some notes about the relevant factors in the various systems that are identified within the outermost circle—the Service Provider's Community. For example, what employment initiative programs are relevant for Autry's parents or for Autry? What educational support programs would help him?

INTERVENTIONS-ACTIVITY PROGRAMMING IN COMMUNITY

Reflection-for-Practice

There are many possibilities for intervention with Autry. Intervention begins from the moment a practitioner and youth meet. As the practitioner begins a relationship with Autry there is an assessment of his development as well as the context in which he lives, works, and plays, which provides ongoing information about points of intervention. You might start with an activity focus—basketball, chess, paintball, or something else that interests Autry. As the relationship develops you will also be giving him opportunities to develop social skills and building his success and therefore his self-esteem. Helping him find and join local clubs will increase the opportunities he has to meet youth his own age that are acceptable to his father as well as Autry. The family may need some assistance as well with understanding the postsecondary system and other medical options for his sister or with changing the home environment to better manage the respiratory health concerns.

FINAL REFLECTION: YOUTH

Here is a personal reflection written by a youth for the The Letters of Hope Project. The project is a collection of letters from youth worldwide who have survived hopelessness and now want to give hope to other youth struggling to get to the other side. The project is led by filmmaker Andree Cazabon, who is collecting the letters for a book and will use the proceeds to further support youth who need to find hope in their lives. You can learn more about the project at www.andreecazabon.ca/letters-of-hope-project.

Considering your own social and geographic environment, what is available locally that you would use to help Autry and his family?

Amanda, 24 years old, Quebec province

I was sad, angry, and rebellious when I was 13 and taken out of my home. In photos I can see the emptiness . . . the sad vacant eyes filled with hopelessness. I had lost my father at a very early age. A lot of people say he was not a great father or husband but I never really was able to judge because I was 3 when he died. My mother remarried very quickly and her second husband had a special attraction to little girls. At a very young age I did not really appreciate his "special attention" and I reported him constantly to the police and school authorities, but people were very slow to intervene. We even moved jurisdictions to avoid being watched by the police. It was when I was 7 that everything got worse. My stepdad took to humiliating me and beating me daily to punish me for reporting him. I started dieting and hating myself. He spent 6 months in jail. My mother got cancer just after that and it became very obvious without him around that she had a drug problem. I am not sure if the drug problem got worse when she got cancer or if that is why she slept so much and allowed him to mistreat my siblings and I.

When I went into care at 13, I was immediately diagnosed with seven mental disorders. I did not question anyone, assuming doctors knew best. I got put on a lot of drugs and they felt the best place for a troubled kid like me was group homes. I finally got a subsidized apartment when I was 16. It was so much better than the group homes. I could finally decide when to go to bed, when to eat and when to shower. It is very stressful to not be able to make simple decisions like that for years. I had to work full time to cover the rent and food my last year in high school. It was really hard but I graduated with honors.

When I went to college I had no idea the dorms close at breaks sending typical students home or to Florida, but leaving youth without family homeless. I never considered the fact that dorms might close knowing how expensive those rooms were and no social worker or staff thought to tell me. So I was homeless in college my first 2 years at every break. It was really tough at Christmas break, which was 5 weeks long at my college. I got through and graduated. I even spent a year as a Rotary Ambassadorial scholar abroad. I will get my master's degree soon and have a 3.8 GPA at a pretty prestigious graduate school. Oh and I am not mentally ill . . . the contextually insensitive doctors may have been or maybe the staff who benefited from my diagnoses were. I am not homeless anymore. I pay my rent, have savings, and found a home.

I think it was not me, it was the situation I was put in, that made my life so difficult. I was obviously very capable with the right supportive network. Maybe you can offer to be a support to homeless youth or someone aging out of care? If you are a youth who is homeless, parentless, or in foster care the one thing I can suggest is find people who believe in you and make a point of finding a few good people not quite as stressed as you are to befriend and support you: whether that is through church, a community center, school, or work, those people can get you through the rough patches, point you toward opportunities, and celebrate your successes.

A big thanks to every scholarship agency, the Rotary District 6690, the Orphan Foundation of America, teachers, staff, friends, honorary relatives, and coworkers who sent me socks, sent me books, sent me cookies, covered a semester of tuition, tutored me, hugged me, sent me Christmas and birthday emails, told me I was smart, proofread admission and scholarship essays, and helped me find my way.

CHAPTER 6

THE SELF

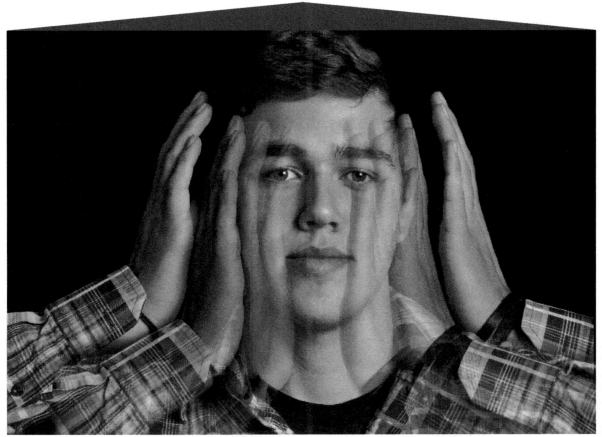

Photo by Laine Robertson

CHAPTER OBJECTIVES

- Explore the self domain and introduce some basic skills and knowledge that inform how practitioners use self during interactions with young people and families.
- To introduce the concept of using self to **be** in interaction.
- To explore reflective practice in detail.
- To introduce the subdomains of boundaries and self-care and develop basic skills in these domains that will deepen and advance as practitioners become more experienced.
- Explore the self in intervention component of practice.

Youth work is enriched and fraught will all the emotions, challenges, struggles and discoveries that are part of being human. Workers try their best and learn from their successes and failures. Central to this process is self. Workers bring self to the moment and learn from their feelings and insights as they interact with and learn from youth. Workers do their homework . . . so they can understand how their histories bias and influence their interactions. They also try to be aware of their feelings of fear, anger, joy, excitement, boredom, sadness, etc. as they interact. Youth work, in this context, is a process of self in action. Workers use self to inform and be in their interactions. (Krueger, 2007b, p. 40)

THE SELF

Child and youth care practitioners understand how the self influences the work that they do with young people and families. Interventions require specific theory and technique, some of which you will learn about in Chapter 13, and the rest of which you will spend your career learning about. In all interventions you must bring who you are to the theory and the technique and you must bring your **self** to the person that you are working with. Insight about your personal and professional development is essential to the work that we do. As Krueger describes in the quote that opens this chapter, self is the foundation for child and youth care practice. You may recall that a core characteristic of practice is its experiential nature. Experiences and reflection on the learning that comes from those experiences develops self-awareness and self-understanding. As illustrated in **Figure 6.1**, self surrounds the six other domains. Practitioners are personally responsible for developing self-awareness through self-inquiry and relational inquiry and have a life-long commitment to developing and utilizing the self to ensure the best practices for young people and families.

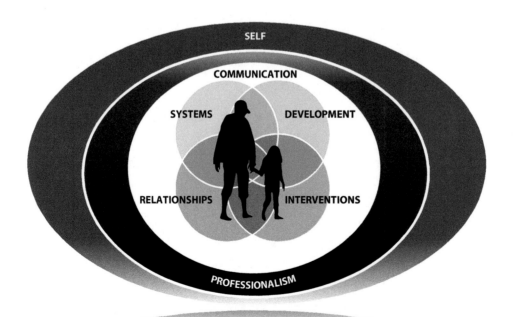

Figure 6.1   The Domain of Self

WHAT IS SELF?

There are many ways of characterizing who you are, who your "Self" is. You began to understand and describe the concept of self in Chapter 3; now we will look at it more closely. When asked who they are, young children will focus on the visible and concrete aspects of self—hair, body size, clothing—and may add family members or activities that they do. They don't notice the internal manifestations of self. This understanding of self changes as children get older. An important developmental task for adolescents is the formation of an identity, which often results in a particular style of dress that represents that identity to the world. As young people leave high school and enter the world of work, this visible identity may come with them. Youth work is particularly challenging at this stage because the identity you carry and the visible manifestations of that identity are, in part, a method for connecting with the youth you work with. Since you look like "one of them" they will relate to you. There is much more to self and identity than the visible manifestations of our being. As young children can already identify, self is shaped by the various milieus and ecosystems that you participate in and is expressed in many different ways, internally and visibly to the people around you.

First, complete the Self-Inquiry exercise at the end of the chapter to identify your "model" of Self or how you characterize your own Self at this point in your life. Through the use of metaphor this exercise helps you develop a personal "theory" or conceptual framework that describes the self. How does your metaphor compare with the model developed to help youth workers understand youth in **Table 6.1** (UNESCO, 2003)?

These eight categories of self can be useful to help you consider the individual aspects of self—found on the left side of the table—and the contributions to defining self that are relational (found on the right side of the table) such as social, family, community relationships and cultural

Table 6.1   Understanding and Identifying Self

PHYSICAL SELF	SOCIAL SELF
• Appearance	• Relationships with female friends
• Involvement in athletics	• Relationships with male friends
• Sense of physical safety	• School/social group membership
• Sense of comfort in body	• Popularity in and out of school
• Disability status	• Social aspirations
SEXUAL SELF	**FAMILIAL SELF**
• Sexual orientation	• Roles as son/daughter, sister/brother, aunt/uncle, mother/father, niece/nephew, grandmother/grandfather
• Sexual values	• Sense of belonging in family
• Sexual feelings	• Familial expectations and aspirations
• Sexual experience	• Balance of future career and family
• Sexual aspirations	

(Continued)

Table 6.1 (*continued*)

CREATIVE SELF	COMMUNITY SELF
• Creative talents or interests	• Group/club membership
• Involvement in hobbies or activities	• Volunteer experience and aspirations
• Creative aspirations	• Activist experience and aspirations
• Creative talents as careers	• Employment experience

ACADEMIC SELF	CULTURAL SELF
• Student achievement	• Ethnic/racial identity
• School/social group membership	• Spiritual/religious identity
• Educational aspirations	• Geographic identity
• Career aspirations	• Socioeconomic identity
	• Cultural aspirations

identity. In essence, these categories provide a set of questions or areas for self-inquiry to identify aspects of your Self and enhance your self-awareness and ability to describe that awareness.

Models, such as Table 6.1, can help people understand the nature of self and develop self-awareness. Models can enhance self-observation or self-consciousness and they can assist with self-inquiry. The **aspects of self**, introduced in Chapter 3, provide a different model or way of thinking about self. In this model (see **Figure 6.2**), the self is composed of values, beliefs, and ethics that are developed through relationships and influence of the collective society and culture that we grow up and live in. Other aspects of self include our thoughts, feelings, and actions as they are expressed in our daily living through our relationships. These aspects of self make up our worldview.

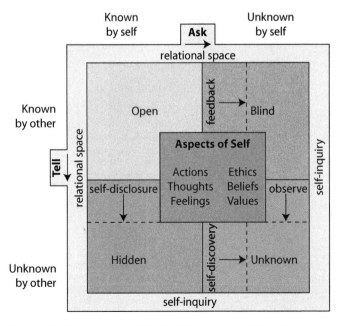

Figure 6.2 Aspects of Self at the Centre of Inquiry

What are ethics, beliefs, and values and how do they relate to our actions, thoughts, and feelings in practice? Ricks (1989) argues that your worldview, composed of ethics, beliefs, and values, is developed from your experiences (social, familial, community, and cultural). From those experiences you develop conclusions (beliefs) about the world, which include judgements about what is most important (your values) and rules that guide how you run your life and behave with others (your ethics). These conclusions are your worldview and it guides your actions, thoughts, and feelings as you interact with others. Together, these form the aspects of your Self that you carry into your practice. Remember in the previous chapter you consider these aspects of self in relation to how you interpreted the circumstances of Autry. Let's look at the aspects of self again and consider them more personally in relation to your own actions, thoughts, and feelings.

Dissonance, through conflicting values and beliefs within your worldview, is associated with feeling uncomfortable, and by critically examining and assessing your worldview you may decide to change certain beliefs or values or to change your behaviour. Sometimes dissonance occurs because you become aware of historical conditions (such as the treatment of First Nations people in Canada or slavery in the United States) and you begin to critically analyze how the dominant views of society have been influenced by historical conditions as well as how language and indeed the culture of the systems in which we work have created conditions that do not match your own consciousness about how to value and treat young people and families. Sometimes dissonance arises when you become aware of how your own behavior is inconsistent with your values and beliefs.

To examine those aspects of self that are central to your practice you need to engage in self-consciousness. Ricks describes self-consciousness as "the capacity to reflect on what I experience. It might be thought of as a kind of preoccupation with cognitive awareness or mindfulness about self-reflection and introspection" (2003, p. 72). She seems to be describing the **reflective practice** subdomain that is essential to practice. Thompson and Thompson (2008) recommend keeping three words, "head, heart, habit," at the front of your consciousness as a reminder to reflect on our thoughts, feelings, and actions in the moment. Doing so will help you identify when habits are hard to change or when the best of plans do not become reality because beliefs or values conflict or the emotional commitment is insufficient.

However, self is not objective and separate; self exists only in relationship to our being with others. "'Being' describes conscious existence. . . . With conscious existence, I am more than a body. I am a being. . . . [with] subjective awareness and an inner capacity to experience and make meaning of my experiences" (Lundy, 2008, p. 209). Subjective awareness and self-consciousness are key components of "being"; however, "being" also exists because of the relationships we have with friends, family, and others, which are embedded within culture and the social system. Shared experiences generate shared meaning, values, beliefs, and ethics, creating a collective worldview held with other members of your family, community, and culture.

The idea of "being," where self is one component of being, leads to a discussion of the relational component of practice (which will be taken up in Chapter 9). Indeed, White (2007) indicates that being mindful and self-aware is only one part of "being" in child and youth care. It is the idea of "being" that makes the other subdomains of self so important. **Boundaries** guide the practice of child and youth care to help you distinguish self from other within the relationships that you have. The **use of self in intervention** puts "being" at the heart of change (Lundy, 2008). Given the nature of the experiences of young people and families that practitioners work with, **self-care** for the practitioner is critical. Identifying and describing the self, using the models just considered, is an essential start to understanding self and the role of self in practice. Once you have some language for describing yourself it is easier to understand why and how the self domain influences all the other domains of practice. **Reflective practice** is the mechanism by which learning occurs and by which the self domain exerts its influence on the other domains. The role of reflective practice in professional development was discussed in Chapter 3. In the next section these concepts are considered in more detail and reflective practice strategies are presented.

REFLECTIVE PRACTICE

My inspiration is life itself and all that comes with living and being.

In a moment, hour, day, month, or even a brief interaction with one person, your whole world can become shattered or enlightened. I treasure each of these interactions knowing that through them I will be a stronger and more self-aware individual than a moment, hour, month, or day ago. ~Vanessa Lalonde (Personal communication, 2009)

The child and youth care practitioner continuously assesses his or her professional skills, knowledge, and personal well-being and reflects on the influence of these factors on day-to-day practice. Self-reflective habits ensure quality care for young people and families as well as enhanced personal and professional growth. Schon (1987) developed a methodology for reflective practice that has been applied to many different professions throughout all phases of their careers. In his model practitioners actively reflect on their professional experiences. They identify feelings and attitudes; determine how those guide the activities they engage in; learn or identify what needs to be different; and apply that new learning to a new situation.

Child and youth care practitioners not only actively reflect on their professional learning, they also actively reflect on their personal history and the influence it has on day-to-day relationships as well as reflecting on their interactions with team members and clients. It is "the journey into self" (Burns, 2012; Fewster, 1990a) that is ongoing throughout the practitioner's career, which distinguishes the use of self in reflective practice.

Practitioners recognize that the self organizes and influences all the other domains. "Growth occurs in a series of moments and interactions, and therefore each moment and interaction has enormous potential" (Krueger, Galovits, Wilder, & Pick, 1999, p. ix) for reflection and for change—both for yourself as a practitioner and for the young people you work with.

Transformative events occur in the minutia of the moment. The event becomes a transformative experience of first-order or second-order developmental change (Maier, 2002) only when the significance of the interaction is noticed by the person and the potential for change is released. Noticing is an important skill for implementing **reflection-in-practice** (Thompson & Thompson, 2008). Your observational skills will help you draw out the aspects of the moment that are particularly significant and to recognize how the context, the system, the organization, or the culture affects your learning. Of course, noticing is influenced by your personal history. The person from a very warm southern country notices the snow differently than someone from a northern country, surrounded by snow for 6–8 months of the year. Less tangible aspects of personal history, such as religious beliefs, family traditions, or habits of friendship and social interaction, also influence what we notice.

Learning in child and youth care practice occurs not just in formal education and training but also through relational inquiry. Through a "process of self-in-action, workers and young people learn about themselves from their experiences together" (Krueger et al., 1999, p. ix). Thus, through both critical reflection on interactions and relationships as well as through asking for or receiving feedback (remember the Johari Window), practitioners learn about themselves and transform their perspectives on self and other.

Reflective practice is not just about revealing aspects of the self, however. Knowledge, theory, and refined skill development is also a focus. The other domains of practice are developed by systematically considering new theory or knowledge and focusing on how it guides or justifies the actions that you take with young people and families. "Systematic practice is about having a plan, albeit one that can be revisited and revised, rather than fumbling about in the dark, hoping that things will work out if we try long and hard enough. But that plan needs to be workable or else it will not provide the structure needed to prevent 'drift'" (Thompson, 2007, p. 81).

Strategies and exercises for reflective practice are found throughout this book. You have already learned about the concepts of reflective practice in Chapter 3, experienced a number of exercises for implementing them, and you will continue to be asked to implement reflective practice throughout the remaining chapters. It will become a seemingly natural part of your self and the development of your knowledge and skill base for professional practice. An essential component of reflective practice, which ensures that change occurs at times when change is difficult, is goal-setting. Setting a goal targets a specific act or a way of thinking for change. Goals should be measurable and attainable and accompanied by strategies that identify how you will achieve your goals. They should focus on what you will do, know, or believe when you have accomplished the change. Strategies are the steps for activities that will help you to accomplish the goal. Evaluating the goal and the strategies is important. A component of reflective practice is checking in to see if you are progressing toward change. Goal-setting is something that we expect of young people that we work with as well as ourselves.

BOUNDARIES

> Boundaries are the interface of intimate communication between people within a particular context. . . . Boundaries are not yours or mine: they are the set of points between you and me where we are both accountable and responsible for communicating and shaping the distinction between us so that we maintain our unique identities and shape a relationship that is specific to us. (Stuart, 2008, pp. 135, 167)

The concept of boundaries is often defined by discussing the consequences of the absence of boundaries. That is, professional literature talks about boundary violations, the damage created when professional boundaries are crossed or when an ethical violation occurs. Boundary violations do not always lead to ethical violations and boundaries and ethics are different. Indeed, boundaries are something that we establish in the context of all our relationships. Fewster (2005) describes boundaries as a "felt energy," which is the edge of your personal energy field as it bumps against the edge of the energy field of another person. Indeed, he says that without boundaries there is no "Self." You have to recognize where you end and the other person begins in order to remain as separate and unique individuals.

Establishing clear personal and professional boundaries helps the practitioner to deliver safe and effective services for young people and families. However, boundaries are fluid in child and youth care practice. They change with the requirements of the relationships that workers have. Practitioners must be open to acting on feedback from those outside the relationship and place authentic relationships at the forefront of their interactions. Not only do they work to identify, develop, and maintain unique and clear boundaries with each client, they are also responsible for helping young people develop and maintain their own boundaries. Since the work of child and youth care is milieu-based, boundaries are not defined in the same manner as other professions, and yet the edges of the boundaries must be very clear for the practitioner within the relationships that they have with young people.

PRACTICE EXAMPLE

Lydia, a youth corrections officer, worked in an open custody program just after graduation with her child and youth care diploma. The youth were 15 to 18 years in age and at age 21, there was often very little age difference between them. She was constantly setting limits for them about swearing in public, horseplay, racist language, and sexual comments toward young women on the street. Unlike what she had been taught to expect in school, though, the youth seemed to have boundaries that stopped them from making sexual comments or flirting with her. She struggled with her own boundaries, though, when one of the young men disclosed that he had been raped in the youth jail and was afraid that his attacker would be placed in the home he was in. She was uncertain how much of her shock and anger to share with him, since "being emotionally involved" was a boundary she tried not to cross. She just wanted to pick him up and cuddle him to make the pain go away. She was also worried that he was unable to set boundaries for himself with other youth and might be victimized again.

Any discussion of boundaries must also include a discussion of limits and of ethics. A fulsome discussion of professional ethics will occur in the next chapter, and the idea of personal ethics was introduced previously. Ethics are the rules that we all hold for "correct" or "right" (morally correct) behaviour. Our personal ethics (based on our values and beliefs, our worldview) influence how we set our boundaries in any given relationship. They also influence what we believe are the limits of other people's behaviour and therefore how we set limits for others.

Limits are the implicit and explicit statements that we make about "appropriate" behaviour as it affects us and those around us. Limits are particularly important in child and youth care because we have a professional responsibility to help young people understand how to govern their behaviours and set their own personal boundaries in relationships with others. Limits are defined, or set, to communicate when you experience the other person's behaviour as unacceptable. Boundaries, on the other hand, involve a judgement call to determine what behaviour is acceptable for you in the context of a particular relationship and a particular environment. Boundaries in practice should be co-created because a core characteristic of practice includes engagement and empowerment as a foundation for practice. To a certain extent, then, limits and boundaries are negotiated between the people involved.

In most professions, personal and professional boundaries are defined separately; however, this division does not work as well for practitioners who work in the milieu (Stuart, 2008). Since practitioners are entering the life-space of young people and families, personal boundaries must also be considered within the milieu. The potential for confusion about boundaries is high and a boundary violation may easily occur without malice or intent, thus leaving the young person further confused and feeling violated. There are several areas where practitioners need to give careful consideration to their boundaries and to communicate or explicitly negotiate boundaries with the young people that they work with (Stuart, 2008). These areas include:

1. **Caring** is a core characteristic of practice and therefore feeling emotional and being "emotionally involved" is part of the work that you will undertake. As a practitioner you must decide when and how to express love and caring to young people (Skott-Myhre & Skott-Myhre, 2007) and help them to shape and understand the boundaries of their caring for you. You must explore different types of love and how those types of love are related to power differentials and to mutuality.

2. **Being personal** requires that you consider your comfort level with self-disclosure. You'll need to reflect on those aspects of self and determine what you want to share. There are many ways to be personal, including identifying and talking about your basic feelings and reactions, your personal history, current issues or concerns, and stories about others. Being personal is important to the young people you work with, they want to know about you, and so considering your boundaries around self-disclosure as well as the youth's boundaries and needs is a must.

3. **Interpersonal separation** is sometimes advocated as the "professional approach"; however, practice exists in a relational space and therefore complete separation is impossible. Practitioners must consider and negotiate in each and every relationship with a young person or family how separate they are. Satisfying interpersonal relationships are part of the personal rewards that motivate you to do this work. How do you understand yourself in relation to the young person or family? How do they understand themselves in relation to you? Are there merged areas?

4. **Touch** is a boundary area that must be addressed in the work that you do with young people. Limits around touch are frequently set for practitioners through the policies of the organization in which they work. The rationale for these limits often relates to the increased incidence of a history of abuse and is motivated by a desire to protect both children and practitioners. Still, young people need to be touched. Horseplay, hugging, or simply reaching out and touching are all part of necessary human contact and part of the developmental needs that children and youth have. It is easier to make a rule about touching (of various forms and types) than it is to talk about what is appropriate and how that might vary according to the individual you are working with, however, it is essential that practitioners determine their own level of comfort and then address the individuality of each young person in this area, shaping boundaries that are unique to each relationship.

5. **Social networking technology** has changed the nature of boundary-setting, information-sharing, and communication. Social networking sites were developed as a way to stay in touch over long distances and to share information in a semi-private space with friends, relatives, and perhaps even coworkers. However, they are actually semi-public spaces where practitioners need to give some consideration to how boundaries will define their information-sharing. Decisions about who to be "friends" with and how to determine the privacy settings are all part of the new requirements when technology becomes part of our relational spaces.

Boundary work needs to be integrated with the nature of the interventions that practitioners use.[1] Children who have been abandoned may interpret limit-setting interventions such as time-outs as further abandonment. Young people who are extremely needy may be rejected by practitioners who feel inundated by such demands, or alternatively, practitioners who enjoy being needed may cross boundaries and take on too much responsibility with needy clients (Fewster, 2005). Boundary-setting requires an awareness of your own relational history, particularly around issues of caring, self-disclosure, interpersonal separation, and touch, as well as the ability to take responsibility for yourself but not for the other person's aspects of self. Boundaries look different in the various milieus in which practitioners work, so consideration of context and boundaries is essential. Organizational systems and cultural background of yourself and the

---

[1] For some detailed examples of how boundary considerations are integrated with intervention and some additional information on energetic boundary work, see Fewster (2005).

young people and families you work with will play a role in setting boundaries. Understanding of these aspects will develop as your practice matures.

> . . . no boundaries, no Self–no Self, no relationships. Or as Andy Turner, one of my more positively focused colleagues, puts it: "know boundaries, know Self–know Self, know relationships." (Fewster, 2005, p. 13)

USE OF THE SELF IN INTERVENTIONS

> Entering into this flow of experiencing as it is occurring, and helping the child to live differently. . . . This joint experiencing between child and worker, and the facilitation of the opportunity for change within this joint experiencing, is the major difference between our work and other intervention efforts that rely upon interpretative insight, alteration of value orientation, behaviour modification, education, and so on. (Garfat, 2002, n.p.)

The practitioner examines the influence of self on others, cultivating and developing checks and balances to ensure that interactions are consistent and constructive. Practitioners take into consideration their individual values, beliefs, and opinions, and the effects that these have on their actions with young people, families, and coworkers. However, the use of self goes beyond the checks and balances that are expressed in boundary-setting and the reflective practice necessary to examine the effects we have on others. Practitioners take themselves into their interventions in a unique manner, which is variously described as "being at the heart of change" (Lundy, 2008); the "flow of immediacy" (Guttman, 1991); "presencing" (Ricks, 2003); a "journey into self" (Fewster, 1990a); "self in action" (Krueger et al, 1999); or "co-created, connected experience" (Garfat, 2008).

The idea of being present (presencing) means that the practitioner is observing self and other; being aware of the thoughts and feelings unfolding in their own conscience and identifying thoughts and feelings as they arise in the interaction within the child (Ricks, 2003). This use of self is **interactive** (not historical as in stories about the self); **immediate** (thoughts and feelings are conscious and one may choose to share them); and **child-centred** (decisions about communication are made on the basis of the child's needs). Presencing requires a high degree of skill in **reflection-in-action** (Thompson & Thompson, 2008) or **self-consciousness**. "When using self-consciousness, I make the observations and make meaning of my observations. To do this, I must be able to observe, know that I am observing, know what I am observing, and know that I am reflecting on and making meaning of what I am observing. This is a complex process and one that becomes more complex in the larger contexts of work, school, and community: in other words when I am engaged in relatedness" (Ricks, 2003, p. 72).

One of the unique aspects of the relational child and youth care perspective is the knowledge and awareness of **self in the moment of relational interaction**. The concept developed initially from self psychology with the idea that self-awareness was fundamental to the development of a relationship with another (Ricks, 1989). It has evolved and been expressed as becoming fully present (Fewster, 1990b); keeping things clear (Fewster, 1990b); and self-awareness and separation from self (Garfat, 1998). Ricks describes it as "consciously interacting with myself within my interactions with others. In turn, this results in greater understanding of the subsequent interactions that we create" (2003, p. 71).

When one becomes really skilled at this, it becomes integrated as a way of being with others. You can't turn it off. In each and every relationship, personal and professional, you are in a heightened state of awareness of your values, thoughts, feelings, and sensations, and have an understanding of those in the context of your history and the history of the other person. Fewster, (1990b) describes this as being fully present and attentive, in tune with the sensations and feelings experienced at the moment. It requires taking a moment to transition by acknowledging thoughts and feelings and letting them go. It also requires the ability to let go of hidden "baggage," thoughts and emotions that might influence our interactions with the other. Guttman (1991) focuses on the immediacy of the experience whereby the practitioner is simultaneously immersed in a situation or series of events and must select a specific event out of the stream of events to respond to. Ricks describes presencing as an "immediate engagement within the context in which I both observe and co-create while having awareness of what is unfolding within my conscience, within my self-consciousness and within the interaction" (2003, p. 73). It is the interactive and immediate nature of the concept that is unique to child and youth care practice.

Garfat and Charles (2010) introduce us to the idea of "meaning-making." Meaning-making requires that you accept that there is no such thing as an objective reality and that everything that we see, hear, and feel is subjectively interpreted through our experience. We all have a perceptual frame, which is an integral part of our self. This perceptual frame is our predisposition to structuring our experience in the world and it significantly influences our practice interventions. Meaning-making is influenced by personal history, previous caring experiences, peers, culture, and family. In short, meaning-making is influenced by the aspects of self, as previously described.

SELF-CARE

> It is common knowledge that the quality of care and training of children is directly related to the sense of well-being experienced by their care-givers. . . . In fact, a decisive factor in group care work is whether there is or is not "ample care for the caring." (Maier, 2006, p. 92)

Practitioners must value self-care as an essential component of healthy practice. Self-care strategies need to be integrated into daily practice because a practitioner's health and well-being is essential to providing good quality care to young people. Thus practice requires continuous reassessment of personal well-being. Self-care is essential for doing any job well; simply to take care of ourselves and stay healthy is important. However, in child and youth care the work is often with young people who have experienced significant trauma and/or behave in ways that are not socially acceptable. The work creates stress when practitioners experience vicarious trauma through the experience of abusive behaviour directed toward the adults and caregivers working with hurt and traumatized young people and families. To help understand the mechanism by which helping places practitioners at risk, this section briefly outlines some information and theory about vicarious trauma, stress, and burnout and describes some strategies for self-care.

Stress is both "good" and "bad" and the determination of which one, lies with the person who is experiencing the stress. When a particular event, situation, environmental condition, or developmental phase in our lives creates "stress," it is due to our unique perception and feelings associated with the event. Stress can also be related to a sequence of "daily hassles," none of which individually are stressful, but in totality they may be overwhelming. Stress represents an imbalance between a person's capacity to respond to environmental demands and the actual demands and is actually a physiological response, whether it occurs through daily hassles or a sudden traumatic event. During a stress response energy levels are increased (to manage the event) as adrenalin is produced and at the same time the body readies itself for fight or flight by increasing the heart rate, tightening muscles, and decreasing blood flow to areas of the body that are not absolutely essential for responding (such as digestion). If the event is not managed or resolved, then the energy and the resources of the body are consumed and the person become anxious, tired, and sick because the energy stores are reduced. In addition, certain organs are targeted for less energy and others receive an abundance of energy. Finally, if stress continues, then the body can no longer produce enough energy to maintain simple daily activity and the person become chronically stressed. The organs in the body are more susceptible to disease or difficulty under chronic stress.

PERSONAL REFLECTION

I know that as stress increases for me I drink more coffee and eat less. I also know that if the stressor is sudden and situational (a family member in the hospital) that I suddenly get cold, my metabolic rate shoots up, and I use up significantly more calories. All of this contributes to almost instant weight loss and a pit in the bottom of my stomach (which is really the coffee) that makes it uncomfortable to eat. I get very focused and need to "do things" both as a distraction and to try and resolve the situation. Over time and with reflection I've learned to stop drinking coffee and pay attention to eating healthy, regular meals.

Carol Stuart

Alternatively, when events exceed a person's ability to cope with them, he or she may enter a crisis state. Crisis states require immediate intervention in order to reduce the level of stress and assist the person to cope. Child and youth care practitioners are often required to intervene during crisis states; however, without good self-care they may find themselves in a crisis state, seeking intervention for their own mental health as a result of compassion fatigue, vicarious trauma, or burnout.

The four domains that may lead to a crisis state are:

• **Developmental events** in life such as graduating from school or adding a new family member can create stress. While developmental events are routine in the flow of life, they can create stress and potential crisis when they are surprising or accompanied by unusual circumstances. Returning to school and having a child are two routine developmental events that should not cause undo stress, but if they occur together and one is unexpected the perception of the person involved may cause a significant amount of stress that exceeds their capacity to deal with either event;

• **Situational stress** results from sudden and traumatic events that are often catastrophic. A car accident, sudden unemployment, or physical assault are examples of situational events that create stress and may lead to crisis.

- Transformative events, whether sudden or gradual, can create inner conflict and anxiety that may result in **existential crisis** and **stress**. In a profession that requires constant self-reflection and awareness of self in relationship with "other," there is great potential for inner conflict and existential crisis as new insights into self occur.

- Finally, **environmental** conditions such as disasters that lead to extreme trauma or repeated exposure to potential dangers that are a risk to physical or emotional self also create stress. Life in a war zone, caring for angry and physically acting-out teens, youth work involving outreach to gang members, and community violence prevention are all examples of environmental conditions that have the potential to exceed your ability to cope, leading to stress and possible crisis (James & Gilliland, 2013).

Vicarious trauma is a secondary stress disorder that occurs when practitioners have prolonged and repeated exposure to traumatized young people and families who are in crisis. Sometimes called **compassion fatigue**, the continuous work of processing the loss, grief, and anger of others who have been traumatized leads to the practitioner absorbing the life events and feelings of those they are working with and experiencing their inner world vicariously (James & Gilliland, 2013). Recent research indicates that child and youth care practitioners work with traumatized young people (98% reported doing so) and that they show evidence of secondary traumatic stress symptoms (66%) indicative of vicarious trauma (Bloom, 2009). Practitioners are vulnerable to vicarious traumatisation because they empathetically connect to their clients' feelings and because vicarious experience can also include feelings of pride and accomplishment as well as grief and pain, the reward felt for helping and the sense of pride and accomplishment in the successes of others also puts them at risk. Vicarious trauma accompanied by on-the-job stress can lead to burnout.

Burnout is one of the reasons that self-care is essential to good practice. Burnout is a state of physical, mental, and emotional exhaustion that results when ongoing stress consumes the resources that are present for coping with events in life. Research on burnout has conceptualized it as consisting of three factors; emotional exhaustion, depersonalization, and reduced personal accomplishment (Savicki, 2002). It results from long-term involvement with emotionally demanding situations and includes symptoms such as physical exhaustion, feeling helpless and hopeless, being disillusioned, and carrying a negative attitude toward work and life in general (James & Gilliland, 2013). It develops slowly over a long period of time and therefore prevention is critical because recovery is difficult. Burnout is developmental and involves the socialization process of entering the field of practice as well as chronic stressors that preclude opportunities for reflection and consolidation of learning. Research on burnout among child and youth care practitioners (Savicki, 2002) pointed to the uniqueness of the milieu-based environment. High levels of continuous contact with clients in their daily living space combined with high levels of independence in moment-to-moment decision making and high levels of constraint by organizational regulations and procedures proved to be a dangerous combination, unless the team environment offered high levels of coworker support, which could be preventative.

Additional important considerations in burnout are the conditions within the organization, which may not match the practitioners' needs for autonomy, reward, community connection, or support of their worldview. In addition to organizational variables the dimensions of culture related to work values such as equality versus power status, flexibility versus predictability, individualism versus collectivism, and balanced lifestyle versus career achievement were important dimensions of burnout.

In a study of burnout among child and youth care practitioners in 13 cultures, Savicki (2002) concluded that cultural variations affected burnout.

> Career success may make work so important to child and youth care workers that the difficulties they face on the job take on immense proportions. Without balance or other facets of life to counteract work-related stress, it may be that workers in high career success cultures feel trapped by their jobs without a venue for discharge of accumulated work stressors. Low power distance cultures offer an opportunity for workers to have more influence and control at work; thus they may feel a greater sense of accomplishment because they are more directly responsible for their actions. (p. 89)

Savicki further noted that burnout among child and youth care practitioners was lower when the work environment was characterized by high peer cohesion, high supervisor support, a task-focused orientation, autonomy, innovation, and coping styles that emphasized dealing directly with the course of stress. There was also less work pressure and less coping through escape. Prevention and remediation of burnout is both an individual and an organizational responsibility and burnout is mediated by cultural considerations related to the work environment.

Deciding how to take care of yourself as a practitioner is a very individual decision because each person's stress is individually triggered, and different strategies will be required. Self-care is essential to prevent vicarious trauma and burnout and to provide better care and counselling to the young people and families with which we work. There are a variety of strategies for self-care that include incorporating regular physical exercise, quiet time, time with friends, and hobbies and recreational pursuits that practitioners can explore. However, there is another essential aspect of self-care that involves ensuring time and space for reflective practice, as well as knowledge about the need for self-care outlined above.

Reflective space can be considered in three different contexts:

1. **Personal reflective space** involves maximizing the potential for time and attention to your own critical reflection before, during, and after practice-based interaction.
2. **Dyadic reflective space** can be effectively found in supervision, mentoring, and coaching scenarios with coworkers.
3. **Group learning/reflective space** encourages you to consider how courses, team meetings, conferences, and projects can be used to energize and transform practice through self-reflection (Thompson & Thompson, 2008). It is also something that must be organizationally supported.

Personal Reflective Space

In order to enhance your ability to make personal reflective space a part of your day-to-day responsibilities, you will need to attend to several different aspects of your practice. Doing so will enable you to develop a deeply self-reflective practice as well as ensure self-care. In *The Critically Reflective Practitioner* (Thompson & Thompson, 2008) there are five important components to making personal reflective space a part of your day, which are illustrated using the following questions.

1. **How am I managing my work pressures and when was the last time I said no to a task?** Being able to manage work pressures ensures that we have time for reflection. Helpers have trouble saying no because it implies that they are not helpful, but among other skills this is an essential skill to managing the pressures of work.

2. **How am I influencing this situation, and what role do I have in shaping this relationship or interaction? What impact is it having on me?** These simple questions will enhance your ability to identify the areas that are important aspects of self and therefore increase your self-awareness.

3. **What imaginative and creative solutions or ideas can I bring to this situation?** Answering this question encourages us to be critical free thinkers, an essential component of reflective practice.

4. **How does this fit into the bigger picture?** It is easy to get caught up in minutia of the day-to-day and forget about how the work fits into the broader world and may, or may not, be consistent with our vision for how the world should be.

5. **What is my focus here?** Instead of just going with the flow, it's important to have a sense of the goals in the work that we do. This will help the young people and families that we work with to achieve their goals.

Making space to engage in reflective practice can be difficult, especially when you consider the different types of reflection ("in," "on," "for" practice) and the many aspects of self-inquiry that can be part of that reflection. Addressing the questions above will ensure that you build in some time and space (mind space, emotional space, or physical space) to consider additional reflection. They will also help you to identify early signs of burnout in yourself because if you can't focus or you don't care about the bigger picture and everything you do has become "rote" rather than fun and creative, those early signals of burnout will be evident as you take some personal reflective space.

Dyadic Reflective Space

You will consider the role of supervisors and mentors in your professional practice in the next chapter. They are one of your most important dyadic resources for reflective space. Very often practitioners need someone else to help with reflection. Coworkers, mentors, and supervisors act as mirrors or echo what practitioners do to help them "see" and "hear" differently. The **Johari Window** described in Chapter 4 includes the concept of relational space and illustrates how receiving feedback can help you understand your blind spots. Supervisors can identify when an enhanced self-care program might be critical, either because of signs of vicarious trauma or burnout or because experience tells them that your working conditions are likely to create an increased level of stress. They can ask you the questions in the foregoing section to help you seek that personal reflective space and can create that space with you.

Group Reflective Space

Opportunities for learning and reflecting on the work you do, while learning something new, provide a fresh perspective on day-to-day problems. These opportunities are important aspects of self-care that must be balanced with the pressures of work. Learning can take place in conferences, workshops, training seminars, and/or additional postsecondary education courses but it can also be part of committee work, special projects, and team meetings in the workplace. Supportive organizations provide these opportunities for their staff. It is helpful to think of these opportunities in terms of what they target (knowledge, skills, core value development) and to consider how to best make use of the opportunity. Some knowledge of your personal learning style will also help so that you don't get caught in a session that is frustrating and does not match your own unique method of learning. It's also important to include a reflection-for-practice component that helps you transfer your learning back to the work you do with young people and families. Then, not only will you return to the work refreshed, having taken care of yourself, but your clients will benefit from your learning.

SUMMARY

The domain of self surrounds all the other aspects of the work that you do. This chapter has helped you understand two different models for describing your self, one that focused on your identity(s) and the other that explained further the aspects of self that you bring to your work with young people. Further exploration of the knowledge and skills of reflective practice was introduced and will be added to throughout the rest of the book. You were introduced to the subdomains of boundaries, use of self in intervention, and self-care. Stress, vicarious trauma, and burnout are occupational hazards in the work of child and youth care practice and taking care of the most important tool that you have in your work, the self, through creating reflective spaces is essential to an extended career in the field.

The next chapter considers how the domain of professionalism builds upon the domain of the self. With self as a foundation the practitioner can begin to understand the professional culture of the field, its core issues, and develop competence in additional skills and knowledge that will be widely applicable to work with young people and families.

Photo by Laine Robertson

CHAPTER EXERCISES

SELF-INQUIRY

Experience: A Metaphor for Self

Pause for a moment and consider who you are. Your *Self*. Consider your Self as a whole. Find a metaphor for the whole. Perhaps you are a "cake," a "car," a delicious "vegetable curry," or a large "deciduous forest." The metaphor doesn't matter, except that it should be meaningful to you, and we will examine it a little more closely. Your "whole" works well together most times. Occasionally you may need to go in for repair, or an ingredient is missing, a part of you is sore and aches.

Metaphorically there are many ingredients or "parts." Identify the parts of your "self." What are these? Describe the parts in detail.

Reflection-for-Practice

Consider how you would describe these aspects of self without the metaphor. How many aspects of self are there? Which parts of the self are visible to whom? Which parts will be visible to youth? To coworkers? Who or what had a significant role in shaping parts of your Self?

THOUGHT, FEELING, ACTION (HEAD, HEART, HABIT)

Experience: Unexplained Habits

Consider for a moment something that you do on a regular basis that is associated with an uncomfortable feeling. Perhaps you are embarrassed or feel frustrated with yourself. That action is likely also associated with some self-deprecating thoughts such as "I'm such an idiot!" or "Why did I do that again!" Describe what you are doing, the associated feelings, and the thoughts that run through your head as you do this. Record these on the left side of the box below.

Reflection-in-Practice

Consider the definitions of beliefs, values, and ethics described in the centre of the box and create statements that identify your general beliefs, values, and ethics associated with this action and the uncomfortable feeling. Record these statements on the right side of the box.

Aspects of Self

ACTIONS, FEELINGS, THOUGHTS	WORLDVIEW	RELEVANT VALUES, BELIEFS, AND ETHICS
	Values: The positive or negative evaluations of importance that you attach to someone or something based on your experience.	
	Beliefs: Statements you believe are true about your experience of reality.	
	Ethics: A "rule" for behavior that is connected to your values and beliefs and defines the "right" behavior in this circumstance.	

Reflection-on-Practice

Reflect on what you have recorded. Are there inconsistencies or conflicts in your worldview? Does something that you value contradict a belief that you hold? Does this explain your emotions and your confusion?

NOTICING AND DEVELOPING THE CYCLE OF REFLECTIVE PRACTICE

Reflection-in-Practice

Noticing requires that you pay attention to key aspects of a situation. Before we get to the situation, consider the following questions, which you will ask yourself as you move through the experience.

Where am I? How is this environment influencing my actions, thoughts, and feelings?

What values and beliefs are important in this place? How are they different from my values and beliefs?

What stereotypes are present here? How do those limit me or the person I am with?

What assumptions have I made about this situation?

Experience

Of course, you'll need to be involved in a "situation" and there are no guarantees that it will be transformative. A simple situation is meeting a new person. Find someone that you don't know and begin a conversation. Get to know them, and tell them a little about yourself. As you converse try to attend to the questions above and simply "notice." You can write the answers down later if you want.

Reflection-on-Practice

Following the conversation, reflect on what you learned. What did you learn? Share your learning with another person. (Note: Repeat the noticing exercise for additional learning.)

Alternatively, you might use a situation such as beginning a new job, attending a political rally, starting an exercise program, etc.

SELF-IN-ACTION (REFLECTIVE PRACTICE)

Reflection-on-Practice

> Every day the teenage boys, who had become experts (on conscious and unconscious levels) at spotting faces and liars, taught me something about how to "walk the talk" and "be real." They seemed to have antennae that let them know a behavior was out of synch with a feeling, or words were incongruent with actions, and they would tell us with their words and/or confronting or evasive behavior. (Krueger, 2007b, p. 17)

Recall a time when you were "called out" or confronted for not being genuine or honest. Using first person and the aspects of self framework, write the story of what happened.

GOAL-SETTING (REFLECTIVE PRACTICE)

Reflection-for-Practice

Review what you have learned so far about child and youth care practice. Pick one piece of theory or a skill that stands out for you as particularly important. Learning needs to be taken to practice systematically, it doesn't just happen naturally. After identifying what you have learned, make a plan for implementing that learning by answering the following questions:

- What are you trying to achieve? What is your goal?
- How are you going to accomplish that achievement? List the steps to getting there and identify any potential barriers.
- How will you know when you have achieved it? What is your evidence? Can you show someone else that evidence?

ARE PROFESSIONAL BOUNDARIES BLACK AND WHITE?

Experience

Consider the following scenario: You are a practitioner in a community drop-in centre for youth. Many of the children and youth who attend have difficult family situations including violent parents. Some have been involved with child protection services and you are quite familiar with the process by which older children are returned to their families, depending on the nature of the family violence and who it is directed at. Livia, a 16-year-old girl, arrives at the centre this afternoon. You have not seen her for a year or so. She was in a foster home because spousal abuse was redirected at her when she tried to protect her mother. She has dropped by today to let you know that she is back at home and she would like to get involved in volunteering at the centre. You help her with a volunteer application form and, in the conversation, she indicates that she is setting up a series of "safe havens" for herself in case her parents become violent again. She asks if you could be one.

Reflection-for-Practice

How do you respond? What does your own family and cultural background tell you to do? What are the boundary considerations? What would you do if you received a request to be her "friend" from your social networking site before she reappeared at the recreation centre? What about afterward?

MEANING-MAKING (SELF IN INTERVENTION)

Reflection-on-Action

Pause for a moment in your reading (after you finish reading this box.) Go and find a friend, family member, colleague, or roommate and ask them to join you in a short exercise.

Together go to the kitchen and open the fridge. Check out what's inside. If you are hungry, get something to eat.

Take a few minutes to talk with your companion and answer the following questions. You of course have already read the questions (unless you go now) and your companion has not. Notice that I have assumed that you are reading this at home. (My belief about where people study.) Notice that as you are opening the fridge and checking it out, you are also paying attention to the questions and deciding what to respond to.

What was the first thing each of you noticed when you opened the fridge? What was your first thought? How did you feel? Who do you associate with food and mealtime in your family? What were the rituals around that? What is your favourite food and was it in the fridge? Why or why not? Do you and your companion eat together in this house? Why or why not?

Make note of the differences in your answers to these questions and consider the things that influence meaning-making and how they explain the differences. Consider the influences of personal history, peers, culture, family, and previous caring experiences about food.

Ask your companion about his or her responses to those questions and note differences.

ARE YOU STRESSED?

Experience: Stress Check

It has become recognized that stress is about how you perceive events, not the number of things that you are exposed to; therefore, "stress tests" like this one assess behavioural indicators.

Find your stress level right now by completing this test (*www.cmha.ca/BINS/content_page. asp?cid=4–42–216*).

DO YOU FREQUENTLY:	YES	NO
Neglect your diet?		
Try to do everything yourself?		
Blow up easily?		
Seek unrealistic goals?		
Fail to see the humour in situations others find funny?		
Act rude?		
Make a "big deal" of everything?		
Look to other people to make things happen?		
Have difficulty making decisions?		
Complain you are disorganized?		
Avoid people whose ideas are different from your own?		
Keep everything inside?		
Neglect exercise?		
Have few supportive relationships?		
Use sleeping pills and tranquilizers without a doctor's approval?		
Get too little rest?		
Get angry when you are kept waiting?		
Ignore stress symptoms?		
Put things off until later?		
Think there is only one right way to do something?		
Fail to build relaxation time into your day?		
Gossip?		
Race through the day?		
Spend a lot of time complaining about the past?		
Fail to get a break from noise and crowds?		

"Are You Stressed," from the Canadian Mental Health Association (*www.cmba.ca*). Reprinted with permission.

BURNOUT AND PROFESSIONAL PRACTICE

Experience: Symptom Recognition

It is extremely beneficial to recognize the symptoms of burnout before they happen. Early warning signs are relatively individualistic. The state of burnout is characterized by physical exhaustion, feeling helpless and hopeless, being disillusioned, and carrying a negative attitude toward work and life in general. Consider a time in your life when these feelings were present. Using the framework described by Burns (2012), review the 3 to 6 months leading up to these feelings in your mind's eye. Reflect on the psychological, emotional, social, physical, and spiritual symptoms and early warning signs that you experienced.

Reflection-on-Action: Symptom Description

Complete the following chart.

THE SELF	SYMPTOMS	EARLY WARNING SIGNS
Psychological		
Emotional		
Social		
Physical		
Spiritual		

Reflection-for-Practice: Prevention Strategies

Reflect on your own unique constellation of symptoms and early warning signs. Identify any values, beliefs, or personal ethics that are represented in the symptom descriptions and path to burnout that conflict with the importance of self-care. Consider your goals for preventing burnout and consider the organizational context in which you expect to work.

Using the concept of reflective space—personal, dyadic, and group—identify and prioritize strategies for increasing your reflective space in order to meet your goals for preventing burnout.

Values, beliefs, and personal ethics that conflict with self-care:

Goals for preventing burnout:

Strategies to achieve the goals:

CHAPTER 7

PROFESSIONALISM AND PROFESSIONAL CARING IN THE SOCIAL-POLITICAL CONTEXT

Photo by John Campbell

CHAPTER OBJECTIVES

- To understand how child and youth care professionals bring all aspects of the self and personal identity into the sphere of professionalism.
- To understand the requirements that define what a profession is and how child and youth care has worked to meet the challenges of being a profession.
- To examine how the combination of art and science present in professionalism is used in the service of others.

- To review the code of ethics and its commitment to competence, integrity, altruism, and promoting the public good.
- To describe the role of professional development.
- To describe the skills and knowledge required to make effective use of supervision in the context of a mutual relationship.
- To understand the role that professionalism plays in managing the diversity of young people and families and foster an appreciation of how differences based on gender, race, ethnicity, culture, sexual orientation, and/or disability can affect practice.

Professionalism is the area of influence that includes the practitioner's professional demeanour and professional relationships with young people, families, community members, and other professionals. A profession requires the mastery of a complex and distinct body of knowledge and skills that are applied with artistic intuition within the life-space of young people and families. This combination of art and science is used in the service of others. There is a social contract between a profession and society, whereby society provides the privilege of self-regulation, autonomy in practice, and exclusivity in determining the required knowledge in exchange for the assurance of safe and competent service. This means that professions are accountable to the people that they serve and to greater society (Cruess & Cruess, 2008). The development of the "profession" of child and youth care began post–World War II as described in Chapter 2, and practitioners who emerged from the initial educative communities focused on equality of participation and social justice as core values. These values tended to be in opposition to professional values related to autonomy and exclusivity. Political beliefs about how to provide for those less fortunate have also influenced the efforts of the field to professionalize over time.

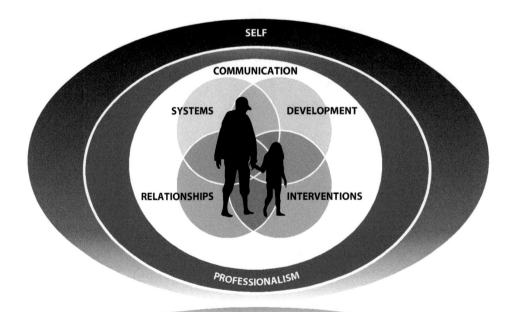

Figure 7.1 The Domain of Professionalism

Many debates in the field have focused on whether child and youth care is a craft or a profession (Dunlop, 2004; Eisikovits & Beker, 1983; Maier, 1983; Stuart, 2001; Thomas, 2004).

> Professional Child and Youth Care is committed to promoting the well-being of children, youth, and families in a context of respect and collaboration. (Mattingly, 1995b, p. 372)

This quote helps us to understand the struggle of child and youth care with the requirements for being a profession. Collaboration, which is part of practice, seems to go against the recognition that a profession would receive for its authority and expertise. Authority and expertise provide a profession with the exclusive rights to the knowledge of that profession. Debates about professionalism have typically focused on the functional view of professionalism. Under this view, the requirements of a profession include:

- Formal education
- Organized/distinct body of knowledge
- Clientele and colleagues that recognize authority
- Professional culture or association
- Autonomy and self-regulation (Berube, 1984; Kelly, 1990)
- Service to people
- Code of ethics

The next section considers some of the issues raised by the functional view of professionalism as faced by the profession in North America. Additional research is suggested to understand the nature of these issues and to track the progress of the field as it professionalizes.

Professional Education

Professional education in child and youth care is quite recent. As outlined in Chapter 2, in Canada, the first postsecondary education programs began because individual agencies providing services for young people (usually residential services) were providing training to their workers to enhance their competence, and they lobbied the government in Alberta, Ontario, and British Columbia to develop educational programs in accredited institutions. In the United States, postsecondary education is embedded as a specialty within departments that provide education, psychology, or leisure studies programs, and most child and youth care practitioners receive their training "on the job." The increasingly available provision of university-level education paves the way for research and the development of new knowledge specific to the field; however, debates continue about the role of experience versus the role of theory in knowledge generation. These debates are layered with more recent critical perspectives or postmodern views of professionalism, which question "the underlying assumptions and beliefs about knowledge, power, and standardized approaches to practice" (Pence & White, 2011, p. xvi).

Research and Knowledge Generation

The requirement that a profession have an organized and distinct body of knowledge implies that theory and "truth" are learned through formal education. One of the core characteristics of child and youth care practice is experiential learning, a characteristic that conflicts with the functional view of professionalism that formal knowledge and formal education are the best mechanisms for learning. In child and youth care practice, the process of change is constant; therefore, defining what constitutes the body of knowledge is related to both abstract truths and to relational moments, and is grounded in personal experience. Formal education in child and youth care goes beyond basic transmission of knowledge and theory, and also requires the practitioner to engage in self-reflection, to examine personal experience and values and to understand their dynamic within practice. Research and knowledge generation in child and youth care is active and often that research is field-based and grounded in relational methodology that matches the value base of the field. Research and theory in child and youth care is explored further in Chapters 9–12.

Being Distinct and Being Recognized

Child and youth care practitioners have repeatedly tried to define what they do (See Appendix A) and to educate other professions about the approach. As members of multidisciplinary teams, practitioners often struggle to be recognized by other professionals, and want to be valued for their expertise in a time when inter-disciplinarity is common and other professionals often cross the boundaries of professional definitions (Salhani & Grant, 2007). Leaders in the field have acknowledged that practitioners need to stop trying to define and defend themselves and simply get on with doing what they do (Charles et al., 2005), but they must at the

Tips and Resources

Definitions of child and youth care

Association of Child and Youth Care Practice (ACYCP): www.acycp.org

Council of Canadian Child and Youth Care Associations (CCCYCA) Scope of Practice: www.cyccanda.ca

same time directly address the power differentials that exist among professions. Practitioners must understand how to both explain what they do and how to advocate, with professionalism, for the young people and families with which they work (Salhani & Grant, 2007). This approach will both help to professionalize the field and will help individual practitioners achieve recognition within the team.

Association Membership

Professional associations for child and youth care exist in most provinces and many states in North America and there are two national coalitions (ACYCP and CCCYCA) that address professional issues. Belonging to a professional association is a basic expectation for most professions, particularly because **autonomy** as a profession often means that professionals are self-employed. Not only does an association represent a group of people with common interests and backgrounds, but often the association also provides practice liability insurance; legal control over who can practice or not; and regular conferences and upgrading of educational qualifications. Membership in child and youth care professional associations is still voluntary. Most people are covered for liability insurance with their employer and the cost of association membership when getting paid so little seems onerous. While union membership often assists with negotiating increased pay, it does not address the need to get together with people from other employing organizations and to lobby for common interests. Associations can operate to further the interests of the field, but they must have a membership base to do so and many child and youth care associations struggle to maintain their membership.

Self-Regulation through Accreditation and Certification

Ensuring that child and youth care practitioners meet an acceptable standard of practice, do not pose a danger to their clients, and provide high-quality care and service requires that practitioners be assessed against an agreed-upon standard of competence.[1] You would not think of going to a hospital that was not "accredited" or of being taken care of by a doctor who was not a registered and certified member of the Canadian or American Medical Association, yet on a daily basis young people are cared for or serviced by people and organizations who are not accredited or certified through a recognized standard. Indeed, physicians have a social contract with the public to provide competent service and are legislated by government (as the representative arm of society) to administer a testing and registration program that assesses new physicians against that standard. Members of the public can call and check a physician's credentials; practicing medicine without a license is illegal. The profession of child and youth care has begun this journey, but has a long way to go (Eckles et al., 2012; Stuart, 2001, in press) and must resolve along the way the debates about what it means to be a profession.

Can You Be Professional without Being Part of a Profession?

The focus and purpose of any professional relationship is the work that the practitioner and the young person are engaged in. This work is based on specialized expertise; it does not begin because of a social or personal relationship. Recall, however, that in child and youth care, interpersonal interactions may appear to be social or personal because the work occurs within the milieu and daily life-space of the young people. Similar to the apparent paradox of what a professional relationship "looks like" in child and youth care, Thomas (2004) concludes that without the professionalization of the field, professionalism of the worker is not possible, and therefore the struggle to professionalize should continue and practitioners should commit to supporting it:

> I would have moved on into the other professions . . . if I had not had the support of other child and youth care professionals, if I had not been presented the opportunities for growth that opened up for me through the profession, or if I had not been able to obtain the education I needed to improve my practice with children, youth and families. That is what the creation of a profession of child and youth care work does, rather than the empty posturing and callow manipulation [observed] in other professions. (p. 274)

Four subdomains of **professionalism** are explored in the rest of this chapter. They more clearly describe the basic competence required to translate the self into professional practice. In the previous chapter, the importance of self-care and how self-care could be achieved by making space for both didactic and group reflection was discussed. These reflection strategies play a

---

[1] Critical postmodern perspectives would disagree with the concept of an agreed-upon standard of competence, since it is based in a set of value judgments and societal beliefs about what is competent. I would agree that a rigidly adhered-to set of standards for competence is insufficient for high-quality care and service because it does not cover every situation and does not address the subtle nuances that are required in relational practice.

different role in the domain of professionalism. Group reflective space is found in training and development opportunities, but these opportunities are also an expectation of professionalism, within the subdomain of **professional development.** Similarly, the subdomain of **supervision** emphasizes the importance of mentors and supervisors for guiding the work practitioners do. The subdomain describes the skills and knowledge required to make effective use of supervision, with the philosophy that supervision is a mutual relationship. Following the guidelines of professional **ethics** and knowing the ethical code of the professional association is a basic expectation, however, ethical codes are not simply "rules" to follow, there is also a systematic decision-making process that helps determine the "right" way to address ethical conflicts. Finally, being a professional demands a certain level of skills and knowledge in managing the **diversity** of young people and families and an appreciation of how differences based on gender, race, ethnicity, culture, sexual orientation, and/or disability can affect the application of skills and knowledge in all of the other domains of practice. The rest of the chapter introduces some key concepts in these areas.

PROFESSIONAL DEVELOPMENT

The practitioner is committed to lifelong learning and professional development, including formal and informal learning opportunities in day-to-day practice and learning through formal education and training. Attending education and training events develops new knowledge and skills in the latest strategies and techniques for helping young people and families to create change in their lives. Professional development also includes self-criticism and reflection on critical comments from others (young persons, parents, partners, colleagues, superiors) in an effort to improve practice. Using the reflective practice model outlined in the **self** domain, practitioners acknowledge mistakes and learn from them, with the goal of improving professional practice. Combining aspects of experiential learning with new knowledge and theory, the practitioner becomes a "knowledgeable doer" who is able to identify and develop **theory-in-practice**. Practitioners seek new knowledge, identify different approaches, and critically analyze both experience and information from facts and theory (Thompson & Thompson, 2008).

As illustrated in **Figure 7.2**, the cycle of experiential learning (Kolb & Kolb, 2005, 2008) is critical to the phases of practitioner development outlined in Chapter 3 and professional development enhances a practitioner's ability to implement theory-into-practice and to recognize their own use of theory-in-practice. By finding space for personal reflection, the practitioner will be able to identify gaps and seek additional knowledge and theory through professional development activities. The group-reflection opportunities in professional development encourage practitioners to plan for implementing and applying new knowledge, and increase the probability that they will successfully incorporate changes into their practice as a result of attending a seminar.

Creating and maintaining a professional development plan that is regularly reviewed and is based on reflection and identification of gaps in knowledge or experience is an important component of professionalism. When practitioners inquire "now what?" of themselves, as in Figure 7.2, it is time for some professional development. There may be a need for additional formal knowledge to process and incorporate into daily work, or perhaps a different type of experience to stretch the active understanding in a different direction. The professional development plan should focus on adding new knowledge or skills to the repertoire or in some cases may create a transformative shift in **aspects of self** through more personal development opportunities. These are both aspects of planning for professional development using the experiential learning cycle.

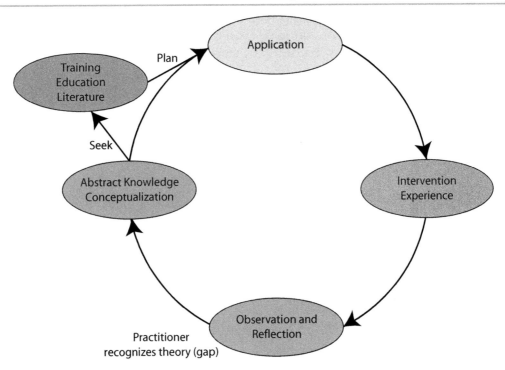

Figure 7.2 Experiential Learning Cycle and Professional Development

---

PERSONAL REFLECTION

Over the last 9 years I have slowly been letting go of my once enforced fundamentalist religious background. Through this letting-go process, all of a sudden one day I realized that I had no idea what I personally held to be true and important, my values and beliefs. I felt completely lost in my personal life as a CYC, I had nothing to base decisions on. Although I was not in therapy at the time, I independently engaged in a sort of reality therapy. I had the room to make my own choices, and I did. In turn I learned all about taking responsibility for the consequences of my decisions, revised my approach, and tried again. This was one of the most liberating and challenging experiences for me as a young woman. As a result of this self-directed reality therapy, I began to rediscover what I truly hold as true and important. I now realize that this will be a lifelong cycle of inquiry for me, and I am beginning to look forward to it instead of dread it.

Lacey Cann (personal communication, March 2009)

Identifying the areas for developing new knowledge and skills is relatively easy when practitioners are new in the job, or when they change from one setting to another because the focus is on the expertise required for a new client group or the particular requirements of the setting. The experiential learning cycle is one tool for identifying the knowledge and skill gaps. Early in a practitioner's career it may also help to identify gaps in the four domains of practice that focus on the day-to-day work that we do with young people and families: **relationships**, **development**, **systems context**, and **interventions**. Experiences in the field, together with the subdomains and the statements about learning outcomes for these domains (Appendix C), can help to identify areas for professional development.

Identifying the new knowledge and skills required when practitioners have been located in a position for some time may be more difficult. Experienced practitioners may need to focus on career development and identify what the next step is in their career to identify professional development opportunities. Learning supervisory skills, project management skills, training and teaching, or public speaking are all generalist skills that can be integrated into practice as the career progresses. Alternatively, practitioners might focus on a different client population or develop skills for working within a different jurisdiction that provides services for young people and families in anticipation of moving to a program in that sector. Learning about critical postmodern perspectives is another option for disrupting practice and defining a different way to *be* and *do* with young people and families.

The nature of learning opportunities in a professional development plan can also be quite varied. Formal education through diploma or degree programs is one option for professional development, but there are also opportunities for conferences, organizational training, specialized internships, committee work, community work, and project development that will add to your knowledge and skills. The nature of a practitioner's learning style and the circumstances of their lifestyle will affect the choices available for professional development. The professional development plan will be ever changing over the practitioner's career.

SUPERVISION

Supervision in child and youth care practice is part of a practitioner's commitment to the provision of high-quality care through facilitating reflective practice. The supervisor, as a senior and more experienced practitioner, has a role to play with younger, novice practitioners; however, both experienced practitioners and novice practitioners have a responsibility to be active in seeking feedback from their supervisors. The child and youth care practitioner uses regular supervision meetings and takes responsibility for initiating reflective conversations and identifying areas that are a struggle. Supervision may occur "in the milieu" just as practice does, or may include formal one-to-one meetings for clinical supervision and/or team supervision. In all cases, the practitioner has a significant responsibility to raise difficult issues and engage in the learning process as part of the **professional** domain of practice.

For novice practitioners, supervision may imply a place where they will be criticized for mistakes. The belief that showing weakness with a supervisor may result in being dismissed could limit the effective use of supervision. Ideally, supervision in child and youth care practice should be a didactic space for reflective practice to incorporate and question social context.

> Supervision is a professional relationship that provides support, education, monitoring of quality, and creates a safe forum to reflect on professional practice. It should encourage constructive confrontation and critical thinking that informs and improves the practice of all parties. Respecting the inherent hierarchy in the relationship, it should accept the responsibility to use power in a thoughtful manner. (Delano & Shah, 2007, p. 7)

An important component of competently using supervision involves identifying and taking responsibility for what is brought to the time spent together, both issues and concerns but also a practitioner's worldview and its influence on how supervision is approached.

Supervision has several important purposes, which practitioners should plan for as they approach supervision sessions. It provides support, education, and a safe forum for exploration of their worldview, and encourages self-monitoring of the practice standard (Delano & Shah, 2007), as well as questioning of the basis for the standard. Many practitioners (and supervisors) only think of supervision in terms of its monitoring or managerial function. It should also focus on the core characteristics of practice, which form a professional worldview, support quality practice, facilitate experiential learning, and mediate between the demands of the organization and the demands of the young people (Sapin, 2009; Thompson, 2007). Providing good care and service to young people and families is a joint responsibility between practitioner, supervisor, and program manager.

Not all programs or services will assign practitioners a supervisor; therefore, it's helpful to broaden the definition of who provides supervision to ensure that a practitioner seeks supervision because supervision is essential to both self-care and the quality of care provided to young people. Supervision can be provided internally, within an organization, or externally, by someone outside the organization. If a supervisor is not assigned to, or the supervisor is "administrative" but not a child and youth care practitioner, practitioners may need to seek out someone else to act as a clinical supervisor/mentor. Table 7.1 describes a two-dimensional framework for thinking about who can provide supervision and the functions or purposes that are appropriate for those supervisors. A single supervisor may provide both functions, or two supervisors can address different supervisory functions. The model that is most appropriate will depend on the service or program, as well as a practitioner's personal preference.

Table 7.1   Supervision Functions, Location, and Hierarchy

SUPERVISOR FUNCTION	ADMINISTRATIVE MANAGEMENT	CLINICAL OR NONMANAGERIAL
LOCATION		
Internal to organization	Practitioner is accountable to a line manager or supervisor with authority for the program. Emphasis is primarily on support and education to do the work as well as monitoring the practice standard through evaluation and/or disciplinary action.	Peer supervision, which could be interdisciplinary or cross-disciplinary. May include group or team supervision. Focus is on a supportive, safe forum for exploring and questioning the professional worldview and debriefing experiential learning. The employer may "expect" this approach and require regular meetings.
External to organization	Practitioner is not directly accountable to the supervisor because the supervisor is contracted by the organization. Emphasis is on education to do the work as well as monitoring the practice standard through program evaluation.	A clinical supervisor or mentor, likely hired by the practitioner for their knowledge and skill in the field, and therefore perceived as an expert. May include group supervision. Focus is on support, safe forum for exploring and questioning the professional worldview, and debriefing experiential learning.

Supervision should be a joint and mutual process (Delano & Shah, 2009; Sapin, 2009; Thompson, 2007). There are many skills and strategies for being a good supervisor, but the practitioner's focus should be on being a good supervisee and preparing for what to expect in supervision as well as how to guide the experience of supervision. Preparation is especially important if the supervisor is not skilled or experienced in the art of supervision, and practitioners may never know until they have entered the relationship what the supervisor's experience is.

In a planned approach to supervision (Sapin, 2009) supervisor and practitioner are both responsible for the following four steps:

1. Preparing for supervision.
2. Establishing the supervision relationship.
3. Examining practice to consider the nature of experiential learning.
4. Moving on.

The steps can be considered from the point of view of both the macro and the micro nature of supervision. Each individual meeting and the overall relationship with the supervisor require this type of planned approach.

When preparing for supervision, practitioners should consider the type of supervision. They require and approach supervision from that perspective. Practitioners who approach supervision from a learning perspective will begin by locating themselves in relation to **aspects of self**. Who am I? What is my worldview? Do I anticipate that personal challenges or professional knowledge will be more important for me? Practitioners who focus primarily on the area of personal challenges may want to engage an external, clinical supervisor or seek an internal colleague from a different discipline without line authority. **Novice** practitioners likely need to develop a good understanding of the standards of practice and to establish their reputation as a good practitioner; therefore, should engage a line supervisor with evaluative responsibility. Practitioners who want to become a certified or registered practitioner will require their supervisor to recommend them to a certification board. Other aspects of finding a supervisor include considerations of identity, including race, gender, disability, religion, sexual orientation (see the section "Diversity"), and how these identity needs may surface in practice. Broad preparation for supervision helps to select a supervisor and be conscious of the concerns or issues that may arise in the relationship. Similar preparation should occur around each supervisory meeting.

A professionally packaged approach (Delano & Shah, 2007, 2009) to supervision implies that the supervisor focuses on support and education. When a supervisor discusses the quality of practice, the focus is on a professional standard. Supervisors focus on the expectations of a professional in their work with young people. However, "Philosophically, child and youth work as a profession is committed to strength-based, competency-based approaches that promote resilience and personal growth, all in the context of a developmental perspective. Therefore, the process of performance management should always have at its core a dialogue about strengths and competence rather than deficits and problems" (Gharabaghi, 2008, pp. 338–339).

Establishing the supervision relationship involves discussing the above areas as well as discussing practical arrangements such as meeting times and location; period of time; formal or informal evaluation of the supervisee and/or the effectiveness of the group relationship; determining the agenda or focus to the session(s); discussing record-keeping; and discussing ethics related to the supervisory relationship (such as confidentiality and reporting to authorities).

Examining practice is of course central to supervision. This examination can focus on four different areas, presented here from the point of view of the practitioner:

1. Monitoring the practice standard by discussing the requirements for certification or registration or engaging in an examination of ethical practice and its meaning (Greenwald, 2008).

2. Professional development through education and training by examining knowledge and skills gaps that can be remediated through additional training or through a focused discussion of theory, drawing on the supervisor's expertise and experience.

3. Supportive care for practitioners through engaging in reflective practice techniques with the supervisor who will challenge aspects of the self that are hidden to the practitioner.

4. Mediating between the demands of the young person, the practitioner, and the organization to help the practitioner understand the organizational and societal context to the work that happens with young people and families.

PERSONAL REFLECTION

It was the first time in my life since middle school that I felt really stuck. I had a really hard time understanding how this case report on my client should look, how it should be organized, etc., so I went to see Tatania (the program manager). Well, trust me when I say I did not expect that meeting to turn out the way it did. As Tatania challenged me on my beliefs and ideas about the report and about who I am and what I believe in as a practitioner, I became completely overwhelmed. She told me she was trying to understand and get a sense of who I was as a practitioner, which is something up to that point I had always thought I was able to do quite well. I had always seen my ability to critically self-reflect as one of my strengths. So now not only do I not understand how the agency wants me to complete the report, but I am having trouble articulating my professional identity. What I learned from that conversation is important. I learned two things.

First, I realized that I needed to strengthen my self-confidence when it comes to my skills and abilities as a worker. In addition to that I needed to strengthen my self-confidence about my personal and professional identity, so that regardless of who it is I am talking to, rather than fear disapproval, I should stand by who I am and what I believe.

Second, how critical and hard on myself I can and tend to be. Therefore, my goals as a practitioner are to identify my defeating thoughts/self-doubt and try to reflect on why I am feeling that way. I would also like to explore my need for approval. For me, relationships are so incredibly important but I am always afraid of failing the relationships in my life (friends, etc.). I believe my fear of disapproval is connected to my lacking self-confidence and thus it has become a goal to explore these feelings and learn how to be more self-assured. So that's what resulted out of that one supervision session. These goals will impact me as a practitioner, change my approach, and how I interact with clients and other professionals.

Vanessa Lalonde (personal communication, March 2009)

Practitioners can prepare for the overall relationship and for each session with the supervisor by considering where priorities lie for discussion and what their needs are. They can expect, or request, that the supervisor will listen and reflect on the discussion, help them process their own answers, and challenge them to think about alternative perspectives. At times they may also expect the supervisor to question the standards of practice, theory, and ethics of practice.

The final aspect of planned supervision is planning for after supervision. It is important to identify what was learned and to make a plan for acting on that learning. Consider the description in the Personal Reflection box below of a supervision session from a practitioner with several years of experience in residential care who has been assigned a one-to-one client to follow up in a program that transitions adolescents to independent living.

Preparation for supervision can be thought of from the point of view of the Johari Window, introduced in previous chapters. In the example described by Vanessa, an enormous amount of learning occurs in the supervisory meeting. Her training as a practitioner had prepared her to engage in self-inquiry, but this supervision session was relational inquiry. She followed up the meeting and reflected on her experience in that relationship. She considered her values, beliefs, and ethics and how they had affected her in the meeting. Previous blind spots were revealed to her through the questioning and probing of the supervisor. She had an identified need going into supervision, but the session became much more than a focus on how to write a report because the supervisor picked up on and challenged her lack of confidence.

ETHICS

The child and youth care practitioner follows a code of personal and professional behaviour in the day-to-day performance of his or her work, and uses a systematic ethical decision-making process to determine the "right" decision when faced with an ethical conflict. Professional codes of ethics are governed by a professional association and the sanctions for not following the code of ethics are determined by those associations. This section also considers the formal guidelines for behaviour within the workplace such as policy and procedure, as well as the norms of professional conduct for engaging with young people and families. Ethics are determined by the nature of the system and the culture of the organization. Professional ethics are typically representative of the professional "group" culture because the profession designs, deliberates, and administers the written code. All these facets contribute to the ethics of professional behavior that a practitioner follows.

Ethics have already been described as an important aspect of our **being**, of who we are in the world and in relationship to others. Indeed, ethics cannot be a distinct and separate part of the work that practitioners do because of the relational nature of the work. Practitioners have an ethical identity that is in large part the reason that they entered child and youth care. The passion

---

Tips and Resources

This article offers an interesting discussion of ethics and morals in professional practice:
www.cyc-net.org/cyc-online/cycol-0507-ricks.html

The Code of Ethics for Youth Work in Aotearoa New Zealand

This code has been collaboratively developed and revised twice. It is expected to have a biennial review to maintain its relevance for the social context of practice. It takes a relational, contextual approach to ethics, which is different from the International Code of Ethics in Appendix B.
www.arataiohi.org.nz/Code

and commitment to "caring" and the sense of being "called" to the practice, which are characteristic of practitioners entering the field, are part of the "ethic of care" that underlies the historical development of the field (Petrie, 2006). This ethic of care is the foundation of relationships and helping in the work that practitioners do with young people and families (Aotearoa, 2011; Austin & Halpin, 1989; Greenwald, 2008).

There are other virtues or ethical principles that are part of the ethical identity of practitioners that could be explored, such as wisdom, temperance, humanity, justice, transcendence, and courage (Greenwald, 2008). Courage, for example, includes the courage to act and "do the right thing" according to our conscience. "Conscience is the inner compass for right and wrong and plays a critical role in providing the focus for noticing and understanding relatedness" (Ricks, 2003, p. 71) and for guiding ethical decisions. As a practitioner's ethical identity combines with a professional identity, they develop an ethical code for professional behaviour. Professional identity and ethical identity overlap to create an ethical model that is consistent with and includes professional codes of behaviour and ethics (Greenwald, 2008).

While each practitioner develops a moral compass or ethical identity, all professional associations also have a code of ethics to which their members are required to adhere. Most also have a disciplinary policy that has sanctions for "breaking" the code of ethics. A code of ethics can be designed as a set of rules or standards for behaviour or as a set of principles to follow in making decisions about how to behave. Consider the difference between the following statements:

> "We will develop, implement, and administer the policies and procedures of our respective agencies and institutions" (Ontario Association of Child and Youth Counsellors Code of Ethics, www.oacyc.org/page4.html).

> "Respects the commitments made to the employer/employing organization" (Code of Ethics: Standards for Practice of North American Child and Youth Care Professionals, www.Pitt.Edu/~Mattgly/Cycethics.html) (Mattingly, 1995b, p. 375)

> "BIG PICTURE: The development of young people is impacted by big picture influences such as social and economic contexts and dominant cultural values. This includes legislation, public policy, economic systems, political systems and cultural values." "23.3 Youth workers and their organisations will ensure that appropriate risk management procedures, systems and paperwork are completed for services, programmes, events or activities organised for and with young people." (Code of Ethics for Youth Work in Aotearoa New Zealand; Aotearoa, 2011, p. 38)

The first statement is like a command. If the organization that the practitioner works for has a policy to report to the appropriate authorities all illegal activity, then he or she would be ethically required to phone the police if a child in care stole an item from a store. The second statement illustrates a statement of principle that might guide the decision about whether to report or not, particularly when another statement from the same code of ethics is considered:

> "Recognizes that professional responsibility is to the client and advocates for the client's best interest" (Mattingly, 1995b, p. 374)

The third statement places the actions of the child in a much larger context and requires teasing apart the influences of criminal law, poverty (perhaps hunger was part of the action), and local culture. It also places responsibility jointly on the practitioner and the organization to examine issues related to risk management (what role did the organization have in prevention of the incident).

The preamble to the *Code of Ethics: Standards for Practice of North American Child and Youth Care Professionals* describes the principle-based approach, which represents the collective conscience of the field.

> As Child and Youth Care Professionals we are aware of, and sensitive to, the responsibilities involved in our practice. Each professional has the responsibility to strive for high standards of professional conduct. This includes a commitment to the centrality of ethical concerns for Child and Youth Care practice, concern with one's own professional conduct, encouraging ethical behavior by others, and consulting with others on ethical issues.
>
> This ethical statement is a living document, always a work in progress, which will mature and clarify as our understanding and knowledge grow. The principles represent values deeply rooted in our history, to which there is a common commitment. They are intended to serve as guidelines for conduct and to assist in resolving ethical questions. For some dilemmas, the principles provide specific or significant guidance. In other instances, the Child and Youth Care professional is required to combine the guidance of the principles with sound professional judgment and consultation. In any situation, the course of action chosen is expected to be consistent with the spirit and intent of the principles. (http://www.pitt.edu/~mattgly/CYCethics.html; Mattingly, 1995b, p. 373)

This North American Code of Ethics, as noted in the foregoing preamble to that code, was intended to be a living document; however, professional associations have adopted it and confirmed it, without making changes or considering the historical or current social contexts. It is considered the primary reference for ethical decision making in the certification program of the Child and Youth Care Certification Board (CYCCB), as outlined in Appendix D. White (2011) astutely notes that in the certification program, ethical competence implies "someone who is capable of correctly reading what is at stake, knowing which specific principles from the relevant Code of Ethics apply, and implementing a course of action that conforms to predetermined standards and principles" (p. 37). This is in sharp contrast to the way "ethics permeate every aspect of human caring practices, and what is considered to be good or right in one context might be quite different in another, casting suspicion on individualist, universalist, predetermined approaches to ethics and professional practices (White, 2011, p. 37).

While a code of ethics, particularly one that outlines principles for decision making, can provide guidance to practitioners, there are additional factors to consider. Ethical principles are set in a social and historical context and should not be read without an understanding of that context (Aotearoa, 2011). Earlier chapters have outlined the social and historical contexts to child and youth care practice in North America and the practitioners are encouraged to find avenues to enlarge their perspective on professional ethics and examine "the value-laden quality of CYC" (White, 2011, p. 47) to arrive at a moral position that goes beyond simply applying ethical codes.

Understanding the process of decision making is an element of competence in ethical decision making (Garfat & Ricks, 1995). There are numerous models for ethical decision making offering variations on the decision-making process; however, the model presented here is grounded in child and youth care practice (Garfat & Ricks, 1995), and while it has been criticized for its focus on the self, to the exclusion of the social and historical context (Slade, 2012; White, 2011), the model provides a beginning practitioner with a process for undertaking self and contextual reflection in the process of making a decision. In this model, as illustrated in **Figure 7.3**, self is central to the process of decision making, and decision making is not a linear process but rather

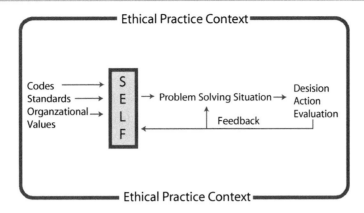

Figure 7.3   Self-Driven Ethical Decision-Making Model

consists of a set of attributes that are possessed by the practitioner and a process to follow for exploring assumptions and decision making.

Reflective practice is central to the model because "in the context of clinical practice, the worker's personal framework, codes of ethics, and standards of practice are confronted, evaluated, and actualized through the self and applied to the situation and the process of problem-solving" (Garfat & Ricks, 1995, p. 395). The practitioner must know the self and be able to identify and articulate their worldview—including values, beliefs, and ethics—and distinguish personal bias from what is the "right thing" under the circumstances.

The ethical practice context includes organizational values and professional standards and codes of ethics. Critical reflection on the values embedded in self, organization, community, and society is essential as is critical reflection on the ethical conflict that is posing the problem to be solved. Practitioners must ask hard questions about beliefs and values and use these questions to examine alternative solutions that might not be obvious at the start. Making a decision and taking action involves personal responsibility and a commitment to overcome barriers that are present to "doing the right thing." Very often practitioners will "know" what is right, but may not act to do the "right thing."

Conscience, as it combines with self-consciousness, plays a role in defining one's ethical identity and makes ethical decisions an evolutionary process. When ethics is thought of as a process there is not one truth, but rather an evolution of truth (Ricks, 2003). This evolution of truth occurs through the evaluation and feedback loop that is a component of decision making, which is part of reflective practice.

DIVERSITY

The child and youth care practitioner respects differences related to cultural and human diversity by attending to differences and similarities in the process of creating change for young people and families. Differences can exist along multiples lines of age, class, race, ethnicity, citizenship, nationality, levels of ability, language, spiritual belief systems, religion, sexuality, educational achievement, and gender (deFinney, 2008; Mattingly et al., 2003), and these differences represent the major factors that set groups apart from one another and give individuals and groups elements of their identity. All these elements of identity and difference are addressed in an integrated manner throughout all other domains of practice.

In addition, the practitioner must recognize that some groups are more vulnerable to oppression and disadvantage and practitioners have an obligation to assist with eliminating these forces. A significant issue in assisting young people and families who belong to oppressed and disadvantaged groups is recognizing diversity, including a continuum of difference, and understanding the implications of a continuum of difference. Skills for assisting young people to overcome oppression are part of the intervention domain, but practitioners must be able to recognize and critically reflect on the implications of differences and the diversity of young people, families, and coworkers. This knowledge and skill builds on the skills of reflective practice to incorporate critical reflection.

Where Do Differences Lie?

> Differences among people exist along the lines of age, class, race, ethnicity, citizenship, and nationality, levels of ability, language, spiritual belief systems, religion, sexuality, educational achievement, and gender.

This is perhaps an obvious statement; you can look around the room and understand that everyone is different. Difference becomes an issue when it is used to classify people and to either limit them based on that classification and/or attempt to understand someone exclusively in terms of that classification. Differences are often understood as an either/or, a singular identity, or something that is vested in the "other."

In reality, we are all unique individuals with multiple identities. Indeed, identity is an evolving concept that can be conceptualized as a borderless map that is influenced by all our previous travels (Little, 2011). Everyone is different, but this idea must not become a reason to ignore the importance of differences. Practitioners must actively seek to understand differences that people experience and build their understanding of those differences in order to be a competent and professional practitioner. While difference can be bounded (a border created around it) according to various categories of difference, such as age or culture, in reality we each follow a different path through these categories and therefore come to a multidimensional identity. It is this identity that makes us different and that practitioners seek to understand in themselves and others. It is important to question individual actions and the actions of the profession, just as Krueger does in an examination of his possible role in social dominance over other groups within the child and youth care profession.

> [A]s I have read more about critical race theory, class, and oppression, I have been wondering how I might have directly or inadvertently contributed to hegemony. What was it I brought to those moments in youth work and my efforts to work with other youth workers to develop a profession that might have inadvertently, or directly, contributed to exclusionary, oppressive, and insensitive practice and relationships with youth? (Krueger, 2007b, p. 57)

Understanding and appreciating difference are critical tasks in three areas of practice: (1) the provision of a safe milieu; (2) the interpretation and application of theory in practice; and (3) the implementation of interventions involving advocacy, engagement, and empowerment.

Using culture as an example, Fulcher reminds us that cultural safety is set within the context of relationship and requires a mutual inquiry "between my culture and yours. Multi-cultural practices provide little guidance for direct action other than to offer a general list of principles" (2003, p. 27). The principle of mutual, relational inquiry can be applied to difference as a result of age, disability, gender, or educational competence, as well as difference based on culture. Fulcher identifies six areas to observe and inquire about that are particularly appropriate to ensure safety within milieu-based work.

1. Dress and public behaviour
2. Interpersonal greetings
3. Dialogue and interpersonal communication
4. Preparation and taking of food and drink
5. Hygiene and personal space
6. Status and hierarchy

Recall that culture is composed of the way of life in a society, including the norms, rules of social interaction, values, beliefs, artistic traditions and objects, legal and social institutions, and religious and political belief systems. As a multicultural society, Canada (and North America) deals with difference on a daily basis; indeed, individuals may blend traditions from different aspects of culture such as religion or ethnicity and may adhere to traditions differentially even though they appear to come from similar backgrounds. This makes the need to observe and discuss difference an important practice skill and requires practitioners to actively help young people to discuss differences.

PERSONAL REFLECTION

Children and Cultural Difference

Children can sometimes have little sympathy for new individuals that come into their lives. For example, a new student coming into a classroom can be judged and maybe even mocked by their peers. What is the reason for this fear? Children are so used to routine and dislike anything that alters it. Whether the student is from another country, another city, a different school, or even a different class, it can be difficult for the student to gain acceptance in a new setting.

Perhaps it is because the new pupil does not know the class routine. When they don't know they are regarded as outsiders. I remember as a child how rude and mean we were to the "new kid(s)." When I was in third grade we had two boys come over to Canada to escape the Bosnian war. We didn't care about their background or care to learn. They didn't know the language and therefore could not be allowed to play, interact, or even learn with us. Through time, we would learn to accept them, not completely as one of our own, but we did become friendly with them after a few months. Others were not as well received, though. We had a friend whose first, middle, and last name were the same; he was mocked the entire year and by the end of the year he had decided to switch schools. I cannot recall specific insults or incidents of embarrassment but I know there were enough to make him leave our school with a sour taste on his tongue and a bruise in his soul. Teasing is a form of bullying that so many children can be blamed for being a part of.

Isaac Ben Weinstock (personal communication, December 2008)

Aboriginal young people and families in Canada and the United States have experienced significant effects from structural, cultural, and personal barriers based on their membership as part of a cultural group that Europeans attempted to assimilate as they colonized North America. As such, they require specific mention relative to the issues that are part of the colonization process. Residential schools for Aboriginal children were created by the government and operated by Anglican and Catholic churches with the explicit purpose of assimilating children into mainstream culture and eliminating their uniqueness as Aboriginal peoples. The schools existed in Canada from 1857 to 1996, when the last one was closed.

Aboriginal children are overrepresented in the Canadian child welfare system and in the youth and adult justice system, and many families struggle on a daily basis with poverty, abuse, and neglect that are the result of several generations who were "parented" by institutions who rejected their culture and worked to destroy those differences. It was an unsafe environment. In 2008, the Prime Minister of Canada apologized to the Aboriginal people. The text of his apology illustrates how actions based on difference can have long-lasting effects on people who are members of that group.

SOCIETY REFLECTS: CANADA APOLOGIZES

Two primary objectives of the residential schools system were to remove and isolate children from the influence of their homes, families, traditions, and cultures, and to assimilate them into the dominant culture. These objectives were based on the assumption that Aboriginal cultures and spiritual beliefs were inferior and unequal. Indeed, some sought, as it was infamously said, "to kill the Indian in the child." Today, we recognize that this policy of assimilation was wrong, has caused great harm, and has no place in our country. Most schools were operated as "joint ventures" with Anglican, Catholic, Presbyterian, or United churches.

The government of Canada built an educational system in which very young children were often forcibly removed from their homes, often taken far from their communities. Many were inadequately fed, clothed, and housed. All were deprived of the care and nurturing of their parents, grandparents, and communities. First Nations, Inuit, and Métis languages and cultural practices were prohibited in these schools. Tragically, some of these children died while attending residential schools and others never returned home.

The government now recognizes that the consequences of the Indian residential schools policy were profoundly negative and that this policy has had a lasting and damaging impact on aboriginal culture, heritage, and language. While some former students have spoken positively about their experiences at residential schools, these stories are far overshadowed by tragic accounts of the emotional, physical, and sexual abuse and neglect of helpless children and their separation from powerless families and communities. The legacy of Indian residential schools has contributed to social problems that continue to exist in many communities today. It has taken extraordinary courage for the thousands of survivors that have come forward to speak publicly about the abuse they suffered. It is a testament to their resilience as individuals and to the strength of their cultures.

Regrettably, many former students are not with us today and died never having received a full apology from the government of Canada. The government recognizes that the absence of an apology has been an impediment to healing and reconciliation. Therefore, on behalf of the government of Canada and all Canadians, I stand before you, in this chamber so central to our life as a country, to apologize to Aboriginal peoples for Canada's role in the Indian residential school system. To the approximately 80,000 living former students, and all family members and communities, the government of Canada now recognizes that it was wrong to forcibly remove children from their homes and we apologize for having done this. (Prime Minister Steven Harper, June 11, 2008, retrieved April 20, 2009, from www.cbc.ca/canada/story/2008/06/11/pm-statement.html)

Dealing with Differences

Understanding differences, engaging with difference, and coming to terms with difference is an essential part of relational inquiry. At the same time, to be able to assess and understand difference, practitioners need a conceptual frame of reference and the flexibility to "stretch" that framework. Gradually incorporating new perspectives and gently stretching their understanding is the nature of gradual transformative change. Stretching too quickly can be dangerous (think about the pictures of yoga practitioners and whether or not you could survive attempting that stretch) and leads to a high degree of anxiety.

Hoskins and Ricks (2008) provide a conceptual framework (theory) for examining differences that builds on the idea of self-consciousness introduced previously and leads to a **co-created consciousness** or relational consciousness that incorporates the belief systems of both people while encouraging each person to explore and stretch their inner framework. The elements of the framework are illustrated in **Figure 7.4**.

Inner stances are the preliminary moral stances that represent values, the **aspects of self** that are held as truths. They include a practitioner's personal ethics and the codes of ethics outlined by the professional association. They are dynamic and changing in relation to the young people and/or coworkers in the practice relationships. They are identified through inquiry, both self-inquiry and relational inquiry (as illustrated in the Johari Window introduced earlier). Inner stances require observation, reflection, and active inquiry. When faced with a conflict related to difference, practitioners must actively inquire about the meaning of the conflict. This is difficult to do in the face of emotional reactions and self-judgemental thoughts.

1. Am I laying blame for this conflict? On whom? What benefit do I gain by doing so?
2. Am I thinking about the relationship? Or am I thinking about a victim and a perpetrator?
3. Am I engaged in binary thinking?
4. Am I able to hold two competing stances at the same time and appreciate their differences?
5. What do I tell myself as I examine these issues? (Hoskins & Ricks, 2008)

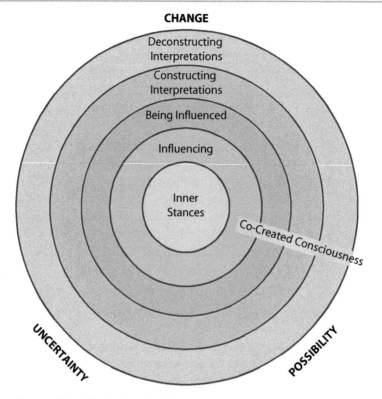

CHANGE

Figure 7.4 Exploring the Experience of Difference

PRACTICE EXAMPLE: KOKO AND HALLOWEEN

Koko was a young woman who immigrated to Canada from Ghana. As a young child she recalled sneaking out of the house on Halloween with her costume hidden in her school bag because her mother forbade her to dress up, explaining that it was "devil worship" and against their religion. Koko did not want to defy her mother, but her teacher expected everyone to dress up and had taught them a lesson in school about Halloween, or "All Hallow's Eve," and its significance to the pagans as well as its relationship to "All Saints Day" on November 1. Saints seemed like a good thing, and getting candy was even better, so she opted to sneak out with a costume. Now, as a child and youth care student she was learning about oppression and discrimination, and the necessity of reflecting on the social structures in which she worked to help young people overcome the barriers they faced because of systemic oppression. Her co-op supervisor in her school-based work setting had asked her to organize the Halloween celebration in the school. Koko found herself reflecting on her own personal experiences and empathizing with the children; she saw little conflict and began to organize a costume parade and plan her own costume. On the other hand, she also began to realize how Halloween represented both a pagan ritual and a fundamental Christian celebration, even though there was no discussion of either value base in the curriculum and realized that she was in a Catholic school but worked with many people who were not active members of the Catholic religion. She became increasingly uncomfortable when she looked around the classroom and realized that there were children who were Buddhist, Muslim, Jewish, Hindu, Sikh, Islamic, as well as Christian and Aboriginal children. She realized that she didn't know much about the beliefs of any of them and wondered if there were any that were feeling pressured to participate. She also began to recognize how the curriculum and the power structure of the school would limit children and parents from speaking out against the celebration. Some of the children had just immigrated this year and she recalled her own experience at the age of 8 and how confused the family had been by the costumed children calling on their door on October 31. Koko consulted with her supervisor and discussed her critical reflection on the structure of the curriculum and her lack of comfort in pursuing the organized celebration. Her supervisor was initially surprised and dismissive of the importance of considering something different, but with some further discussion she encouraged Koko to talk with the children about what their families did for Halloween (if anything). Koko discovered that several did not know what she was talking about (they were recent immigrants) and that at least half the group were discouraged by their families from dressing up. All of them wanted candy, though!

Koko engaged in the questioning process outlined above, initially thinking about Catholics and non-Catholics and blaming the curriculum developed by the government for the irrelevance of Halloween to the students. She recalled how she could hold two different stances as a child and wondered about the ability of these children to do the same thing.

Influencing and being influenced by others is a process by which difference can be understood. It may result in first-order or second-order developmental change, and it may result in maintaining a clear inner stance while observing and understanding the inner stance of the other person. As a child, Koko was influenced by her peers and her mother. Her values and beliefs about Halloween were confused, though ultimately she opted for a stance that was similar to her mothers. When faced with a supervisor with a different inner stance, someone who holds power and authority over her, she struggled and ultimately was successful in maintaining her own inner stance while respecting her supervisors. She didn't have to stretch very far, but she did need to attend to the foregoing questions.

Co-created consciousness encourages you "to think relationally by being conscious of [your] own inner stance, but only in relation to how it affects others and vice-versa" (Hoskins & Ricks, 2008, p. 301). In the process of co-created consciousness, you put your own needs aside to focus on the other person's experience and inner stance. The other person must do the same. Doing so has the potential to create an understanding that is larger than both of you and this is particularly important when dealing with differences. Co-created consciousness means that practitioners understand the relational aspects of their actions, including their critique or judgment of someone who is different.

The final aspect of the theory involves constructing and deconstructing our interpretations with the other person. "Constructions" are the judgements that form our worldview and explain our understanding of what is true and right in this world. **Constructing and deconstructing** involves challenging what is true and being open to challenge about our own truths. It involves conversation, inquiry, and risk and questions such as:

1. Where and how did I learn what I know?
2. What proves that it is true?
3. Can two different points of view be true?

4. Who decides what is true?

5. Who decides what theories, facts, and ideas I learn in school? (Hoskins & Ricks, 2008)

Stretching too quickly to transform your perspective leads to a high degree of anxiety, but on the other hand it may be "absolutely necessary, especially for those working in child and youth care" (Hoskins & Ricks, 2008, p. 289), who may fear losing the essence of the profession by examining the underlying assumptions upon which it is founded. **Novice** practitioners won't be certain what the foundations ("inner stances") of the profession are and may be depending on this book and others to tell them. The foundations of the profession must be critically examined, through a full exploration of the knowledge and theory presented here and engagement in this process of co-created consciousness. When the knowledge presented is different from practitioners' own culture or another aspect of difference, they should question and explore the foundations of that truth.

> Child and Youth Care Workers educated in the Western tradition of bio-psycho-social theories of child and adolescent development have been guided traditionally by values and customs founded in Judeo-Christian traditions. However, when working with children or young people from cultures from different traditions, it is easy to make false interpretations of child or adolescent behaviour, personality development and family practices with substantially deleterious effects on the lives of vulnerable children. As with First Nations, Hispanic and Afro-American children, New Zealand Maori children experienced extreme disadvantage from the application of Western psychological theories and methods used by social and behavioural scientists to investigate Maori character structure. (Fulcher, 2003, p. 21)

The diversity subdomain lays the foundation for examining everything that child and youth care practice has been built on with the understanding that it is founded on Western traditions, values, and morals. The domains of practice (Appendix C) that are focused on working with young people and families draw on two sources: theory developed largely in other disciplines and the grounded theory-in-practice articulated by experienced practitioners and academics. As the domains are examined in later chapters, the diversity ideas and critical thinking introduced here should prompt some critical reflection, not so that practitioners reject these ideas, but rather to question their relevance and identify what may not be useful when they are practicing within the diversity of today's society. It is not sufficient to simply "know" about what the differences are; practitioners must engage and explore those differences.

SUMMARY

This chapter has considered the domain of professionalism describing and laying the foundation for developing new skills and knowledge in all other domains, through effective use of professional development and supervision. An international ethical code for child and youth care practitioners was described along with a theoretical framework for ethical decision making that is consistent with the values and beliefs of the field about the importance of self to the work. Finally, the issues of diversity and difference were considered as part of the professional responsibility that practitioners have to understand, examine, and critically reflect on the nature of difference and how it affects our practice. Diversity was placed in a Canadian and North American context by considering two issues: the treatment of Aboriginal peoples by Canadian society and the highly specific traditions of Halloween as practiced in most of North America. Knowledge and theory about diversity is located in the professional domain to emphasize that practitioners have an ethical and professional responsibility to attend to diversity throughout all the other domains of practice. Critical reflection for understanding and working with diversity in practice are addressed throughout the other chapters in this book as a means of emphasizing and integrating responses to diversity in practice.

Photo by Laine Robertson

CHAPTER EXERCISES

IDENTIFYING PROFESSIONAL DEVELOPMENT NEEDS

Reflection-on-Practice

Make a list of 10 areas (knowledge or skills based) you are uncertain how to approach in your practice with young people and families.

Choose the three most important gaps to complete some research that will identify opportunities for further learning in these areas.

What learning format will you choose (online, classroom, postsecondary credit, literature search, conference workshop, personal counseling)? How does that format fit with your learning style and your lifestyle?

THE MEANING OF SUPERVISION

Reflection-on-Practice

What does "supervision" mean to you? What kinds of thoughts and feelings does it raise? What initial boundaries will you set on your relationship with your supervisor and how will you communicate those? What beliefs are influencing your boundary-setting?

SUPERVISION MODELS AND PROCESS

Experience

Consider the personal reflection provided by Vanessa in the section on supervision. Revisit the scenario with the new information that she is doing some extra contract work in a second program, where she has no formally assigned supervisor.

Theory-in-Practice

Use the four steps to planning for supervision to identify what may have been missed, on the part of both Vanessa and Tatiana, in planning for this supervision session. Identify some concrete strategies that Vanessa could take to implement her new learning.

ETHICAL DECISION MAKING

Experience

Revisit the following scenarios (from Chapter 5) and apply the self-driven ethical decision-making model. Choose one scenario to work with.

1. You need to make a decision about whether to report evidence of neglect during a visit with a family. You are in the practice milieu of family support, or supervised access, and must consider the meaning of making a report, the number of people involved, and the effect of the report in comparison to a different intervention that might mitigate the neglect and assist the family. You are responsible for one or two children and the parents with whom you work. The legislation about abuse and neglect and policies of the program are clear and specific but you may need to look them up.

2. You are faced with a decision about whether to report licensing violations in a foster home or after-school care setting where you are visiting a young person with which you work. In the context of the organizational system, the meaning of making a report, the number of people, and the nature of the effects are much broader and involve more people. There are families and children who may have limited options if the program is closed.

Reflection-in-Practice

As you read the scenarios above (read again if necessary) attend to the thoughts and feelings that are going through your mind. Record them. Consider and try to document your assumptions about "good care versus neglect"; what constitutes justice; and the options available for children when a program is closed.

Reflection-on-Practice

Identify the implications of your initial reactions for the various parties. Identify the various components of the ethical context. Confront and reflect on your aspects of self as they apply to this scenario. What are your values, beliefs, and moral rules as they apply to the scenario?

Reflection-for-Practice

Review the Code of Ethics in Appendix B and determine which principles apply. Which principles offer conflicting guidance? What aspects of your reflection thus far are *not* addressed by the Code of Ethics? What would be the right thing to do? What is the social context of the dilemma? What new information might change your plan of action? Determine a course of action and a plan for how to undertake that action. Consider what sources you would use to evaluate the results.

Readers may wish to review the practice examples provided in the *Code of Ethics for Youth Work in Aotearoa New Zealand* (2nd edition), available at www.arataiohi.org.nz, for additional scenarios for discussion and consideration of an alternative model of ethical conduct.

BINARY THINKING

Experience

In the previous chapter you were asked to consider aspects of who you are.

Table 6.1 identified eight aspects of self. Review the table and the aspects of self and consider how you are different from others in these aspects of self.

Reflection-on-Practice

Are you:

Normal or abnormal?

Straight or gay?

Able or disabled?

Dominant or disempowered?

Reflection-for-Practice

What is your reaction to these labels? How have you used them previously? How does this label influence the way you relate to others or how others relate to you?

COMMUNICATION

CHAPTER OBJECTIVES

- To describe the importance of communication in the day-to-day work of practitioners and how the domains of self and professionalism are expressed through professional communication.
- To introduce basic verbal and nonverbal communication skills.
- To review the role of documentation in professional work with young people and families.
- To explore the impact of digital technology on communication.
- To introduce the importance of teamwork and professional networking.

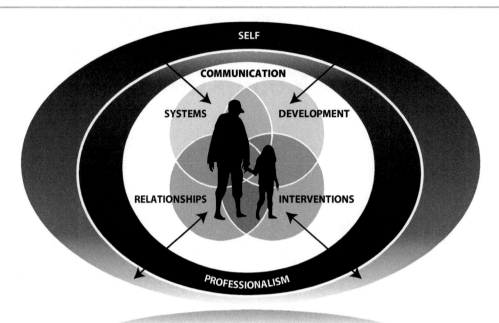

Figure 8.1 The Mediating Influence of Competence in Communication

It is through communication that practitioners establish relationships with people and the quality of service offered by the practitioner is enhanced. Effective communication requires a challenging array of skills; knowledge of relevant policies, procedures, and legislated requirements, and a strong belief in the relevance and importance of communicating with others. Communication is a mediating domain that brings the outer two domains together with the inner four, as illustrated in **Figure 8.1**.

Becoming an excellent communicator involves attending to aspects of self and professionalism as well as observing and listening to others. It requires skills and knowledge in **verbal and nonverbal communication; written communication** in many different forms; the use of **information technology** as a communication tool; and **interaction with professionals and community members** beyond the field of child and youth care. This chapter introduces some basic concepts and skills in the domain of communication.

VERBAL AND NONVERBAL COMMUNICATION

Communication is essential to effectively expressing caring when working with young people, families, colleagues, and the community. The child and youth care practitioner communicates effectively through both verbal and nonverbal avenues to enhance the quality of service and promote understanding and trust. The art of conversation is a critical skill for practitioners because so much of the work occurs in the milieu and is prompted by daily life events (Garfat, 2002). Nonverbal communication involving voice tone, facial expression, and intensity of expression must be appropriate to both the circumstance and to the young person's needs. The practitioner reflects on and evaluates the results of the communication, making any necessary adjustments to be a more effective communicator.

In *Pain, Normality, and the Struggle for Congruence*, Anglin concludes that group homes are "well-suited to providing a sense of intimacy without much of the usual emotional baggage associated with living in a family," and yet young people need to experience family-like relationships "characterized by a sense of belonging, caring, respect, loyalty, trust, generosity" (2002, p. 131). Anglin's research identified that communicating a sense of caring, respect, trust, and belonging occurs through direct contact as well as indirect activities such as report writing and daily life events (making meals, cleaning up play areas, decorating, planning activities). "Rarely is a meal prepared or a resident driven without considerable banter, discussion, argument, or confidence-sharing taking place between care workers and youth" (p. 97). The nature of this communication with young people requires that the practitioner be self-conscious and work toward a co-created consciousness, as is essential for understanding differences.

Verbal and nonverbal communications start with the art of conversation. Conversations develop relationships and help people to find common ground, to get to know and understand each other. Conversations move from "small talk" to a more in-depth "meaningful talk" that helps you to understand the other person's perspective, to a mutual agreement on solutions or "next steps." Conversations with young people happen about and around activities that they enjoy. You won't always move through all the phases of conversation, but being skilled at doing so is essential to practice because it helps connect you to the people that you work with. There are many "microskills" that form a base for all phases of conversation, from small talk to next steps in effective problem solving, and two of these microskills are described here. **Asking questions** and **paraphrasing** are fundamental skills for making people comfortable and for communicating that you understand and care about them.

Questions can be open-ended, to encourage the speaker to provide more information and detail. Questions can also be closed, which may limit or slow conversation about that topic. Open questions generally begin with the "five W's." Who, what, where, when, why, or how? Questions can focus on facts and observations, or on **aspects of self** like thoughts, feelings, actions, values, beliefs, and ethics. What you focus on depends on how well you know the person and where you are in the phases of a conversation. Jumping right in with "How did you feel when your mother abandoned you?" may not be the best option, even though that's the focus of the work that you've been assigned to do with a youth. "What should we do about that?" is one of the last questions you will ask, and comes after some extensive exploration of the topic at hand. The art of child and youth care practice comes with knowing how to bridge from activities to small talk and knowing when to approach emotional conversations by recognizing that an opening has been presented that would let you identify and talk about difficult issues in the midst of the conversation.

Closed questions are most often answered with "yes" or "no" and, while the child or youth might follow up by expanding on the topic, closed questions often shut down conversation or offer disguised advice without fully exploring the issue. Practitioners use closed questions purposefully and cautiously.

Tips and Resources

Open Questions

How do you like the weather?

Why do you like hockey?

Where did you go today?

What do you think?

How do you feel about what happened?

Who are you hanging out with these days?

When do we need to get this done?

Paraphrasing is the art of capturing the meaning of what the speaker is saying in one or two sentences. In "small talk," paraphrasing keeps the conversation going, communicates that you are listening and that you think what the speaker is saying is important, and focuses on something that interests you. In "meaningful talk," where the purpose of the conversation is to explore aspects of the other person's self with the intent of helping, paraphrasing serves the same purposes and additionally acts as a reflection for the speaker to more fully understand their issue. In "next steps," paraphrasing articulates the solution that is mutually agreed upon. Paraphrases must land somewhere between "parroting," which involves repeating word for word what the speaker said, and irrelevancy, which focuses only on what you as the listener are interested in. Picking out key words and reusing them (especially feelings) will help you use the speaker's language to convey your understanding. Using the same language as the young person can be very important if you are working across differences to understand the perspective of the other person.

Empathy is expressed through paraphrasing the emotional content of verbal and nonverbal communications that you receive. Empathy is the capacity to understand someone's experience and their reaction to that experience. Communicating empathy involves much more than just saying "I understand" or "I've been through that experience." When you communicate empathy you place yourself inside the other person's perspective and summarize for them what you see, feel, hear, and think. Since you do not come to the experience with the same background or previous experience you may have a different perspective on the options for reacting to the experience—and this (in part) is the power of communicating empathy. Empathic communication conveys to the other person that they are not alone in the world and it validates their feelings. Often this expression of caring is sufficient to calm and support a young person; however, empathy may also open the door to problem solving. When you empathically communicate your understanding of someone's experience, you can help them manage and problem-solve with a new and different reaction to the experience.

Being an effective communicator requires attention to other microskills of verbal communication and counselling such as summarizing, conveying empathy, and following a problem-solving model, as well as nonverbal skills such as observation, attending, and effective use of facial expressions and body language. While space limits a detailed

---

Tips and Resources

Keeping Conversations Open with Young People

Observe and listen to youth, noting current topics and the language of youth; understand their stories.

Respond to topics that interest you but not as an expert or as an advice giver, simply because you are interested. Ask open questions, even if the answer is obvious to you. You might be surprised.

Check your understanding of what the person means, to make sure you got it.

Don't collude or agree just to gain acceptance; be yourself and express your opinion without expecting them to agree.

Encourage young people to think "out of the box" and try not to close to problem solving too soon.

Reflect later on the conversation, note points where the conversation could have taken a different turn or identify areas where you were uncomfortable or perhaps noted some of the youth being uncomfortable.

Reflect on what you learned from the conversation—fact, insight, or personal challenge.

Consider what aspects of the conversation you might return to another time—picking up for more detail or potential intervention.

(Adapted from Sapin, 2009)

description of verbal (and non-verbal) skills, brief consideration of the importance of nonverbal communication is critical because most of our intent and meaning is communicated through nonverbal means.

How something is said during conversation is often more important than what is actually said. Nonverbal communication involves attending to and understanding facial expressions, gestures, body movement and contact, eye contact, personal space, and vocal tone and quality. You must observe both the other person and your own nonverbal messages. In addition, there are certain rules for etiquette in different cultures and the interpretation of both language and gesture can be different for people from different regions (even in the same country).

Nonverbal communication serves several purposes. It expresses emotion and attitude; reinforces or contradicts what you are saying while offering additional information to the other person; expresses your personality; and plays a role in social rituals. Being genuine and consistent in the messages delivered through verbal and nonverbal communication is a significant factor in communicating trust and caring to the young people and families with which you work. The young people with whom practitioners work have often been subjected to confusing and contradictory messages. Young people who have experienced abuse or neglect are told "I love you" one day, but are abused the next. For the child with a learning disability, "Do the best you can" contrasts with "I'm going to fail you on this assignment because it's messy and disorganized." These messages say different things about acceptance. Children learn very early the meaning of social gestures, facial expressions, and other indicators of nonverbal communication. Consider young babies when they first respond to smiling faces with a smile in return.

Not all young people naturally learn the common social meanings of nonverbal communication. Working with young people diagnosed with autism spectrum disorders such as Aspergers syndrome can be difficult because they are often unable to express or to identify in others the subtleties of nonverbal communication. Social rituals such as small talk may be lost on them without an explicit lesson in what those rituals are for.

Cross-cultural differences in nonverbal communication are an area of intense interest and study, far too vast to cover here. Nonverbal communication requires a person to attend to and understand things such as facial expressions, gestures, body movement and touch, eye contact, personal space, and vocal tone and quality. There are often culturally based rules for etiquette involving these aspects of nonverbal communication. There may be as many differences between people from the same apparent culture as there are differences among people from different cultures. Direct eye contact may indicate attentive listening and respect for the speaker or it may be interpreted as a challenge to authority and power. Averting the eyes may be a sign of respect based on gender or familial relationships and could be dictated by a specific religion or ethnic heritage. A greeting between two people (whether they are strangers, acquaintances, or close friends) could involve handshakes, kisses, hugs, waving, or a simple hello depending on culture, ethnicity, family norms, and the nature of the relationship.

The nuances of communication, verbal and nonverbal, make the evaluation of communicative interactions and seeking feedback about interpersonal communication essential as part of your reflective practice. Chapter 3 provided guidelines for giving and receiving feedback in order to uncover aspects of the self that are "blind" and such feedback is essential to evaluating and enhancing practitioners' communication skills. Knowledge about cultural, ethnic, and religious variations in communication patterns and rituals can be absorbed through observation and through seeking information from expert members of the group. Most people are unfamiliar with their own unique cultural "habits" in nonverbal communication. As the world has opened up to globalization, people who study and document differences based on culture have begun to make examples readily available. Actively seeking this information is critical to culturally sensitive communication and should be learned both by reading the research of others as well as actively inquiring about the cultural habits of people whom you meet because individual variation within the same group can be extensive.

> Experiences in China taught about important differences between auditory and visual syntax. . . . Western children learn more commonly through auditory processes that lead to concepts and models of understanding. By contrast, Chinese children learn through a visual syntax, meaning they create specific word pictures for names, values, and ideas taught by parents and other adults in their lives. (Fulcher, 2003, p. 24)

Seeking information, observing differences in communication, and being open to understanding differences will help practitioners create safe environments for young people and families.

WRITTEN COMMUNICATION

Written communication takes many forms and has many purposes in child and youth care. Practitioners are expected to communicate clearly, concisely, and correctly in written form. The practitioner must choose the appropriate format, material, language, and style suitable to the audience and write according to the style and conventions of the organization, as well as standards of professional practice. Written materials must be checked for accuracy and clarity as well as for neutral language. Child and youth care practitioners are responsible for progress reports, case plans, contact notes and logs, letters, and reports to other professionals. The practitioner has a responsibility to accurately record client interactions and organizational issues that are fundamental to planning and to integrated service delivery. It is necessary to be aware of and to follow the reporting requirements of local legislation and government policy. Writing in child and youth care practice can also take the form of short research reports and reflective process accounts of the work that we do.

While the main purpose of written communication in professional practice is documenting the outcomes of the work that we do with young people and families, writing could also include program evaluations or research reports that systematically investigate the nature and results of a program, or a reflection that focuses on describing practice and the personal or professional impact of the work. Each purpose for writing has a different style and the format used will vary according to the context in which the practitioner works. Most practitioners learn to write in their postsecondary education, but they don't learn specific formats and styles for writing reports at that time because professional reporting formats vary significantly according to the jurisdiction, milieu, and type of clientele with which they work. Report writing tends to fall in the "dreaded paperwork" category and is sometimes viewed as a demand of the organization that has little to do with the actual work with young people. This (limited) view of the value and role of professional written communication is flawed.

Focusing on the idea of social competence, Acorn notes that record keeping and report writing documents our client's history and that "our histories colour who we are, but do not necessarily dictate who we become . . . although history is important to help us understand our clients, history is the past, and your work as a practitioner is to help your clients write their future" (2003, p. 1). Your written communication as a practitioner helps young people "write their future" because it documents their goals and accomplishments and helps other practitioners help young people to focus on how to accomplish their goals. Written communication also provides a means for practitioners to pass on important facts and background information so that young people and families do not have to repeat their stories over and over again. Time together should focus on making a difference rather than getting caught up in previously discussed events. Finally, written communication demonstrates professional responsibility and accountability to other members of the team.

The following guidelines are particularly important when writing reports (of any kind) for young people and families.

1. Focus on strengths and resources while acknowledging problems and concerns. Be sure to list skills, talents, and abilities.

2. Pay attention to cultural beliefs and values as they are expressed by young people because they add context and meaning to the report.

3. Remain true to the purpose of the report: be organized, complete, and concise.

4. Avoid slang, labels, and judgements.

5. Use respectful and objective language that is free from assumption and interpretation. Write what you see and hear and attribute information to the source. Record observable behaviours, including what happened before and after, if appropriate.

6. Identify and write to the appropriate audience, keeping two hidden audiences in mind. Those hidden audiences are the client (young person or family) and "the law." Writing is guided by the question: "If my client read this report, would they understand it, acknowledge its accuracy, and feel respected?" In addition, most recording or reporting once complete and signed can be subpoenaed to court and as such should be precise and clear.

7. "Package" your report professionally, ensuring that it is nicely formatted, on appropriate paper, and checked for spelling and grammar.

8. Pay careful attention to language. Language should reflect the professional terminology of child and youth care practice but at the same time should not be so sophisticated that a client would misinterpret the report. While some additional explanation might be required depending on the developmental capacity of a young person, basic understanding should be possible when the report is read by a young person.

The types of reporting expectations that are part of your role will vary widely according to the milieu you are working in. The following are typical of the requirements of an organization (varied terminology is noted):

1. Running record/contact notes/logbook/session summary

2. Initial assessment/presentencing report

3. Progress report

4. Individual case plan (program plan/plan of care/service plan)

5. Goal review

6. Discharge report/summary of service

7. Observation report

8. Meeting minutes
9. Incident report
10. Communication log

Legislated requirements for reporting vary and are typically set by government and policy jurisdiction. You should become familiar with local requirements, paying particular attention to reporting child abuse and neglect; confidentiality and protection of privacy; reporting timelines and specific requirements for licensed organizations and programs.

While much of your professional writing will be objective accounts focused on young people and families, there are occasions when you will complete **reflective writing** on your practice. Indeed, much of the work and the writing that you have done throughout this book represents reflection on your practice and is therefore reflective writing. Reflective writing is a common form of publication in the field and includes research methodology that is consistent with methods that seek to understand human experience (Krueger, 2007b). Regular reflective writing requires a commitment to making time for writing within a busy schedule and making writing a priority when you might prefer to "be with the kids." Whether reflective writing is shared with others or highly personal like a diary or personal journal, it still has purpose and form.

PERSONAL REFLECTION: LEARNING JOURNAL

I have learned the importance of the context of where I work and how that impacts the focus of my work. I have also learned that all intensely challenging work might not be for me. The worldview and approach to working with youth of the job that I recently quit is so far removed from my own that I just could not stay there anymore. The utilitarian, bureaucratic, top-down dictation of the organization did not allow opportunity for client choice, did not focus on the strengths, assets, and successes of clients, and did not consider family dynamics and interactions as crucial in the assessment, planning, and intervention process. These are all building blocks I use throughout my practice to promote growth in individuals and families. These building blocks are based on the assumptions that people can change and I the practitioner can help, the relationship between the practitioner and client, and the client's circumstances and issues are context dependent, and the change relationship is a mutual journey of inquiry and learning. I have also learned, through the concept of choice, that although I will never find an organization that perfectly fits my worldview and theoretical perspective, there are certain environments I am not willing to work in. With that said, I know that I will need to explore what elements of the work environment I am willing to adjust to, aim to understand, and compromise on.

One main area I need to improve is in adopting a research-reflective approach. Somewhere along the line, I became proud and decided that I needed to prove to others that I already knew everything. Stating that I think I know everything is an overgeneralization, but I do definitely need to embrace inquiry, ask questions, be openly curious to know the underlying meaning of things. I am a very creative, adventurous, optimistic, and realistic person, so I think that as I continue to intentionally and subconsciously discover what I value and hold to be true, I will begin to break down my walls of pride and ignorance that often cause me to not ask "I wonder . . .," "what is a better way . . .," or say "I don't know, but I can and will find out." (L. Cann, personal communication, March 2009)

In the context of professional reflective writing (such as the exercises in this book), the purpose of reflective writing focuses on professional accountability. **Learning journals** are a reflective account of your professional development over time and may extend to become a **professional portfolio** documenting your competence in practice for the purpose of registration or professional certification. Reflective writing documents the rationale for decision making and can be shared with peers for critique and feedback.

Professional reflective writing is not just about your thoughts and feelings; it should include a number of elements that focus on articulating values, beliefs, and ethics that guide practice and illuminate the conceptual rationale behind decisions (Thompson & Thompson, 2008). Reflective accounts should be analytical, connecting values and beliefs to the decisions made and the approaches taken. Analysis looks for trends and patterns, commenting on the significance of issues and the connection between events. Reflective accounts can also identify and critique the assumptions underlying the work and help to develop better approaches. Conceptual thinking should be evident in reflective accounts. Professional reports focused on young people and families follow a theory base implicitly, but they do not explicate theory in the way that a reflective account would. Reflective accounts should also incorporate an understanding of the complexity of practice.

PRACTICE EXAMPLE

Reflective Account: Theory and Case Management

My vision as the case manager is to utilize systems theory and person-centered theory, embedded within a strength-based/resiliency-focused approach. The rationale for this eclectic collaboration is that a strength-based approach will allow myself and potentially Sam and his family to view and/or acknowledge their strengths. More specifically it influences my understanding of the case as the emphasis will be toward Sam's strengths, etc., so that these strengths can be celebrated and utilized as a form of praise for Sam in areas he himself may not have seen in a positive light. The approach will also be resiliency-focused, I will use this approach as it builds greatly on a worker's capacity to empathize and identify a client's protective and risk factors and identify how they have achieved or arrived at the place they are today. (V. Lalonde, personal communication, March 2009)

Becoming skilled at reflective accounts takes time and practice. Investment of the time to reflect on your practice and record that reflection will also improve your professional writing skills. The exercises at the end of the chapter provide several options for reflective accounts linked to the typical observing and recording writing contained in professional practice.

The final area of written communication that may be required of practitioners involves research and program evaluation. Research and program evaluation both involve a skill set that includes identifying the questions that must be answered to explore the effectiveness of interventions or to understand and learn from the experiences of clients. These skills include research design, methodology, data gathering, data analysis, and the reporting and discussion of the findings of the data analysis. Many experienced practitioners are never required to compose research or program evaluation reports and therefore do not regularly practice the skills of doing so. Research and evaluation reports are simply a sophisticated combination of the professional reporting required for your day-to-day work and the professional reflective accounts that discuss your learning and the analysis of that work. When reporting research results you will write objectively following the guidelines that you would use for client reporting, but with a focus on the collective results of your data analysis rather than a single young person. This is followed by a discussion of what was learned from the results in light of theory and previous learning (a reflective account).

INFORMATION TECHNOLOGY AND COMMUNICATION

Child and youth care practitioners need to demonstrate proficiency in using information technology for communication, information access, and decision making. Information technologies improve your ability to complete tasks, communicate with others, problem-solve, and perform research, and have largely replaced handwritten and paper-based communication. Digital technology in today's professional world epitomizes the two-way nature of communication and information-sharing because it allows instant access to information and provides a means of nearly instant (written) communication. Digital technology allows you to research answers to difficult questions; holds information about clients through electronic record keeping; is used for quick and timely communication of information about organizational policies and procedures or client crisis; and perhaps most importantly, in the context of child and youth care practice, digital technology includes the social networking tools by both young people and practitioners. CYC-Net.org, founded in 1998, is just one example of an international networking tool that connects students, practitioners, managers, educators, and researchers around the world, which can be used for consultation and research as well as professional networking.

Using information technology to research and gather information that helps you make good decisions related to the needs of individual clients is essential. This is a different type of research or professional inquiry from the systematic research and program evaluation described previously. This type of inquiry ensures that you have the most up-to-date information and knowledge about how to work with a young person's needs and to construct an appropriate program. In the past, practitioners would rely on knowledge learned in preservice education and during professional development activities to guide their practice with difficult clients and circumstances; however, with the incorporation of information technology into day-to-day practice, ours has become an information-based society.

"Let me Google that" has become the solution to finding the answer to a difficult problem. The difficulty with Internet-based inquiry is that Google will return 15,000 "hits" and does not screen the information based on any criteria that assesses the quality of the information. Academic and professional journals, the previous sources of new ideas and information for problem solving, use a peer-review system to assess the quality of the information before it is reviewed. The ready access to information today means that practitioners must develop the skills involved in making effective use of technology to assist with professional inquiry.

To begin with, Google is not the only source of electronic information. Library databases list hundreds of print journals and full-text online articles that are produced from print-based academic journals using the peer-review system. Searching library databases and effectively using Internet-based search engines require strategies that will quickly retrieve useful sources of information and a method for evaluating the quality of the information. Retrieval is accomplished through the effective use of a keyword search system that will reduce or expand the parameters of a search. Keyword searches operate using "Boolean" operators that combine key words and find information that is associated with both words. Type "autism AND treatment" to retrieve sources that include both. Type "autism OR treatment" to get many more hits that relate to either of these terms. Use strategies to limit where the search engine looks such as requesting Canadian sources, professional journals, academic journals, qualitative research, or evaluation depending on the purpose of the search.

After retrieving a number of articles, the quality of the information must be evaluated. Since the goal is professional inquiry to enhance the work with young people, there are a number of features to be evaluated. Table 8.1 identifies key areas to evaluate and includes questions to ask when assessing information retrieved during professional inquiry.

Table 8.1   Assessing Information Quality during Professional Inquiry

	SCHOLARLY OR PROFESSIONAL JOURNALS	INTERNET-BASED MATERIAL
Determine the type of publication	Newspapers, popular magazines, and scholarly journals are all significant sources of current information, but they vary in their level of **scholarship**. Is the publication representative of an academic discipline or a particular methodology (e.g. qualitative research)? Daily, weekly, monthly, annual schedule of publication?	Is it a commercial, government, educational, or interest-based site? (Check the URL for conventions such as .gov, .edu, .com, or .org.) Who else links to it? Who funds the organization? Why was the page created? Opinion, information, personal site?
Information on the author	Where does the author work? Who sponsored the research or program that is being described? Is the author considered an expert in the field, and what else has he or she written?	Is the actual author noted and what is his or her reputation? Can you verify the reputation anywhere other than the page?
Quality indicators	Editorial board for the publication Is this an opinion piece or a description of an ideal or does it contain systematic research results and interpretation of those results for practice?	Date of last revision? Material is referenced.

(Continued)

Table 8.1 (*continued*)

	SCHOLARLY OR PROFESSIONAL JOURNALS	INTERNET-BASED MATERIAL
	Date of publication (recent?) and date of articles that are referenced (recent?)	
	Who else references the author?	
Peer evaluation	Articles are reviewed by peers, academics, or practitioners prior to publication. These are referred to as "refereed" or "peer-reviewed" publications.	An advisory board or other representative group is identified.
Overall impressions	In reading the article, did it build on your existing knowledge or was it difficult to relate to?	Are there links to additional supporting information?
	Were basic concepts explained?	Does the author attempt to validate the legitimacy of information? How?
	Did the article support or refute an argument, and were examples given?	Can you find similar information in the library?

While information retrieval is critical to professional inquiry and the provision of quality service to clients, information storage has also been improved by digital technology. While paper records may still be kept, most information is now held in electronic form and may be accessed by multiple professionals within the same program or agency. Some aspects of client information are also available through information exchange between agencies and jurisdictions or through common data portals. Practitioners need to pay careful attention to the ethics of confidentiality and protection of privacy related to digital information.

Most organizations use digital technology to record client information and even to guide the assessment of needs of young people and families. Documentation requirements such as regular program planning, discharge reporting, and even daily logs and contact notes are fulfilled using digital technology. The nature of the technology will vary according to the demands of the jurisdiction, program, and individual organization. In the health and justice jurisdictions, access to information on young people is likely facilitated

---

Tips and Resources

Evaluating Websites

www.lib.berkeley.edu/TeachingLib/Guides/Internet/Evaluate.html

www.nlm.nih.gov/medlineplus/webeval/webeval.html

http://libraries.dal.ca/using_the_library/tutorials/evaluating_web_resources/website_checklist.html by secure Internet access and/or organizational "intranets" that connect multiple computers providing organization-wide access from any computer. In the child welfare or the community sector, sharing of electronic networks is less common and consistent and standardized data-gathering is often lacking, although few programs are without basic digital technology for record-keeping.

Communication technology has made relational work challenging over the last 10 to 15 years. Digital technology—including email, cell phones, text message systems, Twitter, social networking sites, blogging, and more—have been incorporated into day-to-day practice and the milieu. These technologies have implications for confidentiality and protection of privacy. Electronic networking requires careful reflection and new approaches to professional ethics related to professional behaviour, boundary setting, and confidentiality.

PROFESSIONALS AND THE COMMUNITY

Child and youth care practice occurs in many different milieus (Chapter 4) and the contact that a practitioner has with other professionals or with community members varies. A **novice** practitioner in a residential group care setting will likely talk to the neighbours as part of good community relations, and will be involved in regular multidisciplinary team conferences on the young people he or she works with. Multidisciplinary team conferences for a youth in residential care could involve a psychiatrist, psychologist, social worker, therapist, teacher, and probation officer, as well as the family. By contrast, a novice practitioner in a community youth work setting would network with other professionals regarding services and opportunities for youth as needed. A community social worker would have information on housing and social assistance; a teacher at an alternative school would have suggestions regarding educational opportunities; and a police officer would be aware of criminal activity posing risk. Professional community relations would be nurtured so that when a youth needed help or information the proper connections could be made. Community relations with neighbours, neighbourhood associations, homeless people, business owners, sports organizers, and so on would all be part of the work of advocating for youth at risk in that community and ensuring that young people are not stigmatized. The communication skills and knowledge required for networking professionally with everyone from neighbours to highly specialized professionals demand all of the skills and knowledge previously described. They also require an understanding of the community context of practice and systemic issues related to communication.

Child and youth care practitioners use effective communication skills with allied professionals and community members by investigating and developing an understanding of the language and concepts used in other professional contexts. Attention is also paid to the diversity of the community in which you work. Best practice requires close cooperation with the community and you must be able to access and utilize information to promote change. In the mental health jurisdiction knowledge of the language and concepts of a psychopathological approach is required for effective communication with allied professionals. In the justice jurisdiction language focuses on criminal activity, restitution, and justice principles. However, when communicating with others about the young people and families that you work with, you will remain true to the social competence values that are core to child and youth care practice and communicate those to the multidisciplinary team.

Social networking is a concept that originates in the discipline of sociology and represents a social structure consisting of people or organizations that are connected together through relationships between members. The concept has been applied in the business and professional community as a verb, "networking," to mean the conscious development of relationships, which will facilitate new ideas, opportunities, and problem solving. The advent of social networking sites on the Internet has added a new dimension to the networking concept. The skills of networking are essential not just for practitioner opportunities and problem solving but also to support young people and families in their communities and ensure that they are not marginalized or limited in their opportunities. Your professional network is a relational and social tool that will help you create change for young people and families.

Professional networking is most effective when you develop a focus or goal to guide the opportunities that you seek out for meeting people. The goals you set might involve your own career or they may be directly related to the work that you do. Your networking goals will provide guidance about the groups that you seek, in order to meet the people that you want to include in your professional network. If the goal of networking is to improve neighbourhood relations between the program, young people, and adult community members, then strategies such as attending a neighbourhood tenants meeting or a local business council will enable the practitioner to meet and converse with local community members. A cultural interest group will help you to better understand the cultural diversity of the community. If the goal is your own professional development, then joining a committee from the child and youth care professional association will develop your network. Similarly, you might seek out committee work within your own agency (e.g., the information technology committee in a hospital setting) that will offer opportunities to meet and talk with

---

Tips and Resources

Goals for Networking

- Develop relationships with local service providers so that youths can be quickly introduced when they express a need for service.
- Increase the reputation of the child and youth care profession with other professionals.
- Career development and additional learning opportunities.
- Improve relations with neighbours and advocate for youth as members of the community.
- Learn more about the culture, religion, and social norms of community members from diverse backgrounds.

---

members of other professional disciplines. Once the opportunities for networking are identified, the skills of conversation are used to learn about issues, interests, and opportunities that are consistent with the goals of networking.

As you network with other professionals you will develop an awareness of their professional language, and you will begin to use and understand terminology that is different from child and youth care terminology. Use of a multidisciplinary language must also be balanced with your use of the child and youth care professional language. Professional language that focuses on young people as competent and depathologizes their actions may appear simplistic.

> In child care, or any social organization I suspect, language is power, or, to be truthful, jargon is perceived as power. How often have you heard that child care, to develop as a profession, must have its own language? When we give in to this belief the result is small "p" political: it becomes more important that we say the "right" thing than it is that we make sense. (Gudgeon, 1991, p. 28)

When child and youth care practitioners use the languages of psychology, medicine, social work, or education to describe their work, they don't clearly communicate the values and beliefs of social competence (Phelan, 2001). Developing a language to describe the complexity of the everyday interactions is essential. Let's look at some different possibilities for describing the same behaviour.

Gudgeon (1991) describes an interaction with a coworker who insists that a young girl is "fixated" on an adolescent boy. Fixated is a term from Freudian psychology indicating obsessive attachment to another individual resulting from failure to achieve developmental tasks in an earlier stage in life. A probation officer might suggest that the young woman is "stalking" the boy. Stalking is a criminal activity that involves harassment and in some countries is a slang term, while in others it is a designation of the criminal code. A social worker might suggest that the young girl is "oppressed" by the male-dominated society and looking for a way to identify with and fit in with her male peers. A teacher might suggest that the girl needs sex education to prevent possible teenage pregnancy that could result from unprotected sex. The child and youth care practitioner (Gudgeon, 1991) suggested that the girl had an adolescent crush and thought this was an opportunity to teach her some skills for flirting with the boy. It also provided an opportunity to teach her how to "read" the social cues about whether the boy returned her interest. In addition, it might provide an opportunity to talk about safety in romantic relationships and could open the door for some future opportunities to discuss sexual relations.

Teamwork, integrated service delivery, and multi-agency partnerships represent varying degrees of the interprofessional context of the work that child and youth care practitioners do, which demand both sophisticated communication skills and a good understanding of context. Teamwork is addressed in the domain of **relationships** because it is a basic requirement for even a novice practitioner. Integrated service delivery and multi-agency partnerships require the networking skills of **mature practitioners**; however, a basic understanding of the terminology and context of integrated service delivery is essential for novice practitioners and is introduced in this section.

Child and youth care practice happens in a team environment. Often that team involves working with other professionals using a multidisciplinary approach. A multidisciplinary team is composed of professionals drawn from an array of disciplines and each professional has an area of expertise. Each team member applies a different area of expertise to the problems at hand, leading to solutions that others might not think of. Each team member also brings their own professional network, broadening the potential for services available for a client. The discussion of client issues among team members and with the young person or family checks professional bias and uses multiple perspectives to empower the client(s) to state what is best for their needs.

Integrated service delivery arises naturally from both teamwork and professional networking within the community. Programs and agencies begin to work together to deliver services so that young people and families do not need to tell their stories multiple times, or be uncertain about where to seek help. The goal of multi-agency integration is to achieve greater efficiency through the collaboration and cooperation of agencies (Chauhan, 2007). Integration of services requires, as a fundamental principle, community involvement in the process of defining needs and creating and delivering services.

"Community" has different meanings. Community can be defined by the geographic and demographic features that government uses to set boundaries for mandated services. Children attending a specific community school must live between "Mountain Street and Hidden Valley Road; north of the main highway." When community members talk about community they are referring to the network of relationships that are present in their community. The "Asian" community or the "Aboriginal people" are communities that extend far beyond a school boundary that defines service provision.

Service providers working toward the integration of services can be caught between these varied definitions. **Table 8.2** outlines some questions that practitioners should consider as they get to know their community, work on professional networking, and strive toward integration of service delivery. Struggling with these questions will help practitioners identify who to talk to as they work to ensure young people receive the services they need.

Exploring the questions outlined in Table 8.2 expands the understanding that practitioners have about service delivery. Networking, multidisciplinary/multi-agency teams, and working with community members to define and deliver services that meet local needs all apply essential components of the communication domain and enhance the work practitioners do with young people and families.

Table 8.2   Considerations for Professional Networking and Service Integration

DIMENSION OF COMMUNITY	COMMUNITY AND PROFESSIONAL CHALLENGES
Location and geographic boundaries	How isolated or rural is the community? What is the size of the population? What are the geographic boundaries for health, social services, education, recreation? What other communities are served by the same decision makers (politicians and civil servants), and how do you communicate with those communities?
Services mandates and jurisdictions • Primary versus specialised services • Professional disciplines and mandates	What health, social services, education, employment, child-care programs are available? What level of government funds health, social, and recreational services? What are the requirements for receiving service? How flexible are the program mandates and which ones are current social issues? Which services are privately funded and by whom? What service does local industry offer to its employees and their families? What is the cost for a young person to engage in a sporting activity? What is the cost for health care? What protection or financial assistance services are available?
Culture	How many different languages are in the community?
	What are the cultural norms for receiving social assistance, counselling, education, health services? Who provides these services and who accesses them?
	What formal organisations exist to assist specific cultural groups? How are they funded and what are their mandates?

Players	Who represents the community view?
• Individual, family, community	Who is the client of the service—child, youth, family, community?
	Who attends which meetings?
Function	What organisations exist in the community and what are their functions? Include groups such as community associations, housing authorities, dance studios, private sports clubs.
• Recreation, child protection, health, social safety net, education	
	How are the various services viewed by government program managers? Is there a relationship between recreation and child protection as functions? Is recreation a program that prevents the need for child protection, or is it a program that young people in need of protection have a right to attend?
Structures	What interorganizational agreements already exist? What interorganizational committees exist and who do they represent?
• Agreements, committees	
	What protocols exist for working together? What interdepartmental committees exist and who is represented?
	Who works with whom informally (and why)?
Mechanisms	What mechanisms are currently used to coordinate services to individuals? What mechanisms are currently used to coordinate programs between groups?
• Case planning, funding, and staffing resources	
	What interdepartmental or intergovernmental mechanisms are currently used to coordinate services to individuals? What mechanisms are currently used to coordinate programs between governments or departments? How is funding determined?
	What are the mechanisms for cost-sharing between departments?
Planning and goal setting	What is the official community plan?
	What are the mandates of the various groups within the community? Which ones are the same?
	What is the official political platform?
	What are the mandates of the various departments providing services? Which ones are the same?
Leadership	Who are the political leaders in the community? Who are the "behind-the-scenes" leaders in the community? Who are the volunteers and what interests do they represent?
Legislation, policy, and standards	What legislation(s) at each level of government affects the groups within the community? What are the policies and procedures that each group brings to their services and to collaboration? What policies and procedures affect them but are beyond their control?

SUMMARY

Communication mediates the way self and professionalism are expressed in the four central domains and is a complex set of knowledge and skills that make the difference between simply caring about young people and families or providing quality care and service that makes a difference in their day-to-day lives. Using communication skills through verbal, written, or electronic means, practitioners work with young people and families, other professionals, and community members to focus on developing relationships; applying the theory and principles of human development; understanding and applying systems thinking; and creating and planning interventions. These domains of practice are explored in the next four chapters.

CHAPTER EXERCISES

Photo by Laine Robertson

"I CARE"

Reflection-for-Practice

How do you communicate to a child or youth that you "trust" them or care about them, or that they should "trust" you?

What do you need to consider for Autry (introduced in Chapter 5) or for the children and youth whose voices are profiled in Chapter 2? How do they understand trust and caring?

What cultural differences do you think there are in the concept of caring for immigrants from a refugee camp or children raised in the deaf culture?

What differences are present for young children as compared to adolescents in how they perceive your caring response?

CULTURAL DIFFERENCES IN COMMUNICATION

Reflection-for-Practice

Consider some of the following and try to identify differences in communication based on country of origin, being part of Deaf culture, youth culture, or among older adults.

How would the following rituals vary according to the context in which they occur (work, school, home, public)?

1. Dining etiquette
2. Cell phone etiquette
3. Simple hand gestures while talking
4. Personal space between people
5. Rude or hostile signs
6. Waiting in line
7. Indicating yes or no nonverbally
8. Greetings such as hellos and good-byes

THE STAFF MEETING

Reflection-on-Practice

Maier describes the dilemma faced by most programs, particularly those who offer full-time care for children: "Towards the end of the allotted meeting time, a residential worker recommended a trade-off in more time with the kids in exchange for less paperwork. This suggestion, which received an affirmative sigh from many workers, reminded the agency director (who chaired the session) that he was about to take up the issue of recording with the care staff. He wanted their assistance in finding ways the agency could more effectively manage their recordings and to verify the residents' progress. He regretted that time had run out too quickly for this 'lively and productive' staff meeting. The issue of alternative ways of recording was recommended as the major topic for next month's staff meeting" (2006, p. 91).

In the staff meeting scenario, workers were willing to trade off less paperwork for more time with the children and the agency director wanted to discuss the issue of "recording" with staff. He felt it was important to manage the recording of the staff so that the agency could "verify the residents' progress."

Which position do you agree with, the workers' or the agency director's?

How does reporting benefit a child or youth? When and how is reporting a hindrance?

OBSERVATION AND RECORDING

Choose someone to observe for a 10-minute period of time. Events such as preparing and eating a meal, meeting a friend, or playing a game will work well for an observation exercise. Following the observation (which you will document), you will write a short report (in the next exercise). If you have video equipment available, then videotape the observation as well (be sure that you have the appropriate consent to videotape).

Experience: Observation

Using either your laptop or a piece of paper, observe the person for 10 minutes. Split the page into two columns. On the left side record in point form the actions of the person during that time. If the person interacts with someone, including yourself, make note of the behaviour of both people. Note facial expressions, hand gestures, vocal tone and quality, body posture, and so on.

Reflection-on-Practice

Review your observations and look for statements that represent inference or interpretation of the person's behaviour. Move these statements to the opposite side of the page, beside the behaviour that led you to this interpretation. If you don't have a "behaviour" recorded, then try to recall what the person did that led you to that interpretation (review the videotape if necessary).

Reflection(s)-for-Practice

Discuss with a colleague the difference between objective and subjective observation and recording. What role does each play in your work with young people?

Return to the observation recording completed previously. Examine your interpretations on the right-hand side of the page. Look for the underlying values and beliefs that are part of your worldview. Consider whether these are consistent with a particular theoretical orientation. Consider your own role—would the observation have unfolded in the same way if you were not there? Examine any sources of complexity and uncertainty that might provide alternative explanations.

Review your observations, inferences, and interpretation. Choose one of the following to focus on and write a brief reflective account.

- Complete a conceptual analysis of the behaviour by applying theory or knowledge that you have learned elsewhere to this observation.
- Complete an analytic account that examines the strengths and weaknesses of the observation record itself, charting what you missed and reflecting on why you think it was missed. Make a plan for improving further your observation and recording skills.
- Choose a nonverbal behaviour evident in the observation. Research and write about alternative interpretations of that behaviour in different cultures or in a different environment.

CONFIDENTIALITY AND PROTECTION OF PRIVACY

Reflection-for-Practice

Review the Code of Ethics for child and youth care practice in Appendix B and identify the statements that are relevant to the recording and sharing of information about a client with other professionals.

What precautions on the part of a practitioner would be required to ensure confidentiality? What precautions would ensure protection of privacy for digitally recorded material on clients? How are these different from a paper filing system?

HOW DIGITAL ARE YOU?

Recalled Experience: Self-Observation

Consider the last 24 hours and try to estimate how much time you spent interacting with electronic or digital equipment. Now estimate how much time you spent in conversation with people. Is there any overlap between the two time estimates? How much of your conversation used digital technology such as Facebook, MySpace, cell phone, email, text messaging? How often did you carry on two different conversations at once—a digital one and a face-to-face one? What were you doing the rest of the time (besides sleeping)?

Reflection-on-Practice

What are the implications of this description of your involvement with technology? How do you feel? What does it mean about your values, beliefs, and personal ethics? Share this reflection with someone from a different generation, culture, or gender. What reaction do you get?

USE OF LANGUAGE

Experience

As you go into practice settings observe and listen for the language that is unique to that setting as well as any differences between the members of the interprofessional team. Make note of terminology that is specialized to that setting or has a unique meaning in the setting.

Reflection-in/on-Practice

Observe your own emotional and cognitive reactions to the terminology that you hear. Take note of the terminology that you are most comfortable integrating into your own lexicon and make note of how that reflects your values and beliefs.

Reflection-for-Practice

Transfer the following table to your professional portfolio (and expand it) then begin to fill it in with common terminology that you hear in the various jurisdictions. Review it on a regular basis and add more terminology as well as your own explanations for what the professional jargon represents. Use child and youth care language when talking with those professionals but connect it to their terminology so they understand the difference.

PROFESSIONAL JURISDICTION	TERMINOLOGY	MEANING/CYC EXPLANATION
Child Welfare		
Health		
Developmental Psychology		
Psychopathology		
Education		
Justice		
Other		

PERSONAL REFLECTION: YOUTH

From Letters of Hope Project (http://andreecazabon.ca/letters-of-hope-project)

To whom it may concern,

I am writing a letter in hopes that it reaches out and finds itself in the hands of someone who really needs it. Let me start by introducing myself: I am a full-time student, female, and have lived on my own since the age of 17.

I first ran away from home when I was 11 years old. I left home because I was being physically abused by my parents. I was shy, scared, and felt as if I had no voice. My lack of confidence was fueled by the fact that I felt no one cared about me. I had no friends at school growing up (largely because I was awkward and afraid), I found no solace at home, and being a kid is just plain tough sometimes.

All this culminated into a lot of self loathing and soon I was using very hard drugs and living on the street . . . I was 12 years old. Children's Aid had become involved with my life, in fact they were there since I was 8. But no one ever listened to me. Not the social workers, not the counselors, not my teachers, not even my friends.

At the age of 14 I found myself at a crossroads. I had just moved into a group home and was forced to go into rehab. I spent 6 months in rehab. I sobered up, but the one thing that kept me going was now gone. Drugs had become a good friend over the years—the kind that never talked back, never yelled at me, and never tried to fix me. What was I going to do now?

A staff at the group home noticed that I wrote all the time. I had even kept a diary of the whole 3½ years that I had spent couch surfing, living on the streets, and bouncing out of foster/group home care. She suggested to me that I channel all of my frustrations and anger that I had for the "system" into writing about my experiences.

I took her advice to heart and have never looked back. I look at this letter almost as if it were a letter to my younger self. There are no regrets. No wishing certain things never happened and no feelings of shame. All I can say for sure is that I am a better person for having been through all of that and for coming out, not a victim, but a survivor.

I hope this letter finds itself into warm hands.

Anonymous

CHAPTER 9

RELATIONSHIPS

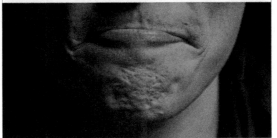

Photo by Laine Robertson

CHAPTER OBJECTIVES

- To describe the nature of relationships within child and youth care practice.
- To explore the role of caring in relational practice.
- To understand the concept of engagement in child and youth care practice.
- To understand how relationship is developed through the use of activities.
- To identify how skilled relational practitioners inter-relate to the professional team(s).
- To introduce the theory of the interventive relationship.
- To introduce research that provides an evidence base for relational interventions.

> A boy, alone, sits on a fence staring sadly, a tear wending its way down his face, at a group of children playing in a yard. This is the lonely isolate, hurting inside to be able to join in, but so threatened by relationships with himself and others that he cannot. (DeNoon, 1965, cited in Trieschman, Whittaker, & Brendtro, 1969, p. 100)

Genuine relationships with young people and families that are based on empathy and positive regard are essential for optimal development. Forming and maintaining relationships is a central strategy for change in child and youth care practice and there has been an evolution in understanding the role of relationship and the implications for practice. Very early in the history of the field, affectionate relationships with caring adults were thought to be the mechanism for saving children from a life of crime and poverty. As the scientific method began to influence the provision of care for young people, proponents of the humanist approach argued that relationships with young people provided a point from which other interventions could be used to create change (Redl & Wineman, 1951). Indeed, the term "relationship beachheads" (Trieschman et al., 1969) was used to illustrate how the relationship was the starting point for change. As the field evolved, the thinking about relationships changed and relationship was seen as a primary tool for change without any additional specific intervention protocol (Fewster, 1990b, 1991). More recently the idea of the **relational process** of intervention with young people and families (Garfat, 2008; Garfat & Charles, 2010) has characterized child and youth care practice.

AN OVERVIEW OF RELATIONSHIP

Novice practitioners are sometimes encouraged to think of their relationship with the youth as that of a "parent," a "mentor," or an older "sibling." While these concepts are worthwhile beginnings, they are insufficient to describe the relationship context within which practice occurs. The developmental status and culture of a young person or family and how it influences their relationship with the practitioner must also be considered. Relationships are multidirectional as well as developmental because they change and evolve over time.

The influences on relationships are multidimensional. For example, young children are particularly susceptible to power and as a result may not express their true feelings and desires when they feel threatened. Teenagers may be resistant to talking and sharing feelings with adults because they are developing their independence. Recent immigrants bring with them the rules and roles of relationships set by the culture of their own countries. Aboriginal peoples in North America have a history of relationships that are different from mainstream society, as well as a history based on how their ancestors were treated. All these pieces form the relational context in which a practitioner engages with people for the purpose of getting to know them and enabling them to change, grow, develop, and meet their goals in life. Practitioners cannot work without the context of relationship; we work from within it and through it. Anglin determined that in "good-enough functioning" group homes workers had "respectful, caring, and engaging relationships" that ensured a "good quality of group home life and healing, growth, and development for residents" who also developed "positive and respectful relationships with peers, family members, staff members, and significant others in community services" (2002, p. 67). Building rapport and relationships was identified as one of the core interactional dynamics in this grounded theory study.

Relationship is the first of four central domains that focus on the skills and knowledge of direct care work, which are required to support young people and families. These domains contain interdependent skills and knowledge that facilitate integrated competence for the mature practitioner. (See **Figure 9.1**.) The **self** comes to every relationship as practitioners bring their values, beliefs, thoughts, actions, and other aspects of self forward. Reflective practice ensures that practitioners pay considerable attention to the nature of their relationships and the mutuality of relationship, which is investigated through relational inquiry. Within the context of relationship the skills of **professionalism** and ethical conduct are expressed through the conscious application of professional boundaries. Practitioners will set limits on their personal disclosure and the nature of intimacy within their relationships with young people with whom they work. In essence, their personal needs must never be primary in the relationship. The focus is always on the young person or family needs. Similarly with coworkers, there are boundaries and limits to the nature of the relationships and how those relationships are expressed within the work setting or in social settings outside of work. All these aspects of the three domains that surround the centre of direct care work are assumed in the discussion within this chapter because they have been previously described.

The domain of relationships overlaps with the other three central domains of practice. Relationships are essential for understanding and assessing **development** and the **systems** in which a child is found. **Interventions** in child and youth care practice cannot be effective outside of the context of relationship and thus we do not attempt therapeutic interventions or methods of developmental practice without relationship. Similarly, we do not attempt to convince a colleague of the need for a different approach without relationship, and we "get to know the neighbour" for the good of the young people in the program. The relationship very often *is* the intervention because relationship is the context within which the young person learns and practices new ways of relating to people.

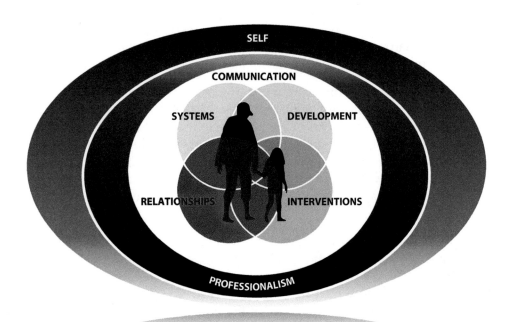

Figure 9.1 The Domain of Relationships

THE RECIPROCITY OF RELATIONSHIP

The interactional nature of relationships provides the forum for human growth and development. Everything that we as people know and understand about ourselves and the work comes to be known through relationship (Fewster, 1990b). The fundamental need that we all have to be loved and cared about is at the core of this domain. The attachment a child feels to caregivers is critical in the healthy development of that child (Maier, 1991). Young people who have learned ineffective relationship patterns lack confidence and a good sense of self (Fewster, 1990b, 2010). In child and youth care practice taking a **relational** view means that you believe that relationship is reciprocal; both caregiver and care receiver are influenced in their development. The historical point of view, which discussed the use *of* relationship (Trieschman et al., 1969), has changed to recognize that problems are interactional and that change has reciprocal effects on both parties in a relationship (Fewster, 1982; Krueger et al., 1999).

A **therapeutic interventive relationship** occurs when the practitioner enters into the "rhythm" (Maier, 1979) or "flow of experience" (Eisikovits, Beker, & Guttman, 1991) of the young person. At the same time, the practitioner has awareness of his or her own history, the context, and the child's needs, and is therefore present in the moment and fully available and responsive to the person. Through the interaction both parties grow and are changed. Any disclosure is an expression of the self, not an expression based on a covert agenda hidden from the young person (Fewster, 1990b, 2010). In short, the relationship *is* the intervention. The therapeutic moment and the environment for the intervention are created together. Novice child and youth care practitioners often say they want to be friends with the young person. As noted earlier, they might frame their relationship as one that is a mentor or "big brother." These descriptions focus on the role the practitioner plays in the relationship and they also focus on the practitioner rather than on the relationship. In relational child and youth care practice the focus is on the relationship (Garfat, 2008).

As noted in Chapters 3 and 6, our relationships with others play a significant role in reflective practice because relationships provide opportunities for feedback and relational inquiry. It is difficult to describe the nature of relationship and identify what it is that two people create when they meet and begin to form a relationship.

Lundy calls it a "we-space" based on "shared experience, shared meaning, shared values, and shared beliefs" (2008, p. 210). Garfat (2008) describes it as a "joining together that creates the in-between between us. It is in this area of joint connectedness where Relational CYC practice occurs. . . . As our relationship with the other develops and we become more familiar, more secure, more intimate, and more vulnerable, the space between us changes" (pp. 8–9) and we become a part of the in-between, it becomes part of "us." Relational practice is an approach to practice that focuses on relationship as the primary ingredient in interventions with young people and families.

While all practitioners have skills and knowledge in relationship development and the sub-domains of relationships, some practitioners focus on relational child and youth care practice. **Mature** practitioners may have preferred ways of thinking and theorizing about interventions based on the context(s) within which they have worked. In essence, a mature practitioner becomes more specialized in the theory of one of the four central domains and relationship is integrated into their practice.

A relational approach to practice focuses on the relationship and its characteristics as the central component of intervention and practice. Relationships can be scary, fun, distant, intimate, sexual, conflictual, and more. Professional practice relationships with young people and families focus on:

- Safety
- Engagement and connection
- Flexibility
- Interaction
- Exploration of self and other
- Meaning-making within the relationship (Garfat, 2008)

Relational practice establishes a balance between self and other in the relationship. Because the relationship is co-created, there is a gentle negotiation and discussion of the nature of the relationship. It is not the practitioner who "creates" the relationship; rather, the child and the practitioner create it together. The ideas of self and "us" exist together in a relational approach to practice. According to Garfat (2008), this is best illustrated by the standard inquiry, offered with genuine interest: How are you? How are we? Both are part of practice. "How are we" addresses the relationship and inquires about how the other person feels about the relationship. It monitors the relationship. "How are you?" is a focus on the other person's aspects of self and acknowledges the separateness of each person in the relationship. Finally, relational practice focuses on meaning-making, the meaning that both people make within the relationship and about the interactions with each other.

Relationships have context that is both shared and individual, as illustrated in **Figure 9.2** (Garfat, 2003; Garfat & Charles, 2010). The relationship between the practitioner and the young person (or family) is central and is characterized by connection and experience. Relationships are sometimes

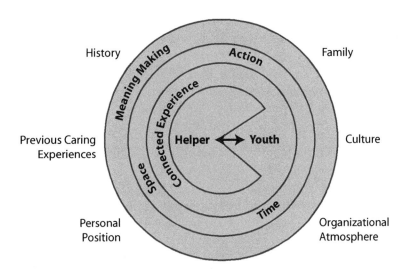

Figure 9.2 A Context for the Interventive Relationship.

From *A Guide for Developing Effective Child and Youth Care Interventions with Families* (Pretext), by Garfat, T., and G. Charles. Reprinted by permission.

"assigned" and at other times "chosen," depending on the milieu that surrounds the relationship. The nature of the milieu (e.g., community, school, residence), factors of time, and the activities that you undertake all affect the connection that is felt between two people. Both people within the relationship make meaning and interpret both the relationship and the actions of the other person.

The **novice** practitioner must consciously be aware of and juggle the many influences on relationship, sometimes "dropping the ball" and consciously picking it up again to inquire "How are *we*?" Mature practitioners seem to smoothly connect with young people, though such connections are still a conscious and thoughtful process. Practitioners consciously examine aspects of context during the relational inquiry that is part of connected experiencing. The Nature of Relationship exercise examines several aspects of context and provides an experience of relational inquiry—or the "how are we?" aspects of relationship.

Within the relationship domain there are five subdomains that represent both the uniqueness of the child and youth care approach to relationship and the skills and knowledge that are required to form relationships in a conscious and helpful manner. The remainder of the chapter explores these subdomains to introduce further the key aspects of relationships as part of practice:

- Caring
- Engagement
- Use of activities
- Teamwork
- Professional relationships

The subdomains are followed by a discussion of **interventive interactions**, which form the basis for a relational approach to intervention in child and youth care practice.

CARING

The child and youth care practitioner values caring for others as an essential component for emotional growth, social competence, and healthy development. Chapter 1 explored the value base of caring and noted that a core characteristic of child and youth care is caring—physically, emotionally, individually, relationally, and collectively. Within the domain of relationships, caring involves the development of a safe and nurturing environment and the teaching of basic self-care skills to clients. Practitioners demonstrate a caring attitude by placing the child at the centre of their day-to-day practice and encouraging the child to care for others.

Caring *about* children, individually and collectively, is something that practitioners bring to their practice. How they communicate that caring in a practical manner and how they teach the child to care about themselves and others will depend on the milieu in which they work. Caring *for* young people implies ensuring that their basic needs are met and that they are healthy. Often practitioners are in a substitute parent role (in-loco-parentis) and therefore the skills of caring **for** children are as essential as caring *about* them.

Most milieus in North America provide food for children and youth, even if it is a simple snack at school in the morning. In residential care, practitioners often shop, prepare meals, and, of course, eat with the children. Novice practitioners may need to learn cooking skills and understand balanced nutrition; food is a necessity but it is also a concrete way to express caring about someone. Celebrations of relationship (birthdays, anniversaries) almost always include food and so its inclusion as a way of expressing caring is natural.

Attending to the inevitable bumps and bruises that are part of childhood is another aspect of caring. It may be easier for children and adolescents to ask for help with their physical bumps and bruises than the emotional bumps and bruises. Taking care of the physical expresses care and concern and may lead to an opportunity to learn about emotional bruising. Of course, sometimes physical bumps and bruises are a symptom of physical abuse or neglect, and gentle questioning about how they happened as well as offering a band-aid, bruise plaster, and sympathy are essential. Practitioners have an obligation to report abuse, and knowing how a child received an injury may be essential to protecting them in the future.

Basic routines and structure are the fundamental backbone of caring in a residential care program. Children feel safe in a predictable routine, where meals occur at the same time everyday and bedtime accompanied by a snack and a story is expected. The space and time components of a milieu should have a familiar structure to them. While residential care is the most obvious example, any milieu should have a structured routine that provides predictability and safety for the young people that inhabit the milieu. In a family-based program, the practitioner helps parents develop that routine and structure, while in an after-school care or drop-in recreation program, structure is created through norms and routines about appropriate behaviour and deciding what the activity is for the day. Simple rituals of greeting and nicknames are predictable indicators of caring that recognize each child's uniqueness and the special relationship you have with them.

"In group care practice it is common that an intense involvement with one child readily creates a demand by other children for equal time. The result may be a rivalrous frown by co-workers, with a possible warning against over-involvement, or at least a curt reminder that not every staff member can afford such a heavy investment" (Maier, 2006, p. 96). Relational practitioners will discuss the nature of their relationships both with the young people and with their coworkers and explore how others feel so that there is a balance between treating everyone as an individual and how that affects group relationships. This type of approach leads to a common understanding and a co-created set of relationships.

Caring *for* young people requires touch as a component of the relationship. Touch is essential for healthy growth and development and yet there are clear cultural, ethnic, and religious differences in norms about touch. In some milieus young people will have histories of interpersonal violence—both sexual and physical—that must be considered. While children need touch, practitioners cannot ignore the fact that children may have been victims and may therefore be particularly sensitive. Practitioners must discuss boundaries and limits and the way in which caring is expressed through touch with the young people and their coworkers.

How people express caring has certain subtleties based on gender and culture. Differences by gender are most evident in the

Tips and Resources

Handbook on Sensitive Practice for Health Care Practitioners: Lessons from Adult Survivors of Childhood Sexual Abuse

www.phac-aspc.gc.ca/ncfv-cnivf/pdfs/nfntsx-handbook_e.pdf

activities that are assigned to men and women and boys and girls related to caring for others. Activities such as cooking, cleaning up, and organizing celebrations often have gendered responsibilities. Norms about the way in which caring is expressed across genders or between adults and children may also be governed by cultural or religious practices. Religious prohibitions may prevent women (or men) from physically touching or looking at children of the opposite sex when they reach adolescence. Young men who are novice practitioners may grow up in cultures where they are expected to live at home until they marry and not be expected to learn how to cook, thus missing an important aspect of being able to offer care to young people.

ENGAGEMENT

> . . . workers deeply involved in the care of children find much personal satisfaction in their practice, but they are simultaneously pulled by the need for neutrality and some may even consider deep emotional involvement as "improper professional" behaviour. (Maier, 2006, p. 100)

Child and youth care practitioners actively develop relationships with a genuine and **empathetic** understanding of the perspective of another person. To be "engaged" with young people or families implies that both parties are meaningfully involved in the nature of the relationship. While therapeutic relationships involve a connection, alliance, or association with a person that is purposeful, goal-directed, and rehabilitative in nature, practitioners are genuinely interested in relating to others—no matter if there is a purpose or not.

Empathy and respect are fundamental to relationships with young people and families. Empathy requires that practitioners recognize and understand the feelings of another person without actually sharing or "feeling" the emotion. Empathy requires tuning in to the other person's emotional state and simultaneously being aware of their own emotional state to be able to recognize the differences. It also requires that they communicate to the other person through words and actions that they have an understanding of how the person feels. Empathy is both an individual and a collective experience. Individually, when people feel understood because their emotions are recognized and valued, the relationship is enhanced. Collectively, the practitioner should have empathy for how the conditions a family, group, or community influence those that belong to the group. Collective empathy means recognizing the injustices in our societal structure and how they limit the potential that people have. It brings to the work a balance between individual responsibility for change and collective responsibility for creating the conditions for success.

Respect in child and youth care practice is based on respect for person, rather than respect for status, beliefs, or opinions (Sapin, 2009). Practitioners must separate the person from their actions and recognize that young people often bring expectations from previous encounters with adults to their relationships. While youth may be disrespectful, the practitioner must continue to offer respect, listen, value, and support young people's achievements while engaging them in talk about feeling disrespected. Sometimes practitioners don't yet know what the achievements of a young person are and thus a respectful relationship is based on potential. Awareness and empathy for how members of a historically oppressed group have been disrespected because of their race, ethnicity, disability, gender, or religion is important. Aside from other aspects of difference and diversity, young people as a group are often disrespected by adults. Their opinions are discounted or ignored in matters that are very important to them. Child and youth care practitioners believe in their potential and actively elicit and respond to their ideas, helping youth implement their ideas.

Engagement is the development and expression of genuine empathy and respect for the other person's position. Youth workers, a specialization within practice, use engagement and/or empowerment as a primary approach to the work that they do. Youth work practitioners fundamentally believe in the young person's right to dignity, privacy, and equality of opportunity (Sapin, 2009). Practitioners develop specific skills and knowledge related to how to engage young people and help them develop the skills that they need to be successful in self-advocacy. Some of these strategies are discussed further as part of the advocacy subdomain in Chapter 12. Some basic concepts are introduced here related to engagement and empowerment.

> Children need opportunities to engage with peers and adults who are models of the competence and social efficacy that children seek. However, they will only feel empowered if their actions make a difference. If organizations are to attract young people to serve their communities, they need to allow "youth culture" to flourish and to allow for diversity of children in terms of age, gender, ethnicity, physical and mental ability, and sexual orientation. Only in this way will the organization support personal and social identity. Adults in young people's organizations need to provide a trustworthy base, maintain a sense of purpose, and understand the issues and needs of children as children define them. When children or youth critically evaluate their own living conditions and identify the underlying causes of problems, they become more able to rise above the constraints imposed by their environment. (Hart, Daiute, Iltus, & Kritt, 1997, pp. 52–53)

In describing the youth participation ladder (Hart et al., 1997), the concepts of engagement and empowerment have found their way into a fundamental orientation to practice that recognizes and respects youth people and their capacities. The concepts involved in a **youth empowerment–engagement** orientation are founded on the belief that youth are capable of decision-making responsibility, and through the process they gain certain essential skills and offer important and otherwise inaccessible insights into the needs of all youth, thus benefiting others. Varying levels of empowerment and participation, as defined by Hart and Schwab (1997), are based on the level of control or power that young people have in decision making and has become an expectation of the work we do.

Participation means that young people are present and participate in activities and the design of activities initiated by adults. This often means that young people are directed by the adults, and that the goal of participation is to develop skills or change individual behaviour (Stacey et al., 2002). Young people who participate are often identified as the leaders in the community and rewarded for their community service. Participation in activities and decisions that affect one's life is a basic right for young people (UNICEF, n.d.).

Empowerment means that young people feel like they are participating and the workers help them to develop the skills to participate and to feel that they have equal influence in decision making. However, the practitioners may not be acknowledging the rights, privileges, and powers that they have (often as paid workers), and the young people (often volunteers) may not be fully aware of all the aspects of the decision making.

Engagement occurs within when young people and adults participate equally and recognize the power imbalance as well as the rights of youth to be treated equally (Stacey et al., 2002). In such circumstances young people are often paid for the work that they do and they are fully aware of the constraints and limitations of the social structures that influence them. These values permeate the work that the group does together.

The ideas of empowerment and children's right to participate in and direct decision making, exemplified in the United Nations Convention on the Rights of the Child (UNCRC), are relatively new and based largely in Western culture (Jefferess, 2002). The potential that there will be cultural differences in how young people are valued and what their rights are must be kept in mind when adopting this orientation. Young people and families from different backgrounds may hold different values about the rights and responsibilities of children and their capacity to participate in determining their own future. Organizing a youth group in a housing project where most tenants are recent immigrants could be challenging and youth empowerment strategies should consider cultural norms and the diversity of participants.

ACTIVITIES AND RELATIONSHIPS

Child and youth care practitioners select recreational activities and day-to-day life experiences for young people as opportunities for developing relationships, engaging in social learning, and developing competence in new areas. Social and recreational activities are essential aspects of daily life for everyone and therefore practitioners working within the milieu from a holistic and developmental perspective help young people learn how to spend their leisure time. As the practitioner participates with a young person in a basketball game, a card game, or a hike in the woods, he or she consciously uses the activity to develop a relationship, to observe and assess the child's needs and responses, and to design new learning opportunities for developmental change. Sometimes the focus of an activity is relational, sometimes the focus is new learning and development, and sometimes it is therapeutic change; therefore, this subdomain overlaps with the use of activities in life-space intervention, as described in Chapter 12.

Within the domain of relationship, activities are opportunities for socializing, creating a shared history and fond memories, or joining together around a common cause. Activities reflect not only individual preferences but also cultural traditions, including the culture of childhood.

When young people play games, they are learning skills and developing knowledge about themselves. Games have rules and structures that teach children how to conform and how to interact in a socially acceptable manner within a competitive environment. These are key skills in today's society that the children you work with may not have naturally developed. Physical activity is an essential component of lifetime health and well-being, one that is often missed when children are troubled and in need of professional expertise. "The strategic use of physical activity for change implies that an individual's sport and fitness programming deliberately incorporates both physical and psychological agendas. A process of personal change initiated through the body is best achieved in partnership with the mind" (Gavin & Lister, 2001, p. 332). Art and imaginative play are also natural forums for expressing feelings and exploring issues in a non-verbal manner. As youth get older and develop independence, helping them to take leadership in planning and organizing activities is important. These are all aspects of using recreation and activities in both a social and a therapeutic manner.

Gavin and Lister (2001) developed an analysis of physical activity requirements along seven psychosocial dimensions. As described in **Table 9.1**, this analysis can be extended to other forms of activity. Some activities are higher on the psychosocial "risk-taking" dimension or the "social-interaction" dimension. Soccer, for example, requires teamwork and social interaction, but less risk-taking than a sport like karate, which is high risk with little social interaction. Sports and activities

Table 9.1 The Psychosocial Dimensions of Play, Recreation, Arts, and Fitness

PSYCHOSOCIAL DIMENSION	DESCRIPTION OF DIMENSION	DESCRIPTION OF ACTIVITY CHARACTERISTICS	EXAMPLES OF ACTIVITIES
Sociability	At the **social** end of the dimension people interact socially through active involvement with others during the activity, including verbal or nonverbal exchanges. **Social** people spend time with others to satisfy personal needs and goals while **nonsocial** people prefer to be alone more often when achieving personal goals.	**Social** sports and activities require interaction to achieve some end. **Nonsocial** activities such as exercising are done individually without social involvement (even though it might be a group event).	Dancing is social. Speed swimming is nonsocial.
Spontaneity	Evaluate the degree to which the individual or activity is flexible and spontaneous versus programmed and controlled. **Spontaneous** people and activities tend to be creative, intuitive, and flexible in thought and action. **Controlled** and analytic activities and people are structured by rules.	**Spontaneous** activities require participants to be creative and reactive to the movements or ideas of others. **Controlled** activities are programmed and structured with particular rules and patterns.	Soccer is spontaneous. Competitive gymnastics and chess are controlled.

(Continued)

Table 9.1 (*continued*)

PSYCHOSOCIAL DIMENSION	DESCRIPTION OF DIMENSION	DESCRIPTION OF ACTIVITY CHARACTERISTICS	EXAMPLES OF ACTIVITIES
Motivation	Evaluate the degree to which the motivation for participation is outside or inside the person or activity. **Extrinsic** motivators include gold medals and praise from others. **Intrinsic** motivators are self-directed, and people are often willing to endure discomfort to participate and feel satisfied.	**Intrinsic** activity requires discipline, initiative, and persistent self-talk to sustain involvement. **Extrinsic** activities have rewards that come from social support, entertainment, or the recognition of others for success.	Marathon running tends to be intrinsic. Football might be extrinsic.
Aggressiveness	Assess the degree of dominance, mastery, or control over situations, objects, and others through **force. Forceful** people are assertive or aggressive and driven to master other people. Submissive people and activities involve compliance.	**Forceful** activities require concentrated physical energy and effort (though not necessarily destruction). **Submissive** activity is more fluid with congruent actions that flow with the energy.	While all martial arts may initially be thought of as forceful, different styles take different approaches. Karate is concentrated and forceful, whereas Aikido uses the force of the other person and flows with that energy.
Competitiveness	People and activities can be characterized by the degree of concern about rivalry and superiority with others on a set of evaluative criteria. **Competitive** people intend to be "the best," whereas **cooperative** people avoid competition and prefer to work with others to achieve an end.	**Competitive** activities pit participants against each other so that there are winners and losers. **Cooperative** activities are devoid of rivalry between participants so that even if the participants are competitive they cannot "win."	"Musical Chairs" is competitive. Building a human pyramid is cooperative.
Mental focus	Evaluate the amount of concentration required to engage in the activity or the amount of concentration capable of being put forward. **Concentrated** people and activities have a singular focus and are difficult to distract. **Dispersed** people and activities require attention to multiple facets.	Participants are required to **concentrate** during the activity, and distraction means they cannot complete the activity. In **dispersed** activities, participants can think freely or wander about unfocused and come back to the activity.	Video games require concentration. Outdoor adventure trips are more dispersed.

PSYCHOSOCIAL DIMENSION	DESCRIPTION OF DIMENSION	DESCRIPTION OF ACTIVITY CHARACTERISTICS	EXAMPLES OF ACTIVITIES
Risk-taking	Evaluate the degree of risk, daring, or **adventure** involved where the psychological or physical well-being of people may be at stake. Risk-takers are daring and expose themselves to potential harm. **Cautious** people and activities offer a high degree of safety and security.	In **adventure** activities participants are required to take chances with physical or emotional safety. In **cautious** activities participants are protected from harm.	Sky-diving is an adventurous activity. A walk in the park is a cautious activity.

for developing relationships can be selected based on the psychosocial needs and existing strengths of the child. The analysis can be extended to include artistic, recreation, and playful activities.

Any activity and any person can be assessed along all seven of the psychosocial dimensions. The dimensions can also be used as a beginning conversation about activities and interests. You can add additional examples of other activities to the chart to create your own ready-made reference.

TEAMWORK AND PROFESSIONAL RELATIONSHIPS

Positive staff teams produce positive youth groups. When staff treat youth with respect and autonomy, delinquent values in the group decrease. When there is a problem-solving focus, even disturbed and troubled youth improve in functioning. Staff who instil great expectations for success foster a student culture with greater interest in school. Students who develop close bonds with the staff are more able to seek adult support and guidance from other adults in their lives. (Brendtro, Ness, & Mitchell, 2001, p. 123)

Child and youth care practitioners work with both multidisciplinary and program teams. Working effectively in a team requires the ability to develop relationships with coworkers as well as with young people and families. **Multidisciplinary teams** meet regularly and bring varied perspectives to the table for discussion on the best programming and intervention approaches. **Program teams** composed of child and youth care practitioners are found in settings where larger groups of children require multiple practitioners. Practitioners need to pay attention to the relationships between team members, engaging coworkers and coming to know and understand their perspective as well as assuming responsibility for collective duties and decisions. On a multidisciplinary team the practitioner represents the child and youth care perspective and in program teams the practitioner focuses on both individual input and collective decision making. Teamwork is essential, not just for the benefit of the young people and families in the program but also as an opportunity for group reflection and renewal.

Teamwork, in a group home setting, is one of the crucial elements of a "good-enough functioning" program. Anglin found that residents needed "to find a sense of comfort and security in the staff team and to know that whatever happened, and whatever they did, the team would remain strong, united, and protective. Only then could the residents let go of their own defences and begin to trust in the adults around them, thus discovering a safe environment within which they could begin their own healing and growth processes" (2002, p. 95).

In a retrospective review of early research on teamwork in residential care, Burford and Fulcher (2006) demonstrated that the (diagnostic) characteristics of residents influenced the way group home teams functioned. Specifically, young people with "power orientations" were more difficult to manage and were associated with power-based responses by staff. The same can be said of any program where the focus is on enhancing the development of young people. In order for teams to become strong, consistent, and clear about their purposes with young people, they must build relationships and rapport with each other, they must be "relational," and they must respect young people and involve them in the decision making.

In all milieus, but most obviously in youth development programs, young people also have a role to play as members of the team and are engaged as capable co-participants on that team, following the principles of engagement described previously. All of the following information on developing teams assumes that youth workers would be using a youth participation and engagement approach.

As with any relationship, team member relationships grow and change over time. A typology of group development, originally proposed by Tuckman (2001), has been adapted to characterize team development and is described in **Table 9.2**.[1]

Table 9.2 Phase of Team Development

PHASE	GROUP STRUCTURE	TASK ACTIVITY
	The nature of relationships among team members.	The way in which members interact to accomplish the task of caring for young people.
Forming	Testing of others' ideas and dependence on others for decisions.	Orientation is to focus on the young people.
Storming	Intragroup conflict regarding the "rules" of the program.	Emotional responses to the demands of young people create disagreement about what to do.
Norming	In-group feeling and cohesiveness develop. New standards evolve and new roles are adopted with individual values; beliefs accepted and a group culture adopted.	Open exchange of relevant interpretations, comfort with expression of personal opinion. Focus is on both the young people and how the team is doing.
Performing	Roles become flexible and functional. Structural issues have been resolved and the structure supports caring for young people.	Interpersonal team relationships become the tool for working with young people. Group energy is channelled into the program so solutions can emerge.
Adjourning	Disengagement, anxiety, and sadness about separation. Feelings are expressed toward team members and leader.	Self-reflection on contribution to the team.

---

[1] These stages of development will be applied again in Chapter 12 when you consider group work with young people.

Relational teams focus on their work together. The skills that practitioners need to be contributing members of an effective team (performing) have already been described in preceding chapters. They include skills such as:

- Accepting and giving constructive feedback to open the "Johari Window"
- Conversational skills including listening, paraphrasing, and questioning
- Professional follow-through on assigned tasks
- Awareness of self (self-inquiry) and articulation of your values, beliefs, and ethics around the issues being discussed
- Reflective observation of yourself and others to learn from each interaction
- Written communication with team members including objective observations and process notes as appropriate
- Relational inquiry, including checking in with other team members about how they think the team is functioning

In child and youth care practice, teams that are performing well have members that make a conscious effort to support each other in both accomplishments and struggles. They share knowledge and are eager to learn from each other. They take the time to discuss and process their feelings so as not to undermine their work together. Empathy is characteristic of effective team members, and it is applied to adults as well as youth members of the team. Team members hold each other accountable for team actions. Finally, all teams have a leader and well-performing teams recognize that sometimes the leader makes difficult decisions that are in opposition to the team views (Krueger, 1990). Such decisions are fully explored and explained, including the recognition of power and the power dynamics of the organization.

There is significant emphasis in practice on the multidisciplinary team and as discussed in Chapter 8, practitioners need to consciously use child and youth care language as part of the multidisciplinary discourse. Anecdotal reports by child and youth care practitioners often indicate a feeling of powerlessness on the multidisciplinary team. Rarely, however, does anyone investigate the actual power of child and youth care practitioners within the team. Because child and youth care work occurs in the milieu, practitioners can control access to the children by other members of the team (Salhani & Grant, 2007). In milieus where child and youth care practitioners provide primary care and support (hospitals, residences, alternative schools and classrooms), other professionals may need the invitation of the child and youth care practitioner to meet with the child. Caution is necessary so that practitioners do not feel powerless and create a dynamic that reduces effective team functioning.

In addition to working on the program team or multidisciplinary team, child and youth care practitioners understand the teamwork necessary for integrated service delivery. Practitioners work in partnership with other professionals and community organizations. The communication skills identified in Chapter 8 are used to create networks and relationships between services and programs, often without a focus on a specific client. Since young people and families often need to access several different services, practitioners should be familiar with the programs, services, and philosophical orientation of organizations that serve the same population. Being familiar with community programs is valuable and essential by itself, but requires that you actively network to develop relationships with service providers and colleagues in other agencies.

Having considered some of the skills and knowledge in the subdomains of relationship, we will now consider research in child and youth care that demonstrates the effectiveness of relational interventions, that is, relationship as an intervention.

RELATIONAL INTERVENTIONS: THEORY AND RESEARCH

Understanding and knowing the other is about the practitioners' ability to go beyond the "file" or the history of the young person in front of them and to truly *know* who that young person is. When a practitioner intervenes in a way that is consistent with their global "knowing" or understanding of the young person (Garfat, 1998), they have a sense of how young people will react to their life experience. **Relational interventions** help the young person understand, cope or develop based on this global understanding. Garfat (1998) studied the meanings embedded in "effective" child and youth care interventions. Meaning-making was explored from the perspective of both the worker and the youth. The **interventive relationship** is a concept that emerged from this research. He found that the young people saw their relationships with the practitioners as "family-like." This seemed to be a way of expressing the deep connection they felt with "their" practitioners. The practitioners felt the same deep connection and understanding of the issues that the youth faced. They "identified" with the youth and their issues and felt bonded. There was an "intimate familiarity" (p. 132).

Garfat also challenged the traditional notion that congruence and consistency among staff in a program is important to effective intervention with young people: "It may be that continuity in the experience of relationship with individual staff may be at least as important as congruence between the youth's varying experiencing of different staff. It also hints at the possibility that staff being congruent with other staff and with program expectations may not always be desirable, . . . all three youth described their relationship with these child and youth care workers as different from their experience of relationship with the other staff in the program" (1998, p. 150). Relational intervention requires an individual approach to the work with each child.

PERSONAL REFLECTION: YOUTH

From Letters of Hope Project (http://andreecazabon.ca/letters-of-hope-project)

Hello my brothers and sisters,

This is what I know about where you are or may have been . . .

In one single moment your whole life can turn around. Your whole world can just can cave in and crash before your eyes and you have no control, even when you try with bare desperation. Then you find yourself just standing there, just staring into the ground, not even able to say a word, because everything is gone. Now, you realize you have nothing, absolutely nothing . . .

You thought what you had before was going to last forever; maybe it was good or terrible where you were. But could you ever imagine what life would be like without your family? Even if you never really knew them, how could they walk away from you or let you walk away? Then there are things you can't imagine seeing, like what will your life look like from now or how your life may have been then.

Life goes on, and you feel heavy . . . heavy with the feeling of guilt, as if maybe it was your fault that you are in the situation you're in. And so you sigh and sometimes you sob. But I promise you, it is not your fault. They left you or they let you go, for whatever reason and that's their fault. You could of only been a beautiful child, they were the adults. They made [their] mind up, and you have to understand how you can move on.

Your biggest challenge will be to make lasting relationships with people who will continue to be there for you, someone you can trust. With all the different placements you will experience and all the different schools you'll go to, it will be hard. A lot of people won't even give you a chance, they'll judge you for being in care and assume things . . . ignore them and don't let them have that power [over] your life. It will be hard to share with people where you live and why you are there, take your time. Just don't get in the habit of telling people things, but not telling them straight . . . you will get caught out and that's worse.

People will love you, you just need to find them and let them find you. Once you do, let them in at your own pace, trusting is a hard thing to do for us, I know. This is the hope I want to share with you. You will not be alone forever. Start by giving your social worker a chance, truly and honestly. You will change, you grow and you will adjust, [your] social worker will be there throughout if you let him or her in. . . . They will guide you through life and offer you intimate advice that will save you from harm, that is [their] vow to us. Remember that you have the right to make decisions that you believe are in your best interest. Make sure you exercise that right, it's the most important one you have while you are in the system.

Finally, you have to go for what makes you happy . . . explore and don't let anyone tell you "you can't" . . . because the sky is the limit for us too, I promise you.

My name is Samuel and I have been through that journey, it has shaped me and made me who I am. I am a good person, who is able to trust others and pursue my life, doing what I love.

I have hit rock bottom in the system, for me that was being in custody. Many times I felt like I had no chance to succeed and do something positive with myself, I felt doomed.

But then I made the decision to trust again—in my social worker to begin with.

Since that time I have gone on to do amazing things, like graduating from high school, completing a degree in my field of passion, winning a provincial championship playing rugby.

I was completely alone once and now, I have people around me that will be there no matter what, and believe in me.

You are not alone, and I believe in you.

Love from your brother Samuel:
Montreal, Quebec

Mann-Feder (2003) found that relationship and behavioural control cannot occur simultaneously. Research indicates that integrating discipline with warmth and acceptance is critical. "To choose one over the other deprives young people in our care of appropriate developmental conditions" (p. 13). Relationship, accompanied by clear explanations, is fundamental to exerting moderate control over young people's behaviour and helping them experience success.

Relationship and the youth's perception of that relationship are also important for success with young offenders. "What is needed is a corresponding intensive "jump" where adult staff make a concerted effort to meet, quickly become familiar with, and even charm the incoming participant. Some may chafe at the recommendation for staff to court and "woo" incoming offenders—but the research is clear: the youth's perceptions of the alliance rules when it comes to outcome" (Clark, 2001, p. 25).

Research indicates the importance of non-parental adults in the lives of youth; however, there is little research on the nature of these relationships (Rhodes & Lowe, 2008; Storer, Barkan, Sherman, Haggerty, & Mattos, 2012). A significant barrier for young people in the child welfare system was found to be the lack of a significant connection between the young people and their caregivers (Storer et al., 2012). A comprehensive literature review and evaluations of factors that influence the effectiveness and closeness of mentoring relationships found that relationship duration and structure as well as relationship skills had an influence on youth outcomes (Rhodes & Lowe, 2008). Young people in an alternative school setting clearly identified the relationship between themselves and the child and youth care practitioner as the basis for positive school outcomes. They identified both passive and persistent engagement strategies of the practitioner in the relational context as important to their success in the alternative school program (McMillan, Stuart, & Vincent, 2012).

Research on a relational approach to intervention indicates that youth experience empathy, respect, and individuality in the context of practitioner relationships. Indeed, research also indicates that relationship is an essential component of helping children learn how to change and control their behavior. The youth's perception of an empathetic and respectful relationship leads to positive outcomes. For practitioners who use relationship as their primary theoretical approach, this is affirming.

SUMMARY

This chapter has described some of the basic concepts and introduced some skills relevant to the domain of relational practice with young people and families. This domain overlaps with those described in the subsequent chapters because relationships enable practitioners to effectively assess developmental needs and systemic contexts and implement additional interventions. The chapter ends with a research example of a practice tool called the Gender-Sensitive Needs Assessment Tool, which illustrates the integration of developmental and relational approaches and appropriately leads to the next chapter on the domain of critically applied human development in child and youth care practice.

RESEARCH EXAMPLE

A Gender-Sensitive Needs Assessment

www.cyc.uvic.ca/naty/guide/index.html

A developmental approach grounded in interactive relationships implies that needs assessment is also interactive and relational. Artz, Nicholson, Halsall, and Larke (2000) developed the "Gender-Sensitive Needs Assessment Tool."

The tool is strongly grounded in the **developmental** and the **relational** child and youth care theoretical orientations. Each question asked of the youth to examine their developmental needs is paired with a question that the youth asks the practitioner about themselves.

Worker asks: Who do you think you can be real (genuinely yourself) with?

Who do you think is real with you?

What makes it possible for you to be real with that person/people?

Youth asks: How did you learn what you need to know to understand my situation?

Have you ever been through the same life experiences as me, or have you only read about them?

What do you need from me so that you can be real with me?

The pilot study of the needs assessment tool indicated that:

- While youth had questions to add, delete, or clarify, they felt that it helped them get to know their worker and to articulate their needs more clearly, simply by thinking about the responses to the questions.

- Practitioners found that the tool itself needed to be integrated into the relationship over time, that there were certain questions that should be asked later in the relationship, and that it took a long time to go through all the questions. The gender-sensitive questions prompted the practitioners to think about these issues and raised more questions for them. Personal boundary issues arose when they felt uncomfortable being asked questions about themselves. They also had trouble moving from the identification of need in the context of a trust-building exercise to what that meant for planning.

- Academic colleagues validated the intent of youth collaboration and suggested that risk assessment needed to be undertaken in conjunction with the needs assessment. The gender and culturally sensitive intent was felt to be important and additional questions were suggested in these areas.

Photo by Laine Robertson

CHAPTER EXERCISES

USE *OF* RELATIONSHIP VERSUS *BEING IN* RELATIONSHIP

Theory-in-Practice

Compare and contrast the following two quotations. The first is from *The Other 23 Hours* (Trieschman et al., 1969) and the other from a 1982 article by Gerry Fewster called "You, Me, and Us."

Which quote resonates for you? What is the difference in the way relationship is conceptualized or interpreted by the authors?

... when a worker speaks of having "established a relationship" with a particular youngster, the implication is that this adult (a "significant other" in contrast to adults in general) communicates readily with the child, is a strong social reinforcer to the child, and is a behaviour model that the child imitates. (Trieschman et al., 1969, p. 54) ... The existence of a "relationship" places the child in a vulnerable position; he can readily be influenced for better or for worse. Thus, it is not enough for the worker to establish a "relationship" with a child, but he must also see to it that he uses the "relationship" in a therapeutic manner. (Trieschman et al., 1969, p. 56)

Most people have little difficulty in accepting the idea that relationships make us what we are. They shape our behaviours and enable us to develop a concept of self. They generate our sense of values from which we make appraisals of who we are and what we do. They are fundamentally the world in which we live. They move with us from experience to experience whether we find ourselves among friends, among strangers, or completely alone. They are not convenient vehicles to be used in a process of coercion disguised by a veil of altruism. As the nutrients of growth and development they are based upon mutual understanding and respect and not upon grandiose theoretical notions. There is a crucial distinction between knowing someone and knowing "about" them. The point to be made is that the child care relationship should not be regarded as some adjunct to a process called therapy . . . the problems are interactional, and change that occurs through an involved relationship has reciprocal effects on both parties. (Fewster, 1982, p. 72)

THE NATURE OF RELATIONSHIP

Experience

The focus in this exercise is on the relationship. In essence, this is a relational inquiry about the nature of relationships. Search through the various relationships that you have and identify three different types of relationships. Because most practitioners are naturally "helpful" try to identify two helping relationships, one in which you were the young person and the other in which you were an adult with a young person. For the third relationship, choose a relationship that was not inherently "helpful."

Reflection-on-Practice

Begin by describing and then categorizing the "not helpful" relationship. What "type" of relationship was/is it? Describe some core characteristics of the relationship and your thoughts, feelings, and actions within the relationship.

Now consider the helpful relationships. Describe some core characteristics of the relationships and your thoughts, feelings, and actions within the relationships. What are the differences and similarities between the relationships when you were a child versus as an adult?

Reflection-for-Practice

What examples do you have in these reflections of being in relationship versus using the relationship?

FAMILY, CULTURE, AND RELATIONSHIPS

Experience

Consider the following and make a note of them (a note to self):

- Something your culture taught you about how to be with others.
- Something your culture taught you about relationships.
- Try to differentiate cultural teachings from family teachings and in a similar manner identify something your family taught you.

Reflection-in-Practice

Now comes the fun part—you'll need a partner. Stand facing your partner and about 15–20 feet (5–7 meters) away. Begin to walk toward your partner slowly. Every two steps, stop and talk with your partner about what is going on. Focus on the questions:

- How are we?
- How are you?

Consider thoughts, feelings, and actions as you walk and share those with your partner in response to these two questions. When you "meet" in the middle, make note of how far apart you are.

Reflection-on-Practice

Sit comfortably and talk about the experience, reflect on the values and beliefs that are represented in your earlier "note to self," and talk with your partner about how those emerged in the exercise.

Reflection-for-Practice

What did you learn? (You can repeat this reflection process and focus on other aspects of context like history or previous caring experiences.)

GENDER, FAMILY, RELIGION, CULTURE, AND CARING

Experience

Picture the relationships that you have with others and focus on the idea of caring for another person and how you express that caring.

Reflection-on-Practice

Identify how your gender, family, religion, and/or culture has defined those expressions of caring. Share your thoughts with a friend or fellow practitioner attending particularly to points of difference between the two of you. Consider how you might need to resolve points of difference in a practice setting.

Reflection-for Practice

How would you engage with a young person to express caring? How would you involve food, what routines would you set up, what special rituals or symbols would express the uniqueness of your relationship?

ENGAGEMENT AND EMPATHY

Experience

When David arrived on the doorstep of the youth shelter at age 16, he had been on the street for 2 years. Prior to that time he had lived in 16 foster homes and three group homes from the time he and his siblings were first removed from his mother at age 3. Over the last 2 years he had grown his hair and wore it in two long braids. He gave his name as "Dave Smith" and indicated that he had always lived in Edmonton, but was tired of hanging out on the street. He wanted to get a job and live independently. Stahl, the youth worker doing intake for the night, didn't believe Dave's last name but said nothing. Stahl's observations of Dave's appearance told him that Dave was probably Cree and Stahl seemed to recall seeing him at the Friendship Centre Round Dance the previous week, but he wasn't sure. Later in the evening when Stahl was sitting around with the group watching a documentary series on the history of Canada, he noticed Dave sitting apart from the group but, unlike everyone else who was complaining about watching a documentary, Dave seemed intently interested in the program. Stahl decided to get to know him a little better.

Reflection-for-Practice

1. Acting as if you are Stahl, come up with three different ways of starting a conversation with Dave that would form a basis for a relationship that could be used to support Dave in the changes that he wants to make in his life.

2. Choose one of the following as an opening line in the conversation and provide a rationale for why you chose it.

    a. Your last name isn't really Smith, is it? It's more likely Cardinal or _____? (light voice tone)

    b. I like the braids; when did you decide to go with the traditional look?

    c. Didn't I see you at the Round Dance last week? (inviting voice tone)

    d. I was at the Round Dance last week and I really enjoyed it. The drummers were great.

    e. What do you think of this documentary? They don't really show the Aboriginal influence very accurately, do they? Louis Riel is really shown as a bad guy and he was a hero in that war.

EXERCISE: THE PARTICIPATION LADDER

Experience

Go to the following website, from the One-Stop Youth Participation Shop, to find an explanation for Roger Hart's Ladder of Participation:

www.fbcyicn.ca/YPS/snack.htm

Consider a program that you have been involved in either as a child and youth care practitioner or as a child or youth. If you can, choose a program that espoused a liberated, participatory philosophy. If you have not been involved in such a program or aren't sure of the philosophy, choose a program that you enjoyed as a youth.

Reflection-on-Practice

Examining the ladder graphic, what level of participation did you have in that program? Write a few sentences on what you think each of these degrees of participation look like.

Reflection-for-Practice

Consider how you will engage young people in decision making in the work that you do.

Theory-in-Action

Choose another model for the continuum of participation and engagement such as the IAP2 Spectrum of Public Participation (Curtis, Lawrence, & Hoffman, 2012, p. 15, *www.mitchellshire. vic.gov.au/community-services/youth-development.aspx*). Contrast this model to the Ladder of Participation.

ORIGAMI

Experience

Find a piece of paper (any paper will do, regular printer paper, a sheet of newspaper, a napkin). Think back a few years to when you were younger and make something from the paper. Something fun. If a friend is close by, ask him or her to do the same thing.

Reflection-on-Practice

After you have finished your creation, share its story with your friend. How did you learn to make this? Who helped you? Taught you? Is your creation unique to your cultural or ethnic history? Are you familiar with what the other person created?

Reflection-for-Practice

What are the childhood activities like this that are common across cultures, languages, AND countries?

ACTIVITY ANALYSIS—AUTRY

Reflection-for-Practice

Autry (introduced in Chapter 5) has had some supportive adult relationships in school but overall he reports that he knows few people. His ability to create relationships seems compromised. Relationships are about a shared history, giving you something to further your relationship.

Develop some open-ended questions that would be appropriate for Autry's age and personality to engage him in a conversation and complete an analysis of his preferences in relation to the seven psychosocial dimensions of activity outlined in Table 9.1. Using what you already know about Autry and the activity analysis, identify three to five activities that you might suggest to Autry that the two of you can do together. Provide a rationale for how it will help you get to know Autry better and what you hope to learn about him.

THERE IS NO "I" IN TEAM!

Theory-in-Practice

Consider a team, or group with a common focus of which you have recently been a member. What stage of team development was present when the team dissolved? Complete an analysis of the stages of team development, providing examples from your experience.

Consider the issues identified in Table 9.2 and think about what might you have done differently to take the team's development further. What support would you need to encourage the team to develop further?

CHAPTER 10

CRITICALLY APPLIED HUMAN DEVELOPMENT

© Jose AS Reyes, 2013. Under license from Shutterstock, Inc.

CHAPTER OBJECTIVES

- To critically explore the role of developmental theory and research within the knowledge and skill base required for child and youth care practice.
- To examine the role of culture and social context in the assessment of a young person's trajectory of growth and development.
- To understand the concepts of risk and resilience within a developmental framework.
- To introduce a perspective on psychotropic medication and its role in correcting behavior, managing symptoms, and remediating childhood mental illness.
- To introduce research that provides an evidence base for developmental interventions.

235

Child and youth care practitioners apply theories of human development to understand the child's current developmental status and are thus able to recognize typical growth and development patterns and trajectories. A social competence perspective helps practitioners recognize the strengths that young people bring to coping with the circumstances that pose risks to their development. Practitioners understand that development and learning occurs over the lifespan and developmental theory helps them understand difficult or unusual behaviour, and puts that behaviour in the larger contexts of total development and the circumstances of family and community.

How developmental theory and research is applied to working with young people varies according to the milieu in which practitioners are located and whether they are working in individual, group, or family contexts. Knowledge and theory of human development are applied to many facets of practice, often in ways that are not obvious, but are essential to supporting young people and families.

A youth worker in a community outreach program designs activities that are developmentally appropriate for adolescents who attend in the evening but may also be designing activities for young parents and toddlers during an afternoon play group. The activities need to accommodate any potential disabilities and be consistent with the common interests of the members of the community. The afternoon play group helps young teen mothers bond to their children through singing games and provides the mothers with the opportunity to socialize with peers. In the evening, a basketball game may be more appropriate than a chess game in an inner-city context, and in a northern First Nations community the basketball game might be followed by a sweat lodge. A family-based child and youth care practitioner helps the parents of teenagers, who also have a preschool child, plan a family outing to the local science centre where all the displays are hands-on. All the children are occupied because the preschooler touches and interacts with everything to stay busy and the teenagers interact with displays about synthesizing music. Learning about science is encouraged along the way. Attention to the social conditions for the family means that the availability of a subsidized family pass creates a less expensive outing for the family. A practitioner in a mental health treatment centre notes the whining and clinging behaviours of a 14-year-old, understanding these as a symptom of an attachment disorder, while at the same time helping the girl plan for attending her first high school dance by helping her choose an appropriate outfit and practice social conversation openers as well as how to respond to any peer pressure to engage in risky activities. Subtle questions and observations about mood and her anxiety level provide information about how her new medication is working and can be relayed to the nurse practitioner.

All of the foregoing examples require a good understanding of human development over the lifespan and integrate that understanding with the domains of **relationship**, **systems context**, and **interventions** as illustrated in **Figure 10.1**. The principles of **diversity** (see Chapter 7) must also be integrated with the developmental domain because the theory and research on human development comes from a Western cultural perspective that may or may not be representative of the development of young people in the rest of the world. While some developmental theorists state that human development is universal, systematic research has demonstrated that universality is lacking.

Developmental psychology has been critiqued by those in the field of child and youth care for falsely claiming that this knowledge base is "true" (Dean, Harpe, Lee, Loiselle, & Mallett, 2008; Pacini-Ketchabaw, 2008, 2012). Practitioners study developmental theory as a starting point for using critically **reflective practice** techniques to ask questions and learn more about applying the concepts of human development to practice in varied contexts.

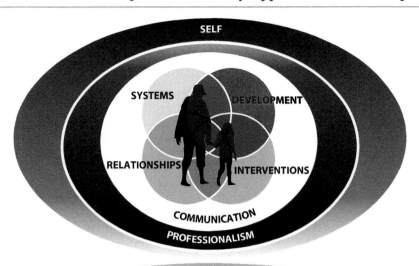

Figure 10.1   The Domain of Applied Human Development

By understanding that developmental theories and research are shaped by value systems, philosophical mindsets, and historical circumstances within specific cultures, students are more likely to appreciate the urgency of understanding and framing African child development within the context of local knowledge, values, traditions, and practices. From "Early Childhood Development in Africa: Interrogating Constraints of Prevailing Knowledge Bases" by Alan R. Pence and Kofi Marfo. In International Journal of Psychology, 43(2). Copyright © 2008 by Taylor & Francis. Reprinted by permission of Taylor & Francis Ltd, http://www.tandf.co.uk/journals.

It is impossible to offer an in-depth introduction to the concepts of human development as they are used in child and youth care practice as well as help practitioners initiate the necessary critical reflection on developmental psychology in a single chapter. Therefore, this chapter introduces some basic ideas by describing the subdomains of applied development and follows up with some exercises that are designed promote critical reflection on the concepts and apply them thoughtfully in practice. The chapter attempts to establish a middle ground between critical reflection and an introductory understanding of how the concepts of developmental psychology establish a theoretical and practical definition of the developmental path of a young person.

The domain of applied human development includes an understanding of **developmental theories** and **patterns of growth and development;** recognizing **risk and resilience** rather than developmental psychopathology; and an understanding of the implications of **psychotropic medication** as they apply to the treatment of mental illness with young people. Prior to considering those subdomains, a basic understanding of what human development is and how child and youth care practitioners think about it is important.

EXPLAINING HOW CHILDREN GROW UP: THE NEW NORMAL

In medieval times children were thought of as **sinful** and parents worked to eradicate evil from the child. The idea that children are a **tabula rasa**, proposed by John Locke in the 17th century suggested that children were malleable by both the good and the evil forces that confront us in this world and everything they interacted with shaped them as either a good or an evil person. In the 18th century, philosopher Jean Jacques Rousseau stressed that children were **inherently good** and, if permitted to grow naturally, without constraints, this goodness would emerge. These ideas represent early theories about the process of child development because they explained to people of that time how children learned, grew, and developed into adults. Today we recognize that there is an interaction between how **nature** and **nurture** influence a young person's development over time. How the balance is defined and which is more important has been an ongoing subject of debate amongst developmental theorists. There is of course a synergistic interaction between the environment and the child that must also be accounted for.

Theoretical explanations for development have become more sophisticated and theorists working in this area, primarily but not exclusively developmental psychologists, have recognized that development does not end with the beginning of adulthood. In fact, new research on brain plasticity indicates that neural pathways are constantly being reprogrammed, with great potential for life-altering changes (Perry & Hambrick, 2008). Child and youth care practitioners take a **lifespan development** perspective on their work, with a focus on social competence. Practically, a lifespan perspective means that:

1. Development and change occurs from birth until death. Every moment of every day is an opportunity for change, growth, and development in all aspects of the person. Even central nervous system structures like the brain continue to grow and develop throughout the lifespan.

2. There are many dimensions to development. Growth and development does not just occur biologically or physically, it also occurs cognitively, socially, emotionally, and spiritually. These areas can be represented by changes in language, behaviour, feelings, relationships, values, and moral commitments.

3. Developmental dimensions do not all develop at the same rate or even in the same direction. This concept is fairly easy to "see" in a child with a physical disability, a disorder that restricts growth, or in a child with a cognitive disability. When a conversation, a game, or a school activity is initiated and the physical size and development of the child is obviously different from his or her thought process, practitioners know that physical and cognitive development have occurred at different rates. Differential rates of development are common in all young people and there may be a difference that requires the practitioner's support to enhance social, emotional, or spiritual growth and development.

4. There are many influences on development, including the individual and the physical, historical, social, political, and cultural environments in which the young person is located. Lifespan developmental psychologists divide these influences into three types (Santrock, MacKenzie-Rivers, Leung, & Malcomson, 2011). **Normative age-related influences** include things such as puberty and menopause or rites of passage such as graduation from high school or an Aboriginal naming ceremony. **Normative historical influences** include events that all of a society experiences such as civil war or the current technological-digital revolution. **Non-normative life events** have a significant influence on individual development but do not happen to everyone and include things like having a parent die during childhood, teen pregnancy, and acute or chronic illnesses.

Judgements about whether a young person's behaviour is normal or abnormal are frequently made without an understanding of the influences behind such a polarized choice. Both the assumptions underlying the theoretical basis of the judgment and the immediate context where a young person exists affect which direction such a choice might be made. Developmental theory has been accepted as "fact" in child and youth care practice, whereas it should be viewed instead as a framework for thinking about young people's behavior (Pacini-Ketchabaw, 2011). A young person's social history, cultural and ethnic background and immediate situational variables all influence whether the behavior is "normal" or adaptive to the circumstances. Similarly, the theorist's social history and cultural and ethnic background affect the theoretical interpretation of what is "normal." Critically reflective theorists in child and youth care argue against using development as a foundation for child and youth care practice and suggest that the emergence of developmental science was a reaction to the focus in the early 20th century on myth, religion, and superstition as sources of guidance for raising children (Pacini-Ketchabaw, 2011). Psychology and developmental psychopathology in particular sought to control, direct, and correct behavior that did not conform to the standards of society. We now recognize that societal standards are framed by the social context and that they do not consider diversity, but rather work toward a universal ideal.[1]

The focus in child and youth care practice is on optimizing children's development and social competence and recognizing the strengths that the young person has while understanding the fluid nature of such concepts as *optimal outcomes, competence*, and even what represents *strength*. Strengths will enable young people to cope with circumstances that pose risks to developmental outcomes. A practitioner's influence on a young person's developmental progress today is set in the larger framework of what the young person needs through the ages and stages of life, some of which we are unable to predict.

Within the **applied human development** domain there are four subdomains that describe how child and youth care practitioners have adapted and adopted developmental theory and knowledge. The skills and knowledge that are required to effectively understand human development are introduced, but you will need to learn much more in order to effectively use and critique theory and research in this domain. This chapter introduces basic concepts in the following subdomains:

- Developmental theory
- Patterns of growth and development
- Linking developmental theory to risk and resilience
- Psychotropic medication

The subdomains are followed by a description of some specific developmental interventions that form the basis for a developmental approach to intervention in child and youth care practice.

DEVELOPMENTAL THEORY

Developmental theory helps us explain the developmental progression that a child would "typically" follow and identifies how to intervene and support optimal development. As practitioners become more experienced they are able to recognize situations when they need to adjust their relationship, activities, expectations, and interaction based on their integrated understanding

---

[1] The question of whether there is a universal ideal or an ultimate truth is a debate beyond the realm of this book.

of developmental theory and the individual needs of the child (Phelan, 2008). Developmental theory is primarily the work of developmental psychologists and child and youth care draws on this work extensively but not exclusively. Practitioners must be prepared to critically examine their theoretical assumptions in light of the social and historical context in which the theory developed.

Theories of development usually focus on one aspect of development and have varied assumptions (theoretical beliefs) about the importance of age and whether development occurs in predictable stages. A theory may also address the question of whether early experiences are important to later development. Theories that include "ages and stages" should enable practitioners to predict when a child will be able to perform a particular task. Knowing the optimal time for learning to read will enable the practitioner to support the child to be successful at the right time. Theories that emphasize early experience and how it influences later development assist practitioners to understand and intervene with adolescents who have been affected by early abandonment. Such early attachment theories have also guided policymakers in decisions about permanently removing children from a family. Theory must always be applied with the critical awareness that it is culturally bound and that it does not explain all aspects of development, nor will theory be universally applicable in all situations. Aboriginal peoples, for example, struggle with the application of the basic principles of attachment theory to the circumstances of their children.

> Bonding and continuity of care are often cited by the mainstream courts as key considerations in decisions relating to the child's best interests, as they attend to what is considered important from an individualist's orientation. While bonding and continuity of care are also considered important within the tribal perspective, they are balanced by other considerations related to the cultural context of the child and his or her best interests. (Richard, 2008, p. 192)

Developmental theories can be grouped into five areas.[2] Theories such as those by Freud and Erikson have a **psychoanalytic** orientation and follow the ages and stages model to predict what tasks children should accomplish at certain ages. **Cognitive** developmental theorists such as Piaget and Vygotsky emphasize the development of cognition and thinking skills. Vygotsky does not use stages in his theory but focuses on information-processing. **Behavioural and social cognitive** theorists focus on learning and environmental factors as the primary mechanisms of development and experiences at all ages are important to growth and development. **Ethological developmental** theorists focus on biology and believe in the importance of critical periods that are represented at certain ages. Early experiences are particularly important and if the critical period is missed, the skill may not develop. The fifth area is **ecological** theory, which suggests that development is influenced primarily by the nature of transactions with many different environments. Ecological theory is discussed further in Chapter 11.

Learning the concepts of these developmental theories is important (but beyond the scope of this book) in order to understand the perspective of psychologists, psychiatrists, and other professionals who are highly trained in normative development, abnormal psychology, and developmental psychopathology. Practitioners must also be able to think critically about the application of these theories to their work. A thorough understanding of the theories of development allows

---

[2] See (Santrock et al., 2011) or another introductory textbook on lifespan development for details.

the practitioner to selectively apply theory and to recognize circumstances in which the theory may not be valid because of individual circumstance or cultural bias.

Rather than focusing on the "abnormal," which takes a deficit-based approach and judges young people in comparison to the predictions of developmental theorists, child and youth care practitioners typically focus on strengths-based assessment within a developmental perspective. Maier (1991) identified two types of developmental change. First-order developmental change is the gradual, incremental change that occurs over time. This orientation to developmental change is common in community-based programs such as after-school care centres, early intervention programs, and family resource programs where they do not have "treatment" plans; instead, practitioners support the family or young person in their development. The promotion of gradual change is embedded in the programs for young people and families who attend and activities are designed that help children develop along multiple dimensions.

Second-order developmental change is similar to the transformative experiences described in Chapter 3. This type of change is expected in residential or out-patient care settings where the young person is transformed in a nonlinear manner. Changes are dramatic and the young person thinks, acts, and feels differently about life (Maier, 1991). Such change does not occur magically in residential care; it occurs in the minutia of daily life, and it requires great persistence on the part of the practitioner along with focused awareness of development and how it interacts with the adult caregiver's development. In mental health and juvenile justice centres the adoption of the strength-based approach to practice is indicative of the developmental Child and youth care approach. From assessment of need, to the identification of outcomes, and the measurement of change and progress, Child and youth care practitioners focus on what the young person or family brings with them (assets) and how to develop additional strengths, rather than focusing on deficits and psychopathology.

Developmental child and youth care theorists believe that development should be viewed holistically, with a focus on strengths and with specific consideration for the child's cultural and familial background. One example of this theoretical approach to development is the *Circle of Courage®*, based on Lakota teachings about child development. This theory proposes four central values as the primary basis for healthy development of young people, as noted in **Figure 10.2** (Brendtro, Brokenleg, & Bockern, 2002; Brendtro, Mitchell, & McCall, 2009).

The values of belonging, mastery, independence, and generosity are the focal points for educating the developing child in traditional Native American culture. From this perspective, any acting-out or difficult behaviour is a symptom of a broken circle that emerges when the environment and caregivers fail to help the child to develop a spirit of belonging, mastery, independence, or generosity. **Belonging** is the sense that

Figure 10.2   The Circle of Courage®
Used with permission of Starr Global Learning Network through Reclaiming Youth International. For related publications and training, see www.reclaiming.com.

children have of membership in a community that cares about them. **Mastery** is their competence in several areas, including self-control, responsibility, and effort and motivation toward their goals. **Independence** is their capacity for decision making and self-discipline. **Generosity** involves their contributions to the community in which they belong. According to this model youth distort feelings of attachment to gang loyalty; skills in problem solving to cheating; a sense of self-discipline to rebellion; or a prosocial attitude to servitude. Such distortions need an encouraging environment that will focus holistically on the young person, developing behaviours and attitudes that are in line with the central values guiding human development. Mastery includes the dimensions of development that are discussed by developmental psychologists (physical, cognitive, emotional, social, and spiritual) and therefore integrates developmental theory from that discipline into a more holistic way of understanding development. This is a model of development that emphasizes values and life-long learning rather than ages and stages as the mechanism for understanding and promoting development.

Strength-based approaches are also found in the positive youth development movement where theorizing about the influences on development includes both personal and environmental factors. This movement promotes the use of **developmental assets** to create "concrete, common sense, positive experiences and qualities essential to raising successful young people. These assets have the power during critical adolescent years to influence choices young people make and help them become caring, responsible adults" (Search Institute, 2012, n.p.). Focusing on supporting the developmental assets leads youth through incremental, gradual, and linear progression toward success and responsibility as adults (first-order developmental change).

Developmental assets include internal strengths and external supports. External assets or supports focus on the roles that family, schools, and community organizations play in supporting healthy development amongst young people. When people, organizations, and communities provide support and empowerment and set boundaries and expectations, young people thrive. Internal strengths include values, social competence, and commitment so that the young people are prepared for challenging situations. The positive youth development approach is present in school-based initiatives, Boys and Girls Clubs, and healthy communities/healthy youth programs across North America.

PATTERNS OF GROWTH AND DEVELOPMENT

Child and youth care practitioners should apply recent research in patterns and trajectories of child and adolescent development as a framework while engaged in the observation and assessment of young people. Patterns of growth and development are culturally and socially based, and while practitioners must be knowledgeable about typical developmental patterns, experienced practitioners access and assess research and theoretical frameworks that detail how culture and social environment influence growth and development. Practitioners also recognize that influence is a multidirectional process and young people influence their cultural and social environments while they grow and develop.

Scientific research, a product of the Western world's approach to knowledge, has demonstrated that the "blank slate" theory of child development is no longer viable. Growth and development is a product of both biological processes (nature) and environmental conditions (nurture). Research offers detailed information on typical development during the pre-natal period as well as during infancy and early childhood when change occurs at a very fast rate. Physical development and some aspects of cognitive and language development are thought to show near universal patterns in the approximate timing of when children display particular skills and abilities. This is most noticeable in the infancy and early childhood phases of life, and there are key points in the prenatal period of growth and development where the actions of mothers and the care that they take with their health can affect the later development of the child. While child and youth care practitioners may be more interested in patterns of growth and development in middle to late childhood and adolescence, these patterns are more affected by the context in which a child is growing up. Knowledge of growth and development in infancy and early childhood helps practitioners identify the relationship between a young person's current skills and behaviours and how environmental conditions affected development and the strengths a young person brings to their interactions with others. Research in the area of neuroscience is helping us understand how young people develop programming within the brain to cope with adversity and help them survive (Brendtro, et. al, 2009).

There are many inventories of expected growth and development for young people and they are primarily based on the idea that at a certain age, the child should be able to perform the expected task and will act in a particular way due to physical, social, emotional, and cognitive development. Patterns of growth and development are grouped into stages of life and described around those important "life transitions." Events such as birth, going to school for the first time, graduation(s), marriages, and the beginning (or end) of specific relationships are thought of as events that distinguish stages in life. These types of events are culturally determined in the context of how family is defined. Additional important contributors to growth and development are school and work. Factors such as going to school, leaving school, getting married (if at all), how family is defined, and what community means look very different in Canada, the United States, Japan, India, Israel, Somalia, Russia, and so on. Even within each of these countries there is significant variation in development based on socioeconomic factors, geography, and individual circumstances.

In North America researchers generally talk about infancy, preschool, school age, adolescence or the teenage years, and early adulthood, middle age, and the elder years. Child and youth care practitioners often seek out developmental understandings beyond the views of developmental psychologists that identify the expected ages and stages for certain tasks or behaviours. This knowledge comes through practitioners' relationships with people and their curiosity. Developmental audits may also address gaps in values and processes of learning (rather than ages and stages) to identify the function of certain behaviors and the relational supports for change within the ecology (Brendtro et al., 2009).

School seems to figure prominently in some of the developmental transitions and markers of development in North America, but school looks very different in other cultural contexts. In Russia and China, for example, children may be selected at a young age to enter specialized sports schools and train for competition in the Olympics. North American children have sports programs built into their school systems (not true in other countries) to enhance their physical development. Japanese children must complete entrance exams for high school as well as university and they attend school on Saturdays and after their "regular" day to study and improve their marks. Some ethnic communities in Canada offer "Saturday school" and families expect their children to go. In some countries young girls may not be allowed to attend school and in India the thousands of homeless children in the slums also may not attend schools. These are basic examples of how the Western perspective is embedded in typical assessment tools that practitioners might use. Practitioners should be aware of the potential limitations and the bias that is embedded in the available assessment tools. Inventories of growth and development are helpful to parents and health practitioners to understand when a child might need further assessment to determine if there is a developmental problem that should receive intervention.

Tips and Resources

The Community University Partnership on Early Childhood Screening at the University of Alberta is investigating the cultural relevance of these tools for immigrants and aboriginal children. Check out their research.

Psycho-Educational Assessment of Aboriginal Children and Youth: A Brief Summary of Issues, Research Findings, and Recommendations

www.cup.ualberta.ca/wp-content/uploads/2011/06/AboriginalAssessmentReport.pdf

Cross-Cultural Lessons: Early Childhood Developmental Screening and Approaches to Research and Practice

www.cup.ualberta.ca/projects-initiatives/ecme/past-projects/early-childhood-screening-in-immigrant-and-refugee-families

Work by Ethno-Med examines the considerations that physicans must make in screening the health needs of immigrants and their young children.

http://ethnomed.org/clinical/pediatrics/developmental-screening-with-recent-immigrant-and-refugee-children

---

Developmental screening inventories focus on young children under the age of 5, and are mandated by federal, provincial, or state legislation. As noted in Chapter 4, child and youth care practitioners are not often working with this age group; however, they may participate in early intervention programs. Of course, children can carry developmental delays forward into their later years, particularly when early intervention was not possible; therefore, understanding both strengths and deficits in relation to typical development can be important. Developmental screening tools identify young children with developmental delays so that interventions can occur when they have maximum effect, during the most rapid period of growth in the early years. Some children who need assistance are not identified until they reach school, at which point intervention may not have the same intensity or effect but is still important.

Developmental screening tools, which use the "ages and stages" approach, are not common for children over the age of 5; however, there are still basic patterns of development that are "expected" by developmental theory and research. Rather than reviewing patterns of development here, use your own developmental experience for the chapter exercises to highlight the concepts of later patterns of development.

Understanding patterns of growth and development helps practitioners to identify

---

Tips and Resources

The following resources are used to complete screening for developmental disorders in several provinces and states, ensuring early intervention and remediation for children with developmental delays or developmental disorders such as autism spectrum disorder.

Nipissing District Developmental Screening

www.ndds.ca/language.php

Ages and Stages Questionnaire

http://agesandstages.com/what-is-asq/

---

what is typical for a child of that age or in that stage of development, and to know when a child requires intervention to support further development. Learning is embedded in development as a life-long process assisting young people to overcome risk and develop resilience to help them manage future challenges.

LINKING DEVELOPMENTAL THEORY TO RISK AND RESILIENCE

Child and youth care practitioners apply developmental theory to assist then to understand difficult and risky behaviours in which young people engage. Ecological theory points to the importance of the environment as well as internal factors that are at play in growth and development. As noted in earlier chapters, child and youth care practice occurs in the milieu and makes use of the milieu for facilitating growth and development. The jurisdiction that a practitioner works within will dictate whether the primary orientation of the program is toward a strength-based approach, a learning and development approach, or a deficit-based approach. Practitioners may be responsible for implementing and advocating for a strength-based approach while working with a multidisciplinary team who is focused on risk and pathology. This section and the next introduce some language and concepts that will help understand the perspectives of other professionals and apply the concepts of growth and development to understanding young people.

In some jurisdictions (often health and criminal justice) risky behaviours are described as a **pathology** that needs to be corrected, and therefore practitioners in those settings also understand the language and theory of developmental psychopathology and are able to translate this language into the language of risk and resilience. Pathology is the study and diagnosis of disease within the field of medicine. The medical approach assumes that symptoms are evidence of illness and by treating the illness, the symptom will be corrected and the individual cured, or the illness managed. Psychopathology applies the medical model of disease to social and emotional problems, which are evidenced by behavioural symptoms. Mental health disorders and mental illness can be corrected with proper treatment and treatment takes a variety of forms, including psychotherapy and drug therapy. Developmental psychopathology is a branch of developmental psychology that studies the development of typical or atypical (abnormal) behaviour and problematic outcomes. Child and youth care practitioners make use of this knowledge with the understanding that development may lead to adaptive outcomes under one set of circumstances, and maladaptive outcomes under a different set of circumstances. Developmental psychopathology attends to the behaviours and symptoms of young people when they deviate from the "norm," and by using a cluster of behavioural symptoms attaches a diagnostic label. The label, provided by the *Diagnostic and Statistical Manual of Mental Disorders* (DSM), offers direction about how to correct the illness. Many labels for children are part of popular culture in North America. Terms such as "manic," "hyper," "retard," and "ADD" are associated with the behavioural descriptions and diagnostic labels in the DSM. They are also associated with significant stigma for young people who carry those labels. Those with symptoms of mental illness are often thought to be acting purposefully, or they and their families may be rejected for being different. There are many factors (internal and environmental) to consider in determining the influences on behavioral symptoms and child and youth care practitioners advocate for a strength-based resilience perspective in the face of the developmental psychopathology orientation found in some settings.

Defining what is typical or atypical depends on the ecological context within which a child is located. Take, for example, this portion of an interview:

> . . . two rival gangs came and used the school as a battlefield and we were unaware that this battle was going on. And when they were finished they decided they would go into the classrooms and rob us. . . . And he said, "what do you have to offer?" And I said, "I have nothing to offer you." And he got upset and he hit me so hard and I thought that was unnecessary. And after he left I realized that I was bleeding, but I had not yet realized he had stabbed me. I then investigated and realized I had been stabbed and thought this was uncalled for.

> Within less than three minutes he was lying on the ground, and I had stabbed him about six times. And I walked away remembering not feeling any remorse, not any pain, that I had done anything wrong. . . . I remember asking myself, "how did you get here?" And I didn't know. I never thought it was possible for a 15-year-old who had grown up in a home where the mother was strict, who was raised with all the positive values that you could be raised with, how that person could have stabbed someone six times, and I wasn't aware of how I had done it. (Magnuson & Baizerman, 2007, p. 273)

From the perspective of developmental psychopathology this young man might be diagnosed as a youth with conduct disorder, void of emotion and remorse. Most certainly the environment in which he lived, which he described as one where violence and beatings were a daily fact of life, would be considered abusive and he would be considered a child in need of protection and therefore be removed from his home and placed in foster care. Of course, he has committed a crime and would therefore be investigated and charged, though self-defense might be a viable court defense. However, this young man was not arrested for the killing and indeed went on to work with young people in prison, to help them become "inventive" without being destructive. Paul Legrange, the youth worker interviewed above, grew up in the townships in South Africa and was describing a day at school when he was 15 years old. He first started carrying a knife at 6 years of age. His experience points to the importance of going beyond the individualistic, deficit-based focus of developmental psychopathology. The experiences described above also reveal the difficulty of imposing the theory and definitions of Western knowledge onto a cultural configuration where social workers carry caseloads of 400 children, HIV/AIDS has killed many family members, and violence has been normalized (Smith & Drower, 2008).

Thinking from a developmental perspective helps practitioners to understand the dangers of seeing behaviours as symptoms of illness, risk factors as variables that lead to a **final** outcome, and outcomes as good versus bad. "In a developmental perspective where risk and resilience modify each other, DSM diagnoses need to be contextualized as either a process variable (i.e., one of many risk variables operating together) or an outcome variable (several stressors or risk factors leading to a final pathway that then in itself becomes another risk factor)" (Carrey, 2008, p. 120). In all cases a mental health diagnosis becomes part of and influences the developmental process.

Recent researchers in the area of resilience (Liebenberg & Ungar, 2008; Ungar, 2002, 2004, 2006) also view **resilience** as a process rather than an outcome and acknowledge the importance of individual, family, and community resilience. According to recent theorists, resilience is more than just a positive developmental outcome for a young person in the face of adverse cir-cumstances. Resilience is equated to capacity by Michael Ungar (2004, 2008) and as a concept resilience is more consistent with the strength-based approach than develop-mental psychopathology. When resilience is represented as capacity, practitioners can-not label an individual youth as "resilient" and expect that his or her developmental path will lead to "normal" or even "accept-able" outcomes. Similarly, they cannot label a youth with pathology and expect that the developmental path will lead to unaccept-able outcomes. Neither can practitioners expect that a predetermined set of factors (individual, family, or community) can be

---

Tips and Resources

Resiliency Interventions

Tribes: A School-Based Curriculum and School Com-munity Development Process

http://tribes.com

Pimatisiwim: A Journal of Indigenous and Aboriginal Community Health, 6(2), is about resilience in the Aboriginal cultures.

www.pimatisiwin.com/online/?page_id=173

---

part of an intervention program to develop the child's resilience and that this will automatically determine a successful outcome. Let's consider what resilience as capacity means and how a view of resilience as capacity needs to be integrated with developmental theory and knowledge of patterns of growth and development.

Resilience as capacity means that practitioners look for capacity in three areas:

- How young people navigate toward resources that sustain their well-being
- The physical and social ecology that provides those resources
- The negotiation between young people, families, and communities about culturally meaningful ways to share those resources (Ungar, 2008)

When children are exposed to risks (e.g., violence, limited family income, communities with limited resources), they are resilient if they can make their way toward the resources that they need to meet their developmental needs. These resources include both individual resources and family and community resources such as the external supports that are part of the devel-opmental assets approach (Search Institute, 2012). As a practitioner you can help children make their way to those resources that will help them cope and you also need to understand their developmental needs, using theory and research. Of course, the family and community must share the responsibility by ensuring that those resources are present and accessible to the child. If Paul was unable to get to school or his mother was not strict and insistent on positive values, his story might be different. These external supports were provided by family and community. Finally, various cultures value such resources differently: education, child protection, medical care, and punishment for violence must be perceived by the community and the youth as help-ful for meeting developmental needs (Ungar, 2008). The variations in culturally meaningful ways of sharing these resources are evident in Paul's story.

Practitioners must understand the young person's developmental needs and how those needs are located in the cultural context as well as what interventions, actions, community resources, and family resources are appropriate for meeting needs and building on existing internal strengths. Resilience as capacity is not a simple matter. Phelps et al. (2007), as cited by Ungar (2008), tell us that only one-sixth of children increased in positive development over time when there was a decreased exposure to risk and decreased pathology. In fact, many children who experienced increased risk or increased behavioural problems also showed increases in positive development and some children declined in positive developmental outcomes no matter what their risk exposure or diagnosis. It is critical in practice to focus on developing competence and strengths in young people through promoting resilience but at the same time to recognize the valuable information provided by assessment and diagnosis of the risks and psychiatric symptoms that often interact with environmental factors.

PSYCHOTROPIC MEDICATION

Psychiatric disorders in childhood often focus on disorders of development such as autism or pervasive developmental disorder, but may also include disorders of behaviour such as conduct disorder or oppositional defiant disorder and disorders of emotion such as anxiety disorder or depression. Child and youth care practitioners focus on social competence, health, and wellness, and psychiatric diagnosis is outside the scope of practice. However, since practitioners work within the multidisciplinary team they must understand the diagnostic categories and treatment approaches, including medications, recommended by other professionals on the treatment team.

Psychotropic medications to control the symptoms of young people's developmental and psychiatric disorders are often prescribed by consulting psychiatrists within specialized milieus and jurisdictions. Child and youth care practitioners working in these jurisdictions need to be familiar with commonly used medications and understand the role of medication and pharmacology and its place in the management of psychiatric disorders. Not all child and youth care practitioners will deal with medication on a regular basis. This domain has specialized application in the health jurisdiction. In other settings, such as schools, community centres, and family-based programs, there will be little need for specific knowledge on medication and its unique role and effects on development and behaviour. In any milieu,

---

Tips and Resources

The Medication Controversy

"If You Meet the Pill Fairy Along the Road, Kill It" (Fewster, 2004)
www.cyc-net.org/Journals/rcycp/rcycp17-1.html

Medication for the Depressed Child: Hope or Harm? (Roberts & Alessi, 1999)
www.cyc-net.org/Journals/rty/rty-4-1-robertsalessi.html

Psychiatric Patients Advocacy Office
www.ppao.gov.on.ca/sys-kid.html

Merikangas, He, Rapoport, Vitiello, and Olfson (2012) challenge the prevailing idea that young people are over-medicated through a comprehensive survey.
http://archpedi.jamanetwork.com/article.aspx?articleid=1465762#RESULTS

Oversight of Psychotropic Drug Prescriptions for Foster Children
www.gao.gov/products/GAO-12-270T

Podcast Interview on the report:
www.gao.gov/multimedia/podcasts/581603

Search *www.cyc-net.org* for additional references and discussion.

however, a small percentage of young people are prescribed psychiatric medications and practitioners must make an effort to seek information specific to those circumstances.

The use of psychotropic medication to control young people's behaviour is controversial in child and youth care practice. It is important to be well informed about the controversy, particularly if you work in a milieu where you regularly distribute medication to young people. It is also important to be well informed about the potential side effects and behavioural effects of various medications as they affect young people's development. Practitioners must make use of research rather than personal opinion to argue for or against medication for particular children.

There are certain milieus in which child and youth care practitioners work regularly with young people who have been prescribed psychiatric medication to correct pathology. Settings such as hospitals and mental health programs include psychiatrists and other physicians who prescribe medication as part of the multidisciplinary team. The child and youth care practitioner in these settings must be familiar with commonly used medications and understand the role of medication and pharmacology and its place in the man-

agement of children's psychiatric disorders. The practitioner applies this knowledge to their relational interactions with young people. Young people may self-medicate though drug misuse and abuse, therefore observation and assessment of behaviour with an awareness of side effects as well as the symptoms and issues of drug misuse and abuse is essential.

Child and youth care practitioners need a basic understanding of common drug side effects (physical, behavioural, emotional, cognitive) as well as symptoms of drug abuse or misuse and how to report observations to the prescribing physician, which will assist with diagnosis and/or adjusting prescriptions. You also need to be clear about your own values, beliefs, and knowledge about the use of psychotropic mediations and if necessary be able to argue for or against the use of medication with a specific child or youth. These arguments involve a secure knowledge of your own aspects of self and some professional research on the specifics of the medication involved.

The focus on strength-based development that occurs in the minutiae of day-to-day life is at the core of developmental child and youth care in multiple settings. It is balanced with the reality of working with a multidisciplinary team that interprets behaviour differently and focuses on change and interventions using other methodologies. The previous sections introduced some basic concepts and language as a foundation for integrating and applying a lifespan development perspective. The next section describes some specific approaches to intervention that arise primarily from a developmental child and youth care approach and are more commonly used by practitioners who specialize in a developmental approach.

APPLIED HUMAN DEVELOPMENT INTERVENTIONS: THEORY AND RESEARCH

While details on child and youth care approaches to intervention will be reviewed in Chapter 12, there are some specific approaches to change that arise from our strength-based perspective on applied human development.

Transitional and transformational objects (Maier, 1991) are examples of interventions that are linked to attachment theory and to social-cognitive explanations of development and are best used in the milieu-based intervention approach of child and youth care. Such objects are items that we are all familiar with in our own lives. They are the emotionally meaningful objects that we have difficulty getting rid of, or that we carry with us to support us in times of crisis. **Transitional objects** are those familiar objects given to children by their caregivers to carry them through a difficult time. A young person who enters a new relationship with a child and youth care practitioner might receive a special stone to symbolize the relationship. A young person with suicidal ideation develops a contract with their practitioner and carries a copy of it with them, along with a promise to call or contact the practitioner as needed. These objects support the young person and represent the attachment that he or she feels to the practitioner. **Transformational objects**, on the other hand, are objects that a young person chooses freely and carries with them mentally or physically. They are associated with a time of transformative growth and change and are a symbolic representation of the transformation. As adults, these are the special items that we are emotionally attached to and cannot throw out, since the object is too invested with memories. For young people, the high school prom ticket, the cheap birthday gift received from a first love, the "colours" associated with their gang, or a crumpled, raggy teddy bear are items full of meaning and transformation. When practitioners ask young people about the meaning of these objects they open a window on their development at that time and come to understand the strengths associated with that time of their life. They can build a bridge to additional transformations that will continue the young person on their developmental path. Transitional and transformational objects offer clues to understanding the resilience of the young person and enable practitioners to help young people further develop their capacity for resilience.

Practitioners also apply learning theory to create interventions that promote change and maximize developmental outcomes for young people. All interactions with young people and families are learning opportunities; the practitioner understands the methods that can be used to facilitate learning and therefore promotes change, growth, and development.

Learning theory uses concepts such as **reinforcement**, **cueing**, **observation**, **role modeling**, **self-talk**, and **social attribution** to explain development. When young people's behaviour is reinforced, either purposefully or accidently, they develop, refine, and repeat that behaviour as a result of the reinforcement. Receiving an "A" in school reinforces studying. Going to a community centre and enjoying oneself, while being recognized by the youth worker for participating, increases the chances that a young person will go again. **Cueing** is simply another term for being reminded. "Do your homework" cues a child to study. A sly wink or a finger to the lips in a "shshsh" motion will remind a child to be polite while listening to an elder. More sophisticated forms of cueing can be developed to help children develop socialization skills like sharing or cognitive skills such as memorizing information.

Child and youth care practitioners can be effective **role models** but they must have the respect and admiration of the young people that they work with in order for those young people to want to imitate them and/or adopt the positive values that they hold. Relationship can be critical for role modeling to be an effective intervention. Young people are likely to perceive popular artists and youth culture icons as role models and attempt to imitate them in dress and behaviour. Observing others can lead to development and change. Young people learn new games, develop social interactions, and understand how to express emotional responses through observing others.

Cognitive processes such as **self-talk** and **attribution** are thought to play a significant role in development. Internal dialogue, including thoughts about the self, influences development in a variety of ways. Attribution involves identifying what, or who, you hold responsible for your success, failure, feelings, or actions. Our brain is always filled with thoughts. The thoughts might involve lists of things to do or remember, ideas that we want to implement, things to tell someone else, or statements about our worth and value and internal or external attributions of responsibility. Autry (whom you met in Chapter 5) attributes his difficulty in school to the administration that doesn't attend to racial slurs as well as to his inability to receive enough to eat. He tells himself that postsecondary education is essential to his life. All these attributions are related to his feeling of helplessness and are important information for designing interventions. Learning theorists suggest that environmental factors have the potential to make a difference in developmental outcomes for young people. For example, a young person with a learning disability who is identified and tested early in school attributes difficulties with reading to the disability and learns strategies that accommodate while going on to university. A young person who is not identified early attributes difficulty to "being stupid" and develops an internal self-talk that reinforces this idea, leading to failure and the possibility of dropping out of high school.

Re-education techniques such as skill-based groups and positive peer culture have become part of the developmental child and youth care orientation. The premise is that the young person developing these skills through a group intervention can learn and apply that learning immediately within the peer group. Such techniques can address either first- or second-order developmental change and are set in a relational interactive context, accomplished within a group process. Re-education principles have a strength-based focus and argue against the medical model with its emphasis on psychopathology, focusing more on supporting the resilience of young people (Farmer, Farmer, & Brooks, 2010; Foltz, 2011). Life skills groups (Durlak, Weissberg, & Pachan, 2010; Taussig & Culhane, 2010; World Health Organization, 2009) and collaborative problem solving (Greene, 2010; Greene, Ablon, & Martin, 2006; Stewart, Rick, Currie, & Riley, 2009) are two examples of "reeducation" often used with young people that have demonstrated evidence of effectiveness.

Positive peer culture (Brendtro & Ness, 1983; Laursen, 2010; Steinebach & Steinebach, 2009) is a peer group intervention that has been used with juvenile centres since the 1970s. "The *peer* group is viewed as a resource rather than a negative influence. In the group, members' problems are identified and worked through to obtain satisfactory solutions. Members offer solutions, provide helpful confrontations, and support displays of behavioural self-control. Instead of focusing on the youth asking for or expecting to receive help, the focus is on their willingness to offer it. Through giving, a group member's self-worth is more likely to increase" (Vorrath & Brendtro, 1985, cited in Moody & Lupton-Smith, 1999).

Parent **reeducation** groups are also useful as adjuncts to family support programs, residential care programs, and even schools. The Triple P-Positive Parenting Program (Sanders, 2003; Sanders, Turner, & Markie-Dadds, 2002) is an evidence-based program of parent reeducation that has spread around the world (Sanders, 2012) and been studied in relation to its applicability with parents of culturally diverse backgrounds (Morawska et al., 2011). Triple P helps parents to experience and learn the values and skills that they may have missed growing up. They become connected to a community that they may not be familiar with due to a transient lifestyle or recent immigration. The program can be built into residential care settings or implemented in community and family to build skills and external supports foster family resiliency.

Therapeutic holding is a controversial technique that purports to use attachment theory and its application to development as a basis. The principle is that genuine attachment experiences are critical for healthy development, that children must be held and cared about in order to survive and grow to their full potential. Such experiences can be provided later in life through therapeutic holding. **Physical restraint** is different from therapeutic holding and is a behaviour management technique used when children who lose control and strike out with aggression are physically held while the staff offer reassurances until control is regained (Jeffery, 2010; Sourander, Ellila, Valimaki, & Piha, 2002). Research on both techniques examines the controversy and the lack of clear theory, research, and policy to guide practitioners in understanding the issues involved.

Attachment theory has been used as a basis for implementing a number of therapies, which often involve the parent or parent figure actively in the therapy. These techniques include therapeutic holding, rage reduction, and thera-play and have been strongly criticized for both failing to match the appropriateness of the adult behavior to the age of the child and for provoking anger or holding children without consideration for their rights or safety (Allen, 2011). Indeed there is evidence that misuse of therapeutic holding techniques and the improper use of physical restraint has caused deaths among young people in care (Allen, 2011; Day, Daffern, & Simmons, 2010; Nunno, Holden, & Tollar, 2006).

Steckley (2012) interviewed staff and young people in an effort to understand the dynamics of physical restraint as it related to young people's unfulfilled need for touch. Her findings clearly indicate the lack of comfort that staff had with physical restraint as well as the anger of young people at something that they perceived as a restrictive infringement on their rights. However, she theorizes that when opportunities for touch and affection are created between young people and practitioners that are developmentally and situationally appropriate, the need for restraint appears to decrease (Steckley, 2010).

The use of physical restraint as a behaviour management technique gives very little consideration to developmental needs. The intent is simply to control the young person's aggressive or out-of-control behaviour. Indeed, reviews of the use of physical restraint and seclusion (another method of controlling aggressive behavior) have indicated that "except for duration, data about the effectiveness of seclusion and restraints were missing, although there is some indication that seclusion and restraints can lead to severe psychological and physical consequences" (De Hert, Dirix, Demunter, & Correll, 2011, p. 221). Public policy, regulations, organizational policy, and rights legislation offer conflicting and varied guidance about how to manage apparently dangerous behaviour by young people by using physical intervention or seclusion. Additionally, there is no clear research evidence of the effectiveness of such techniques and studies purporting to offer such evidence must be critically examined to determine whether their theoretical and empirical foundations are consistent with the outcomes described.

SUMMARY

This chapter has considered the applied human development domain. Theoretical concepts and applied developmental interventions were introduced within four subdomains. Developmental theory and research is based on Western culture and examples of how difficult it is to apply this perspective in a non-Western context were provided to remind you that critical reflective thinking as well as self-reflection is important to understanding the developmental trajectories of the young people with which you work. The domain of applied human development is constantly evolving and professional learning activities will be part of your regular practice. The strengths-based, resiliency-focused orientation of child and youth care practice was contrasted to the deficit-based, psychopathology orientation of other disciplines and jurisdictions in which you may work. Offering a critical perspective to the work of other disciplines becomes a method of advocating for the young people that you work with.

Photo by Laine Robertson

CHAPTER EXERCISES

MY AGES AND STAGES

Experience: Personal Reflection

This reflection has several parts. To begin with, consider your life thus far. How would you describe the stages of your life? What were the important markers of life transitions? What approximate ages did these various stages cover?

Reflection-on-Practice

Draw a timeline of your own development and note critical transitions points in your life.

How would you describe your "stages of development"?

What were the important developmental tasks or accomplishments for you in each stage and what aspect of development did they address—cognitive, emotional, social, physical, spiritual, other?

Would you consider those developmental accomplishments to be "typical" of someone in that stage of development?

What variations do you notice, and how are they related to the environment you grew up in?

Would your "ages and stages" be accurate descriptors in Jamaica, South Africa, Japan, Russia, Columbia, a remote Aboriginal community in Canada, or another country or region?

Theory-in-Practice

Choose a developmental theory such as attachment theory, the Circle of Courage®, Forty Developmental Assets, Maslow's hierarchy of needs, Erikson's psychosocial stages of development, or another developmental theory that you are interested in.

Review several descriptions of the theory and make note of the implications for working with young people. How does the theory explain your own development?

What will you do differently with young people as a result of learning more about this theory?

Observe a young person and look for examples of the theory in action as represented in the young person's behavior. Discuss what you find with someone else—no matter whether they know the theory or not.

WHAT IS HUMAN DEVELOPMENT? WHAT IS NORMATIVE?

Experience: Autry's Development

Recall from Chapter 5: At age 18 Autry is leaving adolescence and entering adulthood. He feels pressured to go to the university and establish a vocation. He also feels pulled to look after his younger siblings. His adolescence was filled with incidents of discrimination based on his ethnic background and these have influenced his developmental path. Autry also faces subtle systemic discrimination because of poverty and lifestyle. Autry's ethnic and cultural background as well as other aspects of diversity have affected his growth and development and will continue to influence his developmental path.

- Consider Autry's childhood development and try to identify normative age-related events, normative historical events, and non-normative life events (make a list). You may need to review Chapter 5 and extrapolate based on the case study outlined there.
- Consider your own childhood development up to the age of 18 and create a similar list to compare to the one that you made for Autry.

Reflection-in-Practice: Similarities and Differences

Reflect on the similarities and differences and consider how you feel and also how you would explain the differences (or similarities) between your own development and Autry's developmental path.

Identify the important dimensions of development for yourself and Autry (social, cultural, physical, emotional, spiritual, and cognitive). Create a bar chart and extend the line in each area to demonstrate whether you were an average 18-year-old in each of these areas. Make a judgment about where to rank your development in comparison to the "normal" bar at age 18 and where to rank Autry's development in comparison to "normal."

Are you normal or abnormal? What defines normal?

Reflection-for-Practice: Language

Reflect carefully on this language (normal/abnormal) and how it values or devalues certain events and people in relation to an artificial (average) standard.

SELF-TALK

Theory-in-Action

Find a quiet space and kneel or sit cross-legged for a brief meditation. The point of meditation is to clear your mind so that nothing is present and you can be in tune to the moment.

Once you are comfortable, close your eyes. Take deep and slow breaths; focus on your breath. See if you can clear your mind. It takes years of practice, so don't expect that it will happen easily. Instead, note the thoughts that come into your mind. Wisk them out again (picture a broom) and do not dwell on them.

When you have finished (5 minutes is maximum), take a few moments to recall and reflect on the thoughts that came to mind. Write them down. Can you identify a source for this "self-talk"? Are your attributions negative or positive, internal or external? How have these thoughts affected your development as a person? What experiences and memories are they related to and how could you develop a different pattern of relating to people? What would you need to do to "re-program"?

PSYCHOTROPIC MEDICATION FOR YOUNG PEOPLE

This exercise involves examining your own values, beliefs, and ethics and doing some research to find support for your views as well as the views of other professionals. Preparing a good argument involves knowing both sides of the debate.

Experience: Recall

Recall an experience that you have had with a young person on psychotropic medication. Briefly describe that experience. What did you observe and experience? Use some of the skills from Chapter 8 to be factual and descriptive and avoid interpretation. Recall and record your own thoughts and feelings at the time. (Use the chart below to make note of your actions, thoughts, and feelings in the top box.)

Reflection-for-Practice

What learning stayed with you from that experience and how did the experience form your values, beliefs, and ethics? Make note of your values, beliefs, and ethics in the lower box on the right. Reminders and examples of the concepts (value, belief, ethic) based on Chapter 3 are provided. Can you offer any theoretical or research-based explanation for your observation of the young person?

RECORD THE EXPERIENCE: NOTE YOUR ACTIONS, THOUGHTS, AND FEELINGS.

ASPECTS OF SELF	EXAMPLES	MAKE NOTE OF ALL YOUR RELEVANT VALUES, BELIEFS, AND ETHICS ABOUT THE USE OF PSYCHOTROPIC MEDICATION.
Values: The positive or negative evaluations	Control is essential. Creativity is good. Distractibility is bad.	
Beliefs: True statements about your experience of reality	Ritalin distorts children's perceptions. Busy and distracted children are unable to learn in school. Ritalin focuses a child's attention.	
Ethics: "Rules" for behaviour	Medicate distractible children. Channel energy into creative activity, supporting strength.	

RESILIENCE ASSESSMENT

Theory-in-Practice

Choose one of the following websites to complete a critical reflection.

Developmental Assets

http://search-institute.org/developmental-assets

Resiliency Canada

www.resiliencycanada.ca/

Alternatively, if your library has Strengths-Based Counselling with At-Risk Youth (Ungar, 2006), explore Chapter 7 and the resiliency inventory.

All of these resources have inventories that assess resilience based on intrinsic personality factors, extrinsic family and community supports, and finally cultural considerations. There are many inventories available on the Web; be cautious and evaluate whether the concept of resilience in such inventories is related to individual factors only, or includes family, community, and culture.

Complete a self-assessment using the list of factors that (one of) these theorists propose will enhance your capacity to deal with adversity. Use a 1–5 rating scale where 1 = not at all and 5 = a lot and determine how much each factor applies to you. Redo the assessment to consider different points in time during your development such as infancy, preschool, school-age, adolescence, and now (adulthood) and note the factors that have changed substantially. Make particular note of periods of your life where you faced adversity or had a difficult time. Does your score change at these times? How do you make sense of the difference—or lack of difference—in the score?

What, if any, factors are missing that you believe contributed to your resilience process, your capacity to cope with adversity? Which factors are not at all relevant for you in your community? How does your culture come into play in this assessment? What are your values and beliefs surrounding these factors and their role in meeting your developmental needs?

EVIDENCE-INFORMED PRACTICE INQUIRY

Experience

Using Google Scholar or the electronic databases of an academic library, search for research findings on one or more of the following:

- Positive peer culture
- Attachment holding or holding therapy
- Physical restraint
- Transitional objects
- Transformational objects
- Circle of Courage®
- Forty Developmental Assets
- Developmental screening tools

Reflection-for-Practice

Review some of the abstracts and summarize the "hits" (items that you found) in relation to the following questions:

- How many publications deal with the specific request that you made and how many are "close"?
- How recent are the publications?
- How many are research reports and how many are theoretical discussions?
- What do the articles identify as "practice implications"?

Based on what you learned, would you use the intervention and under what conditions? What is the evidence that this will be an effective strategy and for whom might it be most effective?

PERSONAL REFLECTION: YOUTH

From Letters of Hope Project (www.letterstoastreetchild.ca)

Dear precious child,

Know that as you read this letter it was written just for you. I knew that one day you would come to hold this book in your hands. I appreciate the beauty of who you are and the journey you have been on to get here. The world is truly a better place because you are in it. Take a moment and celebrate the gift you are; there is only one you in the entire universe. You are here for a specific purpose and your presence in the world makes a difference.

I write from my heart with the energy of healing and ask that you let it surround you. Know that you are loved, and that it is my intention to move you to a deep place of connection within as you read my written words. Often I am asked how I survived the darkest moments of my life, and it's simple— I put my pen to paper. When it seemed that everything I could possibly lose was gone, I would be reminded of the power I could express through my writing. Just breathe and let the words flow, for they bear an important truth for the essence of your soul.

I am not my story. I am a reflection of what I have chosen to do with my life's experiences. As I reflect on my life, I feel gratitude. I have found beauty in places where it is difficult to find. Those who hurt us the most are our greatest teachers and need to be loved and forgiven the most.

If you have been adopted, know that I feel the pain of rejection and abandonment. I understand your confusion. You may not know why those who were supposed to take care of you are not doing so. I know the emptiness you feel in your heart. Know that you are so very special, and that you are loved just for being you. Adopt a family of love within your heart.

If you have been in foster care, know that I feel the loss of identity and not belonging. I know what it's like not to have someone to call "mom" or "dad." I have lived with all my belongings stored in garbage bags, afraid to unpack because I didn't know how long I would be staying. I feel the rage of having no place to call home. I know the anguish of recognizing that I'm a statistic, a file for someone's case load. Know that you make a difference in all the lives you come in contact with, for they witness your resilience. Foster a strong sense of identity and share your talents with the world.

If you have been sexually abused, I weep with you for the innocence that was taken. I remember the nights lying awake in terror, waiting to hear the footsteps coming down the hallway. Taking baths in scalding hot water, scrubbing so hard until the skin was raw, wanting to feel clean only to shake in uncontrollable sobs because it owns the inside of you. Trying to look ugly so the world knows how you feel; trying to look perfect so the world won't see how damaged you are. Know that your tears are beautiful and I honor you for your strength. No one can ever take away the beauty of your healing.

If you have ever attempted to commit suicide, or thought life wasn't worth living, I've felt that despair. A bottle of pills, a slash of the wrists, a letter written for no one to ever read. Lying in bed for days on end wishing it would all just disappear. Know that your life is worth living. I want you to live. People are waiting for you so that they can love you in all the magnificence of who you are. You are so worthy.

If you have been physically abused, I feel the wince of pain with each blow given. I feel your head pounding from tears you're holding back because you dare not show your weakness. I remember lying in a ball, curled up, holding my breath and trying not to move. Trying to hide the bruises that screamed the evidence of what you were denying. Know that you are lovingly embraced by the healing graces of the Universe. Allow yourself to be sheltered in the arms of hope.

If you have been emotionally abused, I hear the voices that scream in your mind, for they also scream in mine. I know how it feels to be paralyzed in fear, thinking you are never good enough. Constantly waiting for the world to collapse around you. Know that you are valued and respected. I believe in you. I offer support and encouragement as you pursue your dreams.

If you have ever suffered with addiction, I know the clutches of the heartbreaking despair it leaves in its path. I've felt the ecstasy of its seduction and promise to take my pain away. The endless, sleepless days with no trace of who I am remaining on my face. The greatest love of your life that everyone wants you to leave. Know that love is the only substance that gives you real peace. Become addicted to becoming the person you are meant to be.

If you have ever given birth only to have your child raised by someone else, I know the sadness of hearing the word "mother." I know what it is like to have all those around you unable to understand that becoming a mother has only proven that you are unable to raise a child. No book you read or advice given to you can ever replace the experience that you never had as a child. I have felt the grief of a childhood robbed. Know that in this moment, you are giving birth to a new you. A you that has all the knowledge needed to give you the best care. A bond has been formed that never can be broken.

If you have ever prostituted yourself, I know the guilt and shame you feel. The confusing identity that comes from selling your body while remaining unattached to your heart. Never understanding the true meaning of love. Know that love is experienced in building a relationship with ourselves. We teach others how to treat us. Respect and honor your body for the gift of life it gives you, celebrate each moment you are given.

If you have ever been homeless, I know the longing of wanting a bed to sleep upon. Wanting to be able to sleep in safety, not in fear. The constant struggle of trying to survive through another day. Know that you are at home when you look within your heart. This is the language of the soul, the place where you are always welcomed.

If you have ever been raped, I feel your agony and the anguish for all that was taken. I replay the scene leading up to it with the constant thought, "I should have known better." I know what it is to lie on an examination table while evidence is collected for a crime that will never be tried. Know that you are heard by the Universe when you say "no." The tears you cry are wiped away with the cleansing power of love.

If you have ever lost a loved one whose life was taken by murder I know the intense grief felt as you are left questioning "why." The moments spent wishing you had said and done so many things when they were still here. Trying to grasp how you can find forgiveness. Know that your loved one is always with you. You will forever carry them within your heart. Cherish the beauty of the moments you were given together.

If . . .

If . . .

If . . .

If you have experienced hope like I have then you know there is a brighter future in store. It is my hope that you may find peace as you begin the journey of becoming whole again. Speak of the tragedies you have witnessed. Express the anger that is pent up within you. Scream at the top of your lungs with all the rage you have held onto. Allow the tears to flow freely even though you fear they may never end. Let your body shake uncontrollably with the sobs of sadness for all that was taken from you. Pound your fists in anger for the innocence that was lost.

This is your time to claim what is rightfully yours. Take back your life and begin to live from a place of personal truth. Surround yourself with people who love and honor you for the beauty of you. Follow your heart and live from a place of passion. Believe in your dreams and the abilities you possess to make them reality.

Until our paths cross again know that I am so very proud of you. I believe in you and love you. I wish you blessings of happiness, hope, and possibility. Let your light shine for the entire world to see!

Blessings,

Violet-Rose 29 years old, Vancouver, British Columbia

CHAPTER 11

THE SYSTEMS CONTEXT

Photo by Laine Robertson

CHAPTER OBJECTIVES

- To introduce "thinking systemically," a conceptual framework that influences how developmental assessment and intervention occurs.
- To consider the environmental conditions in which young people and families live.
- To describe how the historical and cultural environments of young people and families create influence.
- To describe the political, community, and family environment.
- To identify the systems with which the young person, family, and practitioner interact.

263

When child and youth care began shortly after World War II, consideration of the many systems in which young people were embedded wasn't part of the work. Young people were orphans, or thought to be discarded by families struggling with poverty who could not afford to feed them. Taking care of young people was a means of preventing criminal activity, leading them toward a more productive life as adults. In more modern practice, thinking about the young person as a member of many different systems is essential. Not only do practitioners work in many different milieus under various jurisdictions, but young people enter those milieus with preexisting relationships with people and institutions that are not immediately apparent to the practitioners, and yet those "invisible" people and systems may have significant effects on the young person and your work together. Some relationships may be professional, others may be with family members or friends. These relationships are important resources. Research has demonstrated that one of the most important contributing factors to a child's success following placement in residential care is family involvement during the placement (Curtis, Alexander, & Lunghofer, 2001; Frensch & Cameron, 2002).

Using a systemic framework orients the practitioner to the complexity within the young person's environments and helps practitioners to understand environmental influences on development. Central to the systems orientation is the idea that all the components of a system are interrelated. Thus, changes to one part of the system influence other components and affect the possibilities for growth, change, and successful outcomes for the young person and family. Assessing the systems in which young people are involved helps to identify realistic goals for change and assists the practitioner to identify other professionals and programs that will contribute to a successful developmental process. This chapter introduces some basic concepts by considering four subdomains:

- **Systems theory**, which describes what a system is and how different systems operate.
- The **ecological perspective** and **family systems** provide the novice practitioner with two basic frameworks for identifying and describing the components of the environments and systems that are important to the young person.
- The **legal system** of provincial, state, federal and international rules and regulations that affect young people.

THINK ABOUT IT

Consider Autry's (introduced in Chapter 5) circumstances and the many systems in which he is involved, as well as the cultural and ethnic influences on Autry's development. As a young Jamaican-Canadian there are multiple systems that affect Autry. His family, school, peer group, and church are all groups of people with norms, rules, and structures that define how Autry relates to the group and the people within the group. The practitioner who thinks systemically recognizes that Autry's family is likely a strong support for him, providing practical and material support as well as emotional support and guidance. At the same time, Autry returns this support to his family and worries about them, caring for his sisters above himself. Who else does he consider to be part of his family? As a high school graduate he probably has some teachers who were connected with him and were supportive throughout his time at school. He may have seen a counsellor at school or a mental health counsellor in the community. The social trend of increasing enrolment in university has likely affected his goals for the future while at the same time the economic circumstances of the family and the restrictive rules about student loans limit his ability to meet those goals. These are all points of intervention for the practitioner who thinks systemically and there may already be other people in those other systems and environments that Autry has been involved in who are helping him.

Young people live in complex, open systems such as families, schools, and communities. The issues and concerns that they bring to the child and youth care practitioner must be understood within the nature of those systems and how they affect the child. In child and youth care practice, **relationships** are the vehicle by which practitioners humanize the often frustrating and impersonal systems context in which they work. Working relationally brings the **systems context** together with an understanding of **human development** (see **Figure 11.1**) to more comprehensively understand the resources and strengths that young people and families bring to their lives and identify where to intervene and create change.

SYSTEMS THEORY

General systems theory was originally proposed by biologist Ludwig von Bertalanffy in 1928. The scientific analysis of the time assumed that things could be broken into individual components and the effect of each component could be discretely predicted and analyzed in a linear manner. von Bertalanffy suggested that this assumption was incorrect. Basically, he argued that *the sum of the whole is greater than its parts*, by which he meant that when there is a relationship between two or more things, and that when those things work together, they will have a different effect than applying or analyzing the effect of each thing separately. Together, you and I can change the world, but individually even if we add together what we are doing, we don't have the same effect! Systems are thought of as open or closed. You cannot add components to closed

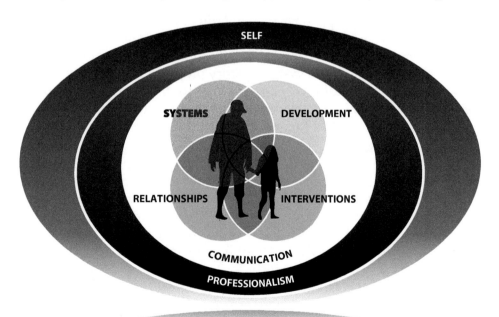

Figure 11.1   The Domain of the Systems Context

systems, and they tend to break down over time, becoming more disorganized, though initially they may appear to be more functional. Consider a car or other mechanical object as a relatively closed system. New ones work really well, look great, and are fun to drive, but eventually they become increasingly noisy, temperamental, and prone to break down. Of course, as this example illustrates, closed systems are a theoretical concept, which do not account for the extent of interrelatedness in an environment. Cars are exposed to weather, repair people, accidents with other cars, even the driver, all of which influence the course of their "breakdown."

The concepts of general systems theory began to enter the social sciences and human services in the 1950s when von Bertalanffy came to Canada. Systems psychology, organizational psychology, and family systems therapy began to emerge as areas of study using system theory concepts. In the late 1970s, ecological systems theory was first proposed as a mechanism for better understanding young people's development beyond the laboratory (where psychologists were studying early childhood development in detail). These new ideas helped explain phenomena such as why, when young people were placed in residential care for a period of time, their behaviours would "correct" and as soon as they were returned to their family and community, the problems would begin again. The ideas of systems theory are also applicable to teams and organizations.

Systems can be as small as a single person and as large as a culture, as determined by the members of the system. Social systems theory draws on general systems theory and proposes that social systems are "open" systems (as opposed to closed or isolated), and that all social systems share common characteristics:

- **Boundaries** are the vague and subjective limits that define a system as separate from the rest of the environment. Boundaries are created by the members of the system to determine who participates in the system and how. Recall the boundaries discussion in Chapter 6? Boundaries are set both individually and collectively.

- **Membership** includes the people who are regularly part of the system and in many ways may be self-defined. Statements such as "I work for . . . ," "This is my family," "I belong to . . ." are all statements of membership in a social system. If members of a system only interact inside the system, then general systems theory proposes that entropy or chaos results, involving a significant expenditure of energy with no useful work being done. In other words, bringing new people into a place of employment is good and, while disagreement may result, systems theory would suggest that remaining closed to input would be worse.

- **Rules and norms** for interaction are defined among members of the system, both within and outside the boundaries of the system. Some rules will be explicit and clearly stated and others are implicit. Implicit rules are not immediately obvious to outsiders who join the organization and must be learned over time. As a new practitioner in an elementary school you will be told what time work starts and ends and some guidelines about how to interact with young people. To learn whether people socialize outside of the school day, you will have to observe and listen closely to find out how members talk about those friendships during school.

- **Functional and structural** relationships among members describe the "on-paper" organizational structure and the functional reporting structure. The organizational structure and the functional structure may be different. In essence, this is the hierarchy and the power structure of the organization. **Complexity** within the system describes the number of connected parts and multiple levels, as well as the entanglement among the parts and members of a system.

- **Feedback** loops are the processes by which information is fed back into the system to help maintain **homeostasis** or equilibrium (balance) within the system. When feedback indicates that the system is moving away from a desirable state, then corrective actions are initiated.

- All systems also have specific **processes for change** and making adjustments to environmental inputs that lead to systemic "learning" and "development." Like individual organisms, systems can change and develop over time. Development is smooth and relatively painless if the system has a process for incorporating change.

Any system can be described and understood in terms of these characteristics and the theory should make predictions about what will happen when change occurs in the system and how to manage change. Systems concepts can be applied to families, friendship groups, businesses, neighbourhoods, religious and ethnic affiliations, governments, and just about anything that involves multiple people and relationships.

Systems theory provides an organizing schema that emphasizes the relationships among the individual, family, service, and community, and describes how these groups work together. This knowledge helps the practitioner to develop integrated and holistic approaches for young people and their families. There are systems and "subsystems" that are related within the larger system of society. As general systems theory became popular in the 1960s and 1970s, researchers and theorists interested in family dynamics began to adapt the concepts to explain family functioning and to guide family interventions.

FAMILY SYSTEMS

Optimal development occurs within the family and surrounding social environment. When young people stray from the path of optimal development, practitioners with a sound knowledge of family systems theory value the family's input and ensure that cultural values and beliefs held by young people and families are respected. Understanding families in the child and youth care approach means meeting them within their own environment, focusing on their needs, and working with daily life events to understand how the precepts of family systems theory work in this particular family (Garfat, 2007; Garfat & Charles, 2010). The family home is a milieu for practice in child and youth care; however, a **mature** practitioner ensures that family issues, ideas, and ideals are respected even when the young person cannot live at home.

Tips and Resources

Learn more about family and the culturally relevant family approaches to Aboriginal Child Welfare.

Putting a Human Face on Child Welfare: Voices from the Prairies
http://cwrp.ca/node/907

Learn more about trauma-informed family-based approaches to working with urban families living in poverty.

Understanding the Impact of Trauma and Urban Poverty on Family Systems: Risks, Resilience, and Interventions.
http://nctsn.org/nccts/nav.do?pid=ctr_rsch_prod_ar
http://nctsn.org/products/nctsn-affiliated-resources/understanding-impact-trauma-and-urban-poverty-family-systems

Family Informed Trauma Treatment Centre
http://fittcenter.umaryland.edu/

Family systems theory follows the basic ingredients and assumptions of social systems theory, however, in applying the concepts to the family the terminology is more specific. Family systems therapists have used these concepts to explain difficult behaviours by family members, thereby guiding intervention with the family. As with other theoretical perspectives, family systems theory is set within a Western approach to the concept of family. Practitioners must think carefully about the transfer of family systems concepts to working with families who have immigrated and/or grown up in a distinct and separate culture within North America. Increasingly family approaches are recognizing the importance of larger forces such as the culture of poverty and its influence on trauma and family violence (Collins et al., 2010).

Family systems theorists began by applying the basic concepts of general systems theory.[1] The family as a system has **boundaries** that vary in the degree to which they are closed or open. **Open** family systems allow and encourage contacts outside of the family (including friendships, social events) and invite others in. **Closed** families are more restrictive and have more rules that limit friendships and socialization with others. Within the basic family system there are **sibling/child subsystems** and **parent subsystems** and each subsystem has a different role and responsibility within the family. There is also the extended family system. Identifying and describing the boundaries of a system, the subsystems, and the open or closed nature of a family is a culturally bound exercise because the family exists within the cultural system.

Family systems concepts have been used extensively within the child welfare jurisdiction to guide policy and practice, and do not always recognize the culturally bound aspects of the theory. Typically, child welfare interventions in families assume a nuclear family boundary and that responsibility for parenting rests with the parents. Members of cultures that don't hold this same bounded view of family have worked to develop alternative approaches. Family Group Conferencing, for example, which emerged from the concerns of the Indigenous Maori population in New Zealand and is used by many Aboriginal Child Welfare agencies in Canada, casts a very wide net in finding the family members to participate in a family conference (Desmeules, 2007). "Pre-conference planning is when the bulk of the work takes place. On average, community facilitators . . . spend 40 to 60 hours over a 4- to 6-week period . . . [and] the widest net is cast by inviting all family and kin, regardless of whether they have been estranged from the child and family for years" (Desmeules, 2007, p. 173). This is a very different approach from meeting just with the parents to discuss options.

Family systems theory assesses family function with the assumption that the family has an emotional climate that is generated by the relationships within the family. Family systems theorists view the parents as key to family function and believe that the parent subsystem should be emotionally cohesive and distinct from the subsystem of the children, for which it has caretaking responsibilities. When conflict or emotional tension arises between the parents, how that conflict is handled is thought to have implications for family functioning. One parent may go to a child to try and relieve that tension. Sharing information, spending time together, and asking the child to perform functions that the other parent might do (ranging from simple chores to caring for other siblings) creates a **triangle** between the parents and the child. Triangulation is thought to

---

[1] The concepts presented here are a brief overview combined from the theoretical works of Murray Bowen (intergenerational transmission), Salvador Minuchin (structural family therapy), Virginia Satir (conjoint family therapy), Carl Whitaker (family systems), Paul Watzlawick (communication theory), and others who had a significant influence on the concepts and language that frame contemporary work with families.

reduce the tension and stabilize the parent subsystem, creating equilibrium or homeostasis in the family system. While this strategy may work for a short while, family systems theory suggests that the triangulated child eventually becomes overwhelmed with the emotional tension and responsibility for maintaining family equilibrium and attempts to **distance emotionally**. The attempts to distance can involve arguments with parents, running away, silence, even the development of a mental illness. Family systems theorists often see these as strategies on the part of the child to bring the parents together over a common cause and at the same time distract them from their own tension in the relationship. Increasingly it is recognized that families are sensitive to the traumatic context of urban poverty and this context creates an emotional climate of trauma and conflict. The conflict does not just sit within the parent subsystem. It is critical to use strategies that include alliances with both primary and extended family systems so that family coping skills are enhanced. It is also essential to recognize the cultural variations in family roles and functions (Collins et al., 2010)

Of course, all of the family systems concepts described above are immersed in cultural assumptions about the nature of family and even then, as societal definitions of family changed and divorce became easier to obtain, the basic concepts seem simplistic when applied to modern families. Modern families in a multicultural society may have one parent, stepparents, same-sex parents, multiple homes, adopted siblings from different ethnic origins, stepsiblings, grandparents living within the home, or may consist of grandparents raising a grandchild as if it were their own (and many more variations). Family systems theory therefore gives practitioners a common language and framework to begin comparing their own definitions of family with those of the program in which they work, and how the young person or family might potentially define their own family. However, given the diversity of family in today's society, it provides only a beginning point.

Not all child and youth care practitioners work with families. Even if the program and milieu in which you work does not encourage family contact, it would be a significant error in judgement not to be aware of the importance of family. The child and youth care practitioner will encounter families in many situations:

- At interdisciplinary conferences
- As parents or older siblings pick children up during school or at community programs
- During home visits
- In the "minds" of children
- In formal family-based intervention programs

The practitioner touches the daily lives of families in many ways, entering relationships and bringing the characteristics of child and youth care practice forward into those relationships (Garfat, 2003; Garfat & Charles, 2010; Shaw & Garfat, 2003; VanderVen, 2003). Child and youth care practitioners simply enter into relationships and into the daily life of the family as they do with young people. In essence, the practitioner is incorporated into the family system, creating relationships with family members and being aware of self and "other" within those relationships. Even within a "closed" residential care setting where the practitioner may never meet the young person's family, the family is brought to the context of the relationship that you have with the young person through the exploration of life-space, and therefore, family relationships should be explored and understood. In family-based milieus where the practitioner enters the family's home, understanding and exploring family relationships (inside and outside the home) becomes a conversation, a focus for relational intervention. Being effective in a relationship with family members requires a significant degree of self-awareness about your own family, including its history, secrets, relationships, culture, and more.

Child and youth care practitioners who work in family homes step into the family activities. They assist with planning recreational activities, getting meals together, or doing laundry and, along the way, help the family to more clearly understand young people and how to support the them toward the goals they have (Shaw & Garfat, 2003). A relational approach means that the practitioner helps the family, through the implementation of relationship, to find more effective ways of interacting and being together (Garfat, 2003). Practitioners help the family focus on social competence and care about each other in their relationships. They implement all the interventions described in Chapter 12, using the family home as the milieu and the family as the group within which change will occur.

Family is just one system in which a young person participates. The ecological perspective is an organizing framework for social systems that helps practitioners understand how development is influenced by multiple systems (Bronfennbrenner, 1979). The ecological perspective is described in the next section and the concepts are applied to understanding how systems affect development and how policy on providing care and intervention with young people has been shaped using ecological ideas.

ECOLOGICAL PERSPECTIVE

The ecological perspective emphasizes the interaction between people and their physical and social environments, including cultural and political settings. Practitioners need to understand how institutional systems such as justice, health, child welfare, and education can help or restrict the growth and development of young people. Practitioners undertake systemic assessments in family, peer, and community systems and believe in the importance of engaging these systems in an effort to meet young people's needs.

The concepts of the ecological perspective were introduced in Chapters 4 and 5. Recall the diagram, illustrated here in **Figure 11.2**, which identifies the many systems that may be present in a child or family's life.

An economic crisis cannot be controlled by parent or practitioner and will affect the family's capacity to provide proper nutrition, dental care, and perhaps even safe housing. Events in a larger system (e.g., political scandals, family income) can impact daily life even when the child is not involved in that system, perhaps because of placement in group home care. Autry worries about his siblings and his parents. If he were placed in a residential group home he would still worry and if his parents could not afford gas to drive and visit him, he would be concerned and possibly angry. Institutional employment policies can strongly influence young people's development within the care system. If there are not enough practitioners to keep children safe or to plan and implement recreational activities, then social and physical development is restricted. A cutback in funding from the local school district for a community school means that the school can no longer be open after school hours and young people in the community (perhaps a community of poverty and prone to higher rates of violence) can no longer attend the local community centre, which was housed in the school. More young people are at risk for violence or entering the young offender system as they search for relationships and social and recreational activities.

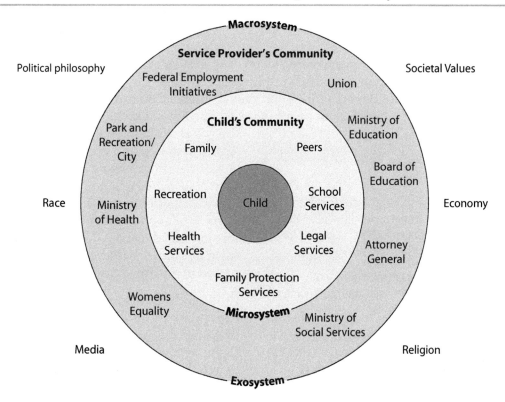

Figure 11.2   An Ecological Description of Influences on Young People, Families, and Service Providers

The ecological perspective was introduced to child and youth care practice as a means for understanding and assessing the influences on young people's development, just as Bronfenbrenner (1979) intended. The developing young person in the centre of the circle in **Figure 11.3** has a basic biological makeup and genetic predisposition but then follows a developmental path that is influenced by the people, environmental spaces, values, and beliefs of the systems in which he or she is living. As practitioners work with and support that young person to be competent and resilient and to maximize development, they assess the environments as well and consider the interaction between the two. Young people are active in influencing their environments and processing the conditions of their environments. Resilience occurs through the processes involved in mutual influences as well as the characteristics and conditions of the environments that surround the young person. How young people understand

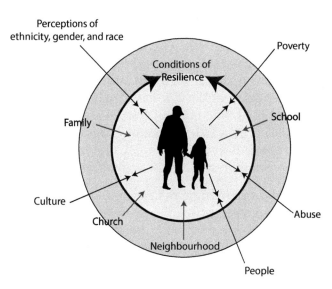

Figure 11.3   Ecological Influences on Development Which Mediate Risk

and interpret poverty, abuse, community violence, gender, race, and ethnicity, varies therefore the same conditions can have different effects.

The family can be a milieu for intervention; so too can the systems in which a child participates present opportunities for intervention (Munger, 1998). In an effort to support young people in their communities, practitioners work in different milieus. Community centers and schools provide an opportunity to work with peers to help a socially awkward child learn and practice social skills and help other young people learn tolerance and compassion for difference. Practitioners may have a conversation with a soccer coach about how to instruct a child with attention difficulties, which supports the development of a life-long passion for sports and teaches the child how to cooperate in groups based on successful participation in a team sport.

Child and youth care practitioners, as they expanded the milieus within which they practiced, began to shift from simply applying a family systems or ecological perspective to the individual development of young people. They now integrate the characteristics of their child and youth care practice into family, school, and community settings, working with the settings as well as individual young people. The previous section discussed how child and youth care practice might work within a family-based milieu as a context for practice. Now let's consider how child and youth care approaches can be integrated into the community ecology. Beyond understanding the influence of the ecology on the individual or the family, the ecological system becomes a locus for intervention and change.

Tips and Resources

Systems of Care is a philosophical approach to working with young people and families who are vulnerable to mental health concerns. Several sites explain the history and philosophy and offer links to other resources.

www.childwelfare.gov/management/reform/soc/
www.aacap.org/cs/systems_of_care_and_collaborative_models/system_of_care_resources

Wrap Around is a specific technology or approach to systems of care and the following sites promote the use of wraparound and provide training and support.

www.wrapcanada.org
www.nwi.pdx.edu

The ecological perspective on development helps child and youth care practitioners put the meaning of young people's behaviour into an environmental context to understand the developmental paths that young people are following. As social service, mental health, education, and even criminal justice systems have recognized that the ecology influences development, policy and intervention programs have focused on change strategies that use the young person's ecology rather than focusing just on strategies for changing individual behaviour. Intervention programs such as multisystemic family therapy (Henggeler, 1993) and Systems of Care (Stroul & Friedman, 1986), sometimes referred to as "Wraparound," are examples of programs that use ecological principles.

Positive youth development (PYD) expands the work of practitioners to include primary prevention. There is evidence that when there is a call to support young people who are troubled, the community tends to believe that this is a call for professional help (Sesma, Marnes, & Scales, 2006); however, if there is a call to help all young people develop to their maximum capacity, then community leaders will volunteer as mentors, leadership programs develop, and community centers attempt to engage *all* young people, creating a system of care. This creates a community-minded approach to ensuring that the assets of all youth are brought forward and supported and the responsibility for the success of young people is vested in their community

(McCammon, 2012). Positive Youth Development and the provision of leadership and mentoring programs that involve community leaders is a mechanism by which child and youth care practitioners can expand their influence and join with young people to create challenges to the underlying societal assumptions about young people as risk-takers or troublemakers.

Systems of Care (Stroul & Freidman, 1986) is an ecologically based intervention model that is consistent with the values, beliefs, and core characteristics of child and youth care practice. As adults and young people with severe mental and physical vulnerabilities have been deinstitutionalized, community-based mental health clinics needed to help people with complex needs, often people whose needs crossed numerous jurisdictions and service providers. Under the Systems of Care approach service provision is coordinated and the philosophical beliefs of partnership and a focus on strengths and competence that are part of child and youth care practice are embedded in the approach.[2]

Systems of Care is an approach to working with children and families that is:

> A comprehensive spectrum of mental health and other necessary services which are organized into a coordinated network to meet the multiple and changing needs of children and adolescents with severe emotional disturbances and their families. (Stroul & Friedman, 1986, cited in Arbuckle, 2006, p. 12)

The Systems of Care approach is appropriate for all young people, although it currently focuses on those with complex needs. It holds three core values. It is **child-centred and family-focused,** meaning that the families determine the nature and mix of services required. It is **community-based,** so that the child is not removed from the systems that already support his or her developmental needs. It is responsive to the **diversity** of young people and families, and therefore responds to the localized "macrosystem" of the child, family, and community (Arbuckle, 2006). Services and the professionals representing those services go *to* the young person and work in his or her milieu. They individualize the environments to meet the needs of the child and they never make decisions without the genuine involvement of young people and their families. The principles of engagement and caring, discussed in Chapter 9 are thought to be applied to all work in a Systems of Care approach.

The Systems of Care guiding principles are presented in **Table 11.1** with examples of how child and youth care practitioners can apply them in the milieu in which they are working, whether that is residential-, school-, or community-based care. Implementing a Systems of Care approach in a community is a task that must be achieved through a coordinated and integrated collaboration of all local service professionals. (See Chapter 8 on integrated service delivery and networking.) While an individual practitioner is unlikely to undertake such an initiative without the support of an agency contracted to deliver the service, you can use the principles of a Systems of Care approach in the work that you do in a community and incorporate the PYD approach. The principles in Table 11.1 are summarized from Arbuckle (2006).

---

[2] Personal reflection: Development of Wraparound is credited in several locations with following the philosophies of Browndale, an Ontario-based residential group care agency that developed in the early 1970s. Browndale offered small, multi-aged, community-based homes where "treatment plans" were individualized and families participated in treatment. I worked in several of those homes. I didn't consider them to be particularly unusual at the time and it was not until much later that I learned that the elements of what we did—family workers, case planning, involving parents in conferences, use of community schools and recreation programs, and so on—were not the "norm" for residential care programs in the late 1970s.

Table 11.1   Principles of the Systems of Care Approach Implemented in Child and Youth Care Practice

PRINCIPLE	CONSIDERATIONS AND STRATEGIES FOR THE CHILD AND YOUTH CARE PRACTITIONER
Comprehensive service provision	Young people "need" services that include recreation, opportunities for friendships, and address basic issues such as transportation and food security. Child and youth care practitioners in the community can facilitate their access to these services and advocate for the essential nature of these services for all young people.
Individualized needs and preferences	Each young person and family is unique and the preferences that they have should be respected and inquired about. What works for one young person or family will not work for another. The practitioner advocates for an individualized perspective.
Least restrictive/most normative environment	As much as possible young people and families should not have to leave their community to receive service. While this might mean initially a more intensive intervention, in the long term the young person will not have to deal with separating from and leaving family. Community-based practitioners hope to eradicate the need for their colleagues in residential care.
Family participation	Families should direct the planning for their children. The practitioner can encourage this by inviting the family's thoughts and supporting them to advocate for their needs and for the child's needs.
Service integration	Complex needs may require services from multiple jurisdictions such as child welfare, mental health, education, and justice simultaneously. Meeting together (with the family) to coordinate is essential, and the practitioner can inquire about timing and location of meetings—even volunteering to set them up in the absence of a formal System of Care.
Care coordination	Sometimes known as case management, it is essential that a single person be identified to coordinate the assessment of the family needs. In some circumstances the child and youth care practitioner might be the appropriate link between systems. In other circumstances, legislation will mandate a child protection worker or a justice worker as the coordinator.
Early identification and intervention	Early intervention has several meanings: early in the development of the child (e.g., prior to school age) or early in the development of the problem (e.g., when risk factors are identified). The premise is the same, intervening and providing assistance should happen as soon as risks are identified.

	Community- and school-based practitioners are in ideal positions to see early signs of potential difficulties with young people, bringing them to the attention of professionals who are in a position to intervene. Child and youth care practitioners are also in an ideal position within the community milieu to play the role of the case coordinator focused on early intervention. They might also identify "community risks" and help the community accept their responsibility to create programs that provide for positive youth development for all young people.
Smooth transitions	Young people experience natural life transitions, often around changes in school (elementary to middle to high school) and as they approach adulthood. The focus on lifespan development suggests that practitioners will support young people through those transitions and will maintain continuity of relationships to support the child.
Protection of rights and advocacy for the child	Child and youth care practitioners should operate from the perspective of the United Nations Convention on the Rights of the Child, and can use the convention to advocate for the needs of young people that they care for, ensuring that their needs are met and individual uniqueness is respected.
Nondiscrimination	The principle of responding to diversity and individual uniqueness runs throughout child and youth care practice. Taking a position of knowing about your own differences and noting your own experiences of discrimination, based on race, class, gender, sexual orientation, disability, religion, or other personal characteristics, enables you as a practitioner to enquire about and be sensitive to the experiences of the young people and families you work with trying to ensure that they have access to the services that they need.

An ecological perspective on young people and on practice implies that a much bigger picture is considered in the work that child and youth care practitioners undertake. The understanding of young people's circumstances is widened and the possibilities for intervention are expanded. Chapter 12 addresses some approaches to intervention and describes further the possibilities for case management from a systemic approach. The final aspect of the systems context that should be considered is the codified societal rules that are documented in the laws of society.

LEGAL GUIDELINES AND PRACTICE

Practice is guided by a set of legal rules governed by provincial and federal legislation concerning young people and families. These laws and guidelines are applied in everyday practice, and changes to the law need to be reviewed and understood immediately. Laws are a representation of the norms, rules, and culture of the dominant society in the country in which practice occurs, and therefore must be interpreted through an understanding of the diversity of people living in that society.

Because each country, state, or province is unique in the specific local legal requirements, and because laws are updated regularly, this section simply points to where to look and points to some of the things that practitioners must consider in their practice. Laws relevant to young people and families include those dealing with:

- Reporting of child abuse and neglect
- The requirement to provide for the education of young people, including those with special needs, and the specifics about how and where education must be provided
- The requirement to attend school prior to a certain age
- Laws related to criminal activity for young people under the age of majority
- Laws related to involuntary commitment due to mental illness as they relate to young people
- Laws related to requirements for developmental screening and health checks for preschool-age children.

Other, perhaps not so obvious laws of relevance include:

- Family laws related to divorce and custody of children
- Legislation about children's advocates (particularly relevant in Canada where independent advocates report to provincial governments)
- Laws related to licensing of children's services and facilities such as daycares, foster homes, and group care settings

Tips and Resources

Provincial, state, and federal laws and regulations can be easily found online using basic search terms that include the area of focus, location, and type of focus. For example, search for "Maryland Youth Laws" or "Canada Family Regulations" using your own social locations to begin narrowing the relevant areas of interest to your practice.

SUMMARY

This chapter has introduced concepts related to systems theory and detailed how those concepts are applied to understand families and to expand your understanding of work with young people and families to account for the multiple ecological contexts in which young people find themselves. The systems context not only helps practitioners assess and understand more clearly the many things that influence human development, it also provides a framework for structuring service provision. Challenges exist to the implementation of these ideas when human services are interdisciplinary, but using a systemic approach encourages novice and mature practitioners to join with other professionals and create higher-quality solutions that emerge from working in an interdependent manner. The challenge to child and youth care practitioners is to bring the unique values and language of the child and youth care approach to those interdisciplinary discussions.

The next chapter describes life-space interventions common to the milieu-based practice of child and youth care and examines "planned" interventions such as group work and advocacy. It describes further the child and youth care approach to intervention in the context of reflective practice and introduces an intervention planning approach that incorporates reflective practice.

Photo by Laine Robertson

CHAPTER EXERCISES

LOOKING FOR SYSTEM CONCEPTS

Theory-in-Action

Take a few minutes to apply the concepts of general systems theory to an organizational set-ting that you "belong to" by answering the following questions. You could choose any of the following systems: your tenants association; your place of work; a sports team or club that you belong to; a community interest group; your professional association; etc.

Describe the **boundaries** of the organization. What is the "outside" environment and what are the limits of the organization? Consider physical, social, or legal boundaries or limits.

Who is a member of the system and what are the requirements for **membership**?

Identify some of the explicit and implicit **rules and norms** for interacting with other members of the organization. Describe the norms for interactions with others outside of the system.

Diagram the organizational chart to represent the **structural relationships** among people within the organization. Think of something that you would like to see done differently and diagram who you would go to, and then where and how the decision to change would be made. This will start to diagram the functional relationships. Compare the two diagrams.

Describe the feedback loop that acts to keep things **balanced** in the organization.

Describe an event that happened outside the system that seemed to have an impact and require some response. How did the system incorporate the new conditions? How did it "learn"?

DEFINING FAMILY AS A CONCEPT

Theory-in-Action

What does "family" mean to you? How do you define the concept? What is the evidence or knowledge that your definition is based on? How do you "know" your definition of family is the true definition? Compare your definition to the definitions of a peer or a young person with which you work.

REFLECTING ON YOUR FAMILY "CULTURE"

Experience

Keeping in mind that culture includes the values, beliefs, and ethics of a group (in this case the family) that lead to personal actions and patterns of behavior (Garfat & Charles, 2010), this exercise asks you to use the concepts of **family systems theory** and the **aspects of self** framework from earlier chapters to describe your family.

Reflection-on-Practice

Membership: Who belongs in your family? How would you describe the subsystems and what are the connections between subsystems? Try to diagram or "map" your family membership and relationships. How has your ethnic or religious heritage contributed to your definition of family?

Roles/Rules/Relationships: Using the idea of "a week in the life of my family," identify the various activities that family members undertake on a routine basis. See if you can identify any family "sayings" that indicate how these activities were attached to various roles (e.g., the oldest child; "mom's job"; "dad's job"; "grandpa's story"). How does gender and age influence the roles and relationships in your family? What changes happened over the years and why?

Open/Closed: Describe your family rules and norms about visitors. How were friends of children and friends of adults incorporated into family activities and under what circumstances?

Stepping Out . . . When you began to see other people's families (in the past and more recently), what did you see and hear in other families that you assumed was characteristic of everyone's family? What was different and surprising? What differences can you attribute to the diverse nature of people such as ethnicity, religion, gender, age, sexual orientation, or disability and what differences are unique to your family?

Reflection-for-Practice

Compare your descriptions above to those of colleagues who have also done this exercise. Make note the differences and similarities, and discuss the influence of culture and the environmental surroundings within which you were raised in on your responses.

PERSONAL CARE RESOURCES

Experience

Using Figure 11.2 as a template (and modifying it if you need to), place yourself in the centre and identify the personal network of resources that support and care for you.

Reflection-in-Practice

What "service providers" are helping you? What family members or friends provide extra support? Which jurisdictions are responsible for the service provision?

Who is your "care coordinator"?

Where do you have control and feel respected? Where do you not?

Reflection-on/for-Practice

After you have finished the picture of your personal care network reflect on two things:

1. What new goals do you have for self-care?
2. What have you learned that might be relevant to working with young people and families from an ecological perspective?

CHAPTER 12

APPROACHES TO INTERVENTION

© Richard Thornton, 2013. Under license from Shutterstock, Inc.

CHAPTER OBJECTIVES

- To introduce some beginning strategies for intervention to help young people and families overcome the challenges that face them.
- To introduce some basic tools and a language for describing the intervention process in child and youth care practice.
- To introduce the concepts of life-space, therapeutic milieu, and daily life-events.
- To introduce the role of advocacy as an intervention.
- To introduce the foundations of group work.
- To review the process for intervention plans, sometimes known as case plans.

The heart and soul of interventions in child and youth care practice: self, relationships, and reflective practice have already been introduced. The nature of the field and the core characteristics have been described, and an understanding of how to meet and engage in relationships with young people has been established—readers may already be engaged. A critical approach to theoretical concepts about human development and the nature of the systems that affect people's daily lives have been introduced and some interventions that arise from these conceptual frameworks have been reviewed. This chapter focuses further on the nature of intervention in child and youth care practice.

Intervention is the act of intervening, or coming between things, to alter or influence the situation in some way. In child and youth care, when you "act" or become involved, you offer your care and attention with an explicit intent to improve the situation and alter or change the young person's development or the circumstances that surround them. Other terms for intervention include "counselling," "treatment," "therapy," "engagement," "support," and "caring." More recently it has been proposed that "pedagogy" is an approach that should replace "treatment" (Gharabaghi, 2013) and recognizes the young person's autonomy and agency as a learner. The domain of intervention includes the practitioner's ability to integrate current theory with the skill, expertise, reflexivity, and self-awareness that are essential for developing, implementing, and evaluating effective intervention programs for young people. Interventions are culturally bound and require **relationships** with young people and families. Interventions are enacted within the **systemic context** of both the practitioner and the client. All four domains surround and support the young person and family, as illustrated in **Figure 12.1.**

There are three essential aspects to the nature of interventions in child and youth care practice: spontaneity, planning, and evaluation of outcomes. Work as a practitioner may not include all three aspects in an explicit manner, though implicitly praxis includes all three aspects. Some

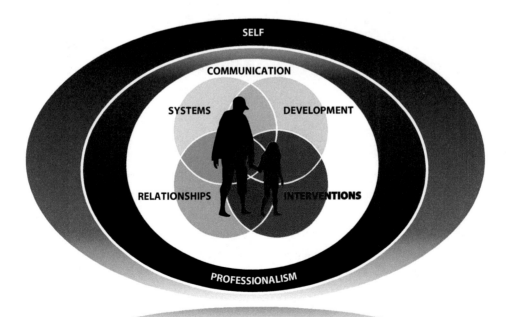

Figure 12.1   The Domain of Intervention

interventions occur spontaneously within the life-space as a response to an opportune moment. These types of interventions are described here in the subdomain of **life-space intervention** and include moment-to-moment opportunities that make use of daily life events, and programmed activities that promote therapeutic and developmental goals for young people. Spontaneous interventions require a theoretical grounding even though they are responsive or reactive to events in the life-space. Planning and evaluation of spontaneous interventions occur in the reflective practice embedded in the experiential learning cycle.

The planning aspect to intervention is more apparent in the **planned interventions** that occur systematically over a period of time and are carefully thought through, based on a theoretical model that guides the implementation of the intervention. Planned interventions involve specific activities that have been predicted to promote certain outcomes, and may occur individually or in groups. Changes as a result of planned interventions are incremental and adjustments are made to the activities based on the reflective observation of incremental change and comparing those reflective observations to the outcomes predicted by the theoretical approach. These types of interventions are only introduced briefly in this chapter. Planned interventions include the subdomains of **advocacy** and **group work**, both of which are essential milieu-based interventions and are therefore discussed separately. There are many theoretical approaches to **planned individual interventions**. These can be adapted for a milieu-based practice, but are most often encountered in the work that practitioners do on multidisciplinary teams and may be carried out by other professionals. These treatment models include cognitive-behaviour therapy, attachment therapy, narrative therapy, brief solution-focused therapy, play therapy, art therapy, and more. These models of intervention are not covered here, and practitioners should seek additional training on the theories and principles of intervention from these perspectives.

The third aspect of intervention is the **intervention plan** and subsequent **evaluation**. Intervention planning involves observing, assessing, planning, implementing, and evaluating the tools and approaches to intervention for a particular client (young person or family). Planning for intervention requires recording and documenting the plans and may also be known as case management, individual-program planning, plans of care, or treatment planning. The terminology used depends on the jurisdiction that funds the program and sets the policy guidelines, language, and terminology involved in planning. While milieu-based interventions are often individualized, it is critically important to document the progress of clients and review that progress to identify and evaluate the interventions that are effective.

Before considering these five subdomains in the domain of intervention, let's return to the ideas introduced in Chapter 9 about the interventive context and consider how the interventive context applies to the process of intervention (regardless of whether these are spontaneous or planned interventions).

Recall that in Chapter 9, we discussed the interventive relationship and the context that surrounds that relationship; this context is captured in Figure 9.2. Recall also that the context surrounding the interventive interaction creates a unique view of the world and brings that view to the interventions that practitioners undertake. As illustrated in **Figure 12.2**, the interventive interaction is centred in a cycle of action and meaning-making that is undertaken by the practitioner with the young person or family.

According to Garfat and Charles (2010), engagement with young people or families during intervention "is facilitated by paying attention to meaning-making and to rhythms"

(p. 66). These are two important aspects of intervention in child and youth care, no matter whether you are intervening spontaneously in the life-space or in a systematic and planned manner. We'll return to rhythm in a moment; let's consider meaning-making.

The cycle of action and meaning-making is best understood from the point of view of the two people engaged in the cycle. As the practitioner observes a youth swearing and throwing his or her school books around the room, the practitioner infers or makes meaning of the actions. What are the possible meanings that can be attributed to this action?

- Frustration and anger because the work is too difficult?
- Fear about an upcoming test?
- Jubilation that school is done for the summer?
- Fear about bullying or violence?

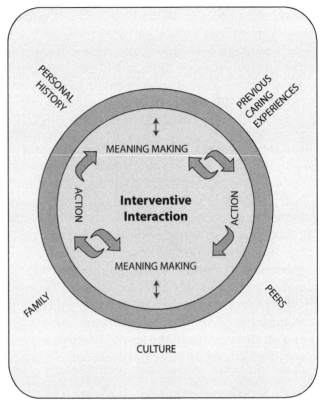

Figure 12.2   The Interventive Interaction
From *A Guide for Developing Effective Child and Youth Care Interventions with Families* (Pretext), by Garfat, T., and G. Charles. Reprinted by permission.

Perhaps the practitioner has never met this young person before and has no information about his or her relationship with school. Even the assumption that these are school books is an initial attempt at meaning-making. Meaning-making occurs through the influence of the practitioner's context. The practitioner was raised in a family, attended several schools, hung out with school peers, and has a set of values and beliefs about school. These, along with knowledge learned in training for practice and during professional development, inform the practitioner's meaning-making and action. Thus, being familiar with societal trends related to young people and families (and other resource materials related to the youth's school performance), the practitioner might recall that:

- Aboriginal youth and youth living in poverty are two groups that are twice as likely to drop out of school.
- Approximately one-fourth of youth in school are verbally victimized and one-twentieth are bullied physically.
- About 4% of young people have a learning disability and it is often comorbid with a mental health disorder.

At this point the practitioner does not have any context for the young person's action, but knows that there are many possibilities, and might take action by inquiring: "Hey, what's going on?" The youth then engages in meaning-making of that action—much of which will be based on an interpretation of the nonverbal tone of the statement, as well as any history from similar interactions. He or she might attribute any of the following meanings:

- Concern, I feel cared about.
- Discipline, I'm in big trouble.
- Help has arrived. . . .

Meaning-making here is also influenced by the youth's context, including gender and the specific milieu that he or she is in at the moment. This example of the meaning-making and action cycle could go on for some time, and as presented involves only the two people. Pause for a moment and imagine several different milieus and the other possible people involved. Perhaps this is actually a classroom and the teacher has called the practitioner to come and help. Perhaps it is the youth's home and the practitioner arrived for a visit. The young person's parents are standing there wondering what will happen next. Perhaps it is a residential care setting, a hospital, an after-school program, and so on.

In his study of "good-enough" group home care, Anglin found that more experienced practitioners were better at "reading young people's behaviour" (2002, p. 118) and were admired by novice practitioners for being able to do so. Anglin also identified that in group home settings pain-based behaviour is an important component of young people's developmental path, and that practitioners may have difficulty making meaning out of this behaviour because they are trying to make things better for youth. However, youth in the study indicated that they could "trace key moments in this learning process back to moments and relationships experienced in the group home settings" (p. 111).

People and practice do not exist in a closed system and this process of meaning-making and action is ongoing in the interventive interaction. Practitioners undertake this cycle of meaning-making with young people and families in life-space interventions, in planned group interventions and advocacy initiatives, and in the planning process that is captured on paper in an individual care plan.

The meaning-making/action cycle just described surrounds the process of the interventive interaction in Figure 12.2. The next section explores the elements of the process of interventive interaction and how they relate to rhythm. Rhythm was the second aspect of intervention. Rhythm is the "in-sync" part of what we do and its importance in intervention is described by several authors (Fulcher, 2003; Garfat & Charles, 2010; Krueger, 2004; Maier, 1987, 1992).

> Rhythm is beat, motion, tempo. Workers and youth moving through the day in and out of synch—a series of upbeats and downbeats. The movement of a group of teenagers from one activity to the next at an easy pace. A discussion of what is to come (foreshadowing) conducted in a firm, reassuring voice. The movement of hands mirroring the flow of the moment. A steady tone of voice that calms rather than excites; or a staccato, jubilant voice encouraging youth to participate in an activity. A body positioned and moving to quell an attack or provide a safe zone of expression. A nonthreatening hand reaching out to assist. A "quick step" and a grasp to avoid being hit. (Krueger, 1996, p. 2)

Rhythmicity comes into many aspects of the interventive interaction. Rhythmicity is critical in spontaneous interventions within the life-space. Timing the moment of intervention is important so that the intervention is received by the young person. Timing involves noticing receptiveness and establishing a momentary sense of bonding and unity (Maier, 1992); it also involves the nature of the daily routines and activities among all members of the milieu. Helping young people transition gently from one activity to the next is part of rythmicity; flowing with them and gently redirecting to the next phase of activity smooths the intervention and the transition.

According to Garfat and Charles (2010), the relational process of intervention involves **noticing**, **reflection**, **preparation**, and **intervention**. The next section compares the relational process of intervening to reflective practice, demonstrating how praxis forms the core of child and youth care interventions. This is the process that forms that interventive interaction as it moves more deeply into relationship.

- Noticing requires the two previously noted skills of **presence** and **understanding of the other** and simply (well it's not really "simple") noticing those elements.
- Reflection requires applying a personal theory[1] to what the practitioner notices to understand it and place it in context in preparation for intervening.
- Preparation involves going beyond the reflection and considering the choices available and the circumstances of time, developmental level, and potential reactions to the intervention that are specific to the young person. Practitioners must also consider how to apply the theory and knowledge available for the intervention.
- Intervention is the action that is taken with the young person, with the intent of facilitating change or enhancing development.

The interventive interaction process, and the components of reflective practice discussed in Chapter 6 form a similar cycle of reflection, meaning-making, and action as described in **Table 12.1**. It is through reflective practice that spontaneity becomes "planned" and the application of life-space intervention and use of daily life events become interventive interactions.

Table 12.1 Comparing the Interventive Interaction and Reflective Practice

INTEVENTIVE INTERACTION (GARFAT, 2004)	COMPONENTS OF REFLECTIVE PRACTICE AND EXPERIENTIAL LEARNING (KOLB & KOLB, 2009; THOMPSON & THOMPSON, 2008)	PRAXIS IN CHILD AND YOUTH CARE
Noticing	= Reflection-in-action	= Reflection-in-practice
Reflecting	= Reflection-on-action	= Reflection-on-practice
Preparing	= Reflection-for-action	= Reflection-for-practice
Intervening	= Theory-in-action	= Theory-in-practice

Noticing is **reflection-in-practice.** You are self-conscious of the internal aspects of your being and you attend to and notice the external environment. All your observations are filtered through your worldview and in order to take you beyond the limits of your worldview it is

---

[1] Personal theories are the concepts and intuition that we develop into an ordered way of understanding the world. They are based on personal experience and learned knowledge integrated into a whole.

helpful to know what to observe. Many of the things that you should observe and notice have been described in the previous chapters. Your reflection-in-practice will attend to:

- The behaviours of the young person
- Components of the systemic context like roles, rules, norms
- Expectations between people
- Rhythm between people
- Connections between systems

Reflecting, as described by Garfat, includes all aspects of reflective practice described in Chapters 4 and 7. Here, let's simplify reflection to include **reflection-on-practice**. As you observe and notice, you draw in previous experiences and your learning from those experiences, you begin to reflect on previous practice as well as the current interaction. You consider knowledge, theory, and the **aspects of self** that are part of your worldview and you consider how those might influence the intervention and the relationship. Reflection-on-practice is essential to help you reach beyond an intuitive response.

> The therapeutic importance of such communications can be under-valued and the chance to build on them [is] lost unless both individual worker and the staff team as a whole are able to locate such interventions within a theoretical framework which will help them understand what is happening and offer some guidance about what to do next. We need to listen to our intuition, reflect on it before we use it, and use it in context by attaching it into our repertoire of more conscious responses. (McMahon & Ward, 1998, p. 39)

Preparing is the phase of **reflection-for-practice**. The practitioner considers his or her readiness to do the intervention, including current feelings and the rhythm of the relationship with the young person. When and where is it best to make the intervention? What does theory direct as the best choice and how do you implement the choice(s) to increase the benefit and the learning. What are alternative interventions and how might those work? What changes need to happen in the milieu to help make this intervention effective? (*Note:* Making changes in the milieu is an intervention and there is more on this type of intervention in the next section.)

Intervening, in the final phase of the interventive interaction, takes the previously described reflection components of the intervention process and puts them together with knowledge and theory to create **theory-in-action** or praxis. You make choices about what to do and intentionally take action, observe, and make meaning out of the result, then initiate another intervention cycle.

While you notice, reflect, prepare, and intervene using the reflective practice cycle, young people follow a similar process of meaning-making and response as part of their developmental process in their own learning. Youth who have participated in an intervention that they felt changed them describe the experience as follows:

1. Experiencing the unreal.
2. Personalizing the intervention.
3. Connecting the intervention to expectations.
4. Experiencing incongruence.
5. Having thinking and feelings stimulated.
6. Making meaning of the intervention (Garfat, 1998).

Not all youth are able to identify and articulate a specific transformative experience as these youth did, but you will learn to trust that the experience of gradual change (first-order developmental change) will be similar to the transformative changes described above.

There are mini-cycles within the intervention process that link **life-space intervention** to **planned interventions** to **planning for intervention** and each intervention builds understanding, relationships, and the developmental path of the young person or family. At first, as a **novice** practitioner you will consciously implement each intervention. There will be times when you are less conscious about it, and then through reflection-on-practice you will build your reflective experience base, which is your personal evidence base, and will be able to respond with more experienced reflection next time. As you follow your own path of professional practice you will become less conscious and methodical, developing into a mature practitioner.

The concepts of the interventive interaction apply during spontaneous interventions in the life-space and in planned group and individual interventions that are more formally structured. They also apply to the process of planning for intervention. Even within the process of planning and documenting what the client needs and how to intervene there must be a formal consideration of the context as well as recognition of the ongoing cycle of action and meaning-making between the practitioner, client(s), and the other professionals who are involved. The rest of this chapter assumes that you will integrate the theoretical framework for interventive interaction described above and offers some reflective exercises to assist with applying the theory of interventive interaction to the five subdomains of:

* Life-space intervention
* Group work
* Advocacy
* Planned intervention
* Intervention plans

THINK ABOUT IT

Autry

There are many possibilities for intervention with Autry. Intervention begins from the moment a practitioner and youth meet. When the relationship begins and the practitioner undertakes an assessment of Autry's needs, strengths, ecology, and the context in which he lives, works, and plays, information about points of intervention is revealed. A practitioner might start with an activity focus— basketball, chess, paintball, or something else that interests Autry. As the relationship develops there will be opportunities to enhance social skills and build success and therefore self-esteem. Helping Autry find and join local clubs will increase the opportunities he has to meet youth his own age who are acceptable to his father as well as Autry. The family may need some assistance with understanding the postsecondary system and other medical options for his sister. The way a practitioner intervenes will differ based on the jurisdiction, program mandate, and milieu that is approaching the intervention. As you read consider the various options for intervention with Autry.

LIFE-SPACE INTERVENTION

Child and youth care practitioners consciously design and plan the physical and the social-emotional environment so that the needs of the young person are met. The activities of daily living, including eating, grooming, hygiene, socializing, and relaxing, promote developmental change. Planned environments integrate developmental, preventive, and therapeutic objectives into the life-space and are sensitive to cultural and human diversity. Practitioners teach basic life skills to young people and help parents teach these to their children, ensuring that physical health and safety is protected and that young people are increasingly responsible for their health and safety as appropriate to their strengths and developmental progress.

Life-space intervention is a primary method of intervention in child and youth care practice and unique to the field. Recent theoretical work in Child and Youth Care has expanded the concepts that were originally developed in residential care to enhance their relevance in multiple settings. Historically the residential setting was considered a therapeutic milieu that could be created and manipulated to create permanent change within the troubled (or emotionally disturbed and angry) young person. Burns (2006) updated the concepts of the therapeutic milieu first described by Redl and Wineman (1952) taking it beyond residential work and the use of routines and rules as well as *in vivo* techniques such as the life-space interview, and expanded the concepts of a therapeutic milieu to schools, community settings, family environments, etc. The concept of the life-space interview as it was originally described within the therapeutic milieu was updated by Wood and Long (1991) to introduce "a therapeutic, verbal strategy for intervention with students in crisis" (p. 5). The young person's reaction to a stressful, emotional incident was processed as a means of changing behaviour, enhancing self-esteem, reducing anxiety, or expanding the young person's insight. The focus of the interview was a conflict between the young person and another person (often the adult caregiver) that had escalated, often out of control. Thus, the intervention became known as Life-Space Crisis Intervention or Life Space Interview (Long, Wood, & Fecser, 2001) and is used extensively in school environments. Similarly, Garfat and Fulcher (2011, 2012) have expanded upon the use of daily life events to acknowledge these everyday events as "the most powerful and relevant opportunities for change" (p. 10). Recent work (Gharabaghi & Stuart, 2013) has reconceptualized life-space from a singular and primarily physical location to a concept that includes multiple dimensions and is characterized by connectivity between places bringing them into an integrated and unified space which does not require a practitioner to be physically present when engaged in an intervention.

This section describes the new thinking about "old" concepts that have formed the basis for life-space interventions in child and youth care practice.

The Life-Space

The concept of life-space originated with Kurt Lewin (1948) who described the life-space as something that included activity, physical space, goals, social interaction, and multigroup membership, as well as boundaries and limits created by self, other, cultural expectations, and norms. Redl adopted and modified the concept in the context of residential treatment as a technique for interviewing children within their "natural habitat or life-space" (p. 41), with the dual purposes of clinically exploiting recent (daily life) events and/or applying "emotional first aid" to assist the child with connecting current behaviours to the broader conditions of his or her life-space. From Redl's pioneering work the terms life-space and therapeutic milieu became synonymous with simply working in the young person's immediate environment.

Recent thinking in child and youth care about life-space has incorporated the concepts of meaning-making and relational engagement to understand life-space as an extension of "the social and psychological constructions of life" (Gharabaghi & Stuart, 2013, p. 4), recognizing the agency of young people and practitioners in the change process. In this reconceptualization of life-space by Gharabaghi and Stuart (2013) there is a singular, unified life-space carried "in imagination, in emotional connection, and in relationship to others, as well as in activities and relationships with people and things that blend into a singular understanding of the space in which we live our life" (pp. 8–9). In this conceptualization life-space has four dimensions. The **physical** dimension is reflected in the five senses as they experience a variety of locations, and our movement within and between those locations. These sensory inputs affect who we are and how we cope with situations presented to us. Sights and smells may carry specific meanings or relational memories. The **mental** dimension of the life-space is present in the thoughts and feelings that are built over time as we make meaning out of the physical dimension of the life-space and how it influences our lives. Therapeutic interventions can help young people to re-story or make new meaning within their life-space. Values and beliefs transmitted through the structures of society, community, and family are also present within this dimension of life-space, providing the opportunity for exploring those mental structures that define right and wrong. The **relational** dimension of life-space attends to what we do with and within our relationships. It includes shared activities, meaning-making, caring about others, and actively engaging to understand the other in relationship to self. Relationships hold us steady, particularly when the physical aspects of life-space present difficulties. The **virtual** dimension of life-space includes those environments that are real and concrete but are often lacking in some aspects of physicality. The technological revolution has provided us with many virtual environments, both safe and unsafe; however, prior to the digital age, imagination, spirituality, and madness were all present as virtual components of the life-space. This way of thinking about life-space opens additional opportunities for life-space intervention that are not confined to a single location, the physical presence of a practitioner, or a bounded social group. When the practitioner recognizes the autonomy and agency of the young person who carries the totality of their life-space with them, any moment becomes a moment for learning. The challenge to a practitioner is to enter that life-space and influence the meaning-making of the young person. With this understanding of life-space, it is now time to turn to a consideration of the therapeutic milieu, most often thought of as representing the physical dimension of life-space within which the practitioner is located. There have been significant shifts in thinking about the nature of the therapeutic milieu as well.

The Therapeutic Milieu

Theorists have been trying to describe the basic components of the therapeutic milieu from the early phases of professional development in child and youth care. According to Fritz Redl (Redl, 1959, 1966; Redl & Wineman, 1952), author of several "landmark" texts in residential care, the concept of the therapeutic milieu is one that emerged initially from Freudian psychoanalysis, where clients experienced a very specific environment and routine to visiting the psychiatrist that followed certain rules and thus enabled the clinician to "analyze" and eventually "cure" the client. The concept was expanded to include removing children from the family and placing them in residential care environments that were designed to support the clinical hour. Redl's initial explanations of the concepts and workings of the therapeutic milieu first appeared in 1959 in a volume of the *American Journal of Orthopsychiatry*. Around the same time, Henry Maier (1957) published in the same journal an article titled "Routines: A Pilot Study of Three Selected Routines and Their Impact upon the Child in Residential Treatment." What Redl didn't realize was that eventually these fundamental environmental routines and relational interactions would not include the "analytic hour" and instead the "other 23 hours" would be seen as the most important ingredient. Lawson (1998) explains that there are two approaches to milieu therapy, the "cultural" and the "additive" models. Either the milieu *is* the therapy (cultural model) or it is an adjunctive support to the clinical hour (additive model).

The **therapeutic** aspects of the milieu originally included:

1. Provision for the basic needs of children, including food and shelter, as well as occupational, recreational, and social needs, structured in a manner that accounts for the child's "developmental phase, pathology, and social background" (Redl & Wineman, 1952, p. 73).

2. Adult caretaking behaviour and activities within the environment that were appropriate to the developmental phase of the child and to their cultural background.

3. The programming and physical environment yielded to the demands of the therapy and the needs of the children "without the overall structure getting entirely lost in the shuffle" (Redl, 1966, p. 75). The demands normally made on children might be forgiven or adjusted in order to focus on the priorities of therapy.

4. The recreational and social aspects of the milieu include therapeutic goals. These were often considered "fringe" goals to the job of the psychiatrist who was unearthing the "root" of the problem or they could be equally valid and important in the "super ego repair" (Redl & Wineman, 1952).

5. The changes created within a therapeutic milieu involved reeducation for the lifetime and the milieu therefore was similar to the environments that the child would return to so that he or she could adjust upon return (Redl & Wineman, 1952).

Designers of residential milieus often modified the environments and created strategies for interaction with the children that followed their own theoretical approaches. Residential milieus have followed theoretical orientations that emphasized:

• Reflecting and analyzing the underlying purpose to the acting-out of the children (psychoanalysis)

• The need for attachment and relationships (attachment)

• Behavioural control techniques (behaviourism) (Mordock, 2002a)

Redl's theorizing about the milieu concluded that "much more work has to be done with the concept of 'setting' to make it clinically more meaningful and that sharper observational techniques, capable of catching 'implied milieu impact,' as well as the 'child's coping with' the experience produced by the setting have to be developed" (1966, p. 91). Redl attempted to define the variables that would need to be measured in order to specifically determine the relationship between clinical inputs and outcomes for young people. He foreshadowed the conclusion that we have come to today: There are mutual influences between the child and the environment and there are too many factors to determine one significant contributing factor, or even the ideal combination of factors.

In his book *Healing Spaces: The Therapeutic Milieu in Child and Youth Work*, Burns (2006) introduces five elements of the environment that can be manipulated and redesigned to meet three essential needs that all developing children have. These basic needs are for safety, inclusion, and affirmation. When **safety** needs are met the child or youth is protected from physical, emotional, and social harm or threats. Beyond safety needs, the need to feel loved and **included** by peers, family, and society is critical. Everyone needs to feel that they are special and cherished and the system(s) that nurture that feeling change as children grow and develop. When safety and inclusion needs are met, children need to feel a sense of affirmation, worth, and self-esteem and the therapeutic milieu contributes significantly to that feeling of self-worth. Burns suggests that there are five elements that should be considered when designing or adjusting the milieu to make it a therapeutic space for young people: physical, emotional, social, cultural, and ideological.

These five elements of the therapeutic milieu were introduced in Chapter 4 and are expanded upon here. According to Redl (1966) and Trieschman, Whittaker, and Brendtro (1969), a conscious awareness of the environmental space, the equipment and items within it, and their effect on the people in that environment are essential. In more modern terminology, this would be referred to as environmental design, focused on the **physical** aspects of the milieu, including the arrangement of furniture and equipment, the actual design of buildings, and the timing involved in presenting and using equipment (including the presence of people and the topics of conversation). Simple things that we take for granted become important in the design of the space in which children live, go to school, or are cared for when they are not at home. There is very little research or writing on the design of physical environments for children in residential care or the effects of design on therapeutic outcomes (Bailey, 2002). However, research into the effects of crowding and controlling access to private space and time for children has clearly indicated that crowding "can increase aggression, withdrawal avoidance, hyperactivity, impulsivity, and competition" (p. 19); therefore, the provision of physical space for the "therapeutic need for physical and psychic privacy" (p. 21) is essential. Art, music, and the concept of beauty are well established as therapeutic healers (Bailey, 2002). Many young people have a history of neglected, deprived, or physically unsafe environments. Physical environments should offer a sense of inclusion and affirmation of children if we are truly listening to them (Fulcher, 2006). Physical environments are inclusive of children when the furnishings are of appropriate size, the space accommodates a wheelchair easily, and interior design reflects the religious and ethnic backgrounds of the people there.

Each person in the milieu brings a unique **emotional** temperament to the environment based on his or her history and current state of being. These emotional temperaments combine to give character to the milieu (Burns, 2006). The emotional history of young people is strongly vested in their family history. Family should be included in any environment designed for children. Family gives to children their sense of identity (Fulcher, 2006), defines how a child includes him or her self in the environment, and often strongly influences self-worth. In group care settings the predictability and emotional stability of the environment—created by the child and youth care practitioners—teaches children trust and helps them learn that they can depend emotionally on their relationships—now and in the future (Fulcher, 2006). How are apprehension, fear, and distrust dealt with in the milieu? Who explains the rules of belonging to the new member of the group, and how is that explanation provided? These are important aspects of dealing with the emotional climate.

Human beings are **social** creatures and the minute-to-minute interactions of the **social milieu** influence safety, inclusiveness, and affirmation needs in young people. The child and youth care practitioner understands that every interaction with children and the shared day-to-day social experiences—those **daily life events**—are opportunities for growth and development. Young people have many relationships: with practitioners, between peers, and between young people, their families and communities. All of these relationships can be brought into or rejected by the milieu in which the young person is involved. Efforts on the part of the practitioner send a message about inclusion and affirmation of the young person is in relation to the rest of their relationships (Burns, 2006). Frequently, in group care settings, these external relationships are interrupted (Fulcher, 2006) by placement decisions. Young people can't be "handled" in the school and are therefore sent to an alternative setting outside of their community, isolating them from friends and family. Young people with difficult emotional and behavioural issues are removed from their family and placed in hospital or residential care. When young people enter a new milieu they encounter membership rituals (Fulcher, 2006) that speak to the social inclusiveness of the environment. What must they do to belong to this group? How do people get to know each other? They also retain social ties to the place they left, and how those are acknowledged in the new milieu provides an important message about affirmation and inclusiveness.

Significant components of the social element of the milieu are the recreational activity structure and the daily routines that are found in all milieus. The setting of routines and predictability in the environment, first studied by Maier (1957), remains a fundamental concept leading to stability and ultimately supporting children's development. A balance between individual and collective needs is necessary in the social environment. Mordock (2002a) described the ideal milieu where one or more unique milieu environments for each child were created within a specific physical setting. Based on the developmental level of a particular child, or set of children, staff would respond with a "specific set of experiences . . . designed to foster the child's growth: The treatment plan for a child included an individualized 'milieu' or a 'specific attitude' about the child's needs and how to consistently respond to them" (p. 30). These specific milieus defined the degree of order and routine; ritual interactions with the children; and directions on how to respond to behavioural disruptions within the group. There could be several such sets of experiences operating within one home, based on the children placed there. Not surprisingly, it was very difficult for the institution to maintain these individualized milieus, so the staff "morphed" these into a single milieu that met the majority of the children's needs (Mordock, 2002b) in relation to structure.

Behavioural control within the environment is an important consideration for the safety of the children and the adults working with them. According to Bailey (2002), authoritarian approaches to behavioural control that involve rigid behavioural expectations have been found to have little long-term or positive effect, and thus residential programs are moving away from control-oriented approaches toward those that promote relational attachment. Children need a sense of freedom or mastery and control over the space in which they live. In part, this is defined by the routines and rituals laid out by the adults and, in part, it is defined by the child's social interaction within the environment.

Play is sometimes viewed as the "work" of children, but children who live in difficult circumstances with poverty, violence, and/or isolating conditions may not experience play during the struggle to survive. Practitioners make use of the social aspects of the therapeutic milieu to design and implement individual and group activities that reflect the significance of play and recreational programming to young people. They analyze the meaning, atmosphere, and the nature of the activities relative to the child's developmental needs and then construct activity plans that are appropriate for the developmental level of the client(s) with which they work. Chapter 9 provided some ideas and a framework for analyzing activities that matches activities to the social and emotional needs of young people in the milieu. Activity programs are one of the core components of treatment in a therapeutic milieu. When working with families, the practitioner assists parents to understand the importance of activities and how to choose developmentally appropriate activities that meet the unique personality needs of their children (VanderVen, 2004).

> . . . the Culture of Childhood refers to the collective folklore of children that is transmitted down the generations, across geographic areas, and among cultural subgroups. The forms and domains of activity that are transmitted include tricks, rituals, sayings, games, crafts, and the like that engage and focus exchanges among children and youth. . . . These exchanges generate changes in children and youth. There are universal patterns found in all cultures that underlie many of the activities in the Culture of Childhood. (VanderVen, 2004, pp. 103–104)

There is a special children's **culture** and an adolescent culture or subculture in which adults are not involved. In child and youth care practice we try to bridge the cultures between young people and adults. Practitioners also work to create an affirming and inclusive culture within the milieu, which is about acceptance and celebration of differences. The cultural element of the milieu involves recognizing the different elements of identity that the young person has (Burns, 2006) and arranging the milieu to recognize these aspects of identity and affirm their importance. Fulcher (2006) calls these differences the cultural and spiritual rhythms of caring. Interventions in the milieu should incorporate cultural rituals with images, sounds, and smells that are apparent as people enter a milieu that incorporates children's culture and accepts diversity. Basic routines such as eating a meal together can identify and teach the etiquette associated with different religious, spiritual, or ethnic backgrounds. Without an awareness of these routines, young people feel excluded or even unsafe in their environment. They ask themselves subconscious questions such as:

- Are there people here like me? (inclusiveness)
- Is my religion (culture, identity, gender preference) acceptable and known here? (affirmation)

Practitioners who attend to the cultural milieu will consciously attend to these questions, seeking answers and making such questions explicit.

The **ideology** is comprised of the ideas, beliefs, and attitudes of each individual in the milieu and the collective "ideals" of the program (Burns, 2006). Fulcher (2006) states that over the last three decades the following "ideologies" have shaped "best practice" in child and youth care and are therefore evident in writing, research, and programmatic descriptions. These ideologies were described in Chapter 2 and along with the theoretical orientation of the program they form the ideology of a milieu.

1. Normalisation
2. Deinstitutionalisation
3. Mainstreaming
4. The "least" restrictive environment
5. Minimal intervention

Research on milieu therapy is limited. "A comprehensive understanding of what milieu is, how it works, and why it is effective, remains elusive" (Lawson, 1998, p. 459). Writers tend to be descriptive and do not identify the underlying theory or specify the concepts and components of the program that are important to a milieu. One of the difficulties with research on milieu therapy is the issue of "drift" over time in the ideology of the model used within the milieu. Even when a program clearly specifies the components of the model it is using, these components may change as staff turnover occurs and children with different needs are added to the group. To assess the outcome of milieu therapy the program must follow children over an extended period of time as well as documenting outcomes when children are successful in that milieu. It is rare that organizations perform follow-up studies of children or even consistently document the outcomes that children achieve while in care. Even more difficult is the description of the exact type of service and the elements of the milieu that are present for a given set of children (Mordock, 2002b). Much of milieu therapy turns on the concept of the therapeutic use of daily life events and the structures and routines present within that milieu.

Therapeutic Use of Daily Life Events

The use of daily life events for therapeutic change to support young people's growth and development is a core characteristic of child and youth care practice (Garfat & Fulcher, 2011, 2012). As can be seen in the early history of the therapeutic milieu, this approach emerged from the premises of psychoanalysts who believed that the **structures** of the psychoanalytic hour were important to encouraging the cure to emerge. Early residential settings focused on the structures and routines as anchor points for young people from chaotic backgrounds. In some residential programs this evolved into point and level (token) systems, based on behavioral psychology, whereby daily life events devolved to opportunities for punishment or reward, rather than relational learning experiences that recognize resilience and **agency***. There is no room within a token economy for meaning-making or the spontaneity of an interventive interaction based on daily life events.

It is essential that daily life events be viewed through the lens of meaning-making that is part of the interventive interaction. "Understanding how young people adapt to and make sense of themselves in context (both past and present), residential workers can reframe all behaviors, even problematic ones, through a lens of strength and adaption . . . a starting point . . . setting the stage for adoption of more pro-social interactions in the future"*. Daily life events are now positioned both as structures and acts of agency by young people, which must be interpreted within an understanding of the young person's context. If a young man comes from a culture where meals are prepared by the women and are large social, family events, he may actively resist being asked to help with preparing or serving a simple meal to his peers. On the other hand, an event may appear to come from nowhere when a young person reacts with anger or aggression to a seemingly routine request. Both offer opportunities for therapeutic intervention.

The use of daily life events extends beyond its original conceptualization in residential care into family and community practice. When the autonomy and the agency of a young person are recognized as primary in their learning during those teachable moments (Swanzen & Marincowitz, in press), then any eventful moment is opened to a therapeutic moment. Meaning-making is again the key. A daily life event is open for therapeutic use when the practitioner and young

---

*From "If I'da thrown that chair at you, it woulda hit you: Seeing difficult behaviors through the lens of meaning and resilience" by Brockett and Anderson-Nathe. In *Relational Child and Youth Care Practice*, 26(2) (in press). Reprinted by permission.

person engage in exploring its meaning together and in learning from each other with the agency of the young person in the learning process being central. "Facilitating meaningful use of events to encourage change implies that adults be more aware of their capacity as a model whilst empowering the child within his/her lifespace, seizing opportunities through seemingly unimportant events out of which a young person's days are constructed" (Swanzen & Marincowitz, in press).

Extending the concept of the therapeutic milieu into the family home by placing practitioners within the home facilitates the use of daily life events as the practitioner joins the family in their routines and activities. Child and youth care practitioners join with families in their homes and help them to structure daily routines and activities that promote safety and affirm the agency of young people and parents (Shaw & Garfat, 2003). The presence of the worker to engage with the family in meaning making facilitates change, growth and development. Presence is both a physical and a relational concept, which opens the possibility that practitioners can insert themselves into daily life events in a relational way without being physically present (Gharabaghi, in press). Because relationships are founded on the feeling of being connected, it is possible to connect with daily life events in a virtual way. Gharabaghi (in press) suggests a variety of strategies for being absent while being a presence in daily life events. Strategies such as providing a family with your personal recipe and asking them to make it together while recalling a story about the recipe brings your presence into their lives. Becoming present through social media—the use of which is a daily life event—provides opportunities for therapeutic use of daily life events, often without physical presence.

The therapeutic use of daily life events, while core to child and youth care from the beginning, has come to focus on the meaning-making inherent within the relational interaction between practitioner and young person or family. It no longer requires a physical presence in the therapeutic milieu and recognizes that as a strategy the therapeutic work focuses both on structure and the agency of young people, balancing the interplay between both.

Life-Space Interview and Life-Space Crisis Intervention

Life-space crisis intervention (LSCI; Long, et. al., 2001) is a structured in-the-moment intervention that was designed to deal with the emotional needs of the young person in a respectful and inclusive manner either before or during a potentially physical altercation. It is a technique that is implemented when the emotional reaction to a "life event" reaches a level that could or does lead to physical or verbal conflict. It provides structured guidelines for **novice** practitioners during the interventive interaction.

> Sometimes after a disturbing experience, children need "first-aid services for the muddled feelings at the time." . . . A friendly worker follows the child and, in the on-the-spot interview, comforts him. The result is a positive milieu impact. At other times the life space interview may be used, shortly after the incident, to umpire quarrels or misunderstandings between two or more children. This application has led some workers to misinterpret the technique as an inquisitional third-degree procedure. Redl stressed the opposite—benign, insightful intervention by a sympathetic adult. (Rabinovitch, 1991, p. 75)

The Life-Space Interview (LSI) involves:

1. Reviewing the incident in a factual manner.
2. Listening to and exploring feelings.
3. Defining the central issue and selecting a therapeutic goal, something that the child wants to change.
4. Exploring and choosing a solution that will lead to meeting the goal.
5. Planning for successful change.
6. Re-integration into the activity space of the milieu.

Long et al. (2001) document both the history of the **life-space interview** technique and the research that has been done on its effectiveness. Several research programs looked at the LSI over a period of 20–25 years, reporting that the LSI was effective to meet developmental needs related to social communication and socialization in groups, as well as other aspects of development. Peer-related crises were identified as the most frequent reason for using a LSI and when LSI is a regular part of the program in a school, with all staff trained in its use, there was evidence of an increase in classroom work, improved self-control, and increased self-initiated requests for assistance and problem solving. Additionally, four of five students could be managed without requiring physical restraint and the extent of physical intervention decreased over the year (Nasland, 1987, cited in Long et al., 2001). The LSI has been modified to incorporate additional ideas about preventing and dealing with physical conflicts as the LSCI (Long et al., 2001). LSCI is intended as a therapeutic intervention that deals with conflict that could escalate to physical aggression toward others. Some programs, particularly residential care, use physical restraint as a last resort for intervention, and intervention in physical conflict is more effective when the emotional environment in the life-space is deescalated and restraint is not necessary. There is insufficient space for a detailed discussion of issues related to physical restraint, and therefore you are referred to professional development sources for further learning. When you

---

Tips and Resources

Therapeutic Crisis Intervention (TCI)
http://rccp.cornell.edu/tcimainpage.html

Non-violent Crisis Intervention
www.crisisprevention.com/Specialties/Nonviolent-Crisis-Intervention

---

consider the interventive interaction and the cycle of meaning-making, you will realize that there are many earlier points for intervention in the emotional escalation during the conflict cycle (Long et al., 2001). However, many **novice** child and youth care practitioners are called upon to learn how to physically intervene in a conflict at some point, early in their career, so proper training is essential.

Life-space intervention offers many possibilities for seemingly spontaneous interventions (interventive interactions), which in reality are thoughtful, reflective, relational engagements with young people and/or their families. The next three subdomains look at the systematically planned group and individualized aspects of intervention. However, as I'm sure you realize now, life-space intervention also involves thought and planning; it is not as spontaneous as it appears. child and youth care practitioners also use systematically planned and prearranged intervention programs within the milieu. Individually and in groups, interventions can be designed and carried out in a pre-agreed and programmed manner as part of the structure and routine of the milieu.

ADVOCACY

Advocacy empowers people to deal directly with their own issues and those of the groups(s) with which they identify. In an ideal world, advocacy would not be required because each and every individual, regardless of the identifiable differences that they have from others, would be heard and respected in their efforts to develop to their fullest potential. Unfortunately, it's not an ideal world, and advocacy is an essential component of intervention in child and youth care practice. child and youth care practitioners believe in the inherent potential of the young person and family and their capacity to grow and change. Practitioners have basic advocacy skills that ensure young people and families have their views heard and considered during the decision-making processes that directly affect them. They understand and demonstrate respect for young people and families, affording them the dignity of self-determination within the context of their developmental capacities. They are also prepared to go beyond basic advocacy for individuals and undertake systemic advocacy.

> The primary goal of child advocacy is to elevate the voice of youth. This means more than empowering youth to speak out on their own behalf. It means more than faithfully replaying their words. The standard to aspire to is articulated in an African proverb: "Don't speak about us, without us." It means speaking together with youth about youth.
>
> Advocacy is often described as a process of empowerment, giving power to others. Advocacy can be more appropriately viewed as assisting children and youth in finding their own power from within and teaching them to use it effectively. (http://provincialadvocate.on.ca/main/en/what/)

The empowerment and participatory approach to practice has always been a hallmark of frontline child and youth care practitioners as they work tirelessly to represent the child's interests; but systemic advocacy has traditionally been a hallmark of social work practice (Anglin, 2001). Recently theorists and practitioners in child and youth care have begun to make use of systems, policies, and national and international conventions such as the United Nations Convention on the Rights of the Child (UNCRC) to guide their work with young people. The fundamental belief behind this approach to practice is that young people are "subjects" not "objects" and as such have both the capacity and the desire to participate not just in the decision making regarding their own lives, but also in the development and implementation of programs and services for themselves and others. Young people have a right and responsibility to participate and they have spent too many years as ignored and disempowered members of society.

There have always been some innovative and pioneering agencies such as McMann Youth Services in Alberta, who had former clients as youth board members in the 1980s, but the beliefs and the theoretical concepts behind these strategies have emerged with greater strength as the profession has advanced and recognized the developmental importance of participation, empowerment, and engagement for young people.

Advocacy requires careful attention to reflective practice and to critical thinking skills. While individual awareness, appreciation, and active inquiry about difference in the context of relationships are essential, these skills are not sufficient in order to professionally assist the young people and families who experience barriers and oppression as a result of their difference. Practitioners must be **critically reflective** with a focus on empowerment, equality, and social justice.

Critical reflection requires not just the self-reflection on "head–heart–habit" as introduced in Chapters 3 and 6, it also includes reflecting on your own worldview and the value base of the social structure around you. Critical reflection on self and on your social structures is an essential tool for applying the lens of diversity to professional practice. In particular, critical reflection on the stereotypes you hold about people with different values and norms than yourself is important. It is also essential to identify the nature of the social structures in which you work, and how they exclude some groups and individuals from accessing opportunities afforded to those with power and privilege (Thompson & Thompson, 2008; Dean, 2012).

Critical reflection transforms your perspective and provides you with direction for changing the way people are treated. Critical reflection will increase your awareness and knowledge of the power dynamics that are present in the social systems in which you work. It is also important to keep in mind a sense of where you can have influence so that you don't feel overwhelmed trying to create change. Your efforts should focus on structures where you and the young people with which you are engaged can have the most influence. Focus on yourself, the young people you work with, and the coworkers who are open to examining their own values and beliefs as places where you can create change. Look for areas, people, or social structures where you can have some influence and target these for discussion about the need for change. You may also need to be creative in your efforts and identify who has influence and who is open to assisting you. Finally, you will need to accept what you cannot influence.

The rest of this section describes some basic concepts underlying the advocacy initiatives that have developed in child and youth care practice, building on the discussion of engagement in Chapter 9. Concepts and strategies discussed here include:

- The principles of the UNCRC
- Youth participation and youth engagement
- Radical youth work

The UNCRC, adopted by the United Nations in 1989, is used in the field of child and youth care for its potential to influence practice.

The UNCRC provides for universal rights for all children around the world, such as:

- The right to an identity
- The right to a family
- The right to express themselves and to have access to information
- The right to a safe and healthy life
- The right for special protection in times of war
- The right to an education
- The right to special care for the disabled
- The right to protection from discrimination

Tips and Resources

Understanding the UNCRC

www.unicef.org/crc/index_understanding.html

This site includes photo essays illustrating the articles of the convention.

- The right to protection against abuse
- The right to special treatment if arrested
- The right to a voice in decisions made about them

The UNCRC has become an important framework for intervention with young people. Interventions using the convention include advocating for children's rights based on the principles of the convention and educating young people about their rights (and responsibilities). Practitioners provide a forum for discussion with young people and a framework for change and personal development as young people participate in the process of ensuring that their rights and the rights of others are protected. Child soldiering, for example, is prohibited under the UNCRC, leading to initiatives on behalf of child soldiers that include former child soldiers speaking to the United Nations and other groups. Schools make use of the UNCRC to educate children about their rights. Young people in care and former young people in care educate other young people and practitioners about their rights and about how to improve conditions in residential care, foster care, and the child welfare system.

Youth participation and youth engagement are advocacy interventions that help young people find their voice and speak about their own needs, alongside the adults that care for and about them. Youth in Care Canada (formerly the National Youth in Care Network) is an example of youth participation in the child welfare sector that has achieved the seventh or eighth rung of Hart's ladder of participation (Hart & Schwab, 1997). The group regularly applies for and receives grants to deliver rights education to young people in care. They train members to do this work themselves, and through this training and other events young people in the care of child welfare authorities in Canada regularly meet to identify service issues that affect them, plan for how to publicize the issue, and develop the skills and confidence to speak with politicians, policymakers, and service providers about how to improve the child welfare system.

> Youth Speak is an event for young people to talk about their concerns, to gain skills through workshops, and to have an opportunity to speak-out in an environment where people are listening. The event consists of time for young people to brainstorm their needs, issues and ideas; attend skill-building workshops that equip them with tools for taking action; and provides them with an opportunity to express their opinions and make recommendations to decision-makers in their lives. (Herbert, 2008, p. 5)

Youth Speak has become a North American phenomena, with the basic principles of youth-driven engagement with social issues and cultural events at the heart of the movement. As with any phenomena, though, there are examples of the movement being adopted for commercial purposes (*http://mtv.in.com/youthspeak/index.php*). There are other examples in the community sector, where the idealism of young people brings strength and energy to projects on environmental issues, children's rights, and community issues. The *Environmental Youth Alliance*

Tips and Resources

Environmental Youth Alliance
www.eya.ca

Youth in Care Canada
www.youthincare.ca/

Youth Speaks Movement

http://youthspeak.ca
http://youthspeaks.org
http://youthspeakcollective.org

is a youth-run organization with multiple funding sources that provides youth employment, focuses on environmental and children's rights issues, and actively recruits and involves "youth at risk" in a variety of projects that produce tangible results such as "green" walking paths and community asset maps that identify service (health, environmental, youth focused, etc.) locations and gaps within a geographic community. Young people learn valuable skills and techniques while both participating and guiding the work of the project.

Bringing young people together to identify and work on common issues is challenging. A planned approach incorporating the concepts of the interventive interaction is essential. As described by Sapin (2009), establishing groups of young people and advocating for change requires:

1. **Identifying a genuine need.** The Youth in Care movement, which has multiple groups locally, provincially, and nationally in Canada, came together around the needs of children in the care of child welfare authorities to be sensitively cared for and heard when they complained about the conditions in which they lived.

2. **Recognizing the potential interest in shared activities.** Youth are concerned about community issues that impact them directly. The need for more recreation space (skateboard parks, for example) or the lack of attention to safety or the environment can provide a focus for action.

3. **Discussing options for change** with young people. The idealism of young people makes it essential that adults facilitate the thinking about what to change and how it should look without taking over and "doing" the thinking. Helping young people develop realistic and manageable options for changing the issues that they want to affect is essential.

4. **Presenting ideas to funders or to management,** with young people is essential. Adults tend to dismiss young people and thus training them in public speaking and delivering their message as well as helping them refine and focus the message increases the chance of success.

5. Getting **financial support** is important to take youth participation beyond tokenism or volunteerism. Youth workers must be careful not to exploit youth participation, particularly when they are getting paid themselves.

6. Meeting with youth group members to **clarify aims and objectives** is an important step in success. It helps young people understand the parameters of what they are able to accomplish and to know when the project is complete as well as provide markers for success.

7. Planning and identifying **resource requirements** with young people not only teaches them valuable skills in planning and budgeting, it sets some realistic parameters around step three, helping to define which options may not be viable.

Youth empowerment and youth engagement involve young people in both self-advocacy and advocacy for societal issues that have been ignored. Issues such as poverty, environmentalism, racism, societies in conflict, and more are addressed jointly by young people and youth workers both as a mechanism for change and an intervention that enhances youth skills and social competence.

Radical youth work is an attitude toward intervention that actively values love and respect for the young people with which we engage. Skott-Myhre (2004) differentiates two types of youth work. "Colonial youth work" is described as that which has as its aim the socialization of youth, particularly "problem" youth, into conformity with the norms of society and culture.

These norms are typically defined by the dominant (and capitalist) majority who hold power. "Radical youth work," on the other hand, steps away from and actively challenges these values and beliefs.

> To truly become effective as a radical youth worker, one must resist the rather small gains to be achieved through "power" in favor of the infinitely rich gains to be achieved by joining in the broadest coalition of human beings to restructure the material conditions within which we all live. This we must do through the radical application of love and production. That is to say we must be guided in what we produce as a field of youth work by principles of loving desire for absolute human connection or the power of love rather than the love of power. (Skott-Myhre, 2004, p. 93)

Radical youth work involves interactions with young people that challenge the existing social and professional structures and policies on both a personal and a political level. It means daring to form an enduring friendship with a youth that could be seen as going beyond the professional boundaries, if such a relationship is mutually agreed to. It means actively forming groups with young people that challenge the political and social structures that restrict or harm our collective existence. Groups such as the Environmental Alliance for Youth or Peaceweavers (Moen, Little, & Burnett, 2004), which actively work to create social change, have radical youth workers engaged with the young people that participate in those movements. It is a specialized intervention that demands careful attention to aspects of self and critical reflection on the nature of social structures.

GROUP WORK

The peer group is a powerful socialization agent and group work provides opportunities for young people to experience social development and to build on their strengths and competencies. All people participate in groups in various forms, with friends, at school, at work, and in the community, and therefore helping young people develop the skills to work out disagreements, make decisions, and understand the power of the group is essential. Practitioners adapt their skills in life-space intervention and their communication skills to function within the group context. The interventive interaction takes on new dimensions when working in a group because there are multiple relationships and cycles of meaning-making and action. Practitioners need to be aware of and be confident enough to deal with group dynamics and ensure that group members are safe and treated with respect. They know the stages of group development and how to introduce new members to the group in a manner that keeps the group functioning effectively. Group work occurs both formally, in prescheduled group times facilitated by the practitioner (within the milieu), as well as informally as the practitioner manages the group dynamics in the milieu.

> Workers' group building efforts serve, essentially, as a source of individual identity formation. In practice, this would mean that a group planning session for an evening of fun would have to include an opportunity for all group members to share their wishes and expectations, searching for common denominators and give-and-take negotiations with regard to expectations that cannot be accommodated on that particular evening. Above all, the evening of fun has to stand as a joint group accomplishment so that members may verify that "I had a part in our having fun." (Maier, 2006, p. 103)

This section focuses on some basic concepts for facilitating groups, such as stages of group development and purposes of group work. Groups of young people, like teams (discussed in Chapter 8), follow stages of development that are thought to have predictable characteristics and struggles.

When working with a group of young people, the practitioner is a member of the group and the facilitator or leader who brings the group together. As the initiator of the group, the practitioner has the additional responsibility to facilitate the process in each of the stages of group development. The purpose of the group, age of the participants, and the nature of the milieu in which a practitioner works will all influence how structured or directive he or she is in any of these stages, but from **forming** through to **performing**, the amount of structure and influence exerted should decrease as the natural leaders within the group emerge and take on more responsibility within the group.

STAGES OF GROUP DEVELOPMENT

- Forming
- Storming
- Norming
- Performing
- Adjourning

Groups form for various purposes with young people. In **issue-based radical** youth work (Magnuson & Baizerman, 2007; Sapin, 2009; Skott-Myhre, 2007), practitioners come together with young people to advocate for social change, influence policy, or change conditions in their community. They have a common interest and purpose to being together. **Counselling** groups (Corey & Corey, 2006) form because young people are referred as a result of a traumatic experience or a specific risk behaviour that is thought to limit their potential. These are very different purposes to a group and each requires a different approach to the work that practitioners do in the group. The experiences dealt with in a counselling group make use of the power associated with knowing that you "are not the only one" and learning from other group members techniques for coping with the issue. Counselling groups can focus on substance use or abuse, sexual abuse, family violence, or specific mental health issues. **Psychoeducational** groups are formed around an identified skill deficit common to group members and have a specific curriculum, as well as some of the characteristics of counselling groups (DeLucia-Waack, 2006). Typical psychoeducational groups include social skills, anger management, life skills, and stress reduction. **Peer helping** groups bring together young people to develop their skills in helping others, which then prepares them for a helping role amongst their peers (Tindall & Black, 2008). These groups build on the social competence and natural helping skills that some young people have. Helping roles may focus on peer counselling, peer tutoring, suicide prevention, play groups, conflict mediation, antiracism, antibullying, and more. **Group care** is a specialized form of group work, characteristic of child and youth care practice, which also requires some consideration of the stages of group development. Group care brings children together, away from their parents, to care for them when their parents cannot. Group care includes foster care, residential treatment, group homes, juvenile detention, and more (Anglin, 2002; Boddy, Cameron, & Moss, 2006; Courtney & Iwaniec, 2009; Fulcher & Ainsworth, 2006; Kendrick, 2007; Peters, 2008; Smith, 2009; Ward & McMahon, 1998).

Groups of young people formed and managed with adult guidance are everywhere, including after-school care settings, recreation centres, sports teams, art classes, and more. Child and youth care practitioners are most often found facilitating groups for the five purposes noted previously. Just as the stages of group development are not clear and discrete, the purposes for groups often mix together. A peer helping group may decide to focus on creating change in the school or community and set up a human rights forum, taking an issue-based approach. Psychoeducational groups frequently occur in a semi-structured format within group care settings.

Intervention skills vary according to the type of group; however, practitioners use common techniques to enhance the group process. Group work and group facilitation skills are essential areas for additional professional development to help the novice practitioner manage the many aspects of intervention. Two strategies for group development will be highlighted here, from the first two phases of group development.

Forming a group requires some consideration of a pregroup stage (Corey & Corey, 2006). At this point the group usually has only one member, the practitioner who intends to bring the young people together. Attending to things like how to attract and select members, orient them to the purpose of the group, set the frequency and location of meetings, and establish an initial climate of safety lays the groundwork for later group functioning. In some settings and group types the pregroup phase is clear, while in others new members have to be integrated into an existing group. All groups, however, have "begun" at some point and often the initial group culture carries on even when all the original members have left. Sometimes this is a conscious decision and sometimes it is a history that is very hard to eliminate.

In the pregroup forming stage considerations have to be given to issues such as:

- How similar versus how different should group members be on dimensions such as age, gender, or common issues?
- How big should the group be based on leadership, type of group, or similarity?
- How long should the group stay together?

CASE ILLUSTRATION

Forest Glen Road has two of our group homes; they are about a block apart. For the entire time that I've worked for this agency, 130 Forest Glen has been the "house with the holes." We are always repairing the drywall. It doesn't seem to matter who the staff are and the youth have changed at least three times; they always have a few that put their fists through the walls. On the other hand, 140 Forest Glen is "the little ones." The youth are less mature and the staff have preadolescent expertise, so we try to place teens who need more work on attachment there. It's a conscious decision.

As the group meets for the first time members will present their "best self" and will need to develop trust, no matter what the purpose of the group. Practitioners can facilitate this process by discussing expectations and developing "group norms" in the first meeting of the group. Brainstorming group norms or group rules helps group members to focus on **storming** and **norming** in a structured and explicit manner. Developing group norms should not be done quickly, nor should the first set of rules posted be accepted at face value. The facilitators should encourage questioning and revisiting norms by group members as trust deepens and develops further. As new members are introduced to the group, rules and expectations about respect,

---

PRACTICE EXAMPLE: SAMPLE GROUP NORMS

Peer helpers (age 12–14 years):

- Listen and don't interrupt
- Be on time
- Suggest ideas
- Have fun
- What happens in the group, stays in the group.

---

caring, group goals, and individual goals all need to be renegotiated over time as members get to know each other. An initial set of expectations for how group members will treat each other and interact lets them develop relationships and begins a discussion that can be returned to when conflict arises.

Group work is challenging and powerful. Groups are composed of peers who have an enormous potential to affect the young people that participate. Peers have something in common—age, gender, trauma, or a desire to help—and these commonalities are what make the group very powerful. The group leader's job is to guide the group dynamics and harness the potential of the group. Balancing individual and group needs, as well as guiding the group through constructive meetings and activities, draws on skills from many other domains and novice practitioners should seek ongoing training in managing groups.

PLANNED INTERVENTION

Practice planning and plan execution is a complex process of decision making amidst current and multiple contexts. It is an iterative process of inquiry interspersed with choice-making among a set of perceived alternatives. A choice at a point in time involves discretionary judgments on the part of practitioners, a process that can be enlightened through self-awareness and a greater understanding of frameworks, models, and interventions. (Ricks & Charlesworth, 2003, p. 4)

Planned interventions arise when practitioners design activities, interactions, and behaviour management methods to support the individual goals and objectives of young people and families. Goals and objectives could be focused around support, treatment, educational, or developmental needs or strengths. Planned interventions are continuously adapted, anticipating the steps and measures required to meet the objectives of the young person or family. Practitioners recognize that the design of these therapeutic interventions and service methods are logically connected to service goals as well as to research-based evidence about effective interventions. Planned interventions include referrals, for example, a service plan for counselling related to substance abuse with another service provider as well as interventions planned and carried out in the milieu by the child and youth care practitioners (e.g., involving a child in a social skills group with other children in the milieu). The basic principles are the same. Interventions are purposeful and consistent with a specific theoretical orientation; guided by agency policy; and individualized to reflect differences in culture/human diversity, background, temperament, personality, and differential rates of development. There are too many theoretical approaches and evidence-based interventions to complete a comprehensive introduction; therefore, a brief illustration of how theory and planned interventions can be implemented is offered through a discussion of a possible set of planned interventions for Autry. The case illustration is followed by a discussion of the application of positive youth development approaches to planned interventions.

CASE ILLUSTRATION: AUTRY

Theory and Planned Interventions

When Autry was age 16, the child and youth care practitioner in his school, Lora, was asked to become involved as a result of an incident during a basketball game when Autry was kicked out of school. Lora knew that the incident was related to racism on the part of the other youth, but Autry didn't want to do anything about it; he felt helpless and didn't believe it would have any effect. He was willing to meet with the practitioner and she decided to try two different interventions with different theoretical rationale.

A simplified view of cognitive-behaviour therapy (CBT) identifies the following basic premise and rationale:

- *Behaviours and cognitions are closely connected. Changing one will change the other.*
- *Your worldview influences your behaviour and mood; therefore, by attending to your thoughts and changing your thoughts you can change your behaviour and mood.*

Lora asked Autry to help organize a Jamaican-Canadian celebration in the school. She could see that he was adopting a negative view of himself and his heritage based on the racism he was experiencing and she knew that there were a number of other peers that were proud of their heritage. She knew that Autry did not have the skills or confidence to organize the day on his own and there were lots of others that did, but she wanted him involved. She assigned him a very specific task: to interview his peers and find out what they thought and how they felt about their heritage. Autry was good at writing and so she asked him to write their stories about immigrating and how they overcame the hurdles they experienced along the way. What Autry found in his writing of the stories was a series of affirming statements that the other youth had used to find strength:

- Jamaicans have spirit and strength.
- I'm stronger and better than those that disrespect and enslave us.
- My family loves me and my community supports me. Together we are powerful.

Gradually he began to tell himself these same affirmations. Lora observed that he seemed taller and was making friends among the organizing group. She asked him to do something else for her.

> *"Storytelling is one of the oldest forms of teaching and healing. . . . Fairy tales, along with the vast collection of myths handed down from culture to culture, are a record of the struggle and the adventure of the human experience . . . the characters mirror the same wide range of fears, trauma, and abuse that many of today's children and youth encounter in the world. These stories mirror the inner reality of most children, and it is the workings of the internal world, the unconscious, where these stories have their greatest effect. . . . The drama of the story symbolically represent[s] the drama of the lives of the audience." (Burns, 2008, pp. xiv–xv)*

There was a peer mentoring program that paired senior students with students in kindergarten and grade 1 at a neighboring school. Lora asked Autry if he would be interested and specifically requested that he find some traditional Jamaican folktales that he could read to the children. He realized that he didn't know any, other than a few scraps that his granny told him before they left for Canada. He asked his mother and father, who started to share some of the folklore from their childhoods. Autry told Lora that he would be happy to tell the stories, but that he couldn't read them because the folktales had an oral tradition. He chose tales that spoke to overcoming powerful beings and battling groups of mythical animals that were trying to hurt you and told these to the children.

Positive Youth Development (PYD) is an orientation to working with young people that emphasizes their strengths and focuses on a primary prevention strategy to build leadership skills and develop community resources to support the growth and development of young people (Catalano, Berglund, Ryan, Lonczak, & Hawkins, 2004; Lerner & Lerner, 2012). In the case illustration, Lora engages Autry in a school-based activity that is not targeted at particular young people, but broadly involves all young people, including those "at risk" in developing their skills for leadership and enhancing confidence.

Positive Youth Development is a theoretical and service delivery orientation that promotes relationship and competence in all aspects of development and fosters identity, self-efficacy, and hope for the future. Opportunities for prosocial involvement and recognition for positive behavior are provided through PYD programs (Catalano et al., 2004), which involve all young people. Lerner and Lerner (2012) distill the characteristics of PYD to the "5 C's": competence, confidence, connection, character, and caring. They theorize that "young people whose lives incorporated these Five Cs would be on a developmental path that results in the development of a Sixth C: Contributions to self, family, community, and to the institutions of a civil society. In addition, those young people whose lives contained lower amounts of the Five Cs would be at higher risk for a developmental path that included personal, social, and behavioral problems and risks" (p. 6). Thus there is believed to be a close connection between the prevention of risk and the positive development of young people.

Model programs in PYD include Big Brothers, Big Sisters and the 4-H movement, among others. Involving young people at risk in these programs can be part of a planned intervention building on their strengths and assets and encouraging the local community to be supportive and mindful of all their young people (McCammon, 2012). Such interventions are not just focused on the individual; they are also focused on young people's ecology and the community that surrounds them. Consideration of this type of approach and recording PYD programs as interventions on the written plans developed with young people and families is often neglected, when in fact such activities are a core and fundamental approach to helping young people (Vander Ven, 2004).

INTERVENTION PLANS

This section describes the importance of creating a written plan for intervention. The planning process has different labels in various jurisdictions and so here it is simply called an **intervention plan**. Other terminology includes individual program plan (IPP), individual education plan

(IEP), case management, treatment plan, support plan, or plan of care (POC). Planning for intervention involves both a **process** of planning and **reports** that document the plan for a specific young person or family during the work that practitioners are involved in. Most organizations and jurisdictions working with young people have a regular cycle of planning and reporting and have a very specific format, often with unique software that guides the process; therefore, only the phases of the process are outlined here because the specifics of the format will be determined by the organization for which a practitioner works.

Planning for intervention includes the process of observing, assessing, planning, implementing, and evaluating specific interventions. The planning process cannot be undertaken without being intentionally relational (Bellefeuille & Jamieson, 2008), even in the planning work that child and youth care practitioners do. The process incorporates relationship, human development, and an ecological perspective to determine the needs of the young person or family. Intervention plans should be driven by goals that are important to, and developed by, the young people for whom the plan is being made. Even in advocacy work the group undertakes a planning process. Planned interventions and methods for achieving those goals can then be matched to the needs, strengths, and ecology of the young person.

Observation is one component of assessment that identifies strengths, determines needs, and leads to specific goals for change. The child and youth care practitioner has strong, objective observation and reporting skills. These skills are used to assess and evaluate the daily interactions in a group environment and observe events related to the client intervention plan(s). Developmentally appropriate opportunities are created in which children can experience success. Observing, assessing, and reporting occur in the life-space with **contact notes** and **daily logs**, which are summarized at regular intervals into assessments and intervention plans. Regularly scheduled summaries, progress reports, and plans of care or treatment plans are essential to the reporting, ongoing assessment, and evaluation process.

Assessment is a component of planning that directs the practitioner's observation toward specific areas of interest that measure developmental progress or describe the systems and ecology that influence development for a specific young person. Assessment tools and the focus of observations are guided by the jurisdiction in which practitioners work. Juvenile justice is interested in criminal behaviours, restitution, expressions of remorse, and planning to prevent future illegal activities. Child welfare, on the other hand, is interested in safety for the children and ensuring that basic developmental needs are fulfilled. Educational programs focus more on assessing school performance and intellectual capacity and health care programs assess for symptoms and opportunities for intervention. Positive Youth Development is interested in identifying and building strengths and confidence.

Planning requires that practitioners identify needs, strengths, and goals for change or enhancement with the young person or family. A goal states what the young person or family wants to accomplish, written in a way that makes it clear when the goal has been met. Intervention strategies follow logically from the goal statements. Young people and families can often describe roughly what they want to achieve (the goal) but the reason that they are working with a practitioner is because they don't know what steps to take to accomplish the goal. Practitioner's expertise comes into play and they design strategies that will help young people and families achieve those goals. These are the planned interventions. They may be strategies that practitioners implement or a referral may occur to another professional with a different expertise.

Planning is useless without knowing that the goals have been accomplished. **Evaluating** progress is critical to recognizing successful outcomes for young people as well as for improving practice and service delivery. Practitioners return to the process of observation and assessment to determine whether the outcomes have been achieved. Evaluation is a systematic process that often has a theoretical basis to identify the expected outcomes. Regular reviews are necessary to identify outcomes and assess additional areas of need or strength. Assessment and evaluation are a process of assigning meaning to information that is gathered and integrated into a comprehensive whole. In general, this meaning-making involves applying a set of criteria that are grounded in theoretical orientations (Ricks & Charlesworth, 2003). In current terminology this is evidence-based practice, which documents the success a program has with a specific method of working with young people. Intervention plans are part of a cyclical process: As the end of a cycle is reached it starts again, assessing, planning, implementing, and evaluating.

SMART GOALS

Specific
Measureable
Achievable
Realistic
Time-limited

1. The group will increase the awareness that teachers have of human rights violations against youth with disabilities and young people of colour in the school by the end of the first semester.
2. Jorge will make two friends in the community, whom he plays with on a regular basis, by the end of the summer.

SUMMARY

This chapter described a theoretical framework for intervention that is based on the relationships that you develop with young people and families. The subdomains of life-space intervention, planned intervention, advocacy, and group work introduced some specific theories and techniques or strategies that a novice practitioner can use to guide his or her practice. These strategies draw on the knowledge and skills of the other domains of practice discussed earlier and are integrated into a reflective practice framework to help you become an experienced practitioner and grow into a mature practitioner. The area of intervention plans was briefly introduced as a general review of a planning framework that guides most practitioners and their organizations toward systematic planning and evaluation to demonstrate the effectiveness of child and youth care interventions.

Photo by Laine Robertson

CHAPTER EXERCISES

THINK ABOUT IT

Intervention Is the Heart of Child and Youth Care

Take a few moments to "take apart" this quote.

How do you define "intervention"?

What do you think "heart" means in this statement?

How do you think intervention in child and youth care is different from intervention as it is defined by other professions?

THINK ABOUT IT

The Role of Self and Relationship in Intervention

Choose one of the following phrases from the child and youth care literature, which describe the role practitioners play as they take "self" and "relationship" into their interventions in a unique manner:

- "Being at the heart of change" (Lundy, 2008)
- The "flow of immediacy" (Guttman, 1991)
- "Presencing" (Ricks, 2003)

- A "journey into self" (Fewster, 1990a)
- "Self in action" Krueger et al., 1999)
- "Co-created, connected, experience" (Garfat, 2008)

What does the phrase mean to you?

Identify an intervention that you have done with a child that captures the concept described by this author and write about it.

Find a copy of the original source (see the reference list at the end of the book) and compare your meaning-making of the phrase to the author's original words.

RHYTHM

Experience

There are many possibilities for experiencing rhythm and the effects of falling "out of synch." Try one of the following:

- Toss a frisbee back and forth. As soon as you catch it, let it go again. When the rhythm is going well, purposefully try and break the rhythm with your partner and see what happens.
- Notice your daily activities—the repetition, the timing, who else is involved. After several days of noticing, break routine. Walk a different route, eat at a different time, phone a friend instead of texting. What happens? How do other people react?

Reflection-on-Practice

Identify an experience that you have had with a child that successfully captures the concept of "rhythmicity" and compare it to the "out-of-synch" experience that you just had.

Reflection-for-Practice

Consider the concept of rhythmicity as you understand it from this exercise and identify how you can bring additional rhythmic interactions into your practice with young people.

ENVIRONMENTAL DESIGN: PHYSICAL MILIEU

Experience

Burns suggests the following exercise to involve young people (in any milieu and of any age) in assessing and designing the physical environment (2006, p. 21).

Gather the young people into a group and let them know that you want to find out how to make the classroom (residence, hospital, community centre) safer and more welcoming or inclusive. Explain that you might not be able to do everything, but you want everyone's ideas.

You are going to make three lists:

- Furniture and equipment
- Floors and walls
- Lighting

Ask the group to brainstorm and write everything down. Start with one area and then go to the next. After all the ideas are out and on paper, go back through and ask the group to eliminate ideas that are too expensive for this place. Note that they are really good ideas and, if appropriate, talk about who we could share the ideas with so that people know how to build good spaces for young people.

This exercise would also work during a family meeting. Try it in your own home, with family or roommates.

Reflection-for-Practice

How will the changes that are recommended affect the safety, self-esteem, and sense of inclusion of the people affected by the change?

Theory-in-Action

The exercise considers three aspects of the environment; what other characteristics of the physical environment might you consult with children about? (*Hint:* Consider your five senses.)

MEANING-MAKING AND PHYSICAL CONFLICT

Experience (imagined) with Reflection-in-Action

Recall a time when you were so angry and frustrated that you might have wanted to lash out and hurt someone. Take a moment to replay the incident in your mind and remember the emotions and thoughts associated with the incident. Scan and note all the emotions and thoughts. Anger of course is one aspect, but what other emotions were present? Was there also fear? Intimidation? Embarrassment? Identify what you were thinking and feeling. How did you control yourself?

Now, you are going to introduce some new elements into the experience. Imagine that a large and strong person noticed your anger and heard what you were saying. As part of the intervention he or she grabbed you from behind and wrapped your arms and legs up so that you couldn't move. Identify how you feel, what you are thinking, how you respond (in this imaginary scenario).

Reflection-on-Action

Next, take a few moments to reflect on both the real and imagined parts of this scene and explore the other aspects of self that both guided you in this incident and also may influence your interventions with young people when conflict escalates to a physical level.

Reflection-for-Practice

What values are evident?

What are your beliefs about physical conflict, and about your role in physical conflict between others?

What are the ethics or current "rules" that govern your actions in response to physical conflict?

THE STRUCTURE OF DAILY LIFE EVENTS

Within the many different milieus where young people are found, there are elements of social control that are the rules of daily life in that milieu that help adults guide children toward being social citizens. They are the **laws** and **rules** of the program and they are set within the social and cultural expectations of the country. Examples include:

- Make a straight line to go into the school.
- No spitting.
- No guns allowed.
- Clean your bedroom on Friday afternoon.

Fact is: These laws and rules don't always ensure compliance, so practitioners need to support young people's agency or compliance as appropriate in the moment while maintaining a practice focus on social competence and enhancing development.

Experience

Choose a milieu and identify three "rules" that children typically have difficulty following or remembering. Design a "fun" activity or direction for each rule that will help them be successful in remembering and following the rule without being punished.

Reflection-for-Practice

Review the activities that you have designed and determine whether the activities work with children who are age 5. What about age 15? How would you adapt the activities for differences in culture, gender, disability, or sexual orientation? How would you adapt for two, 10, or 30 children? What would you do if it was just "a stupid rule" and one of the young people advocated for a change?

UNCRC

Think about It

Review the list of universal rights that are described in this chapter and apply them to the description of Autry's life and family outlined in Chapter 5.

- Which rights are being violated? Can you find the specific articles in the UNCRC?
- What could you initiate to advocate on Autry's behalf to ensure that his rights are no longer violated?

- What could you initiate to advocate with Autry to correct the rights violations and educate others?

FOR THE "SAKE OF THE GROUP"

Experience

Recall the formal groups in which you participated as a young person. You may be able to recognize some of the stages of group development and identify the purpose of the group. In this reflection, focus on your individual needs and goals when you joined the group and how those were balanced with a collective set of group goals.

Reflection-on-Practice

How did you feel when your personal goals were not met? What are your beliefs about the value of group work with young people? What did you learn individually from the experience and what did you learn from the group?

Reflection-for-Practice

Each group member brings a different context to their meaning-making.

Consider all the meaning-making/action combinations possible in a group of six to eight young people.

The complexity of practice requires *Noticing, Reflecting, Preparing, Intervening* simultaneously with six to eight young people.

CAREER ACCOMPLISHMENTS

What Next?

As you come to the end of this book I hope that you are inspired to learn more, to be immersed in a reflective practice that keeps you living in the moment, in relationships with young people and their families. child and youth care practice is evolving and whether you are a novice, experienced, or mature practitioner you will evolve along with the field. In less than a century, the field has expanded in North America from a base in residential care to a field that spans health, education, justice, and social service jurisdictions, and includes practitioners working directly with young people as well as supervisors, managers, educators, researchers, and consultants. Practitioners are found in communities, schools, hospitals, after-school care, mental health centres, juvenile justice programs, youth leadership programs, and more. The characteristics of child and youth care outlined in Chapter 1 have remained core to practice throughout this time of professionalizing the field.

If you are just beginning your journey as a child and youth care professional you have many things to look forward to:

- Young people and families who deserve to be cared about to bring forward their strengths and resilience.
- The challenges of caring, genuine listening, and honest communication.

- The joy and fresh perspectives that young people bring to life.
- Learning about the many different ways that others understand the world.
- Life-long relationships.
- Increasing awareness of self and other.
- Moments that can only be experienced "in the milieu," where daily life happens.

The aspects of self, skills, and knowledge that you have learned about throughout this book are just the beginning. Your developmental journey as a child and youth care practitioner will go much further with a combination of good planning and caring relationships. The final exercise in this book is to get you started on furthering that journey.

Personal Reflection

Use Appendix C, which outlines a set of competencies expected of novice practitioners, to complete an assessment of your current knowledge and skills.

Review the reflective exercises that you have engaged in while reading this book.

Now imagine that it is 30 years from now. You are a mature practitioner in the field. What have you accomplished over your career? (How has the field changed?) Look back over 30 years and record what you have done.

Now come back to the present; identify and record three goals that will start you on that 30-year journey. If you aren't sure how to take the first few steps toward accomplishing your goals, meet with a more experienced practitioner and ask for some strategies.

Afterword

Throughout the first edition and in the second edition you have read a series of personal reflections written by youth for the *The Letters of Hope Project*. The project is a collection of worldwide letters from young people who have survived hopelessness and now want to give hope to other young people struggling to get to the other side. Led by filmmaker Andrée Cazabon, the project is collecting letters of hope into a book and will use the proceeds to further support young people who need to find hope in their lives. You can learn more about the project and read additional letters at *www.andreecazabon.ca/letters-of-hope-project*. The final letter that is reproduced here is intact with the dialect of both the street and today's text messages and illustrates the power of hope, love, and radical youth work. Both Andrée and John use their gift for art as part of their youth work. They illustrate the passion of youth workers who are "untrained" and yet through their talents have had a significant impact on troubled young people. They represent the core and the origin of the profession, a core that those of us that have committed to professional education must not neglect or reject, but rather must go forward in partnership.

PERSONAL REFLECTION: YOUTH

It was late, I was riding three deep wid a couple of my peoples thru a certain part of my city. I remember I had a couple hundred dollars on me and my cell phone. I wasn't supposed to out there I was on house arrest from a robbery charge and it was the first hot day of the spring. We had a few girls wid us but we still wanted some weed. So we went to the only place we knew we could grab some at 3 in the morning. . . .

We pulled into the parking lot of a housing complex off of Jane street to get the weed. It was only about two minutes. We were buying from a "Friend" and was pulling out when we noticed that three bikes where blocking the road. Something told me "hide my money now". Before I could tell the driver to watch out he had a long 357 nozzle on his jaw. We were all pulled out. We were all 19, all had graduated last year but my boy had a new car already. We looked like we were making a lot of loot from the outside so these fools we trying to find out how. I wasn't selling at the time (house arrest) but my boys were. They were robbed–the driver lost a thousand dollars that day and eventually lost his car, my boy in shotgun got his dope robbed and I was almost stripped searched because they couldn't even find a nickel on me. I was born and raised in the ghetto (which do exist in Toronto fuck what any mayor says) so I knew about intuition, street smarts and all that so I hid my loot proper. I grew seeing people get robbed, shot, stab in front of my young eyes so I never blinked when the robber put a gun to my forehead. I knew the guy and was a killer (yet) so I told him flat I got no loot I'm not a hustler. Then things got really scary, he passed the gun to one of his little soldiers. This youth was only bout 15 and looked confused and stupid as fuck. I know this kid would shoot me cuz I just don't think he was thinking for himself to often at that point in his life. He just wanted to be down with the strongest crew in our area. He pulls back the hammer as says. . . . It don't matter what he said I knew I was about to die. I realized that I wasn't afraid to die until I started to think about all the stuff I never did yet. Like I said I was not gangster but u don't have to be to get caught up sometimes. I'm still here so I don't have to finish this story. But it did make me begin to appreciate life in a whole new light. I realized that I have to think about what I do. Is it worth it? Will it benefit me in the long run? If I do this do I even have a long run? . . . I don't preach but I'll say dis. . . . I will not let the world use me and throw me away. Fuck dat. I must survive and live my dreams. I will not let no one speak for me. I will not let this capitalistic world where silent murder is rewarded with prestige take my soul because every day that I live and grow makes my ancestors proud. I am now an art student at Ryerson. I had to give up a lot to get here. And there are many places that I had to avoid to get this far. U must stay strong because it is only u and me and people like us that the world forgot that can actually change it. Revolution is in the hand of the oppressed so right there where u are a potential soldier in the army for real justice, in the fight against hunger and injustice. Reach out to ur elders tell them your story and listen theirs. Maybe you will realize what I did. . . . The hardship I went thru was training for the revolution ahead. And only by fighting for your rights will ever be free.

UhUru (FREEDOM in Swahili)
John, 20 years old, Toronto, Ontario

PROFESSIONAL ASSOCIATIONS DEFINE THE SCOPE OF CHILD AND YOUTH CARE PRACTICE

Scope of practice definitions focus on the boundaries of expertise because definitions help regulate and define the field for legislation that restricts who can practice as a "Child and Youth Care" practitioner and whether a practitioner is ethical within their area of expertise. This is a tough call when we are "experts in the art of living" (Mayer, 1958, p. xvi).

The *Ontario Association of Child and Youth Counsellors* (OACYC) offers the following definition of the Scope of CYC Practice.

> "The assessment of maladaptive behaviour patterns and social-emotional functioning in children, adolescents, and young adults and the prevention and treatment of conditions in the individual, family, and community, in order to develop, maintain, and promote emotional, social, behavioural, and interpersonal wellbeing within the context of daily living." © Adopted March 2004 by the OACYC

For additional information on the OACYC Scope, explore their website at *www.oacyc.org*.

The *Child and Youth Care Association of Alberta* (CYCAA) has defined the scope of practice as follows:

> Regulated members certified by the College may, within the practice (Child and Youth Care Counsellor and/or Child and Youth Care Worker), perform the restricted activities of understanding and providing the Life Space Intervention through the following methods:
>
> - Provision and maintenance of a therapeutic milieu
> - Knowledge and application of human developmental theories in the context of group/family dynamics.
> - Development, implementation and maintenance of progressive care plans including release or post placement planning and support with a strong family reunification focus.
> - Develop therapeutic relationships with children/youth, families, and important contributors to the child's/youth's well being.
> - Collaborate within multi-disciplinary teams including recommendations made to team members.

The Scope of Practice conforms to the format required by the Health Professions Act. (www.cycaa.com/pdfs/scope%20of%20practice%20questionnaire.pdf)

The *Canadian Council of Child and Youth Care Associations* (CCCYCA) has adopted the following Scope of Practice.

> The practice of Child and Youth Care occurs within the context of therapeutic relationships with children and youth who are experiencing difficulties in their lives. Intervention takes place within the family, the community and other social institutions, and centres on promoting emotional, social and behavioural change and well-being within the context of daily living. (www.cyccanada.org, retrieved June 2009.)

CODE OF ETHICS

STANDARDS FOR PRACTICE OF NORTH AMERICAN CHILD AND YOUTH CARE PROFESSIONALS

International Leadership Coalition of Professional Child and Youth Care

June 1995

PREAMBLE

Professional Child and Youth Care is committed to promoting the well being of children, youth, and families in a context of respect and collaboration. This commitment is carried out in a variety of settings and with a broad range of roles including direct practice, supervision, administration, teaching and training, research, consultation, and advocacy. In the course of practice Child and Youth Care Professionals encounter many situations which have ethical dimensions and implications.

As Child and Youth Care Professionals we are aware of, and sensitive to, the responsibilities involved in our practice. Each professional has the responsibility to strive for high standards of professional conduct. This includes a commitment to the centrality of ethical concerns for Child and Youth Care practice, concern with one's own professional conduct, encouraging ethical behavior by others, and consulting with others on ethical issues.

This ethical statement is a living document, always a work in progress, which will mature and clarify as our understanding and knowledge grow. The principles represent values deeply rooted in our history, to which there is a common commitment. They are intended to serve as guidelines for conduct and to assist in resolving ethical questions. For some dilemmas, the principles provide specific or significant guidance. In other instances, the Child and Youth Care Professional is required to combine the guidance of the principles with sound professional judgment and consultation. In any situation, the course of action chosen is expected to be consistent with the spirit and intent of the principles.

PRINCIPLES AND STANDARDS

I. RESPONSIBILITY FOR SELF:
  A. Maintains competency.
    1. Takes responsibility for identifying, developing, and fully utilizing knowledge and abilities for professional practice.

---

2. Obtains training, education, supervision, experience and/or counsel to assure competent service.

B. Maintains high standards of professional conduct.

C. Maintains physical and emotional well-being.

1. Aware of own values and their implication for practice.

2. Aware of self as a growing and strengthening professional.

II. RESPONSIBILITY TO THE CLIENT[1]

A. Above all, shall not harm the child, youth or family.

1. Does not participate in practices that are disrespectful, degrading, dangerous, exploitive intimidating, psychologically damaging, or physically harmful to clients.

B. Provides expertise and protection.

1. Recognizes, respects, and advocates for the rights of the child, youth and family.

C. Recognizes that professional responsibility is to the client and advocates for the client's best interest

D. Ensures that services are sensitive to and non-discriminatory of clients regardless of race, color, ethnicity, national origin, national ancestry, age, gender, sexual orientation, marital status, religion, abilities, mental or physical handicap, medical condition, political belief, political affiliation, socioeconomic status.

1. Obtains training, education, supervision, experience, and/or counsel to assure competent service.

E. Recognizes and respects the expectations and life patterns of clients.

1. Designs individualized programs of child, youth and family care to determine and help meet the psychological, physical, social, cultural and spiritual needs of the clients.

2. Designs programs of child, youth, and family care which address the child's developmental status, understanding, capacity, and age.

F. Recognizes that there are differences in the needs of children, youth and families.

1. Meets each client's needs on an individual basis.

2. Considers the implications of acceptance for the child, other children, and the family when gratuities or benefits are offered from a child, youth or family.

G. Recognizes that competent service often requires collaboration. Such service is a cooperative effort drawing upon the expertise of many.

1. Administers medication prescribed by the lawful prescribing practitioner in accordance with the prescribed directions and only for medical purposes. Seeks consultation when necessary.

2. Refers the client to other professionals and/or seeks assistance to ensure appropriate services.

3. Observes, assesses, and evaluates services/treatments prescribed or designed by other professionals.

[1]Client is defined as the child, family, and former clients.

H. Recognizes the client's membership within a family and community, and facilitates the participation of significant others in service to the client.

I. Fosters client self determination.

J. Respects the privacy of clients and holds in confidence information obtained in the course of professional service.

K. Ensures that the boundaries between professional and personal relationships with clients is explicitly understood and respected, and that the practitioner's behavior is appropriate to this difference.

   1. Sexual intimacy with a client, or the family member of a client, is unethical.

III. RESPONSIBILITY TO THE EMPLOYER/EMPLOYING ORGANIZATION:

A. Treats colleagues with respect, courtesy, fairness, and good faith.

B. Relates to the clients of colleagues with professional consideration.

C. Respects the commitments made to the employer/employing organization.

IV. RESPONSIBILITY TO THE PROFESSION:

A. Recognizes that in situations of professional practice the standards in this code shall guide the resolution of ethical conflicts.

B. Promotes ethical conduct by members of the profession.

   1. Seeks arbitration or mediation when conflicts with colleagues require consultation and if an informal resolution seems appropriate.

   2. Reports ethical violations to appropriate persons and/or bodies when an informal resolution is not appropriate.

C. Encourages collaborative participation by professionals, client, family and community to share responsibility for client outcomes.

D. Ensures that research is designed, conducted, and reported in accordance with high quality Child and Youth Care practice, and recognized standards of scholarship, and research ethics.

E. Ensures that education and training programs are competently designed and delivered.

   1. Programs meet the requirements/claims set forth by the program.

   2. Experiences provided are properly supervised.

F. Ensures that administrators and supervisors lead programs in high quality and ethical practice in relation to clients, staff, governing bodies, and the community.

   1. Provides support for professional growth.

   2. Evaluates staff on the basis of performance on established requirements.

V. RESPONSIBILITY TO SOCIETY:

A. Contributes to the profession in making services available to the public.

B. Promotes understanding and facilitates acceptance of diversity in society.

C. Demonstrates the standards of this Code with students and volunteers.

D. Encourages informed participation by the public in shaping social policies and institutions.

Retreived from *www.pitt.edu/~mattgly/CYCethics.html*. Also available at *http://cyccanada.ca*, *www.cyc-net.org/fice-curr.html*, and *www.acycp.org/standards/standards.htm*.

APPENDIX C

COMPETENCIES OF CHILD AND YOUTH CARE PRACTICE

The domains of practice and elements of performance identified here were developed during a research project and community consultation in 2006. In the first edition they were reproduced just as they were developed for that project. The writing of the first edition of this text and the subsequent revisions to the text for the second edition made it impossible for me to publish this appendix without revision. As the field of child and youth care has evolved and scholars have engaged in critical reflection on our roots, our knowledge, our skills, and even our attitudes, I felt that I had to reflect some of that debate in these competencies as well as in the book. Skills, attitudes, and knowledge are not neutral; they reflect a particular context, culture, and language for a professional group. The original competencies in this appendix were developed specifically in the context of mental health in Ontario, Canada. As noted in the text, child and youth care practice exists in multiple settings, with diverse young people and families. I have updated language and made it more strength-based, resilience focused, and reflective of material that has been published between 2006 and 2013. It is not my intent that these competencies be "the standard"; rather, it is my hope that they engage practitioners, supervisors, and scholars in debate—as suggested by Pence and White (2011)—about the ultimate aims of practice, ethical obligations, and practical responsibilities of caring for young people, advocating for change, and leading the field toward respectful and just interventions that enhance the lives of young people and families who struggle.

The original report and competencies can be found in Stuart, C., & Carty, W. (2006). *The role of competence in outcomes for children and youth: An approach for mental health.* Toronto: Ryerson University. Available at http://digitalcommons.ryerson.ca/cyc/2/. The elements of performance listed in the following domains and subdomains were adapted from other documents on certification and training or from focus groups completed with mental health supervisors of Child and Youth Care practitioners. As such these competencies are grounded to the field of practice and have been enhanced by more recent child and youth care literature reviewed in the writing and revision to this book. Each element of performance is "referenced" to the original source as follows:

- (AB)—CYCAA (2000). *Certification Manual* (Professional Manual). Edmonton: Child and Youth Care Association of Alberta.
- (FG)—focus groups.
- (MN)—Johnston, R. M. (1997). *Comprehensive Competency-Based In-Service Training: A Training Needs Assessment for Residential Child and Youth Care Workers.* Barrie: Institute for Human Services–Canada.

- (NACP)—Mattingly, M., Stuart, C., & Vanderven, K. (2002). Competencies for professional Child and Youth Care. *Journal of Child and Youth Care Work, 17,* 16–49.
- (ON)—Ontario Ministry of Training, Colleges and Universities. (2002). *Child and Youth Worker Program Standard.* Retrieved December 3, 2004, from www.edu.gov.on.ca/eng/general/college/progstan/humserv/echildyt.html.
- (QU)—National Training Program (2002). *Skills for rehabilitation intervention.* Unpublished draft.

I. SELF

Description of Domain

Self is seen as foundational to child and youth care practice. Each of the other six domains is developed within the context of the self as the mediator of knowledge and skills. This is the area that includes the practitioner's responsibility for self-awareness and a life-long commitment to developing and utilizing self to ensure the best practices with children and youth. Graduates have insight into the factors of their own development and the impact of self factors on practice interventions. *(FG)*

Three assumptions about how child and youth practitioners' work with the self are important considerations for this domain: (1) Growth occurs in a series of moments and interactions, and each moment and interaction has enormous potential; (2) work with youth is a process of self in action, workers and youths learning about themselves from their experiences together; and (3) competent practice is continuously interlaced with other spheres of knowledge, skills, and preferred values that are learned concomitantly with the practice.[1] They are aware of and act on the limiting effect of professional client boundaries on the relationship. (NACP) This domain addresses areas of reflective practice, boundaries, self in intervention, and self-care.

Knowledge Foundations

The graduate should have knowledge and comprehension of the following areas in order to achieve the learning outcomes within this domain.

1. Core values and attitudes in Child and Youth Care Practice (AB Professional Issues/Attitudes/Self-Care and Personal Development/Knowledge)
2. Models for self-awareness and self-appraisal (AB Self-Care and Personal Development/Attitudes) *(FG)*
3. Models for time management *(FG)*
4. Theory and symptoms of burnout and stress (AB Self-Care and Personal Development/Skills)
5. Vicarious trauma, critical incident stress reactions, and other occupational stressors inherent in child and youth care practice (AB Self-Care and Personal Development/Attitudes)

---

[1] See Krueger, Galovits, Wilder, & Pick (1999). A Curriculum Guide for Working with Youth: An Interactive Approach. Milwaukee: University Outreach Press.

6. Accepted boundaries in professional practice (Note: Also in Professionalism but key here) (ON-v.s. 6.1, NACP IA) *(FG)*

7. Stress management, self-care, and wellness practices (NACP IA, IB3b2, ON-v.s. 6.4) (Note: Also in Professionalism but key here) *(FG)*

8. Personal goal setting and life-long learning (ON-v.s. 6.3) *(FG)*

9. Agency, personal, and professional support systems (AB Self-Care and Personal Development/knowledge) *(FG)*

10. Local professional support services (NACP IA, QU, AB Self Care and Personal Development/Knowledge)

Reflective Practice

The child and youth care worker (recent graduate) continuously assesses his/her professional skills, knowledge, and personal well-being and reflects on the impact of these factors on his/her day-to-day practice. *(Outcome)* (QU 401–8, AB) *(FG)*

Graduates develop self-reflective habits that ensure quality care to children and youth and enhance personal and professional growth. *(Clarification)*

Elements of Performance

The child and youth care practitioner:

1. Critically reflects upon his/her personal biases and cultural values and their implication for practice. (NACP IIB1a, QU, MN 805–1) *(FG)*

2. Performs ongoing self-assessment relative to personal strengths and limitations; feelings and needs; and his/her role in interactions with children, youth, families, and other members of the professional team. (QU 401–8, MN 802–1, 833–2, NACP IB3a1, IVB1f) *(FG)*

3. Uses reflective tools such as supervision (ON-vs. 6.2), personal journaling, and other reflective exploratory methods to learn from his/her interactions with young people and families. (NACP, AB Self-Care and Personal Development/Skills)

4. Routinely seeks guidance and feedback from supervisors and peers (AB Self-Care and Personal Development/Skills) to challenge his/her role in therapeutic interactions. *(FG)*

5. Understands and incorporates "standing back" in order to assess objectively. (QU 402–7,402–8)*

6. Articulates his/her own learning style. (ON-g.e.d. 4.4)

7. Recognizes the importance of self awareness and its implications for practice and modifies behavior to reflect this knowledge. (QU 407–1, MN 833–2, NACP IVB2a) *(FG)*

8. Reevaluates goals and make adjustments.

Boundaries

The child and youth care worker (recent graduate) demonstrates an awareness of professional and personal boundaries to maintain a safe and effective service for children, youth and families *(outcome)*. (QU, AB Relationship Development/Attitudes, MN, NACP)

Boundaries are fluid and change with the requirements of the relationships that workers have. Practitioners must be open to acting on feedback from those outside the relationship and place authentic relationships at the forefront of their interactions. *(Clarification)*

Elements of Performance

The child and youth care practitioner:

1. Recognizes the practitioner's responsibility to maintain clear boundaries and ensures that therapeutic relationships do not devolve into social relationships. (AB Relationship Development/Attitudes)
2. Demonstrates the ability to set, maintain, and communicate appropriate boundaries (NACP IVB2f) in a manner that is authentic, respectful, honest, and clear. (AB Relationship Development/Attitudes, ON-v.s. 6.1)
3. Describes his/her own needs and feelings and keeps them in perspective when professionally engaged. (NACP IB2d1) *(FG)*
4. Maintains the necessary distance to gather the facts and describe them objectively (QU 402–7, 402–8) while engaging in an authentic relationship.
5. Actively seeks and integrates feedback to set his/her boundaries in relation to clients' needs within the relationship.

Use of Self in Intervention

The child and youth care worker (recent graduate) examines the impact of self on others, cultivates and develops checks and balances *(FG)* to ensure that interactions are consistent and constructive. Practitioners take into consideration their individual values, beliefs, and opinions and the effects these have on their actions with clients and coworkers. *(Outcome)* (NACP, ON-g.s. 11.5)

Elements of Performance

The child and youth care practitioner:

1. Regularly and systematically evaluates how his/her actions affect young people and families and inform practice. (QU401–8, 407–2, 407–4) (ON-g.s. 11.5)
2. Accepts, evaluates, and acts upon feedback from others (client, family, colleagues, supervisors) in an effort to improve practice. (QU, ON-v.s. 1.4, g.s. 11.6) *(FG)*
3. Examines how his/her own attitudes and reactions impact interventions and adapts practice accordingly. (NACP, MN 802–2, QU401–8, ON-g.s. 11.5) *(FG)*
4. Summarizes his/her own skills, knowledge, and experience realistically. (ON-v.s. 7.1)
5. Takes responsibility for his/her own actions and decisions. (ON-g.s. 11.7, QU 408–3) *(FG)*
6. Integrates self-awareness with current research and practice knowledge to develop, implement and evaluate effective programs and services for clients. (NACP)
7. Plans interventions (momentary and systematic) that incorporate an awareness of his/her own self as well as the worldview of the client and the context *(FG)* within which both are located.

Self-Care

The child and youth care worker (recent graduate) values self-care as an essential component of healthy practice. Graduates demonstrate an integration of self-care strategies into daily practice. *(Outcome)*

They understand that CYC practitioners' health and well-being must be accounted for and that practice requires continuous reassessment of well-being. *(Clarification)* (AB Self-Care and Personal Development)

Elements of Performance

The child and youth care practitioner:

1. Demonstrates an awareness of self as a growing and strengthening professional. (NACP) *(FG)*
2. Maintains a healthy lifestyle including adequate rest, recreation, and diet. (AB Self-Care and Personal Development/Skills)
3. Incorporates "wellness" practices into his/her own lifestyle. (NACP IB3b1)
4. Self-assesses for signs of burnout (AB Self-Care and Professional Issues) and applies self-care strategies that promote personal and professional growth. (ON-v.s. 6.4, MN 802–4)
5. Identifies and analyzes occupational stressors in both self and environment and demonstrates adequate coping strategies. (AB Self-Care and Personal Development/Attitudes, MN 802–5)
6. Establishes reasonable and realistic personal goals in relation to self-care (ON-v.s. 6.3), physical, emotional, and spiritual well-being. (AB Self-Care and Personal Development)
7. Accesses and utilizes appropriate resources to build and maintain a support network. (NACP IB3b3).
8. Obtains training, education, supervision, experience, and/or counsel to assure competent service. (NACP IB2e2, ON-v.s. 6.2, QU 407–4, AB) *(FG)*
9. Applies time management skills for an organized practice that balances the process of therapeutic relationships with required professional tasks. (ON-v.s. 6).

II. PROFESSIONALISM

Description of Domain

Professionalism is the area of influence that includes the professional presentation of the practitioner and their interpersonal interactions with young people, family, community, and other professionals. The focus of the interactions is on the work that they are engaged in, not a social or personal relationship. The domain addresses areas of ethics, professional identity and professional behaviours, supervision, and how diverse identities are managed in a professional context.

Knowledge Foundations

The graduate should have knowledge and comprehension of the following areas in order to achieve the learning outcomes within this domain.

1. History of the CYC profession including the legalities of professional regulation (NACP-IA, AB)
2. History of social services, justice environments, mental health treatments, and the historical treatment of "people" (e.g., the convenience of warehousing) including the legal approaches to the care and treatment of children and youth in these systems and the history of political, social, and economic factors that contribute to racism, stereotyping, bias, and discrimination. (MN 801–1, 830–1 NACP IIA) *(FG)*
3. Procedures for children's advocacy and grievances. (AB Community Development/ Knowledge, NACP-IA) *(FG)*
4. The legal rights, protections, and responsibilities regarding legal procedures that pertain to child and youth mental health. (MN 801–2) *(FG)*
5. The laws, standards, guidelines for collaboration, and policies relating to the interface between systems, such as mental health, juvenile justice and child and family services, and how these impact services offered to young people and families. (MN 801–5; 801–6; AB, NACP-IA) *(FG)*
6. Accepted boundaries in professional practice. (NACP-IA, ON-v.s. 6.1) *(FG)*
7. Stress management and wellness practices. (NACP-IA) *(FG)*
8. Change theory, the impact change has on work groups. (MN 830–4) *(FG)*
9. Policies and regulations of their professional association, including the code of ethics and a process for ethical decision making. (AB Professional Issues/Attitudes/Knowledge, NACP IB4c)
10. Cultural structures, theories of change, and values that lead to culture variations *(FG)* among families and communities of diverse backgrounds. (NACP IIA, AB)
11. Cross-cultural communication. (NACP IIA)

Ethics

The child and youth care worker (recent graduate) follows a code of personal and professional behaviour in the day-to-day performance of his/her work and uses an ethical decision-making process to help him/her make decisions when rules for behavior conflict. *(Outcome)*

These professional code(s) of ethics are governed and sanctioned by the professional association and include the formal codes of employment within the workplace, as well as the less formal norms of professional conduct for engaging with young people and families (NACP, AB). *(Clarification)*

Elements of Performance

The child and youth care practitioner:

1. Conforms to agency guidelines relating to attendance, punctuality, personal appearance, sick and vacation time, and workload management. (NACP IB2c1a) *(FG)*

2. Demonstrates an awareness of how personal and professional values influence practice including how beliefs, values, and attitudes influence interactions with clients and coworkers. (NACP March Draft I B-2a(1)) *(FG)*

3. Follows the guidelines of the relevant Child and Youth Work code of ethics at all times. (MN 801–12; NACP I B4c, AB)

4. Distinguishes between ethical and legal issues and applies an ethical decision-making process including:
   * Identifying the problem.
   * Identifying the potential issues involved.
   * Reviewing the relevant ethical guidelines.
   * Obtaining consultation.
   * Considering *possible* and *probable* courses of action.
   * Enumerating the consequences of the various alternatives.
   * Deciding on what appears to be the best course of action. (AB Professional Issues/Skills)

5. Applies the agency policy, laws, and professional code of ethics relating to confidentiality. He/she selects and communicates information that is pertinent to the needs of parents, colleagues, and collaborators as appropriate. (QU 408–2, QU 401–21 AB Professional Issues/Skills, NACP IB4 a-c, ON- VS5.4, MN 801–12, 801–6) *(FG)*

6. Follow the agency policy, laws, and professional code of ethics relating to conflict of interest. (AB Professional Issues/Skills) *(FG)*

7. Demonstrates appropriate use of power and authority and performs this role while showing respect for the people over whom he/she uses his/her authority. (QU 405–5) *(FG)*

8. Accesses and applies relevant laws and licensing regulations related to violations and reporting of a child's right to a safe, secure, and nurturing environment including the procedures and reporting related to crisis intervention and management of aggression. (NACP IB5a, MN 801–3, 808–8)

9. Demonstrates advocacy skills to ensure that young people and families have their views heard and considered during decision-making processes that directly affect them. (NACP IB6f) *(FG)*

Professional Development

The child and youth care worker (recent graduate) is committed to life-long learning and professional development including formal and informal learning opportunities in day-to-day practice and through formal education and training. *(Outcome)* (Alberta Professional Issues/Attitudes, NACP1B2e(2); ON- VS 7)

He/she is capable of self-criticism and accepts critical comments from others (young persons, parents, partners, colleagues, superiors) in an effort to improve his/her practice. He/she acknowledges mistakes and learns from them in order to improve his/her professional practice. He/she asks for help when he needs it. *(Clarification)* (QU 407–1, 407–4; AB)

Elements of Performance

The child and youth care practitioner:

1. Maintains membership in a professional organization. (AB Professional Issues/Skills)
2. Interprets and discusses current professional issues, future trends, and challenges in child and youth mental health. (NACP IVB2k, ON-VS 7.10) *(FG)*
3. Accesses and applies the professional literature, particularly in the relevant areas of evidence-based practice. (NACP March Draft I B-1(a) (IB2e1); AB Professional Issues/Attitudes, ON-VS 7.10) *(FG)*
4. Determines through self-assessment his/her current skills and knowledge and to identify and engage in professional development activities. (NACP IB2b1, ON-VS 7.1, 7.2, 7.3; MN 830–3, AB Self-Care and Personal Development/Skills) *(FG)*
5. Transfers and adapts current knowledge and skills to new contexts. (ON-VS 7.4) *(FG)*
6. Explains the nature of CYC practice to the public and other professionals. (AB Professional Issues/Skills) *(FG)*

Supervision

The child and youth care worker (recent graduate) demonstrates a commitment to the provision of high-quality care through reflective practice and therefore engages in the regular supervision process, taking responsibility for initiating reflective conversations. (AB-Professionalism/Attitudes)

Elements of Performance

The child and youth care practitioner:

1. Understands the agency organizational structure and how decisions are made within that structure, including the roles of the youth and youth care worker. (MN 830–2) *(FG)*
2. Develops and implements personal and practice goals in collaboration with his/her supervisor. (AB Professional Issues/Skills) *(FG)*
3. Employs effective and appropriate problem-solving strategies (NACP VB8i) by recognizing issues, consulting as appropriate, choosing from and implementing a variety of strategies within the context of agency policy and procedure. (AB Professional Issues/Skills, MN 802–2) *(FG)*
4. Critically evaluates personal performance and when requested participates in a peer feedback process. (AB Professional Issues/Skills, QU 407–6) *(FG)*

Diversity

The child and youth care worker (recent graduate) respects differences related to cultural and human diversity by attending to differences and similarities in the process of creating change for young people and families. *(Outcome) (FG)*

He/she is aware of the eight major factors that set groups apart from one another, and that give individuals and groups elements of identity: age, class, race, ethnicity, levels of ability, language, spiritual belief systems, educational achievement, and gender differences, and addresses issues related to these elements of identity throughout all other domains of practice (NACP). *(Clarification)*

Elements of Performance

The child and youth care practitioner:

1. Describes the importance of working with those whose values are different from his/her own. (NACP March Draft I B-2a(1); MN 801–11) *(FG)*

2. Analyzes personal biases and stereotypes about others based on age, class, race, ethnicity, ability, language, spiritual beliefs, education, and gender. (NACP IIB1a) *(FG)*

3. Analyzes the interaction between his/her own cultural values and the cultural values of others. Discovers his/her limitations in understanding and responding to cultural and human differences and seeks assistance when needed. (NACP IIB1b/c, MN 805–1) *(FG)*

4. Supports young people and families to access resources and services that advance cultural understanding and appreciation of human diversity. (NACP IIB1f/g, AB Systemic Frameworks/Skills, Community Development/Skills)

5. Supports young people families and programs in overcoming barriers to services that are created as a result of cultural and human diversity. (NACP IIB1h)

III. COMMUNICATION

Description of Domain

This is the area where relationships with people are established and the quality of service is enhanced through the ability to communicate effectively. This is an area of influence that surrounds four other domains of practice and is the domain through which aspects of the self and professionalism are expressed. Practitioners analyze their audience to identify what is required and to match those needs with the most appropriate means of communication in written, spoken, and visual messages. (ON-v.s. 8.6) The domain addresses verbal and nonverbal, written, electronic communication, and communications with professionals and the community.

Knowledge Foundations

The graduate should have knowledge and comprehension of the following areas in order to achieve the learning outcomes within this domain.

1. Communication theory (verbal and nonverbal) (NACP IVA) *(FG)*

2. Cultural differences in communication styles (NACP IVA, MN 805–1, QU) *(FG)*

3. Developmental differences in communication, including the influence of developmental disorders or diagnosis of mental illness (NACP IIIB2b, IVA, MN 804–1) *(FG)*

4. Family dynamics and communication patterns, including attachment theory as it relates to communication style (NACP IVA, MN 806–1) *(FG)*

5. APA guidelines

6. Computer literacy (NACP, ON-v.s. 8.4, MN, QU 402–12) *(FG)*

7. Use of electronic databases (ON-v.s. 8.4, QU) *(FG)*

8. Team building

9. DSM-V (AB Mental Health/Knowledge) *(FG)*

10. Licensing and program standards related to documentation (MN 801–13) *(FG)*

Verbal and Nonverbal Communication

The child and youth care worker (recent graduate) communicates effectively to enhance the quality of service and promote understanding and trust and is able to evaluate the results of the communication and adjust in order to improve effective communication. (ON-v.s. 8.7) *(Outcome)*

Communication is essential to expressing care and working effectively with young people, families, colleagues, and the community.

Elements of Performance

The child and youth care practitioner:

1. Demonstrates a variety of communication skills including:
   a) Active listening *(FG)*
   b) Empathy and reflection of feelings *(FG)*
   c) Appropriate nonverbal communication (eye contact, tone of voice, facial expression, spatial proximity, and body position) relative to culture, context, and status of the person *(FG)*
   d) Questioning for information and feelings
   e) Use of "door openers"
   f) Appropriate use of challenging and self-disclosure to promote change in the child's perspective on problem behavior
   g) Assertiveness (NACP IIB2a, IVB1b, QU 405–18, MN 806–6, 836–2, ON-g. e.d. 3.1, AB Relationship Development/Skills)

2. Demonstrates clear, concise, and accurate interpersonal communication (QU 408–5, 408–1, MN 803–17) according to the identified need, context, goal of communication, law/regulation, and ethics involved. (ON-v.s. 8.1, 8.6, NACP IVB4g).

3. Demonstrates sensitivity to cultural and human diversity (QU 405–19, MN 805–2) *(FG)*

4. Communicates respect and warmth *(FG)* using culturally appropriate gestures, mannerisms, and conventions such as eye contact, social distance, matching, and mirroring and (AB Relationship Development/skills) recognizes and adjusts verbal and nonverbal communication for the effects of age, cultural and human diversity, background, experience, and development. (NACP IIB2d, IIIB2b2, IVB1a)

5. Communicates with and assists clients (to a level consistent with their development, abilities, and receptiveness) to understand relevant information about legislation/regulations, policies/standards, and supports pertinent to the focus of service. (NACP IIIB2e, IVB1c)

6. Demonstrates an ability to communicate intervention strategies to clients and relevant others to promote understanding and enhance implementation. (Ministry, 10, ON-v.s. 1.1, 4.13, QU 401–21) *(FG)*

7. Demonstrates appropriate boundaries and limits on the behavior using clear and respectful communication. (NACP IVB1f, MN 807–2) *(FG)*

8. Describes objectively the nonverbal and verbal communication between-self and others (including supervisors, clients, and/or peer professionals). (NACP IIB2b)

Written Communication

The child and youth care worker (graduate) demonstrates accurate recording of interactions and issues that are fundamental to planning and to integrated service delivery. He/she is able to communicate clearly, concisely, and correctly in the written form. (ON-v.s 8) Graduates apply the appropriate format, material, language, and style suitable to the audience. (NACP 4 g, ON-g.s. 1.1) He/she produces information according to the style and conventions required, and will have checked written materials for accuracy and clarity. (ON-g.s. 1.6)

Elements of Performance

The child and youth care practitioner:

1. Demonstrates clear, concise, and accurate communication (AB Professional Issues/Skills, MN 803–17) in written material.

2. Evaluates communications and adjust for any errors in content, structure, style, and mechanics. (ON-g.s. 1.8) *(FG)*

3. Identifies, collects, analyzes, and presents relevant information in written form according to identified needs, agency policy, and any licensing, program standards, or legislated guidelines. (ON-g.s. 7, M N803–15, NACP IVB4f) *(FG)*

4. Writes reports that can be reviewed by both clients and professionals that are detailed, accurate, and timely using objective, culturally sensitive language and professional presentation (i.e., technical skills, grammar, spelling). (NACP IIB2f, AB Client Service Planning/skills) *(FG)*

5. Accurately records relevant interactions and issues in the client–practitioner relationship following client interactions (individual, group, and/or family). (MN 801–16, QU 401–10, NACP IVB4f, AB Relationship Development/Skills)

6. Maintains accurate records for health-related issues such as medication. (AB Basic Care/ Skills)

7. Demonstrates competence in the creation and completion of various client reports (regular progress reviews, case plans, critical incident reports) and program documents. (ON-v.s. 8.2) *(FG)*

8. Acknowledges the use of material from other sources according to the conventions of the medium used. (ON-g.s. 2.6)

Digital Technology

The child and youth care worker (recent graduate) demonstrates proficiency in using information technology for communication, information access, and decision making. *(Outcome)* (NACP, k)

Digital technologies facilitate and enhance the completion of tasks, communication, problem solving, and performing research. *(Clarification)* (NACP, MN, QU, ON-g.s. 3.6)

Elements of Performance

The child and youth care practitioner:

1. Selects and applies the use of suitable software, equipment, and tools for communication. (ON-v.s. 8.4) *(FG)*
2. Evaluates digital communications and adjusts for errors in content, structure, style, etc. (Ministry 18)
3. Chooses the format (e.g., memo, illustration, multimedia presentation, or diagram) appropriate to the purpose. (ON-g.s. 1.2, NACP IVB4g)
4. Critically analyzes digital sources of information and knowledge for rigour and evidence of credibility in relation to the purpose for which the information will be used.
5. Demonstrates an ability to use electronic databases for record-keeping with clients. *(FG)*
6. Takes the necessary precautions to protect confidentiality and privacy in digital communications.

Professionals and Community

The child and youth care worker (recent graduate) demonstrates effective communication skills with allied disciplines and the community by investigating and developing an understanding of the language and concepts used in those contexts. *(Outcome)*

The graduate recognizes that best practice requires close cooperation with the community and that the ability to access and utilize information to promote change is essential. He/she understands that the language and concepts of psychopathological approaches is required so that effective communication with allied professionals may take place. *(Clarification)* (AB, MN)

Elements of Performance

The child and youth care practitioner:

1. Applies verbal and written communication skills with multidisciplinary team members and professionals in the community.
2. Identifies and utilizes language and concepts used in the field to effectively communicate with allied professionals and to advocate on behalf of the client. (AB Mental Health/ Attitudes, NACP IVB4d) *(FG)*
3. Analyzes and communicates information about clients that is critical to those in other systems and actively seeks information from same (AB Systemic Frameworks/Skills,

MN 801–14, NACP IVB4d), particularly in relation to involving allied professionals (practitioners) in the assessment and planning process. *(FG)*

4. Acknowledges and respects other disciplines in program planning, communication and report writing using multidisciplinary and interdisciplinary perspectives. (NACP IVB4h) *(FG)*
5. Communicates the expertise of the child and youth care profession to the multi-disciplinary team members. (NACP VB10a, ON-v.s. 6.7) *(FG)*
6. Communicates effectively with family members about the needs of the young person. (NACP) *(FG)*.

IV. CRITICALLY APPLIED HUMAN DEVELOPMENT

Domain Description

The area of influence where practice is guided by theories of development applied to an understanding of a young person's current developmental status. The focus is on developing social competence and recognizing the strengths that the young person can bring to coping with environmental or physiological circumstances that pose risks to normative developmental outcomes. Practitioners are oriented toward lifespan development and apply developmental theory to understanding behavior and placing it in the larger context of the totality of development, the environmental and cultural context of the young person. (adapted AB, NACP) *(FG)*

The domain includes developmental theories, patterns of growth and development, psychotropic medication, and the application of developmental theory to understanding risk and resilience.

Knowledge Foundations

The graduate should have knowledge and comprehension of the following areas in order to achieve the learning outcomes within this domain:

1. Life Span Human Development with a focus on children and adolescents (MN 804–1, 821–1, NACP IIIA) *(FG)*
2. Developmental Theory
   a. Physical
   b. Cognitive
   c. Psycho-Social
   d. Language
   e. Moral
   f. Spiritual (MN 804–1, NACP IIIA)
3. Exceptionality in Development as it relates to Mental Health
   a. Psychopathology
   b. Physical disability
   c. Cognitive disability

  d. Intellectual disability
  e. Psycho-social disability (MN 804–4, 821–1, NACP IIIA)
4. The Language of Psychopathology (DSM-IV) (AB Mental Health/Knowledge) *(FG)*
5. Research on Risk and Resilience
6. Psycho-Pharmacology (AB Basic) *(FG)*

Developmental Theories

The child and youth care worker (recent graduate) knows and understands current research and theory in human development with an emphasis on synthesizing several theoretical perspectives and applying them to practice in work with children and youth. *(Outcome)*

At the level of beginning practice, graduates will demonstrate knowledge and basic application of the theories, primarily through observation and assessment. They will be able to critically describe the historical context of developmental theory and identify its relevance for young people from diverse backgrounds. As experience increases, practitioners will increasingly recognize opportunities for adjusting their own interactions with children and youth based on an integrated understanding of developmental theory and the environmental context. *(Clarification)*

For example, an experienced practitioner may engage a 16-year-old in an idealistic conversation about the unfairness of nuclear war while at the same time engaging in parallel play activities rather than competitive games because the youth cognitively is curious and can discuss and think at the necessary level of abstraction but socially has difficulty understanding the rules of cooperative or competitive games.

Elements of Performance

The child and youth care practitioner:

1. Identifies and explains children's developmental stages with reference to specific theories in different domains (cognitive, physical, emotional, and spiritual) and across different contexts. (AB Lifespan Development/Skills, Basic Care/Attitudes, NACP IIIB1a)
2. Analyzes the developmental appropriateness of environments for meeting the individual needs of clients. (QU 402–9, ON-vs 4.1, NACP IIIB1b, AB) *(FG)*
3. Interprets behaviors (young people and adults) with reference to developmental norms, tempered by an understanding of the cultural relevance of those norms. (QU, MN 804–1, AB Lifespan Development/Skills) *(FG)*
4. Applies interventions consistent with a child's developmental stages when appropriate. (QU 403–5, MN 804–1, NACP IIIB3b, AB Lifespan Development/Skills) *(FG)*
5. Assists clients to access programs and resources that support healthy development. (NACP IIIB4a, MN 804–1)
6. Integrates the developmental domains to examine a young person's development in a holistic manner within their social and cultural context. (AB Lifespan Development) *(FG)*
7. Understands that children's early developmental experiences and their social and cultural context significantly affect their adult maturational status (AB Lifespan Development) and

applies that understanding to problem behaviors that are reflective of developmental lags in specific domains. (MN 821–1, 803–4, 808–1, QU 401–2, NACP IVB3b) *(FG)*

8. Identifies and describes developmental issues to ensure service plans accurately reflect child or adolescent needs. (AB, MN 804–1, 821–1)

9. Assesses the effects of separation and loss on development. (MN 803–10, MN 806–1, 823–2, AB Therapeutic Environments/Attitudes)

Patterns of Growth and Development

The child and youth care worker (recent graduate) applies recent research in patterns and trajectories of child and adolescent development to observation and assessment of young people in his/her care while critically questioning the social and cultural context within which research and theory exist. *(Outcome)*

Elements of Performance

The child and youth care practitioner:

1. Describes the typical and atypical patterns of physical, social, and intellectual growth and development for young people and critically analyzes the binary concept that exists between typical and atypical. (AB Lifespan Development/Skills, MN 804–1, 821–1) *(FG)*

2. Incorporates culturally specific development norms into practice application (AB Lifespan Development/Skills, NACP II3b/c, MN 805–2) *(FG)*

3. Recognizes when development has occurred at different rates, in different developmental domains, for example, the physical, spiritual, emotional, and cognitive domains (AB Lifespan Development, MN 804–2, 804–4) *(FG)*

4. Identifies and describes delays in a variety of developmental domains when they are apparent in a young person in his/her care. (MN 804–2, 804–4, 821–1, NACP IIIA, AB Lifespan Development/Skills) *(FG)*

5. Is knowledgeable in specific subject areas such as substance abuse, suicide, sexual abuse, teen pregnancy, trauma, and adoption and understands how these issues are impacted by the young person's age and developmental status. (MN 822, 824, 831, 833, 835)

Application of Developmental Theory to Risk and Resilience

The child and youth care worker (recent graduate) understands developmental theory in the context of environmental risk and the factors that develop a young person's capacity for resilience. *(Outcome)*

Elements of Performance

The child and youth care practitioner:

1. Applies interventions consistent with a child's developmental stages (AB Lifespan Development/Skills) and understands the symptoms of psychiatric disorders from the perspective of risk. *(FG)*

2. Explains and understands unusual behaviour from the perspective of developmental theory, resilient survival in the face of adversity, and/or psychiatric diagnosis. (MN 804–4)

3. Demonstrates an understanding of developmental theory to critically analyze how childhood disorders described in DSM-V are evidenced in behavior *(FG) and de-pathologizes behavior that is adaptive in the face of ecological risk.*

4. Understands the developmental issues surrounding various disorders such as attention-deficit disorder, conduct disorder, and others identified in DSM-V, and modifies intervention plans accordingly. (MN 821–2) *(FG)*

5. Understands developmental issues that arise in the context of environmental risk and modifies environments and interventions accordingly.

Psychotropic Medication

The child and youth care worker (recent graduate) is familiar with commonly used medications and understands the role of medication and pharmacology and its place in the treatment and management of psychiatric disorders. The practitioner applies this knowledge to the observation and assessment of young people. Furthermore, the child and youth care worker is aware of the symptoms and issues of drug misuse and abuse. *(Outcome)*

Elements of Performance

The child and youth care practitioner:

1. Lists and understands commonly prescribed medications, their indications and side effects. (AB Basic Care/Knowledge, MN)

2. Administers medication prescribed by the lawful prescribing practitioner in accordance with the prescribed directions and only for medical purposes. (NACP VB2c3) *(FG)*

3. Observes, assesses, and provides feedback for the evaluation of prescribed medications. (adapted NACP VB2c2, ON-vs 4.12) *(FG)*

4. Seeks consultation on side effects when necessary. (NACP VB2c1, AB Mental Health/Skills, MN) *(FG)*

5. Provides information regarding medication to client and family as required. *(FG)*

6. Understands the need for documentation related to medication. (MN) *(FG)*

7. Knows the principal drugs used by youth and their behavioural and physical manifestations and can recognize when youth are using/abusing drugs. (MN 822–4, AB Mental Health/Knowledge)

V. SYSTEMS CONTEXT

Description of Domain

Systems thinking is a central organizing and conceptual framework of child and youth care practice *(FG)* and the lens through which assessment and intervention in the young person's life occurs. It is the area of influence that requires the practitioner to incorporate the environmental conditions into his/her work: the historical and cultural environment of the young person; the political, community, and family environment; and all systems within which the young person, family, and practitioner interact. The systemic framework orients the practitioner to the client's situation and the complexity of interrelated structures within their environment. (adapted NACP, AB Systemic Frameworks)

Systemic assessment facilitates the identification of realistic goals for change and assists the practitioner to identify individuals and programs that will contribute to a successful treatment process. Central to the systems orientation is the notion that all the components of a system are interrelated. Thus, changes to one part of the system influence other components affecting the possibilities for growth, change, and successful outcomes.

The domain addresses the areas of systems theory, ecological perspective, legal guidelines and practice, and family systems.

Knowledge Foundations

1. Ecological and systems theory (MN 801–1, 832–1, Child Welfare, NACP IIIA, AB Systemic Frameworks/Knowledge) *(FG)*
2. Provincial and federal legislations applicable to young people and families (AB, NACP IA)
3. Children's rights (NACP IB6b)
4. Procedures for children's advocacy and grievances (AB Community Development/knowledge, NACP-1A) *(FG)*
5. Family systems theory (MN 832–1, NACP IIIA, AB Working with Families/Knowledge) *(FG)*
6. Cultural and human diversity in the professional environment (NACP IIA, IIB2g) *(FG)*
7. Current and emergent trends in society, services, and the profession (NACP IA, IVB2k)

Systems Theory

The child and youth care worker (recent graduate) understands systems theory as a central organizing and conceptual framework for practice. *(Outcome)*

The systemic framework provides an organizing schema that emphasizes the relationships between family, service, and community systems and enables the worker to develop integrated and holistic approaches for young people and their families. *(Clarification)* (AB Systemic Frameworks)

Elements of Performance

The child and youth care practitioner:

1. Understands and describes the concepts of systems theory as they apply to working with young people and families. (MN 832–1, NACP IIIA) *(FG)*
2. Understands and analyzes the web of systems and subsystems and the socioeconomic and political environment within which practice occurs. (MN 803–7, AB Systemic Frameworks) *(FG)*

3. Utilizes the concepts and language of systems theory to *identify* the relevant subsystems in which a young person participates and the interrelationships between those systems that may influence their developmental path. (AB Lifespan Development/Systemic Frameworks) *(FG)*

4. Incorporates a systemic/ecological approach into intervention plans. (AB Systemic Frameworks/Skills)

Ecological Perspective

The child and youth care practitioner (recent graduate) understands an ecological perspective that emphasizes the interaction between persons and their physical and social environments, including cultural and political settings (NACP, 24). The emerging child and youth care practitioner understands how institutional systems such as justice, mental health, child welfare, and education serve to impact young people and understands the importance of interacting with these systems in an effort to meet young people's needs (AB). *(Outcome)*

Elements of Performance

The child and youth care practitioner:

1. In collaboration with the young person's family and the multidisciplinary team, assesses the impact of the environment: the cultural, economic, physical, emotional, social, spiritual, and/or psychosocial contexts in which a client and his/her family lives and functions. (ON-vs 2.1)

2. Assesses the social ecology of young people by identifying relevant social systems and their components; describing the relationships, rules, and roles within the systems; and developing connections among the people in the child's social systems. (NACP IVB3a, AB Systemic Frameworks/Skills) *(FG)*

3. Analyzes current and emergent trends in society relative to the impact on services for young people and the profession. (ON-vs 7.10, NACP IA, IVB2k)

4. Modifies individual intervention plans to reflect differences in culture, ethnic, and religious backgrounds accounting for diversity within individuals and groups. (NACP IIB3d, QU, MN 805–2) *(FG)*

5. Discusses how services and programs need to accommodate the social, political, and economic realities of today. (NACP IVB2k)

Family Systems

The child and youth care practitioner (recent graduate) understands that optimal development occurs within the family and surrounding social environment. Practitioners have a sound knowledge of family systems theory and value the family's input, ensuring that cultural values and beliefs held by young people and families are respected. (adapted AB)

Elements of Performance

The child and youth care practitioner:

1. Describes the development of the family over time and in the context of their social and cultural norms. (NACP IIIA) *(FG)*

2. Identifies and describes a family's strengths, roles, rules, and relationships to each other. (QU 401–15, MN 832–3) *(FG)*

3. Understands and applies family systems theory to assessment, planning, and intervention. (MN 832–1) *(FG)*

4. Explores the cultural, spiritual, and socioeconomic status of the family to inform his/her understanding of the young person's developmental needs. (AB Lifespan Development/Attitudes) *(FG)*

5. Identifies and analyzes his/her own family history and its affect on his/her relationships with young people and families. (MN 803–6, AB Work with Families/Skills) *(FG)*

Legal Guidelines and Practice

The child and youth care practitioner (recent graduate) understands how his/her practice is guided by a set of legal rules by provincial and federal legislation governing young people and families. These laws and guidelines are considered and applied in everyday practice. (MN, ON). *(Outcome)*

Elements of Practice

The child and youth care practitioner:

1. Knows, understands, and follows relevant laws, regulations, legal rights, and licensing procedures governing practice. (NACP IA, IB5a, ON-vs 4.3, MN 807–1, 830–1)

2. Describes the legal rights and responsibilities enshrined in provincial, national, and international laws and covenants that pertain to care providers, families, young people, youth in care, and juvenile offenders (MN 801–2, ON-vs 4.3)

3. Describes the relevant legal protections from abuse, disclosure of personal information, and protection from exploitation that are accorded to young people. (MN 801–6)

4. Describes the local reporting protocols when legal protections are violated. (MN 801–3, 808–8, AB Basic Care/Skills)

VI. RELATIONSHIPS

Description of Domain

Genuine relationships are a critical area of influence based on empathy and positive regard for young people and families when promoting optimal development. Forming and maintaining relationships is a central change strategy in Child and Youth Care practice. This domain addresses learning outcomes for caring, teamwork, use of activities, engagement, and professional relationships.

Knowledge Foundations

The graduate should have knowledge and comprehension of the following areas in order to achieve the learning outcomes within this domain:

1. Characteristics of healthy interpersonal relationships (NACP IVA)

2. Characteristics of a helping relationship (MN 806–5, 836–1, NACP IVA, AB Therapeutic Environments/Knowledge) *(FG)*

3. Individual counseling and communication skills (MN 806–6, NACP VA)

4. Activities of daily living *(FG)*

5. Principles of activity programming (NACP VA) *(FG)*

6. Therapeutic use of activities for enhancing development (MN 807–8, AB Relationship Development/Skills) *(FG)*

7. Nutrition: Canada Food Guide (AB Basic Care/Knowledge)

8. First Aid *(FG)*, fire safety (AB Basic Care/Knowledge)

9. Principles of the therapeutic milieu (MN 807–6) *(FG)*

10. Team development and roles (ON-vs 5.6, gs 5.3) *(FG)*

11. Principles of experiential learning (AB Therapeutic Environments/Attitudes)

12. Strategies to build a professional support network (NACP IA, IB3b3)

Caring

The child and youth care worker (recent graduate) values caring for others as an essential component for emotional growth, developing social competence, and promoting healthy development (NACP attitude 7) *(Outcome)*

Graduates understand that relationships are developed in a safe and nurturing environment and they teach basic self-care skills to their clients, ensuring that their physical health and safety are protected. They demonstrate a caring attitude by placing the young person at the centre of their day-to-day practice and encourage the young person to care for others. (AB Basic Care) *(Clarification)*

Elements of Performance

The child and youth care practitioner:

1. Demonstrates that the young person's health, safety, and well-being are foremost in care provision. (AB Basic Care/Attitudes)

2. Demonstrates affection and physical contact that is sensitive to cultural and human diversity as well as the needs of the young person. (NACP IIb2d)

3. Responds to help-seeking behavior while encouraging and promoting several alternatives for the healthy expression of needs and feelings. (NACP IIIB2b3, QU 406–3) *(FG)*

4. Implements daily routines as both a mechanism for life skill development and a means of ensuring a stable, safe, and nurturing environment. (AB Basic Care/attitudes) *(FG)*

5. Modifies the therapeutic milieu to address the child's needs within the context of the group. (AB Group Interventions/Skills) *(FG)*

6. Plans for and designs activities related to good hygiene, healthy eating habits, physical recreation, and other factors contributing to a healthy lifestyle. (AB Basic Care/Skills) *(FG)*

7. Designs and maintains inviting, hygienic, and well-repaired physical environments, equipment, and supplies that positively support activities of daily living, hence caring and concern. (NACP VB6c, MN 807–1, 807–3) *(FG)*

Engagement

Child and youth care workers (recent graduates) engage in active development of therapeutic relationships and genuinely develop an empathetic understanding of the perspective of another, be it client, family, coworker, community member, or fellow professional. *(Outcome)*

Therapeutic relationships involve a connection, alliance, or association with young people, families, and/or other service recipients and providers that is purposeful, goal-directed, and supportive of the young person. (ON VS glossary) While the primary focus in the work of the discipline is the therapeutic nature of the relationship, practitioners are genuinely interested in relating to others—no matter if there is a purpose or not. *(Clarification)*

Elements of Performance

The child and youth care practitioner:

1. Demonstrates that effective therapeutic relationships are focused on the here and now of daily life events and develops relationships with service recipients that are caring, purposeful, goal directed, and supportive within mutually determined boundaries. (NACP IVB2c, IVB2e) (AB Relationship Development/Attitudes) *(FG)*
2. Demonstrates the capability of being a dynamic, available, and accessible presence (QU 405–1) based on congruence, genuineness, and authenticity. (NACP VB9h, AB Relationship Development/Attitudes) *(FG)*
3. Applies relational strategies such as consideration, safety, trust, availability, and empathy. (QU 405–17)
4. Assists clients to identify personal issues and make effective and healthy choices. (NACPv-VB9f) *(FG)*
5. Modifies decision-making authority and responsibility with young people in a manner that is appropriate to the developmental status of the child/youth. (QU 405–4, MN 807–2)

Use of Activities

The child and youth care worker (recent graduate) selects recreational activities and day-to-day life experiences that are opportunities for developing relationships, engaging the young person in social learning, and developing competence in new areas. (AB, QU) *(Outcome)*

Elements of Performance

The child and youth care practitioner:

1. Adapts skills for building relationships to a variety of therapeutic situations and in response to the young person's unique mental health issues and cultural circumstances. (Ministry, ON-vs 1.5) *(FG)*
2. Makes conscious use of relationship to create changes in the young person's pattern of interpersonal interactions within the day-to-day environment. (NACP VB8b, VB9h, AB Therapeutic Environments/Skills)

3. Recognizes "teachable moments" and effectively utilizes events/situations that offer opportunities for social learning. (MN 807–10, AB Therapeutic Environments/Skills) *(FG)*

4. Rearranges and redesigns the milieu so that learning situations arise.

5. Selects community-based opportunities for formal and informal recreation and social interaction that promotes competency for the child and develops community supports (positive youth development approach). (AB Systemic Frameworks/Knowledge) *(FG)*

Teamwork

The child and youth care worker (recent graduate) demonstrates the ability to work with multidisciplinary teams and programming teams, assuming responsibility for collective duties and decisions as well as representing the child and youth care perspective on the team. (adapt ON VS) *(Outcome)*

Elements of Performance

The child and youth care practitioner:

1. Explains and maintains appropriate boundaries with professional colleagues. (NACP IB2d2, IVB4b)

2. Demonstrates an ability to establish and maintain effective relationships within a team environment by acting professionally; negotiating and resolving conflict; acknowledging and respecting cultural and human diversity; and supporting team members. (NACP IIB2h, IVB4a) *(FG)*

3. Assumes responsibility for collective duties and decisions including responding to team member feedback. (NACP IVB4c)

4. Builds cohesion among team members through active participation in team-building initiatives. (NACP IVB4e)

5. Understands and completes the various tasks required of him/her as group members. (ON-gs 5.6)

6. Contributes his/her own ideas, opinions, and information while demonstrating respect for others. (Ministry 22, ON-gs 5.6) *(FG)*

Professional Relationships

The child and youth worker (recent graduate) demonstrates an understanding of integrated service delivery by working in partnership with other professionals and community organizations. (AB) *(Outcome) (FG)*

Elements of Performance

The child and youth care practitioner:

1. Establishes and maintains a connection, alliance, or association with other service providers to enhance quality of service. (NACP IVB4i)

2. Encourages collaborative participation by professionals, young people, family, and community to share responsibility for client outcomes. (NACP IVB2j) *(FG)*

3. Develops and maintains relationships with community members and neighbors in order to identify community standards and expectations for behavior that enable young people and families to maintain existing relationships. (NACP IV 2l, AB Systemic Frameworks/Skills) *(FG)*

4. Assesses the social ecology of young people by identifying relevant systems; identifying and describing the relationships, rules, and roles in the social systems; and developing connections among the people in the young person's various social systems. (NACP IIIB, IVB3a, AB Systemic Frameworks/Skills) *(FG)*

VII. INTERVENTIONS

Description of Domain

Intervention is the area of influence that includes the professional practitioner's ability to integrate current knowledge of human development with the skill, expertise, objectivity, and self-awareness essential for developing, implementing, and evaluating effective intervention programs for young people. The goal of any intervention is to further the child's development and/or support resilient behaviour.

The domain includes the following areas: life-space interventions, daily life events, activity programming, planned interventions, advocacy and group work, and intervention plans.

Knowledge Foundations

The graduate should have knowledge and comprehension of the following areas in order to achieve the learning outcomes within this domain:

1. Therapeutic milieu and environmental design (MN 807–6, NACP VA)
2. Principles of psychoeducational interventions such as aggression replacement training, life skills training (QU 402–9)
3. Principles of life-space intervention (Gharabaghi & Stuart, 2013)
4. Crisis theory and the role of crisis and trauma in children's behaviour (MN 808–13, 821–2) *(FG)*
5. Principles of conflict resolution (ON-gs 5.7, NACP VB8i) *(FG)*
6. Principles of social support and positive youth development
7. Theories of personal change
8. The principles of evidence-based treatment and practice
9. Research methodology (ON-vs 4.10) *(FG)*
10. Group theory *(FG)*
11. Principles of Narrative Therapy (AB Individual Interventions/Skills)
12. Principles of Solution focused therapy (AB Individual Interventions/Knowledge)
13. Canada Food Guide dietary recommendations
14. St. John First Aid Certification or equivalent and CPR (AB Basic Care/Skills) *(FG)*

Working with the Life-Space

The child and youth care worker (recent graduate) understands that every interaction with the young person, as well as the day-to-day life experiences shared with a young person, are opportunities for growth and development and integrates this understanding into his/her relationship, communication, and activities within the life-space. *(Outcome)*

This is the essence of child care, whereby life-space intervention can simultaneously address basic needs and the developmental change process. *(FG)* Practitioners develop activities and strategies for interventions to ensure that developmental needs are satisfied throughout all phases of the planning and intervention process. *(Clarification)* (adapted NACP, AB)

Elements of Performance

The child and youth care practitioner:

1. Recognizes and uses "teachable moments" in the life-space of the young person and in the therapeutic environment, thereby enabling the child to develop positive self-regard and social competence. (AB Therapeutic Environments/Attitudes, MN 807–10)

2. Arranges the milieu so that learning situations arise and thereby capitalizes on each "teachable moment" as an opportunity for social learning. (QU 404–5, AB Therapeutic Environments/Skills)

3. Creates on-the–spot adjustments to interventions as events unfold (QU 403–10)*(FG)*

4. Applies life-space interview techniques to that young people's autonomy and capacity for learning is supported. (NACP, MN 808–6) *(FG)*

5. Assesses the situation in the milieu and in individual interaction and selects the appropriate approach to an interventive interaction. (NACP VB8d) *(FG)*

6. Demonstrates proficiency in guiding young people's behavior by:

    a) Using techniques in keeping with the level of the young person's understanding (designing the social and emotional environment; social modeling; cueing; encouraging; structuring rules and routines; supporting agency while clarifying consequences).

    b) Outlining expectations with clear, coherent, and consistent language within developmentally appropriate boundaries and guidelines.

    c) Empowering young people's decision making.

    d) Employing at least one method of conflict negotiation and resolution (MN 808–5, NACP IIIB3d, VA, VB9g/k, AB Therapeutic Environments/Skills, Basic Care/Attitudes) *(FG)*

7. Understands and applies the principles of crisis management, including:

    a) Describes his/her own personal strengths and limitations in responding to crisis situations.

    b) Explains how to avoid unnecessary risks and confrontations.

    c) Dressing for interventive contact.

    d) Employs a variety of skills to defuse a crisis and restore the client to calm behaviour.

    e) Describes and applies the principles of physical intervention according to a recognized and approved model. (QU 405–12, MN 808–6, 808–21, 808–30, NACP VB9l) *(FG)*

8. Uses technology to connect with young people in their life-space with due consideration for safety, support, and engagement.

Daily life events

The child and youth care practitioner (recent graduate) understands and facilitates the planned arrangement of the therapeutic milieu and can describe the relationship of developmental processes to the activities of daily living including eating, grooming, hygiene, sleeping, and rest. *(Outcome)*

Planned environments integrate developmental, preventive, and therapeutic objectives into the life-space through the use of methodologies and techniques sensitive to culture and human diversity. Connections are facilitated between components of the life-space to maintain a healthy and growth-facilitating environment for the young person. *(Clarification)* (NACP)

Practitioners have a level of expertise in teaching basic care skills to their clients, ensuring that the client's physical health and safety are protected. They demonstrate a caring attitude by placing the child at the centre of their day-to-day practice.

Elements of Performance

The child and youth care practitioner:

1. Demonstrates that the child's health, safety, and well-being are foremost in care provision. (NACP, AB Basic Care/Attitudes, MN 808–24)
2. As appropriate and within a youth engagement framework, designs and implements activities of daily living that are consistent with the child's developmental status and cultural and/or religious background.
   * Clothing is well maintained, reflecting the age and background of the child
   * Pleasant and inviting mealtimes that encourage social interaction
   * Bedtimes and rest opportunities that are developmentally appropriate
   * Clean and well-maintained bathroom facilities that allow developmentally appropriate privacy and independence
   * Adequate personal space for safe storage of personal belongings
   * Personal definition through decorations that do not exceed reasonable propriety
   * Understands that routines and rules are essential for a safe environment and are opportunities for life-skill development (MN 807–1, 807–3, NACP IIIB3b, VB6b, AB Basic Care/Attitudes/Skills)
3. Administers medication as prescribed. (NACP VB2c3, AB Basic Care/Skills) *(FG)*
4. Uses structure, routines, and activities to promote effective relationships. (MN 807–7, NACP IVB2i)
5. Incorporates role modeling of social behavior (AB Therapeutic Environments/Skills) and provides cues and practice to facilitate the development of social skills (NACP IVB2h).
6. Teaches age-appropriate life skills using a systematic approach, within daily interactions. (AB Basic Care/Skills)

Activity Programming

The child and youth care worker (recent graduate) designs and implements individual and group activities that incorporate an understanding of the significance of play and recreational programming and their usefulness as teaching and learning tools. *(Outcome)* Practitioners are able to analyze the meaning, atmosphere, and the nature of the activities relative to the child's developmental needs. (NACP, QU)

Elements of Performance

The child and youth care practitioner:

1. Understands the principles of activity programming and adapts and modifies to suit the needs of the children and to encourage their involvement in the activities. (NACP VA, V5g, MN 802–9, 807–8) *(FG)*
2. Designs and implements activity programs that account for age, developmental status, cultural, and/or ethnic background as well as the unique treatment objectives of the child. (MN 809–1, NACP IIB3b/c, VB5d, VB6b, AB Client Service Planning/Attitudes)
3. Describes, locates, and critically evaluates community resources for programs and activities and as appropriate connects young people and families to them. (NACP IIIB1c, VB5h, MN, ON-vs 3.3) *(FG)*
4. Demonstrates skills in several domains of activity including arts, crafts, sports, games, and music. (NACP VB5b, QU, MN 807–4)
5. Makes use of space, equipment, time, and props to facilitate the treatment objectives. (NACP VB4c, AB Individual Interventions/Skills)
6. Identifies and describes how his/her own childhood activity experiences and skills are related to adult interests and skills and to his/her current work. (NACP VB5a, AB)

Planned Interventions

The child and youth care practitioner (recent graduate) understands the need to plan and continually adapt interventions, anticipating steps and measures required in meeting objectives and the best means to attain them. Practitioners are able to participate in the selection of goals or objectives from treatment and educational and developmental plans and assist in the design of activities, interactions, and management methods that support these goals and objectives. Practitioners are able to recognize that the design of these therapeutic interventions and service methods are logically connected to service goals. *(Outcome)*

Practitioners recognize that interventions may be formal (service plan) or informal (life-space interventions) and that their basic principles are the same. They are purposeful and consistent with a specific theoretical orientation guided by agency policy and individualized to reflect differences in culture/human diversity, background, temperament, personality, and differential rates of development. (adapted QU, NACP, AB) *(Clarification)*

Elements of Performance

The child and youth care practitioner:

1. Understands and employs intervention programs that comply with regulations and that take into account:
   a) The legal framework under which the request for services falls
   b) The ultimate goal of the intervention

c) An understanding of the clinical aspects and dynamics of the young person and his/her situation

d) Emergencies

e) The resources, strengths, and vulnerabilities of the young person and his/her original environment

f) The resources of the intervention milieu and the social environment of the young person

g) The points of view expressed by the young person and his/her parents

h) The points of view expressed by partners in the intervention

i) Prescribed time periods (QU 403–2)

2. Describes and identifies a theoretical/empirical rationale for a particular intervention. (NACP VB3e, AB Individual Interventions/Skills) *(FG)*

3. Applies basic strategies that encourage the client's participation in assessment and goal-setting as well as in intervention planning and assists in the development of individual, educational, and developmental treatment plans. (NACP IIB2e, IVB1e, IVB2g, QU 403–15, MN 803–2) *(FG)*

4. Describes and participates in the evaluation of realistic goals with client and family. (ON-vs 4.4, MN 837–4) *(FG)*

5. Understands and demonstrates effective and appropriate problem-solving strategies. (MN 802–2, NACP VB8i) *(FG)*

6. Understands the need to collaborate with others for appropriate service and delivery (ON-vs 4.5) and is able to arrange for the necessary resources to assist in the attainment of goals. *(FG)*

7. Demonstrates at least one method or technique for the resolution of conflicts when necessary. (NACP VB8i) *(FG)*

8. Describes the protocol for interventions in suicidal situations. (QU 405–13, 808–31) *(FG)*

9. Understands basic principles of intervention for people addicted to drugs. (QU 405–14)

10. Demonstrates an awareness and knowledge of a descriptive model for the cycle of violence and is capable of applying intervention techniques aimed at defusing violent behavior. (QU 405–11)

11. Identifies the need for and contributes to a plan for a child's transition into appropriate community resources. (AB Client Service Planning/Skills)

Advocacy

The child and youth care practitioner (recent graduate) understands the child and families' potential and capacity to grow and change and demonstrates basic advocacy skills that ensure that young people and families have their views heard and considered during the decision-making processes that directly affect them. (NACP B6b-c) *(Outcome)*

Practitioners understand that advocacy for the young person, family, and community leads to empowerment. They understand the need for and demonstrate respect for young people and families, affording them the dignity of self-determination within the context of their developmental capacities. *(Clarification)*

Elements of Performance

The child and youth care practitioner:

1. Understands how to advocate for the rights of child, youth, and families to secure proper services. (NACP IB6a/d, VB10f, AB Therapeutic Environments/Skills) *(FG)*

2. Utilizes and shares the input of children and families in determining interventions. NACP IIB2e, IVB1e, IVB2g, QU 403–15, MN 803–2)

3. Teaches client self-advocacy skills. (AB Community Development/Skills)

4. Understands the importance of facilitating client advocacy groups. (AB Community Development/Skills)

5. Assists in the identification and exploration of programs and incentives in the community. (NACP IIIB1c, VB5h, MN)

6. Understands how to promote positive youth development options as well as programs that reflect unique, cultural, spiritual, linguistic, and cognitive status. (AB Client Service Planning/Attitudes) *(FG)*

7. Creates opportunities that encourage young people and families to contribute to programs, services, and support movements that affect their lives by sharing authority and responsibility. (MN 803–2, NACP IVB2g)

8. Demonstrates respect for the privacy of clients and holds in confidence information obtained in the course of professional service. (AB Professional Issues/Skills) *(FG)*

Group Work

The child and youth care practitioner (recent graduate) understands that the group is a powerful socialization agent that provides opportunities for its members to experience social development and to build on their existing strengths and competencies. *(Outcome)*

Practitioners are able to describe psychoeducational, therapeutic, and peer helping groups and the developmental stages of groups. Practitioners demonstrate an ability to adapt their behavior management and communication skills to function within the group context. They demonstrate a confidence and competency in dealing with group dynamics at a basic level and ensure that group members are treated in a respectful and safe manner. (AB, MN, NACP, ON) *(Clarification)*

Elements of Performance

The child and youth care practitioner:

1. Investigates and applies an understanding of the cultural, spiritual, socioeconomic status, and other personal characteristics of group members in their everyday practice (AB Group Interventions/Skills) *(FG)*

2. Demonstrates basic group facilitation techniques that take into account the phases of group development and the individual developmental needs of the client. (NACP IIIB3d, MN 807–6)

3. Knows, understands, and utilizes basic group facilitation skills including active listening, questioning, summarizing, coordinating, seeking input, encouraging, gate-keeping, standard-setting, feedback, and self-disclosure. (AB Group Interventions/Skills)

4. Explains how individual goals fit into group goals and activities. (adapted, AB Group Interventions/Skills)

5. Understand principles involved in mediating group process by encouraging both individual and group prosocial behavior (i.e., acceptance of a newcomer, scapegoating, subgroup resistance, and collaboration around goals and activities that promote the welfare of the group). (NACP VB7c, AB, MN 807–6)

6. Contributes to the maintenance of a positive helpful climate of communication and exchange and demonstrates an ability to keep conflicts in perspective and redefine problems. (QU 405–19)

7. Participates in the regular assessment of the group's progress and interactions and suggests adjustments when necessary. (ON-vs 1.4, gs 5.8)

8. Identifies and describes personal bias (AB Relationship Development/Skills) in an effort to remain objective while working with groups of children. (NACP IIB1a) *(FG)*

9. Creates and arranges opportunities for group members to experience social development in formal and informal group settings. (AB Group Interventions/Skills)

10. Describes the process of planning and implementing group activities while taking into consideration group process variables and teaching objectives. (AB Group Interventions/Skills, MN 807–6)

Creating Intervention Plans

The child and youth care practitioner (recent graduate) demonstrates observation and reporting skills that illustrate assessment and evaluation of processes and events in relation to the intervention plan(s) in order to create developmentally appropriate opportunities in which young people can experience success. The practitioner understands the critical importance of evaluations in ensuring successful outcomes for children and youth. *(Outcome)*

Observation is a process of monitoring progress and identifying strengths and weaknesses, which leads to defining the intervention methods required for success in goal attainment. Observing, assessing, and reporting occur both moment to moment and in regularly scheduled summary intervals (NACP, ON, MN, AB). Practitioners understand that evaluations are based on a theoretical approach and that regular reviews are necessary to meet the young person's needs These skills ensure that adaptations to planned interventions will meet young people's needs and developmental status, as well as addressing ecological and environmental influences. *(Clarification)*

Elements of Performance

The child and youth care practitioner:

1. Observes the child or youth in the following development areas:
   * Physical
   * Sexual
   * Cognitive
   * Emotional
   * Moral
   * Social
   * Attachment bonds (QU 401–9, MN 821–1)

2. Understands a variety of checklists, inventories, and other systematic assessment tools. (ON-vs 4.2, AB Individual Interventions/Skills, NACP, QU 402–4, MN 801–16) *(FG)*

3. Observes, and contributes to the assessment and evaluation of treatments/services prescribed or designed with other professionals. *(FG)*

4. Examines client information and selects relevant, important, and useful observations related to the client needs and identified problems. (ON-gs 7.4) *(FG)*

5. Reflects on and analyzes the observations collected to identify needs, strengths, vulnerabilities, and resources and formulate plausible clinical hypothesis. (QU 402–6) *(FG)*

6. Observes and monitors the child's behavior for indicators of change related to the service plan and assesses the child's progress. (AB Program Development/Skills, Client Service Planning/Skills, MN) *(FG)*

7. Demonstrates objectivity by recognizing and describing his/her own attitudes and reactions in observations. (QU401–9) *(FG)*

8. Understands and participates in needs assessment (NACP VB3a) and identifies specific goals that are achievable and measurable. (AB Program Development/Skills, Client Service Planning/Skills, QU, MN 837–4, ON-vs 4.4) *(FG)*

9. Examines the totality of the child's social-ecological environment (AB Therapeutic Environments/Attitudes, Client Service Planning/Attitudes) and assists in the evaluation of the developmental appropriateness of environments for meeting the individual needs of clients. (NACP IIIB1b) *(FG)*

10. Understands and describes the strategies that encourage client and family participation in assessment and goal-setting. (NACP VB3c, QU 403–4, 403–15, MN 803–2) *(FG)*

11. Examines client and family needs in relation to community opportunities, resources, and supports. (NACP IIIB1c, VB10c, ON-vs 4.6) *(FG)*

12. Understands the contribution of research that is designed, conducted, and reported in accordance with high-quality child and youth care practice and recognized standards of scholarship and research ethics. *(FG)*

13. Understands the significance of evaluating the strategies used (with the client and family) and makes the necessary adjustments as a result of evaluation to attain the identified goals. (ON-vs 4.14) *(FG)*

14. Contributes to the assessment and monitoring of progress with the client and team and revises plan as needed. (NACP VB3h, ON-vs 1.4)

15. Applies knowledge gained from ongoing (formative) and outcome (summative) evaluations to specific activities and activity programs. (NACP VB5e5, AB Client Service Planning/Attitudes)

16. Understands how to select clear, specific, measurable goals that are based on a theoretical foundation for developmental and behavioral change and that specify indicators of goal achievement. (AB Program Development/Skills, Client Service Planning/Skills)

17. Participates in the comparison, ranking, and testing of strategies and contributes to recommendations for courses of action throughout the evaluation process.

18. Participates in recommending and identifying timelines and persons responsible for each stage. (AB Client Service Planning/Skills)

19. Consults with other team members and other disciplines to ensure a thorough evaluation takes place. *(FG)*

APPENDIX D

Competencies for Professional Child & Youth Work Practitioners

REVISED 2010

HISTORY OF THE COMPETENCIES

This document is the result of many years of work by North American Child and Youth Care Professionals. Initial development was undertaken by the North American Certification Project (NACP), sponsored by the Association for Child and Youth Care Practice. Some practitioners worked directly with the data, and in drafting and editing various sections of the document. More colleagues than can be named responded with expert opinions and additional information when called upon. This document articulates the competencies necessary for fully professional practice across the various settings in which Child and Youth Care Professionals work.

In May 2007, the Association for Child and Youth Care Practice (ACYCP) organized the Child and Youth Care Certification Board (CYCCB), an independent non-profit corporation, to oversee the implementation and further development of the professional credentialing program created by NACP. In March 2010, the Competency Review Committee of CYCCB completed a review of the competencies and recommended language changes to better reflect diverse settings and evolving practices. These changes are included in this document.

The Association for Child and Youth Care Practice accepted the original competency document at the annual meeting on October 20, 2001 in Lexington, Kentucky. The revised document was accepted in April 2010.

The Council of Canadian Child and Youth Care Associations (CCCYCA) and its provincial members have reviewed the competencies and determined appropriate educational prerequisites. Each provincial association determines how the competencies are recognized within that province's certification program for child and youth workers. Workers who transfer between jurisdictions should check with the relevant provincial association.

PROJECT ORGANIZATION

The North American Certification Project (NACP) arose from a broad opinion that North American certification for Child and Youth Care Practitioners was urgently needed. This project was a joint response of:

> Association for Child and Youth Care Practice (ACYCP formerly NOCCWA)

1

> Canadian Council of Child and Youth Care Associations (CCCYCA)
> International Leadership Coalition for Professional Child and Youth Care Work (ILC)

The NACP project was under the overall leadership of David Thomas, and had three working groups:
> **Resources**, public relations, and networking: David Thomas
> **Competency development**: Martha A. Mattingly
> **Structure** and implementation of the credential: Martha Holden

These organizations formally supported the NACP:
1. Academy of Child and Youth Care Professionals
2. Albert E. Trieschman Center
3. Association for Child and Youth Care Practice (formerly NOCCWA)
4. Child Welfare League of America
5. Council of Canadian Child and Youth Care Associations (CCCYCA).
6. International Coalition for Professional Child and Youth Care Work (ILC).
7. National Resource Center for Youth Services

GUIDING FOUNDATIONS OF THE PROJECT

The project was guided by the following description of the field and guiding principles.

Description of the Child & Youth Care field
Professional Child and Youth Care Practice focuses on infants, children, and adolescents, including those with special needs, within the context of the family, the community, and the life span. The developmental ecological perspective emphasizes the interaction between persons and their physical and social environments, including cultural and political settings.

Professional practitioners promote the optimal development of children, youth, and their families in a variety of settings, such as early care and education, community-based child and youth development programs, parent education and family support, school-based programs, community mental health, group homes, residential centers, day and residential treatment, early intervention, home-based care and treatment, psychiatric centers, rehabilitation programs, pediatric health care, and juvenile justice programs.

2

HISTORY OF THE COMPETENCIES

Child and youth care practice includes assessing client and program needs, designing and implementing programs and planned environments, integrating developmental, preventive, and therapeutic requirements into the life space, contributing to the development of knowledge and practice, and participating in systems interventions through direct care, supervision, administration, teaching, research, consultation, and advocacy.

Guiding principles

1. **Inclusion:** All national, state, and local organizations, as well as persons concerned with setting standards for Child and Youth Care Practitioners are invited and encouraged to participate.
2. **Credibility:** The process is based on standards which are professionally recognized and established by respected assessment methods.
3. **Generic Standards:** The standards are based on standards applicable to all child and youth care practice areas.
4. **Reciprocity:** The credential is designed to support and encourage reciprocity
5. **Ethics:** The certification process and standards are based on the Standards for Practice of North American Child and Youth Care Professionals developed by the Association for Child and Youth Care Practice (ACYCP) and the International Coalition for Professional Child and Youth Care Work (ILC). Other ethical statements can be included as the collaboration develops.

LEVELS OF CERTIFICATION NEEDED

Discussions in a variety of professional forums have led to the conclusion that three levels of certification in Child and Youth Care Work can be considered: entry level, professional level, and advanced level. The focus of this document is the professional level.

WORK OF THE COMPETENCY GROUP

Clarification of the task

This was an unfunded project with all participants, who were mature practitioners and academics in the profession, volunteering their time. Documents related to standards and competency in the field were collected and reviewed (Appendix B).

The task of the domain teams partly resembled a meta-analysis. The database

3

HISTORY OF THE COMPETENCIES

reflected the wisdom of our past, but the field has changed and continues to evolve. The domain team members had an understanding of these changes and at least an educated guess about future directions. In a sense, we stood on these documents in order to look ahead.

The task was to use the documents as useful, but to also include our interpretation of meaning, fill in gaps, remove what was not useful, articulate new directions, make the language clear and direct, and establish congruence with current scholarship.

The process

From the database four domains were identified: Professionalism, Applied Human Development Relationship and Communication, and Developmental Practice Methods. An additional domain, cultural and human diversity, which did not emerge from the database, was added. It is likely that culture and human diversity did not emerge from the data base since many documents were older and our discussion of culture and diversity is a more recent phenomenon.

The field of child and youth care operates within a developmental ecological perspective. As such, this perspective is also applicable to the practice of the art and science of child and youth care. The domains of practice have application in a range of contexts. Organizing the competencies into discrete elements is useful for observing, assessing, and testing specific areas and for the design of training curricula. Professional practitioners have fully integrated the attitudes, skills, and knowledge components into any action they engage in and they adjust their practice according to the context. Skills are demonstrated within a context in a manner that demonstrates the practitioner's awareness of the meaning, atmosphere, and nature of the activities in that context. Communication with a supervisor, for example, is different from communication with a youth, yet the basic skills would be described in the same manner. It is the context within which the action occurs and the integration of the appropriate attitudes and knowledge that differentiate the application. While the skills and knowledge within a particular subcategory of a domain are described in a generic manner, when they are integrated with the foundational attitudes for each contextual layer, their unique qualities emerge. It is intended that each domain be developed by the professional practitioner at the professional level through the contexts of application: self, relationship, environment, organization (system), and culture. The integrated qualities of a professional practitioner are detailed in Appendix A.

Organizing the competencies within the contexts of practice will be a future project.

4

HISTORY OF THE COMPETENCIES

Editing

The compiled work of the domain teams contained the material needed for the competency document. This work was revised and edited by Martha Mattingly and Carol Stuart. Karen VanderVen served as an additional editor.

The draft document was posted on the ACYCP web site for comment. Comments received were considered and revisions made.

Revisions to the Competencies

The original competency document and the professional certification program that is based upon them were developed by the North American Certification Project (NACP), a sub-committee of the Association for Child and Youth Care Practice (ACYCP). Both are owned by ACYCP. Through a licensing agreement, the competencies and certification program are made available to the professional community by the Child and Youth Care Certification Board (CYCCB), a non-profit organization formed by ACYCP to oversee the implementation of the certification program.

Recommendations for changes to the competency document are periodically made by CYCCB. These are submitted to ACYCP for review and approval before being included. A full review of the competencies will be conducted periodically to assure that the document continues to describe the field as it evolves.

In 2009 and 2010, the competency document was reviewed by the Competency Review Committee of CYCCB. This ad hoc committee was assigned the task of checking the document for language and practices that have changed over the 10 years since the original competency document was compiled. The committee included practitioners drawn from diverse settings with mature knowledge of practice within their setting. The committee focused on adjusting the competency language to better represent the wide diversity of settings within the field. Limited editing of competency descriptions was also undertaken.

The CYCCB Competency Review Committee included:

Carol Stuart, Ph.D., CYC-P, Chair
Faculty, School of Child and Youth Care
Ryerson University
Toronto, Canada

5

REVISIONS TO THE COMPETENCIES

Pam Clark, M.S.W.
Member, Strategic Planning Group
National Partnership for Juvenile Services
Columbus, Indiana

David Connolly, CYC (Cert.), B.A.
President, Canadian Council of Child and Youth Care Associations

Deborah Craig, M.A.
Director, Next Generation Coalition
Forum for Youth Investment
Kansas City, Missouri

Frank Eckles, B.A., CYC-P
Board President
CYCCB
College Station, Texas

Kelly Frank, B.S.
The Journey
Indiana Courage to Lead
Indianapolis, Indiana

James Freeman, B.S.
Training Director
Casa Pacifica
American Association of Children's Residential Centers
Camarillo, California

Michael Gaffley, Ed.D., CYC-P
Special Project Manager & Program Professor
Fischler School of Education & Human Services
Nova Southeastern University
North Miami Beach, Florida

Ellen S. Gannett, M.Ed.
Director, National Institute on Out-of-School-Time
Wellesley Center for Women
Wellesley College
Wellesley, Massachusetts

6

REVISIONS TO THE COMPETENCIES

John Korsmo, Ed.D., CYC-P
Faculty, Western Washington University
Woodring College of Education
Bellingham, Washington

Judy Nee, M.A.
President & CEO
National After School Association
Washington, DC

Bonnie Politz, M.P.A.
Center for Youth Development and Policy Research
Academy for Educational Development
Washington, DC

Andy Schneider-Munoz, Ed.D., CYC-P
Vice President
Center for Youth Development and Policy Research
Academy for Educational Development
Washington, DC

Janet Wakefield, M.S.
Director & CEO
The Journey
Indiana Courage to Lead
Indianapolis, Indiana

7

REVISIONS TO THE COMPETENCIES

COMPETENCY DOCUMENT

EDUCATIONAL REQUIREMENTS

The objective of the North American Certification Project (NACP) is to set credentialing standards for North America. However, it is important to recognize that there are significant differences between the United States and Canada, particularly in relation to educational programs.

In the United States, the baccalaureate degree from a regionally accredited college or university will be the minimal educational requirement to engage in the certification process at the professional level. The educational requirement will be waived for an applicant who can document five years or more of experience in the field for a 7-year grandfathering period that ends December 31, 2012.

Educational standards for engaging in the certification process for Canadians will be determined by the professional child and youth care community in Canada, using the structures in place (motions passed at the ACYCP Annual meeting on November 10-11, 2000).

It was further understood, but not the subject of an ACYCP motion that the credential planning and implementation group could specify whatever specific coursework and training may be deemed appropriate. Such requirements would be for those applicants not using the waiver of the educational requirement.

In Canada the educational requirement to engage in the professional level will include a minimum of one of the following:

1. Diploma (2 years or more) from a program in Child and Youth Care studies at a provincially accredited college.
2. Baccalaureate degree in CYC or a related field from a provincially accredited college or university.

For a 7-year period (2006 - 2012) following the implementation of NACP certification, the educational requirement will be waived for anyone with 5 years experience who was employed as a CYC practitioner at the time of, or prior to, implementation. This period ends December 31, 2012.

8

THE COMPETENCIES

FOUNDATIONAL ATTITUDES FOR PROFESSIONAL CHILD AND YOUTH CARE WORK

The Child and Youth Care Professional demonstrates the following attitudes which underlie all professional work:

> accepts the moral and ethical responsibility inherent in practice
> promotes the well-being of children, youth and families in a context of respect and collaboration
> values care as essential for emotional growth, social competence, rehabilitation, and treatment
> celebrates the strengths generated from cultural and human diversity
> values individual uniqueness
> values family, community , culture and human diversity as integral to the developmental and interventive process
> believes in the potential and empowerment of children, youth, family and community
> advocates for the rights of children, youth, and families
> promotes the contribution of professional child and youth care to society

9

THE COMPETENCIES

THE COMPETENCIES

I. PROFESSIONALISM

Professional practitioners are generative and flexible; they are self-directed and have a high degree of personal initiative. Their performance is consistently reliable. They function effectively both independently and as a team member. Professional practitioners are knowledgeable about what constitutes a profession, and engage in professional and personal development and self-care. The professional practitioner is aware of the function of professional ethics and uses professional ethics to guide and enhance practice and advocates effectively for children, youth, families, and the profession.

A. Foundational Knowledge
> History, structure, organization of Child and Youth Care Work.
> Resources and activities of CYC
> Current and emergent trends in society, services, and in CYC
> Structure and function of Codes of Ethics applicable to practice which includes the Code of Ethics, Standards for Practice of North American Child and Youth Care Professionals (www.acycp.org)
> Accepted boundaries in professional practice
> Stress management and wellness practices
> Strategies to build a professional support network
> Significance of advocacy and an array of advocacy strategies
> Relevant laws, regulations, legal rights and licensing procedures governing practice

B. Professional Competencies
1. Awareness of the Profession
a. access the professional literature
b. access information about local and national professional activities
c. stay informed about current professional issues, future trends and challenges in one's area of special interest
d. contribute to the ongoing development of the field

10

THE COMPETENCIES

2. Professional Development and Behavior
  a. Value orientation
    (1) state personal and professional values and their implications for practice including how personal and professional beliefs values and attitudes influence interactions
    (2) state a philosophy of practice that provides guiding principles for the design, delivery, and management of services
  b. Reflection on one's practice and performance
    (1) evaluate own performance to identify needs for professional growth
    (2) give and receive constructive feedback
  c. Performance of organizational duties
    (1) demonstrate productive work habits
      (a) know and conform to workplace expectations relating to attendance, punctuality, sick and vacation time, and workload management
      (b) personal appearance and behavior reflect an awareness of self as a professional as well as a representative of the organization
  d. Professional boundaries
    (1) recognize and assess own needs and feelings and keeps them in perspective when professionally engaged
    (2) model appropriate interpersonal boundaries
  e. Staying current
    (1) keep up-to-date with developments in foundational and specialized areas of expertise
    (2) identify and participate in education and training opportunities

3. Personal Development and Self Care
  a. Self awareness
    (1) recognize personal strengths and limitations, feelings and needs
    (2) separate personal from professional issues
  b. Self care
    (1) incorporate 'wellness' practices into own lifestyle
    (2) practices stress management
    (3) build and use a support network

4. Professional Ethics
  a. describe the functions of professional ethics

11

THE COMPETENCIES

b. apply the process of ethical decision making in a proactive manner

c. integrate specific principles and standards from the relevant Code of Ethics to specific professional problems

d. carries out work tasks in a way that conforms to professional ethical principles and standards

5. Awareness of Law and Regulations

a. access and apply relevant local, state/provincial and federal laws, licensing regulations and public policy

b. describe the legal responsibility for reporting child abuse and neglect and the consequences of failure to report

c. describe the meaning of informed consent and its application to a specific practice setting

d. use the proper procedures for reporting and correcting non-compliance

6. Advocacy

a. demonstrate knowledge and skills in use of advocacy

b. access information on the rights of children, youth and families including the United Nations Charter on the Rights of the Child

c. describe the rights of children youth and families in relevant setting/s and systems advocate for the rights of children, youth, and families in relevant settings and systems

d. describe and advocate for safeguards for protection from abuse including institutional abuse

e. describe and advocate for safeguards for protection from abuse including organizational or workplace abuse

f. advocate for protection of children from systemic abuse, mistreatment, and exploitation

12

II. CULTURAL AND HUMAN DIVERSITY

Professional practitioners actively promote respect for cultural and human diversity. The Professional Practitioner seeks self understanding and has the ability to access and evaluate information related to cultural and human diversity. Current and relevant knowledge is integrated in developing respectful and effective relationships and communication and developmental practice methods. Knowledge and skills are employed in planning, implementing and evaluating respectful programs and services, and workplaces.

THE COMPETENCIES

A. Foundational Knowledge

The professional practitioner is well versed in current research and theory related to cultural and human diversity including the eight major factors which set groups apart from one another, and which give individuals and groups elements of identity: age, class, race, ethnicity, levels of ability, language, spiritual belief systems, educational achievement, and gender differences.

> Cultural structures, theories of change, and values within culture variations
> Cross cultural communication
> History of political, social, and economic factors which contribute to racism, stereotyping, bias and discrimination
> Variations among families and communities of diverse backgrounds
> Cultural and human diversity issues in the professional environment

B. Professional Competencies

1. Cultural and Human Diversity Awareness and Inquiry

   a. describe own biases

   b. describe interaction between own cultural values and the cultural values of others

   c. describe own limitations in understanding and responding to cultural and human differences and seeks assistance when needed

   d. recognize and prevent stereotyping while accessing and using cultural information

   e. access, and critically evaluate, resources that advance cultural understandings and appreciation of human diversity

   f. support children, youth, families and programs in developing cultural competence and appreciation of human diversity

   g. support children, youth, families and programs in overcoming culturally and diversity based barriers to services

2. Relationship and Communication Sensitive to Cultural and Human Diversity

   a. adjust for the effects of age, cultural and human diversity, background, experience, and development on verbal and non-verbal communication

   b. describe the non-verbal and verbal communication between self and others (including supervisors, clients, or peer professionals)

   c. describe the role of cultural and human diversity in the development of healthy and productive relationships

   d. employ displays of affection and physical contact that reflect sensitivity for individuality, age, development, cultural and human diversity as well as

13

THE COMPETENCIES

consideration of laws, regulations, policies, and risks

e. include consideration of cultural and human diversity in providing for the participation of families in the planning, implementation and evaluation of services impacting them

f. give information in a manner sensitive to cultural and human diversity

g. contribute to the maintenance of a professional environment sensitive to cultural and human diversity

h. establish and maintain effective relationships within a team environment by: 1) promoting and maintaining professional conduct; 2) negotiating and resolving conflict; 3) acknowledging and respecting cultural and human diversity; and 4) supporting team members

3. Developmental Practice Methods Sensitive to Cultural and Human Diversity

a. integrate cultural and human diversity understandings and sensitivities in a broad range of circumstances

b. design and implement programs and planned environments, which integrate developmental, preventive, and/or therapeutic objectives into the life space, through the use of methodologies and techniques sensitive to cultural and human diversity

   (1) provide materials sensitive to multicultural and human diversity

   (2) provide an environment that celebrates the array of human diversity in the world through the arts, diversity of personnel, program materials, etc.

   (3) recognize and celebrate particular calendar events which are culturally specific

   (4) encourage the sharing of such culture specific events among members of the various cultural groups

c. design and implement group work, counseling, and behavioral guidance with sensitivity to the client's individuality, age, development, and culture and human diversity

d. demonstrate an understanding of sensitive cultural and human diversity practice in setting appropriate boundaries and limits on behavior, including risk management decisions

III. APPLIED HUMAN DEVELOPMENT

Professional practitioners promote the optimal development of children, youth, and their families in a variety of settings. The developmental-ecological perspective emphasizes the interaction between persons and their physical and social environments, including cultural and political settings. Special attention is given to the every

14

THE COMPETENCIES

day lives of children and youth, including those at risk and with special needs, within the family, neighborhood, school and larger social-cultural context. Professional practitioners integrate current knowledge of human development with the skills, expertise, objectivity and self awareness essential for developing, implementing and evaluating effective programs and services.

A. Foundational Knowledge
The professional practitioner is well versed in current research and theory in human development with an emphasis on a developmental-ecological perspective.
> Life Span Human Development
> Child/Adolescent Development (as appropriate for the arena of practice), including domains of
> Cognitive Development
> Social-emotional Development
> Physiological Development
> Psycho-sexual Development
> Spiritual Development
> Exceptionality in Development including at-risk and special needs circumstances such as trauma, child abuse/neglect, developmental psychopathology, and developmental disorders
> Family Development, Systems and Dynamics

B. Professional Competencies
1. Contextual-Developmental Assessment
  a. assess different domains of development across various contexts
  b. evaluate the developmental appropriateness of environments with regard to the individual needs of clients
  c. assess client and family needs in relation to community opportunities, resources, and supports

2. Sensitivity to Contextual Development in Relationships and Communication
  a. adjust for the effects of age, culture, background, experience, and developmental status on verbal and non-verbal communication
  b. communicate with the client in a manner which is developmentally sensitive and that reflects the clients' developmental strengths and needs
    (1) recognize the influence of the child/youth's relationship history on the development of current relationships
    (2) employ displays of affection and physical contact that reflect sensitivity

15

THE COMPETENCIES

for individuality, age, development, cultural and human diversity as well as consideration of laws, regulations, policies, and risks

(3) respond to behavior while encouraging and promoting several alternatives for the healthy expression of needs and feelings

c. give accurate developmental information in a manner that facilitates growth

d. partner with family in goal setting and designing developmental supports and interventions

e. assist clients (to a level consistent with their development, abilities and receptiveness) to access relevant information about legislation / regulations, policies / standards, as well as additional supports and services

3. Practice Methods that are Sensitive to Development and Context

a. support development in a broad range of circumstances in different domains and contexts

b. design and implement programs and planned environments including activities of daily living, which integrate developmental, preventive, and/or therapeutic objectives into the life space through the use of developmentally sensitive methodologies and techniques

c. individualize plans to reflect differences in culture/human diversity, background, temperament, personality and differential rates of development across the domains of human development

d. design and implement group work, counseling, and behavioral guidance, with sensitivity to the client's individuality, age, development, and culture

e. employ developmentally sensitive expectations in setting appropriate boundaries and limits

f. create and maintain a safe and growth promoting environment

g. make risk management decisions that reflect sensitivity for individuality, age, development, culture and human diversity, while also insuring a safe and growth promoting environment

4. Access Resources That Support Healthy Development

a. locate and critically evaluate resources which support healthy development

b. empower clients, and programs in gaining resources which support healthy development

16

THE COMPETENCIES

IV. RELATIONSHIP AND COMMUNICATION

Practitioners recognize the critical importance of relationships and communication in the practice of quality child and youth care. Ideally, the service provider and client work in a collaborative manner to achieve growth and change. 'Quality first' practitioners develop genuine relationships based on empathy and positive regard. They are skilled at clear communication, both with clients and with other professionals. Observations and records are objective and respectful of their clients. Relationship and communication are considered in the context of the immediate environment and its conditions; the policy and legislative environment; and the historical and cultural environment of the child, youth or family with which the practitioner interacts.

A. Foundational Knowledge
> Characteristics of helping relationships
> Characteristics of healthy interpersonal relationships
> Cultural differences in communication styles
> Developmental differences in communication
> Communication theory (verbal and non-verbal)
> Group dynamics and teamwork theory
> Family dynamics and communication patterns, including attachment theory as it relates to communication style

17

B. Professional Competencies
1. Interpersonal Communication
    a. adjust for the effects of age, cultural and human diversity, background, experience, and development of verbal and non-verbal communication
    b. demonstrate a variety of effective verbal and non-verbal communications skills including
      (1) use of silence
      (2) appropriate non-verbal communication
      (3) active listening
      (4) empathy and reflection of feelings
      (5) questioning skills
      (6) use of door openers to invite communication, and paraphrasing and summarization to promote clear communication
      (7) awareness and avoidance of communication roadblocks
    c. recognize when a person may be experiencing problems in communication due to individual or cultural and human diversity history, and help clarify the meaning of that communication and to resolve misunderstandings

THE COMPETENCIES

d. assist clients (to a level consistent with their development, abilities and receptiveness) to receive relevant information about legislation/regulations, policies/ standards, and supports pertinent to the focus of service

e. provide for the participation of children/ youth and families in the planning, implementation and evaluation of service impacting them

f. set appropriate boundaries and limits on the behavior using clear and respectful communication

g. verbally and non-verbally de-escalate crisis situations in a manner that protects dignity and integrity

2. Relationship Development

a. assess the quality of relationships in an ongoing process of self reflection about the impact of the self in relationship in order to maintain a full presence and an involved, strong, and healthy relationship

b. form relationships through contact, communication, appreciation, shared interests, attentiveness, mutual respect, and empathy

c. demonstrate the personal characteristics that foster and support relationship development

d. ensure that, from the beginning of the relationship, applicable procedures regarding confidentiality, consent for release of information, and record keeping are explained and clearly understood by the parent/caregiver and by the child, as appropriate to his/her developmental age. Follow those procedures in a caring and respectful manner

e. develop relationships with children, youth and families that are caring, purposeful, goal-directed and rehabilitative in nature; limiting these relationships to the delivery of specific services

f. set, maintain, and communicate appropriate personal and professional boundaries

g. assist clients to identify personal issues and make choices about the delivery of service

h. model appropriate interpersonal interactions while handling the activities and situation of the life-space

i. use structure, routines, and activities to promote effective relationships

j. encourage children, youth and families to contribute to programs, services, and support movements that affect their lives by sharing authority and responsibility

k. develop and communicate an informed understanding of social trends, social change and social institutions. Demonstrate an understanding of how social

18

THE COMPETENCIES

issues affect relationships between individuals, groups, and societies

l. identify community standards and expectations for behavior that enable children, youth and families to maintain existing relationships in the community

3. Family Communication

a. identify relevant systems/components and describe the relationships, rules and roles in the child/youth's social systems and develop connections among the people in various social systems

b. recognize the influence of the child's relationship history and help the child develop productive ways of relating to family and peers

c. encourage children and families to share folklore and traditions related to family and cultural background. Employ strategies to connect children to their life history and relationships

d. support parents to develop skills and attitudes which will help them to experience positive and healthy relationships with their children/youth

4. Teamwork and Professional Communication Skills

a. establish and maintain effective relationships within a team environment by: promoting and maintaining professional conduct; negotiating and resolving conflict; acknowledging individual differences; and, supporting team members

b. explain and maintain appropriate boundaries with professional colleagues

c. assume responsibility for collective duties and decisions including responding to team member feedback

d. use appropriate professional language in communication with other team members, consult with other team members to reach consensus on major decisions regarding services for children and youth and families

e. build cohesion among team members through active participation in team-building initiatives

f. collect, analyze and present information in written and oral form by selecting and recording information according to identified needs, agency policies and guidelines. Accurately record relevant interactions and issues in the relationship

g. plan, organize, and evaluate interpersonal communications according to the identified need, context, goal of communication, laws/regulations, and ethics and involved. Choose an appropriate format, material, language, and style suitable to the audience

h. acknowledge and respect other disciplines in program planning, communi-

19

THE COMPETENCIES

cation and report writing using multidisciplinary and interdisciplinary perspectives. Communicate the expertise of the profession to the team

i. establish and maintain a connection, alliance, or association with other service providers for the exchange or information and to enhance the quality of service

j. deliver effective oral and written presentations to a professional audience.

k. demonstrate proficiency in using information technology for communication, information access, and decision-making

V. DEVELOPMENTAL PRACTICE METHODS

Practitioners recognize the critical importance of developmental practice methods focused in CYC practice: Genuine Relationships, Health and Safety, Intervention Planning, Environmental Design and Maintenance, Program Planning and Activity Programming, Activities of Daily Living, Group Work, Counseling, Behavioral Guidance, Family (Caregiver) Engagement, Community Engagement. These are designed to promote optimal development for children, youth, and families including those at-risk and with special needs within the context of the family, community and the lifespan.

A. Foundational Knowledge

> Health and safety
> Intervention theory and design
> Environmental design
> Program planning and Activity Programming including
  • developmental rationales
  • basic strategies of program planning
  • specific developmental outcomes expected as a result of participating in activities
  • principles of activity programming, e.g. activity analysis, adaptation, strategies for involving youth in activities
  • relationship of developmental processes to the activities of daily living (eating, grooming, hygiene, sleeping and rest)
  • the significance of play activities
  • community resources for connecting children, youth and families with activity and recreational programs
> Behavioral Guidance methods including conflict resolution, crisis management, life space interviewing
> Behavior Management methods
> Counseling Skills

20

THE COMPETENCIES

Competencies for Professional Child and Youth Work Practitioners 2010
Copyright (c) 2010 Association for Child and Youth Care Practice
All Rights Reserved.

> Understanding and Working with Groups
> Understanding and Working with Families
> Understanding and Working with Communities

B. Professional Competencies

1. Genuine Relationships

    a. recognize the critical importance of genuine relationships based on empathy and positive regard in promoting optimal development for children, youth, and families (as fully described in Section III)

    b. forming, maintaining and building upon such relationships as a central change strategy

2. Health and Safety

    a. environmental safety

        (1) participate effectively in emergency procedures in a specific practice setting and carry them out in a developmentally appropriate manner

        (2) incorporate environmental safety into the arrangement of space, the storage of equipment and supplies and the design and implementation of activities

    b. health

        (1) access the health and safety regulations applicable to a specific practice setting, including laws/ regulations related to disability

        (2) use current health, hygiene and nutrition practices to support health development and prevent illness

        (3) discuss health related information with children, youth and families as appropriate to a specific practice setting

    c. medications

        (1) access current information on medications taken by clients in a specific practice site

        (2) describe the medication effects relevant to practice

        (3) describe the rules and procedures for storage and administration of medication in a specific practice site, and participate as appropriate

    d. infectious diseases

        (1) access current information on infectious diseases of concern in a specific practice setting

        (2) describe the components relevant to practice

        (3) employ appropriate infection control practices

21

THE COMPETENCIES

3. Intervention planning

   a. assess strengths and needs

   b. plan goals and activities which take agency mission and group objectives, individual histories and interests into account

   c. encourage child/youth and family participation in assessment and goal setting in intervention planning and the development of individual plans

   d. integrate client empowerment and support of strengths into conceptualizing and designing interventions

   e. develop and present a theoretical/empirical rationale for a particular intervention or approach

   f. select and apply an appropriate planning model

   g. select appropriate goals or objectives from plans, and design activities, interactions, and management methods that support plans in an appropriate way

   h. work with client and team to assess and monitor progress and revise plan as needed

4. Environmental Design and Maintenance

   a. recognize the messages conveyed by environment

   b. design and maintain planned environments which integrate developmental, preventive, and interventive requirements into the living space, through the use of developmentally and culturally sensitive methodologies and techniques

   c. arrange space, equipment and activities in the environment to promote participation and prosocial behavior, and to meet program goals

   d. involve children, youth and families appropriately in space design, and maintenance

5. Program Planning and Activity Programming

   a. connect own childhood activity experiences and skills, and adult interests and skills, to current work

   b. teach skills in several different domains of leisure activity

   c. assist clients in identifying and developing their strengths through activities and other experiences

   d. design and implement programs and activities which integrate age, developmental, preventive, and/or interventive requirements and sensitivity to culture and diversity

   e. design and implement challenging age, developmentally, and cultural and human diversity appropriate activity programs

     (1) perform an activity analysis

22

THE COMPETENCIES

(2) assess clients interests, knowledge of and skill level in various activities

(3) promotes clients participation in activity planning

(4) select and obtain resources necessary to conduct a particular activity or activity program

(5) perform ongoing (formative) and outcome (summative) evaluation of specific activities and activity programs

f. adapt activities for particular individuals or groups

g. locate and critically evaluate community resources for programs and activities and connect children, youth, and families to them

6. Activities of Daily Living

a. integrate client's need for dignity, positive public image, nurturance, choice, self-management, and privacy into activities of daily living

b. design and implement, and support family members and caregivers to implement, activities of daily living, which integrate age, developmental, preventive, and/or interventive requirements and sensitivity to culture and diversity

(1) age and cultural and human diversity appropriate clothing

(2) pleasant and inviting eating times that encourage positive social interaction

(3) age and developmentally appropriate rest opportunities

(4) clean and well maintained bathroom facilities that allow age and developmentally appropriate privacy and independence

(5) personal space adequate for safe storage of personal belongings and for personal expression through decorations that do not exceed reasonable propriety

c. design and maintain inviting, hygienic and well maintained physical environments and equipment and supplies which positively support daily activities

d. encourage client development of skills in activities of daily living

(1) personal hygiene and grooming skills

(2) developing and maintaining of areas related to daily living e.g. maintaining living space, preparing and serving meals, cleanup

(3) socially appropriate behavior in activities of daily living: respecting other's privacy, expected grooming and dress for various occasions

7. Group Process

a. assess the group development and dynamics of a specific group of children and youth

23

THE COMPETENCIES

b. use group process to promote program, group, and individual goals
c. facilitate group sessions around specific topics/issues related to the needs of children/youth
d. mediate in group process issues

8. Counseling

a. recognize the importance of relationships as a foundation for counseling with children, youth and families. (as fully described in Section III, Relationships and Communication)
b. has self awareness and uses oneself appropriately in counseling activities
c. able to assess a situation in the milieu or in individual interaction and select the appropriate medium and content for counseling
d. able to make appropriate inquiry to determine meaning of a particular situation to a child
e. assist other adults, staff, parents and caregivers in learning and implementing appropriate behavioral support and instruction
f. employ effective problem solving and conflict resolution skills

9. Behavioral Guidance

a. assess client behavior including its meaning to the client
b. design behavioral guidance around level of clients understanding
c. assess the strengths and limitations of behavioral management methods
d. employ selected behavioral management methods, where deemed appropriate
e. assist other adults, staff, and parent and caregivers in learning and implementing appropriate behavioral guidance techniques and plans
f. give clear, coherent and consistent expectations; sets appropriate boundaries
g. evaluate and disengage from power struggles
h. employ genuine relationship to promote positive behavior
i. employ developmental and cultural/diversity understandings to promote positive behavior
j. employ planned environment and activities to promote positive behavior
k. employ at least one method of conflict resolution
l. employ principles of crisis management
   (1) describe personal response to crisis situations
   (2) describe personal strengths and limitations in responding to crisis situations

24

THE COMPETENCIES

Competencies for Professional Child and Youth Work Practitioners 2010
Copyright (c)   2010 Association for Child and Youth Care Practice
All Rights Reserved.

(3) take self protective steps to avoid unnecessary risks and confrontations

(4) dress appropriately to the practice setting

(5) employ a variety of interpersonal and verbal skills to defuse a crisis

(6) describe the principles of physical interventions appropriate to the setting

(7) conduct a life space interview or alternative reflective debriefing

10. Family (Caregiver) Engagement

a. communicate effectively with family members

b. partner with family in goal setting and designing and implementing developmental supports and/or interventions

c. identify client and family needs for community resources and supports

d. support family members in accessing and utilizing community resources

e. advocate for and with family to secure and/or maintain proper services

11. Community Engagement

a. access up to date information about service systems, support and advocacy resources, and community resources, laws, regulations, and public policy

b. develop and sustain collaborative relationships with organizations and people

c. facilitate client contact with relevant community agencies

25

THE COMPETENCIES

GLOSSARY

Agency   Term often used to refer to a social service organization; however, in the context of structuration theory it refers to the capacity of an individual to advocate for him- or herself and to exert influence within the environment. It is the capacity to be an agent of change.

Almshouse   Charitable housing providing accommodation for the poor and needy, based on European Christian traditions dating back many centuries. Commonly known as a poorhouse.

Behaviourism   Behavioural theorists focus on behaviour as a reaction to environmental conditions with little to no mediation of responses by thought or emotion. Behaviours are repeated because an environmental circumstance reinforces that the behaviour is effective. Initially "thought" was viewed as simply internalized speech (a behaviour), but later work in cognitive behaviourism acknowledged that thought could be characterized as an environmental stimulus and/or reinforcement for behaviour.

Boundaries   Imaginary lines or limits that we draw that indicate to others how personal we might be within a relationship. All relationships have boundaries, whether they are personal or professional.

Bourgeoisie   Generally known as the middle class in society; usually city-dwelling merchants, tradespeople, artisans, and later bankers and entrepreneurs, from medieval France.

Burnout   A term used in human service professions, burnout is a state of physical, mental, and emotional exhaustion that results when ongoing stress consumes the resources that you have for coping with events in your life. Burnout involves three factors: emotional exhaustion, depersonalization and reduced personal accomplishment. Prevention is essential since it develops slowly over a long period of time, making recovery difficult. (See also *Vicarious Trauma* and *Compassion Fatigue*.)

Certification   Process of determining that a professional is competent to practice and has a basic set of knowledge and skills that is consistent with the expectations for a professional child and youth care practitioner. Some certification programs have more advanced levels of practice but in all cases there is a set of standards that must be met.

Childrearing   Refers to the actions, activities, and interactions by parents or caregivers that are part of the process of training and raising children to become adults as defined by society.

Chronosystem   Timing of changes in individual and social ecology.

Compassion Fatigue   Seen in trauma victims and those who work closely with young people and families who have been traumatized or are in crisis. It is a gradual lessening of compassion for practice over time, and results from the demanding nature of showing compassion over long periods of time for individuals who are suffering. Symptoms can include hopelessness, decrease in pleasure, continuous stress and anxiety, and a negative attitude. (See also *Burnout* and *Vicarious Trauma*.)

Competence Ability to perform a particular job; requires both knowledge and skill.

Conceptual Framework Acts like a map by outlining possible courses of action or presenting a preferred approach to an idea or thought. The concept is similar to *theory* in the way that it helps to relate ideas and concepts to each other, revealing connections within the material presented and helping to guide practice and research. (See also *Theory*.)

Conservatism Political view that advocates for maintaining the existing traditions. This may mean supporting existing wealth and power as well as strong religious (Christian) leanings and often a very traditional definition of family. Conservatism has the greatest variation in philosophy from country to country.

Contact Notes/Daily Logs Practitioners record observations, events, and information about the young people that they work with in the form of contact notes or daily logs. These are intended as objective recording available to colleagues and could in some circumstances be subpoenaed to court.

Culture Composed of the way of life in a society, including the norms, rules of social interaction, values, beliefs, artistic traditions and objects, legal and social institutions, and religious and political belief systems.

CYW Child and youth worker.

CYC Child and youth care or child and youth counsellor (used by Ontario Association (OACYC) and also by the Government of Alberta).

Developmental Milestones Approximate ages at which children are expected to perform certain tasks such as smile, recognize faces, crawl, sit up, talk, play cooperatively, and so on. They predict the usual course of development for young children.

Developmental Psychopathology Branch of developmental psychology that studies the developmental mechanisms that lead to typical or atypical (abnormal) developmental pathways and problematic outcomes. *Pathology* is the study and diagnosis of disease within the field of medicine, which assumes that symptoms are evidence of illness and by treating the illness you can correct the symptom and cure the individual.

Dichotomous Having two sides or parts, or being split.

Disability Any form of impairment that significantly affects one or more life activities, as compared to what is considered the norm in society. Disability can be due to physical, cognitive, sensory, intellectual, or chronic illness; it can be present at birth or develop during the lifetime.

Discipline Branch of knowledge with a specific focus and orientation to the world in a specific subject area. Disciplines are collectives of people holding degrees with the same specialization. Disciplines represent some collective interests that correspond to a common intellectual interest and the instructional tasks of a group of academics. Each discipline has its own body of knowledge and preferred ways of training and educating its members. Each discipline develops its own pedagogy and curriculum that is accredited by its respective professional organization. Child and youth care is an evolving practice-based discipline. In the recent past people have come to the practice from the disciplines of psychology, sociology, medicine, social work, and education.

Disorder Quite simply, the absence of order and therefore a state of chaos. In the medical world a disorder is associated with signs and symptoms that can be physical, emotional, or cognitive and do not follow the usual pattern (are chaotic). The symptoms cluster together and when there is a common or recognized cluster a physician will label the cluster as a disorder. Disorder is also associated with terms such as disease and abnormal.

Diversity   Presence of difference or variety amongst a socially defined group. Incorporating diversity in practice involves recognition and respect for the differences that exist between individuals and groups, and acknowledgment of the rights of individuals who do not have the same access to equal opportunities as a result of their difference.

Dominant Discourse   Unquestioned values and beliefs of the collective members of society about what is "right" and what is "normal" that directs the language of intervention theory and the worldviews of practitioners.

Ecological Systems Model   Theoretical model to describe the systems that affect the development of a young person. (See *Macrosystem, Exosystem, Mesosystem, Microsystem, Chronosystem*)

Ecology/Ecological Perspective   Emphasizes the interaction between people and their physical and social environments, including cultural and political settings. The ecological perspective considers how institutional systems such as justice, health, child welfare, and education can help or restrict the growth and development of children and youth.

Educateur   Term equivalent to the professional child and youth care practitioner that is used in Quebec and some European countries.

Educateur Specialize   Originating in France (1942), the title given to European professional practitioners who work with children as total life specialists, in the life-space of the child. Having been formally trained and educated, these individuals possess high professional status.

Educative Communities   Self-sufficient group living situations, often rural and/or farm based, founded in Europe in the late 1700s. Children and adults lived together, implementing the principle that basic household work contributed to a sense of community and self-worth. Communities are focused on the ideals of social justice, freedom, and self-sacrifice. The principles of these communities in modern times are found in the therapeutic community movement, for adults with developmental disabilities, mental health, and/or addictions.

Educative Milieu (Community)   Environment that is specialized to focus on providing instruction and education, including social education, by the social pedagogue or educateur who operate with children actively participating in daily life and decision making.

Emotional and Behavioural Disorder   Broad term used to describe an emotional and/or behavioural state that is in some way not "normal." Often abbreviated EBD; used commonly in mental health jurisdictions. This does not mean that the person has been diagnosed with a specific disorder or disturbance, but rather implies that the person is somehow different than what is considered "normal" for other individuals of the same age or developmental maturity.

Engagement   Present when young people and adults participate equally and recognize the power imbalance as well as the rights of youth to be treated equally. In such circumstances young people are often paid for the work that they do and they are fully aware of the constraints and limitations of the social structures that influence them. These values permeate the work that the group does together. Variations of engagement include participation and empowerment, each of which has a particular meaning along a continuum.

Ethics   Set of rules that guide behaviour and determine what is right or wrong. When they are "codified" and written down by a group that agrees to adhere to them, they become a "code of ethics." Ethics are related to values, beliefs, and ideologies.

Eurocentric Centering on or deriving from Europe. A tendency to interpret and emphasize the world with European values, perspectives, and experiences.

Evidence-Based Practice Specific guidelines about service practices, including referral, assessment, outcome management, quality improvement, and case management, that have resulted from the application of research that examines the impact of specific practices on outcomes for young people. It also refers to knowledge gained through research about the impact of treatments on the mental health of young people.

Exosystem Outside systems that are indirectly related to a child.

Family Traditionally known as the social unit, linked by kinship, that resides together in a household. Family is the primary means by which a child becomes socialized and learns his or her culture. This narrow view has expanded and developed over time: no longer assumed to possess kinship ties, or live in the same residence, changing landscapes of what constitutes a family have prompted many new and varied definitions of what family is.

First-Order Developmental Change Gradual, incremental change that occurs over time. This orientation to developmental change is common in programs where clients do not have "treatment" plans, where activities are designed that help children develop further in multiple dimensions, often called support plans.

Holistic Approach or a view that incorporates the "whole" in theory or practice. A holistic approach to child development considers all systems and aspects of change within the individual child: physical, spiritual, social, cognitive, emotional, etc.

Humanist Explanations for behaviour that focus on the experiences and perceptions of the individual. Humanists acknowledge the importance of choice in determining behaviour and focus on the person's capacity for self direction. Existential and phenomenological approaches are other terms used within this broad theoretical orientation.

In Care Generally refers to those children and youth who have been removed from their home by child protection authorities due to abuse or neglect concerns and placed in foster care or residential care until they return to their family, are adopted, or achieve adult independence. The placement is court-ordered and the government is considered to be the one with parental responsibilities. (See also *Looked-After Children*.)

Integrated Service Delivery Integration or bringing-together of the many professionals and/or services that young people and families may access for assistance. The purpose is to integrate and coordinate efforts, including communication and assessment of needs and resources. May also be referred to as *integrated case management* relative to a single client. Integration reduces costs and enhances the client experience because there is less duplication of resources and less need to retell the story for each practitioner.

Interventive Interaction Cycle of action and meaning-making that is undertaken by the practitioner with the young person or family. The cycle involves noticing, reflecting, preparing, and intervening or taking action.

LGBTQ2S Lesbian, gay, bisexual, and transgender, queer, two-spirited; acronym used to describe the spectrum of diversity in sexual orientation and gender identity.

Liberalism Political orientation that focuses on the freedom of the individual and on social equality. Traditional liberalism recognizes the need to support those less fortunate in the short term in order to protect them or provide opportunities for success.

Life-Space Intervention Primary method of intervention in child and youth care practice that uses the milieu to promote change and development. Interventions include spontaneous (or apparently spontaneous) strategies that occur as a result of planned environmental design, routine daily activities, relational interventions, and momentary interactions. The therapeutic use of daily life events in residential or other settings where there is a shared life-space with clients. Daily life events are used by the practice team to help young people gain understanding of their life experiences.

Life-Span Development Perspective on human development that is characterized by the belief that development is a life-long, multidimensional, multidirectional, contextual process of growth and regulation of self.

Looked-After Children The term holds specific meaning in England, where it originated in 1989. It is similar in meaning to the term "*in care.*" Looked-after children are in the care of or are provided accommodation on behalf of the local child protection authority for a minimum 24 consecutive hours. The term encompasses cases where the court has issued a court order as well as voluntary placements (e.g., respite care). (See also *In Care.*)

Macrosystem Beliefs, values, and rules of society and culture.

Mainstreaming Consistent with the normalization principle, mainstreaming involves placing young people with cognitive or social deficits into regular social or educational environments. The mainstream movement became most popular in the education system in the 1970s, when young people, who previously attended schools dedicated to those with intellectual deficits, were placed in classrooms in regular schools. The model included both segregated classrooms and full integration into regular classrooms, often with an educational aid.

Mental Health More than the absence of mental disorder or illness, mental health is a consistent state of well-being whereby people can cope with daily stresses and contribute to their communities.

Mesosystem Relationships between two or more microsystems.

Microsystem Immediate systems in which a child is located and the people, activities, and spaces he or she engages with or in (e.g., family, peers, school).

Milieu Environment or setting, including the physical, social, cultural, ideological, and emotional elements.

Nature versus Nurture Debate Argument amongst theoreticians and researchers about whether genetics (nature and the genetic coding of personality, development, intelligence, physical characteristics, etc.) is more important in determining the potential of a person versus the role of the environment (nurture and the social, relational, economic, and cultural factors) in determining potential and success.

Normalization Principle Principle initially applied to the design of programs and environments for people with intellectual and physical disabilities, which separated the person from the disorder or disease. The principle of normalization encouraged professionals to design environments that approximated average social milieus recognizing the "person" and moving away from the medical model of treating just the disease.

Paradigm Way of thinking that incorporates the collection of values, ideas, assumptions, and practices that make up how a group or community interprets the world. A conceptual framework that includes the commonly accepted views of a particular group of people.

Pervasive Developmental Disorder (PDD) Diagnostic category of pervasive developmental disorders (PDD) was a category within the DSM-IV, which referred to a group of disorders characterized by delays in the development of socialization and communication skills. Within the group were autism, Asperger syndrome, Rett syndrome, and childhood disintegrative disorder. In the DSM-V revisions the category was eliminated and subsumed into autistic disorder.

Positive Youth Development (PYD) Intentional, prosocial approach that engages young people within their communities, schools, organizations, peer groups, and families in a manner that is productive and constructive; recognizes, utilizes, and enhances youths' strengths; and promotes positive outcomes for young people by providing opportunities, fostering positive relationships, and furnishing the support needed to build on their leadership strengths (*www.findyouthinfo.gov/ youth-topics/positive-youth-development*).

Practice Application of knowledge to professional work. We prepare for practice early in our adult life by going to college or university or undertaking similar training in our chosen field. Professional practice is based on the knowledge generated by the discipline, and disciplines evolve and develop in response to developments and work in society as a whole.

Praxis Process of putting theoretical knowledge into action through the reflective understanding of the person implementing the action. Praxis is more than simply application of knowledge; it is reflective learning and inquiry leading to enhanced competency.

Presencing Immediate and active engagement with another person in which the practitioner both observes and co-creates the meaning of the moment while being aware of what is unfolding within his or her own conscience.

Presenting Problem Term used to describe the reason that a young person has been referred for service. Very often the presenting problem is not the issue that needs to be resolved, particularly when the problem is considered in light of the family, neighbourhood,

or societal circumstances that surround the young person.

Professional Regulation When members of a profession are required to ensure that all other members practice ethically and with a level or standard that is determined by the senior members of the field. Usually professional regulation involves legislation that recognizes the authority of the profession to self-regulate.

Psychoanalytic Explanations for human behaviour originated in Freud's approach to understanding problems. The concepts are embedded in Western culture and have generated numerous additional theoretical orientations. Individual behaviour is explained by the "depth" of the psyche (the unconscious mind) as it interacts with the conscious mind (the ego). The concept of the unconscious influence of the mind has strongly influenced the field of child development.

Psycho-educateur Educateur who specializes in psychology (rather than education and learning) and helps people who have emotional and behavioural disorders. (See also *Educateur*.)

Psychological Construction Concept (childhood, in this case) that can be defined, described, and scientifically "measured." Therefore, "childhood" has a beginning, an end, and particular characteristics which present the "average" view of what childhood is. (See *Social Construction* for another way of thinking about the concept of childhood.)

Psychopathology Applies the medical model of disease to social and emotional problems, identifying disorders in mental health and mental illness that can be corrected with proper treatment.

Radical Youth Work Joining with young people to challenge the existing social and professional structures and policies on both a personal and a political level. It may result in an enduring friendship with a youth that could be seen as going beyond the professional boundaries, if such a relationship is mutually agreed to. It means actively forming groups with young people with the intent of challenging the political and social structures that restrict or harm our collective existence.

Relational Child and Youth Care Theoretical orientation that believes that relationships and attachment are fundamental tools for developing social competence and enhancing development with young people.

Relational Inquiry Process of asking for feedback and disclosing to others your internal being in order to reflect on their responses and learn more about yourself in the context of relationships.

Relational Space Space that surrounds the relationship and the people within that relationship. The connected experience between two people is not limited to the present. Both people who enter a relationship carry aspects of previous connections and relationships into the space between them.

Relationship Domain of practice with a highly specific knowledge and skill base. It is the "space" in which you learn about yourself, apply your skills and theory, and integrate new experiences in a process of continuous growth as a practitioner.

Resilience Ability to cope and recover productively when faced with stress, change, or trauma. Children and youth are resilient if they can make their way toward the resources that they need to meet their developmental needs. These resources include individual, family, and community resources.

Restorative Justice/Practices Practices that emerged from the juvenile justice system and involve forming healthy relationships and repairing broken ones through discussion with all parties who harm and are harmed during a conflict or criminal activity.

Scholarship Rigorous and accurate information that builds on previous knowledge.

Scope of the Field Defines the boundaries of a field of study and is broader than the scope of practice of an individual. (See *Scope of Practice*.)

Scope of Practice Within a given profession, the scope of practice defines the "territory" in which practitioners operate. It describes what practitioners are trained to do and what is involved in typical practice. Scope of practice definitions focus on the boundaries of expertise because they help regulate and define the field for legislation, which will restrict who can call themselves a child and youth care practitioner and whether a practitioner is ethically within their area of expertise.

Second-Order Developmental Change Dramatic changes that occur in the way the child thinks, acts, and feels differently about life. This type of change is expected in residential or out-patient care settings where the child or youth is transformed in a nonlinear and dramatic manner.

Self-consciousness Acute sense of self-awareness. It requires the capacity to reflect on what a person experiences and to develop a mindfulness that includes self-reflection and introspection. It is observation of the self and making meaning of the observations while engaged in action. Self-consciousness can be debilitating for shy and introverted people. However, it is an essential skill for self-aware practitioners.

Social Construction In contrast to a *psychological construction*, social construction is a concept (childhood, in this case) whose meaning has been collectively defined (or constructed) by members of a particular society. The construction is therefore reflective of the norms, values, and treatment of "immature people" in a specific society and culture. The social construction of childhood in a single society may vary according to socioeconomic, gender, or race differences. Children also play an active role in the determination of the social construction of childhood.

Social Democracy   Similar to *Liberalism* in its support for social equality; however, the needs of the community or society are often prioritized over the rights of the individual. Social democrats work through democratically elected governments to redistribute wealth and correct social injustice to protect minorities, the marginalized, and those in need of chronic support.

Social Model of Disability   Sees disability as a problem created by society. Seeks equality in accessibility for those with a disability, expecting that society will adapt, not that the person needs to adapt.

Social Pedagogue/Pedagogue   Alternative term that is used in Sweden, Denmark, and Germany (among others). (See *Educateur*.)

Socialism/Communism   Political orientation that advocates for communal ownership and production of goods and services with both the benefit and the costs being equally distributed. It is characterized by working-class struggles for equality against capitalists who hold wealth and power. Structures of power are unnecessary and all people should have access to decision making and the benefits of those decisions.

Structuration Theory   Argues that structure and agency are locked in an interdependent/dependent relationship through perpetual co-creation. Societal structure directs agency of individuals and individuals create societal structure.

Supervision   Professional relationship that provides support, education, and monitoring of quality, and creates a safe forum to reflect on professional practice.

Symbolic Interactionism   Theoretical orientation that emerged from the work of Max Weber related to organizational behaviour and the functioning of bureaucracies in the 19th century. It became a framework for the study of human behaviour in the 1960s and focuses on the behaviour of groups of people (rather than individuals). Behaviour is a result of "ascribed meaning," which is determined based on social interaction. Meaning is modified in an ongoing manner through individual interpretation.

Tabula Rasa   Idea that children were a "blank slate," proposed by John Locke in the 17th century, suggested that children were malleable by both the good and the evil forces that confront us in this world and everything they interacted with shaped them as either a good or an evil person.

Theory   Set of interrelated concepts that provide an explanation for a behaviour or phenomenon; there are several levels of theory. *Implicit or tacit* theories are the personal explanations of the world that each person has. *Explicit* theories are the principles or foundations that might direct an organization or agency to operate in the way it does. *Formal* theories are developed by scholars in an attempt to universally explain and predict behaviour and phenomenon. Formal theories include hypothesis and can be tested through research. (See also *Conceptual Framework*.)

Therapeutic Milieu   Environment that is specialized for therapeutic treatment and intervention.

Token and Level System   System of reward and punishment in which children receive tokens or points for good behaviour. Tokens can be exchanged for material rewards or a higher "level" with more freedom and privileges.

Vicarious Trauma   Secondary stress disorder that occurs when practitioners have prolonged and repeated exposure to traumatized young people and families who are in crisis. The continuous work of processing the loss, grief, and anger of others who have been traumatized leads to the practitioner absorbing the life events and feelings of those they are working with and experiencing their inner world vicariously. (See also *Compassion Fatigue* and *Burnout*.)

Worldview   Mindset of the practitioner. Attitude is composed of values, beliefs, and ways of being that form your worldview represented by the expression of specific moral values, ethical commitments, and orientations to the world.

Youth   Period between childhood and adulthood beginning at the onset of puberty and lasting until physical and psychological maturity is reached, in early adulthood. The ages that define youth vary by culture and jurisdiction.

Youth Development Worker   Alternative terminology used by practitioners who focus primarily on adolescents and work primarily in community-based settings with a focus on youth leadership skills.

Youth Work   Alternative terminology used by practitioners who focus primarily on adolescents and young people and work primarily in community-based settings.

REFERENCES

Acorn, G. (2003). *Writing matters: An introduction to record keeping and report writing for front-line workers*. Sarnia, ON: S.E.E.K. Publishing.

Adlar, E. M., Paglia-Boak, A., Beitchman, J. H., & Wolfe, D. (2007). *The mental health and well-being of Ontario students 1991–2007*. (No. 23). Toronto: Centre for Addiction and Mental Health.

Ainsworth, F. (2006). Group care practitioners as family workers. In L. C. Fulcher & F. Ainsworth (Eds.), *Group care practice with children and young people revisited* (pp. 75–86). New York: Haworth Press.

Allen, B. (2011). The use and abuse of attachment theory in clinical practice with maltreated children, part II. *Treatment. Trauma, Violence, and Abuse, 12*(1), 13–22. doi: 10.1177/1524838010386974

Alliance to End Homelessness. (2012). *Report card on ending homelessness in Ottawa Jan to Dec 2011* (L. Browne, Ed.). Ottawa, ON: Author. Retrieved from www.endhomelessnessottawa.ca/homelessness/2011_Report_Card.cfm.

American Psychological Association (APA). (2012). *Facing the school dropout dilemma*. Washington, DC: Author. Retrieved from www.apa.org/pi/families/resources/school-dropout-prevention.aspx.

Anglin, J. (1999). The uniqueness of Child and Youth Care: A personal perspective. *Child and Youth Care Forum, 28*(2), 143–150. doi:10.1023/A:1021945306842

Anglin, J. (2001, December). Child and Youth Care: A unique profession. *CYC-Online, 35*. Retrieved from www.cyc-net.org/cyc-online/cycol-1201-anglin.html.

Anglin, J. (2002). *Pain, normality, and the struggle for congruence: Reinterpreting residential care for children and youth*. New York: Haworth Press.

Aotearoa, Inc. (2011). *Code of ethics for youth work in Aotearoa New Zealand* (2nd ed.). Retrieved from www.arataiohi.org.nz.

Arbuckle, M. B. (2006). Systems of care principles and practice: Implementing family-centred care for families and children with complex needs. In M. B. Arbuckle & C. A. Herrick (Eds.), *Child and adolescent mental health: Interdisciplinary systems of care* (pp. 3–30). Sudbury, MA: Jones & Bartlett.

Artz, S., Nicholson, D., Halsall, E., & Larke, S. (2000). *Final report: Developing a gender sensetive needs assessment tool for youth* (File No. 3510-U1). Retrieved from http://web.uvic.ca/cyc/naty/Final_Report.pdf.

Ashworth, J., Bockern, S. V., Ailts, J., Donnelly, J., Erickson, K., & Woltermann, J. (2008). An alternative to school detention. *Reclaiming Children and Youth, 17*(3), 22–26.

Askeland, L. (2006). Informal adoption, apprentices, and indentured children in the colonial era and the new republic, 1605–1850. In L. Askeland (Ed.), *Children and youth in adoption, orphanages, and foster care: A historical handbook and guide* (pp. 3–16). Westport, CT: Greenwood Press.

Austin, D., & Halpin, W. (1989). The caring response. *Journal of Child and Youth Care, 4*(3), 1–75.

Bailey, K. A. (2002). The role of the physical environment for children in residential care. *Residential treatment for children and youth, 20*(1), 15–27. doi: 10.1300/J007v20n01_02

Bates, M. (2006). A critically reflective approach to evidence-based practice. A sample of school social workers. *Canadian Social Work Review, 23*, 95–109.

Beker, J. (1977). On defining the Child and Youth Care profession: VI (editorial). *Child Care Quarterly, 6*, 245–247. doi: 10.1007/BF01554244

Bellefeuille, G., & Jamieson, D. (2008). Relational-centred planning: A turn toward creative potential and possibilities. In G. Bellefeuille & F. Ricks (Eds.), *Standing on the precipice: Inquiry into the creative potential of Child and Youth Care practice* (pp. 35–72). Edmonton, AB: MacEwan Press.

Bellefeuille, G., McGrath, J., & Jamieson, D. (2008). A pedagogical response to a changing world: Towards a globally-informed pedagogy for Child and Youth Care education and practice. *Children and Youth Services Review, 30*(7), 717–726. Doi: 10.1016/j.childyouth.2007.11.013

Beneteau, C. (1993). My developmental stages as a Child and Youth Care student. *Journal of Child and Youth Care, 8*(3), 35–40.

Berube, P. (1984). Professionalization of child care: A Canadian example. *Journal of Child Care, 2*(1), 1–12.

Beukes, K., & Gannon, B. (1996). *An orientation to Child and Youth Care.* Cape Town: National Association of Child Care Workers. Retrieved from www.cyc-net.org/reference/refs-history%20-%20beukesgannon.html.

Bezchilbnyk-Butler, K. Z., & Virani, A. S. (Eds.). (2007). *Clinical handbook of psychotropic drugs for children and adolescents* (2nd ed.). Boston: Hogrefe & Huber.

Bloom, M. (2009). *Secondary traumatic stress: The hidden trauma in child and youth counsellors.* Master's thesis, Wilfrid Laurier University, Waterloo, ON.

Boddy, J., Cameron, C., & Moss, P. (Eds.). (2006). *Care work: Present and future.* London: Routledge.

Brendtro, L. K. (1990). Powerful pioneers in residential group care: A look at our roots and heritage. *Child and Youth Care Quarterly, 19*(2), 79–90. doi: 10.1007/BF01273351

Brendtro, L. K., Brokenleg, M., & Bockern, S. V. (2002). *Reclaiming youth at risk: Our hope for the future* (2nd ed.). Bloomington, IN: National Educational Service.

Brendtro, L. K., & Hinders, D. (1990). A saga of Janusz Korczak, the king of children. *Harvard Educational Review, 60*(2), 237–246.

Brendtro, L. K., & Ness, A. E. (1983). *Re-educating troubled youth: Environments for teaching and treatment.* Hawthorne, NY: Aldine De Gruyter.

Brendtro, L. K., Mitchell, M. L., & McCall, H. J. (2009). *Deep brain learning: Pathways to potential with challenging youth.* Albion, MI: Circle of Courage Institute and Starr Commonwealth.

Brendtro, L., Ness, A., & Mitchell, M. (2001). *No disposable kids.* Longmont, CO: Sopris West.

Brendtro, L. K., & Shahbazian, M. (2004). *Troubled children and youth: Turning problems into opportunities*. Champaign, IL: Research Press.

Brockett, S., & Anderson-Nathe, B. (in press). If I'da thrown that chair at you, it woulda hit you": Seeing difficult behaviors through the lens of meaning and resilience. *Relational Child and Youth Care Practice, 26*(2).

Bronfennbrenner, U. (1979). *The Ecology of human development: Experiments by nature and design*. Cambridge, MA: Harvard University Press.

Brown, J. L., & Thompson, M. (Eds.). (1978). *Unconditional care: A human approach to the profoundly retarded*. Toronto: Canadian Educational Programmes.

Brynelson, D., Cummings, H., & Gonzales, V. (1993). Infant development programs. In R. Ferguson, A. Pence, & C. Denholm (Eds.), *Professional Child and Youth Care* (2nd ed., pp. 162–187). Vancouver: University of British Columbia Press.

Burford, G., & Fulcher, L. C. (2006). Resident group influences on team functioning. In L. C. Fulcher & F. Ainsworth (Eds.), *Group care practice with children and young people revisited* (pp. 177–208). New York: Haworth Press.

Burns, M. (1999). *Into the dark forest: Therapeutic storytelling*. Kingston, ON: Child Care Press.

Burns, M. (2006). *Healing spaces: The therapeutic milieu in child care and youth work*. Kinsgston, ON: Child Care Press.

Burns, M. (2008). *Into the dark forest: Therapeutic storytelling* (Revised ed.). Kingston, ON: Child Care Press.

Burns, M. (2012). *The self in in Child and Youth Care: A celebration*. Kingston, ON: Child Care Press.

Campaign 2000. (2011). *Revisiting family security in insecure times: Report card on child and family poverty in Canada*. Toronto, ON: Author. Retrieved from www.campaign2000.ca/reportcards.html.

Carrey, N. (2008). Building a better mousetrap: Risk and resilience processes, the DSM, and the child psychiatrist. In L. Liebenberg & M. Ungar (Eds.), *Resilience in action: Working with youth across cultures and contexts* (pp. 111–136). Toronto: University of Toronto Press.

Catalano, R. F., Berglund, M. L., Ryan J. A. M., Lonczak, H. S., & Hawkins, D. J. (2004). Positive youth development in the United States: Research findings on evaluations of positive youth development programs. *Annals of the American Academy of Political and Social Science, 591*(1), 98–124. doi: 10.1177/0002716203260102

Charles, G., & Gabor, P. (2006). An historical perspective on residential services for troubled and troubling youth in Canada revisited. *Relational Child and Youth Care Practice, 19*(4), 17–24.

Charles, G., & Garfat, T. (2009). Child and youth care practice in North America: Historical roots and current challenges. *Relational Child and Youth Care Practice, 22*(2), 17–28.

Charles, G., McElwee, N. C., & Garfat, T. (2005). Child and youth care in North America. In P. Share & N. C. McElwee (Eds.), *Applied social care: An introduction for Irish students*. (pp. 30–41). Dublin: Gill and Macmillan.

Chauhan, V. (2007). Partnership working in the voluntary and community sector. In R. Harrison, C. Benjamin, S. Curran, & R. Hunter (Eds.), *Leading work with young people* (pp. 232–244). London: Sage.

Chen, X. (2005). *Tending the gardens of citizenship: Child saving in Toronto 1880's–1920's.* Toronto: University of Toronto Press.

Child Labor Public Education Project (CLPEP). (2009). *Child labor in U.S. history.* Retrieved from www.continuetolearn.uiowa.edu/laborctr/child_labor/about/us_history.html.

Child Soldiers International. (2012). *Louder than words: An agenda for action to end state use of child soldiers: Report summary and ten-point checklist to prevent the involvement of children in hostilities in state armed forces and state-allied armed groups.* London: Author. Retrieved from www.child-soldiers.org.

Child and Youth Care Association of Alberta (CYCAA). (2000). *Certification Manual (Professional Manual).* Edmonton, AB: Child and Youth Care Association of Alberta.

Chipenda-Dansokho, S. (n.d.). *The determinants and influence of size on residential settings for children.* Chicago: Chapin Hall Center for Children at the University of Chicago.

Clark, M. D. (2001). Influencing positive behavior change: Increasing the therapeutic approach of juvenile courts. *Federal Probation, 65*(1), 18–27.

Collins, K., Connors, K., Davis, S., Donohue, A., Gardner, S., Goldblatt, E., et al. (2010). *Understanding the impact of trauma and urban poverty on family systems: Risks, resilience, and interventions.* Baltimore: Family Informed Trauma Treatment Center. Retrieved from http://nctsn.org/nccts/nav.do?pid=ctr_rsch_prod_ar.

Colón, A. R., & Colón, P. A. (2001). *A history of children: A socio-cultural survey across millennia.* Westport, CT: Greenwood Press.

Colton, M., & Helljnckx, W. (1994). Residential and foster care in the European community: Current trends in policy and practice. *British Journal of Social Work, 24,* 559–576.

Corey, M. S., & Corey, G. (2006). *Groups: Process and practice* (7th ed.). Belmont, CA: Thomson Brooks/Cole.

Cortiella, C. (2011). *The State of Learning Disabilities. New York: National Center for Learning Disabilities.* Retrieved from www.ncld.org/types-learning-disabilities/what-is-ld/state-of-learning-disabilities.

Costello, E. J., Mustillo, S., Erkanli, A., Keeler, G., & Angold, A. (2005). 10-year research update review: The developmental epidemiology of child and adolescent psychiatric disorders: Methods and public health burden. *Journal of American Child and Adolescent Psychiatry, 44*(10), 972–986. doi: 10.1097/01.chi.0000172552.41596.6f

Courtney, M., & Iwaniec, D. (Eds.). (2009). *Residential care of children: Comparative perspectives.* New York: Oxford University Press. doi:10.1093/acprof:oso/9780195309188.001.0001

Cruess, R., & Cruess, S. (2008). *The healer and the professional in society.* Retrieved from www.afmc.ca/social-professionalism-e.php.

Curtis, P. A., Alexander, G., & Lunghofer, L. A. (2001). A literature review comparing the outcomes of residential group care and therapeutic foster care. *Child and Adolescent Social Work Journal, 18*(5), 377–392. doi: 10.1023/A:1012507407702

Curtis, T., Lawrence, K., & Hoffman, B. (2012). *Enhancing youth engagement toolkit.* Mitchell Shire Council, Australia: Intralink Consulting PTY Ltd. Retrieved from www.mitchellshire.vic.gov.au/community-services/youth-development.aspx.

Day, A., Daffern, M., & Simmons, P. (2010). Use of restraint in residential care settings for children and young people. *Psychiatry, Psychology and Law, 17*(2), 230–244. doi: 10.1080/13218710903433964

Dean, M. (2012). *Diversity in practice: A critical exploration of residential care practice with minoritized children and youth.* Master's thesis. Retrieved from: http://dspace.library.uvic.ca:8080/handle/1828/4216.

Dean, M., Harpe, M., Lee, C., Loiselle, E., & Mallett, A. (2008). "Making the familiar strange": Deconstructing developmental psychology in Child and Youth Care. *Relational Child and Youth Care Practice, 21*(3), 43–56.

deFinney, S. (2008, April). It's about us: Diversity and social change in Child and Youth Care research and practice. Paper presented at *Child and Youth Care in Action: Connecting Across Contexts,*Victoria, BC.

De Hert, M., Dirix, N., Demunter, H., & Correll, C. U. (2011). Prevalence and correlates of seclusion and restraint use in children and adolescents: a systematic review. *European Child and Adolescent Psychiatry, 20*(5), 221–230. Doi: 10.1007/s00787-011-0160-x

Delano, F., & Shah, F. (2007). Using the "Professional Package" to help supervisors confront in a culturally sensitive manner. *Relational Child and Youth Care Practice, 20*(1), 5–11.

Delano, F., & Shah, F. (2009). Defining supervision in a professionally packaged way. *Relational Child and Youth Care Practice, 22*(1), 49–57.

DeLucia-Waack, J. L. (2006). *Leading psychoeducational groups for children and adolescents.* Thousand Oaks, CA: Sage.

Denholm, C., & Watkins, D. (1993). Canadian school-based Child and Youth Care. In R. V. Ferguson, A. Pence, & C. Denholm (Eds.), *Professional Child and Youth Care* (2nd ed., pp. 79–104). Vancouver: University of British Columbia Press.

Desmeules, G. (2007). A sacred family circle: A family group conferencing model. In I. Brown, F. Chaze, D. Fuchs, J. Lafrance, S. McKay, & S. T. Prokop (Eds.), *Putting a human face on child welfare: Voices from the prairies* (pp. 161–188). Ottawa, ON: Prairie Child Welfare Consortium/Centre of Excellence for Child Welfare.

Dewane, C. J. (2006). Use of self: A primer revisited. *Clinical Social Work Journal, 34,* 543–558. doi: 10.1007/s10615-005-0021-5

Doiron, M. (2006). Foreign credential recognition and immigrant labour market integration, Integrating internationally educated physiotherapists. *Human Resources Skills Development Canada.* Retrieved from www.hrsdc.gc.ca.

Dolan, P., Canavan, J., & Brady, B. (2006). Connecting with practice in the changing landscape of family support training. *Child Care in Practice, 12*(1), 43–52.

Dreikurs, R., & Soltz, V. (1964). *Children: The challenge.* New York: Hawthorne Books.

Dunlop, T. (2004). Framing a new and expanded vision for the future of Child and Youth Care Work: An international, intercultural and trans-disciplinary perspective. *Journal of Child and Youth Work, 19,* 254–267.

Durlak, J. A., Weissberg, R. P., & Pachan, M. (2010). A meta-analysis of after-school programs that seek to promote personal and social skills in children and adolescents. *American Journal of Community Psychology, 45*(3), 294–309.

Eckles, F., Carraway-Wilson, C., Zwicky, D., Rybicki, M., Stuart, C., Curry, D., et al. (2012). Workforce crisis and opportunity: The evolving field and emerging profession. *Journal of Child and Youth Care Work, 24,* 54–76.

Eisikovits, Z., & Beker, J. (1983). Beyond professionalism: The Child and Youth Care worker as craftsman. *Child Care Quarterly, 12*(3), 93–112.

Eisikovits, R. A., Beker, J., & Guttman, E. (1991). The known and the used in residential Child and Youth Care work. In J. Beker & Z. Eisikovits (Eds.), *Knowledge utilization in residential Child and Youth Care practice* (pp. 3–23). Washington, DC: Child Welfare League of America.

Evenson, J., & Barr, C. (2009). *Youth homelessness in Canada: The road to solutions.* Retrieved from www.raisingtheroof.org/Get-Informed/Resources.aspx.

Farmer, T. W., Farmer, E. M., & Brooks, D. S. (2010). Recasting the ecological and developmental roots of intervention for students with emotional and behavior problems: The promise of strength-based perspectives. *Exceptionality, 18*(2), 53–57. doi: 10.1080/09362831003673051

Federal Interagency Forum on Child and Family Statistics. (2012). *America's children in brief: Key national indicators of well-being.* Washington, DC: U.S. Government Printing Office. Retrieved from www.childstats.gov/pubs/.

Ferguson, R., & Anglin, J. P. (1985). The child care profession: A vision for the future. *Child Care Quarterly, 14,* 85–102. doi: 10.1007/BF01113404

Ferguson, R., Pence, A., & Denholm, C. (1993). The scope of Child and Youth Care in Canada. In R. Ferguson, A. Pence, & C. Denholm (Eds.), *Professional Child and Youth Care* (2nd ed., pp. 3–14). Vancouver: University of British Columbia Press.

Fewster, G. (1982). You, me and us. *Journal of Child Care, 1*(1), 71–73.

Fewster, G. (1990a). *Being in child care: A journey into self.* Binghampton, NY: Haworth Press.

Fewster, G. (1990b). Growing together: The personal relationship in Child and Youth Care. In J. Anglin, C. Denholm, R. Ferguson & A. Pence (Eds.), *Perspectives in professional Child and Youth Care* (pp. 25–40). New York: Haworth Press.

Fewster, G. (1991). The third person singular: Writing about the child care relationship. *Journal of Child and Youth Care Work, 7,* 55–62.

Fewster, G. (2001). Turning myself inside out: My personal theory of me. *Journal of Child and Youth Care, 15*(4), 89–108.

Fewster, G. (2004). Editorial: If you meet the pill fairy along the road, kill it. *Relational Child and Youth Care Practice, 17*(1), 3–10.

Fewster, G. (2005). Making contact: Personal boundaries in professional practice. *Relational Child and Youth Care Practice, 18*(2), 7–13.

Fewster, G. (2010). *Don't let your kids be normal: A partnership for a different world.* Cowichan Bay, BC: Influence Publishing.

Foltz, R. (2011). Re-ED principles in evidence-based standards. *Reclaiming Children and Youth, 19*(4), 28–32.

Freeman, J. G., King, M. & Pickett, W. (2011). *The health of Canada's young people: A mental health focus* (Catalogue No. 978-1-100-19335-9). Retrieved from www.phac-aspc.gc.ca/hp-ps/dca-dea/publications/hbsc-mental-mentale/index-eng.php.

Frensch, K. M., & Cameron, G. (2002). Treatment of choice or a last resort?: A review of residential mental health placements for children and youth. *Child and Youth Care Forum, 31*(5), 307–339. doi: 10.1023/A:1016826627406

Fulcher, L. C. (2003). Rituals of encounter that guarantee cultural safety. *Relational Child and Youth Care Practice, 16*(3), 20–27.

Fulcher, L. C. (2004). Programmes and praxis: A review of taken-for-granted knowledge. *Scottish Journal of Residential Child Care, 3*(2), 33–44.

Fulcher, L. C., (2006). The soul, rhythms and blues of responsive Child and Youth Care at home or away from home. In L. C. Fulcher & F. Ainsworth (Eds.), *Group care practice with children and young people revisited* (pp. 27–50). New York: Haworth Press.

Fulcher, L. C., & Ainsworth, F. (2006). Group care practice with children revisited. In L. C. Fulcher & F. Ainsworth (Eds.), *Group care practice with children and young people revisited* (pp. 1–26). New York: Haworth Press.

Fuller, S., & Martin, T. F. (2012). Predicting immigrant employment sequences in the first years of settlement. *International Migration Review, 46*(1), 138–190. Doi: 10.1111/j.1747-7379.2012.00883.x/full

Garfat, T. (1991). Definitions of Child and Youth Care: Responses to Billy's mother. *Journal of Child and Youth Care, 5*(1), 1–14.

Garfat, T. (1998). The effective Child and Youth Care intervention: A phenomenological inquiry. *Journal of Child and Youth Care, 12*(1–2), 1–122.

Garfat, T. (2001, January). Developmental stages of Child and Youth Care workers: An interactional perspective. *CYC-Online, 24.* Retrieved from www.cyc-net.org/cyc-online/cycol-0101-garfat.html.

Garfat, T. (2003). Working with families: Developing a Child and Youth Care approach. In T. Garfat (Ed.), *A Child and Youth Care approach to working with families.* (pp. 7–37). Binghamton, NY: Haworth Press.

Garfat, T. (2007, August). Who are we working with?: A short history of Child and Youth Care involvement with families. *CYC- Online, 103.* Retrieved from www.cyc-net.org/cyc-online/cycol-0708-garfat.html.

Garfat, T. (2008). The interpersonal in between: A explanation of relational Child and Youth Care practice. In G. Bellefeuille & F. Ricks (Eds.), *Standing on the precipice: Inquiry into the creative potential of Child and Youth Care practice* (pp. 7–34). Edmonton, AB: MacEwan Press.

Garfat, T., & Charles, G. (2010). *A Guide for developing effective Child and Youth Care interventions with families.* Capetown, South Africa: Pretext.

Garfat, T., & Fulcher, L.C. (2011). Characteristics of a relational Child and Youth Care approach. *Relational Child and Youth Care Practice, 24*(1–2), 7–19.

Garfat, T., & Fulcher, L. (2012). Characteristics of a relational Child and Youth Care approach. In T. Garfat & L. Fulcher (Eds.), *Child and Youth Care in practice.* Capetown, South Africa: Pretext.

Garfat, T., McElwee, N. C., & Charles, G. (2005). Self in social care. In P. Share & N. McElwee (Eds.), *Applied social care: An introduction for Irish students* (pp. 108–126). Dublin: Gill and Macmillan.

Garfat, T., & Ricks, F. (1995). Self-driven ethical decision-making: A model for Child and Youth Care. *Child and Youth Care Forum, 24*(6), 393–404.

Gavin, J., & Lister, S. (2001). The strategic use of sports and fitness activities for promoting psychosocial skill development in childhood and adolescence. *Journal of Child and Youth Care Work, 16*, 325–339.

Ghandour, R. M., Kogan, M. D., Blumberg, S. J., Jones, J. R., & Perrin, J. M. (2012). Mental health conditions among school-aged children: geographic and sociodemographic patterns in prevalence and treatment. *Journal of Developmental and Behavioral Pediatrics, 33*(1), 42. doi: 10.1097/DBP.0b013e31823e18fd

Gharabaghi, K. (2008). Professional issues in Child and Youth Care practice. *Child and Youth Services, 30*(3/4).

Gharabaghi, K. (2012). *Being with edgy youth.* New York: Nova Science.

Gharabaghi, K. (in press). Becoming present: The use of daily life events in family work. *Relational Child and Youth Care Practice, 26*(2).

Gharabaghi, K. (2013). From treatment to pedagogy: A conceptual approach. *Relational Child and Youth Care Practice, 26*(1), 20-32.

Gharabaghi, K., & Stuart, C. (2013). *Right here, right now: Exploring life-space interventions for children and youth.* Toronto: Pearson.

Gibbs, L., & Gambrill, E. (2002). Evidence-based practice: Counterarguments to objections. *Research on Social Work Practice, 12*, 452–476. doi: 10.1177/1049731502012003007

Gilmore, J. (2010). Trends in dropout rates and the labour market outcomes of young dropouts. *Education Matters: Insights on Education, Learning and Training in Canada, 7*(4), Retrieved from www.statcan.gc.ca/pub/81-004-x/2010004/article/11339-eng.htm.

Greene, R.W. (2010). *Collaborative problem solving: The model and its application across settings.* New York: Guilford Press.

Greene, R.W., Ablon, S. A., & Martin, A. (2006). Innovations: Child psychiatry: Use of Collaborative Problem Solving to reduce seclusion and restraint in child and adolescent inpatient units. *Psychiatric Services, 57*(5), 610–616. doi: 10.1176/appi.ps.57.5.610

Greenwald, M. (2008). The virtuous Child and Youth Care practitioner: Exploring identity and ethical practice. In G. Bellefeuille & F. Ricks (Eds.), *Standing on the precipice: Inquiry into the creative potential of Child and Youth Care practice* (pp. 169–204). Edmonton, AB: MacEwan Press.

Griffin, S. (2009). The spatial environments of street-involved youth: Can the streets be a therapeutic milieu? *Relational Child and Youth Care Practice, 21*(4), 16–27.

Griffin, S. (2011). *Negotiating Duality: A Framework for Understanding the Lives of Street-involved Youth Dissertation.* Retrieved from: http://hdl.handle.net/1828/3395

Gudgeon, C. (1991). Politics and the language of Child Care. *Journal of Child and Youth Care, 5*(1), 27–32.

Guttman, E. (1991). Immediacy in residential Child and Youth Care work: The fusion of experience, self-consciousness, and action. In J. Beker & R. A. Eisikovits (Eds.), *Knowledge utilization in residential Child and Youth Care practice* (pp. 65–84). Washington, DC: Child Welfare League of America.

Hallstedt, P., & Hogstrom, M. (2005). Social care: A European perspective. In P. Share & N. McElwee (Eds.), *Applied social care: An introduction for Irish students* (pp. 17–29). Dublin: Gill and Macmillan.

Hart, R., Daiute, C., Iltus, S., & Kritt, D. (1997). Developmental theory and children's participation in community organizations. *Social Justice, 24*(3), 33–63.

Hart, R., & Schwab, M. (1997). Children's rights and the building of democracy: A dialogue on the international movement for children's participation. *Social Justice, 24*(3), 177–182.

Health Canada, (1999). *Healthy development of children and youth—The role of the determinants of health* (Catalogue No. H39-501/1999E). Retrieved from http://publications.gc.ca/pub?id=85463&sl=0.

Heeney, B., & Watters, C. (2009). "Stomping out stigma": Summit conferences for youth. *Relational Child and Youth Care Practice, 22*(1), 34–44.

Helmer, J., & Griff, M. (1977). Child care work: A definition for the profession. *Child Care Quarterly, 6*(2), 144–146. Doi: 10.1007/BF01554703

Henggeler, S. W. (1993). *Multisystemic treatment of serious juvenile offenders: Implications for the treatment of substance abusing youths* (Research Monograph 137; NIH Pub. No. 93–3684). Rockville, MD: National Institute on Drug Abuse.

Herbert, N. (2008). *Youthspeak 2007: A time for action*. New Westminster, BC: Federation of BC Youth in Care Networks. Retrieved from http://fbcyicn.ca/wp-content/uploads/2010/03/YouthSpeak-2007-Final-Report.pdf.

Heydenberk, R. A., & Heydenberk, W. R. (2006). The conflict resolution connection: Increasing school attachment in cooperative classroom communities. *Reclaiming Children and Youth, 16*(3), 18–22.

Heywood, C. (2001). *A history of childhood: Children and childhood in the West from medieval to modern times*. Malden, MA: Blackwell.

Hoskins, M., & Ricks, F. (2008). Experiencing differences: The challenges, opportunities and cautions. In G. Bellefeuille & F. Ricks (Eds.), *Standing on the precipice: Inquiry into the creative potential of Child and Youth Care practice* (pp. 281–309). Edmonton, AB: MacEwan Press.

Howard, M. O., McMillen, C. J., & Pollio, D. E. (2003). Teaching evidence-based practice: A new paradigm for social work education. *Research on Social Work Practice, 13*, 234–259. doi:10.1177/1049731502250404

Hunt, D. E. (1987). *Beginning with ourselves: In practice, theory and human affairs*. Cambridge, MA: Brookline Books.

Hunt, D. E. (1992). *The renewal of personal energy*. Toronto: Ontario Institute for Studies in Education.

Itard, J. M. G. (1962). *The wild boy of Aveyron*. New York: Appleton-Century-Crofts.

James, R. K., & Gilliland, B. E. (2013). *Crisis intervention strategies* (7th ed.). Belmont, CA: Wadsworth/Thomson Learning.

Jean Marc Gaspard Itard. (2008). In *New world encyclopedia*. Retrieved from www.newworldencyclopedia.org/entry/Jean_Marc_Gaspard_Itard?oldid=680597.

Jefferess, D. (2002). Neither seen nor heard: The idea of the "child" as impediment to the rights of children. *Topia, 7*, 75–98.

Jeffery, K. (2010). Supportive holding or restraint: terminology and practice. *Paediatric Nursing, 22*(6), 24–28.

Jones, H. D., & Vander Ven, K. (1990). Education and training for Child and Youth Care practice: The view from both sides of the Atlantic. *Child and Youth Care Quarterly, 19*(2), 105–121. doi: 10.1007/BF01273353

Juul, K. D. (1990). Child and Youth Care in American and Europe: A history of fruitful mutual influences in special education and in therapy. *Child and Youth Care Quarterly, 19*(2), 91–103.

Kelly, C. S. (1990). Professionalizing Child and Youth Care: An overview. In J. P. Anglin, R. V. Ferguson, C. J. Denholm, & A. R. Pence (Eds.), *Perspectives in professional Child and Youth Care* (pp. 167–176). New York: Haworth Press.

Kelly, R. (2009). Draw a circle and be sure to include me in it: Restorative practices with children under 12. *Relational Child and Youth Care Practice, 22*(1), 18–31.

Kendrick, A. (Ed.). (2007). *Residential child care: Prospects and challenges*. London: Jessica Kingsley.

Kidd, S. A., Miner, S., Walker, D., & Davidson, L. (2007). Stories of working with homeless youth: On being "mind-boggling". *Children & Youth Services Review, 29*(1), 16–34. doi:10.1016/j.childyouth.2006.03.008

Kolb, A. Y., & Kolb, D. A. (2005). Learning styles and learning spaces: Enhancing experiential learning in higher education. *Academy of Management Learning and Education, 4*(2), 193–212. doi: 10.5465/AMLE.2005.17268566

Kolb, A. Y., & Kolb, D. A. (2008). Experiential learning theory: A dynamic, holistic approach to management learning, education and development. In S. J. Armstrong & C. V. Fukami (Eds.), *The Sage handbook of management learning, education and development* (pp. 42–68). London: Sage Publications. doi: 10.4135/9780857021038.n3

Kolb, D. A. (1984). *Experiential learning*. Englewood Cliffs, NJ: Prentice-Hall.

Krueger, M. (1982). *Job satisfaction for child care workers*. Milwaukee, WI: Tall Publishing.

Krueger, M. (1991a). Coming from your center, being there, meeting them where they're at, interacting together, counseling on the go, creating circles of caring, discovering and using self, and caring for one another: Central themes in professional child and youth care. *Journal of Child and Youth Care, 5*(1), 77–87.

Krueger, M. (1991b). A review and analysis of the development of professional Child and Youth Care work. *Child and Youth Care Quarterly, 20*(6), 379–388. doi: 10.1007/BF00757496

Krueger, M. (1996). *Nexus: A book about youth work*. Milwaukee, WI: University Outreach Press.

Krueger, M. (2002). A further review of the development of the Child and Youth Care profession in the United States. *Child and Youth Care Forum, 31*(1), 13–26.

Krueger, M. (Ed.). (2004). *Themes and stories in youth work practice: In the rhythms of youth*. New York: Haworth Press

Krueger, M. (2007a). Four areas of support for Child and Youth Care workers. *Families and Society: The Journal of Contemporary Social Services, 88*(2), 233–240.

Krueger, M. (2007b). *Sketching youth, self, and youth work*. Rotterdam, The Netherlands: Sense.

Krueger, M., Galovits, L., Wilder, Q., & Pick, M. (1999). *A curriculum guide for working with youth: An interactive approach*. Milwaukee, WI: University Outreach Press.

Krueger, M., & Stuart, C. A. (1999). Context and competence in work with children and youth. *Child and Youth Care Forum, 28*(3), 195–204. doi: 10.1023/A:1021943811869

Langaard, K., & Toverud, R. (2009). Caring involvement: A core concept in youth counselling in school health services. *International Journal of Qualitative Studies on Health and Well-being, 4*, 220–227. doi: 10.3109/17482620903116198

Lasson, S. M., Nobs, I. K., & Anglin, J. P. (1990). FICE: Striving to build a world in which children can live. *Child and Youth Care Quarterly, 19*(3), 187–198. doi: 10.1007/BF01088453

Laursen, E. K. (2010). The evidence base for positive peer culture. *Reclaiming Children and Youth, 19*(2), 37–42.

Lawson, L. (1998). Milieu management of traumatized youngsters. *Journal of Child and Adolescent Psychiatric Nursing, 11*(3), 99–107. doi: 10.1111/j.1744-6171.1998.tb00021.x

Learning Disabilities Association of Canada (LDAC). (2002). *Official definition of learning disabilities*. Retrieved from www.ldac-acta.ca/en/learn-more/ld-defined.html.

Lerner, R., & Lerner, J. V. (2012). *The positive development of youth: Report of the findings from the first eight years of the 4-H study of positive youth development*. Retrieved from www.4-h.org/about/youth-development-research/positive-youth-development-study/.

Lewin, K. (1948). *Resolving social conflicts*. New York: Harper & Brothers.

Liebenberg, L., & Ungar, M. (Eds.). (2008). *Resilience in action: Working with youth across cultures and contexts*. Toronto: University of Toronto Press.

Lindsey, D. (2004). *The welfare of children*, (2nd ed.). London: Oxford University Press.

Little, J. N. (2011). Articulating a Child and Youth Care philosophy: Beyond binary constructs. In A. Pence & J. White (Eds.), *Child and Youth Care: Critical perspectives on pedagogy, practice, and policy* (pp. 3–18). Vancouver: University of British Columbia Press

Long, N., Wood, M. M., & Fecser, F. A. (2001). *Life-space crisis intervention: Talking with students in conflict* (2nd ed.). Austin, TX: Pro-Ed.

Luft, J. (1970). *Group processes: An introduction to group dynamics* (2nd ed.). Palo Alto, CA: Mayfield.

Lundy, T. (2008). Presence and participation: Being at the heart of change. In G. Bellefeuille & F. Ricks (Eds.), *Standing on the precipice: Inquiry into the creative potential of Child and Youth Care practice* (pp. 207–230). Edmonton, AB: MacEwan Press.

Magnuson, D., & Baizerman, M. (Eds.). (2007). *Work with youth in divided and contested societies*. Rotterdam, The Netherlands: Sense.

Maier, H. W. (1957). Routines: A pilot study of three selected routines and their impact upon the child in residential treatment. *American Journal of Orthopsychiatry, 27*(3), 701–709.

Maier, H. W. (1977). Child welfare: Child care workers. In *Encyclopedia of Social Work, 1977* (Vol. 1, pp. 130–134). Washington, DC: National Association of Social Workers.

Maier, H. W. (1979). The core of care: Essential ingredients for the development of children at home and away from home. *Child Care Quarterly, 8*(3), 161–173. doi: 10.1007/BF01554603

Maier, H. W. (1983). Should Child and Youth Care go the craft or the professional route?: A comment on the preceding article by Zvi Eisikovits and Jerome Beker. *Child Care Quarterly, 12*(2), 113–118. doi:10.1007/BF01151598

Maier, H. W. (1987). *Developmental group care of children and youth: Concepts and practice*. London: Haworth Press.

Maier, H. W. (1991). Developmental foundations of Child and Youth Care work. In J. Beker & R. A. Eisikovits (Eds.), *Knowledge utilization in residential Child and Youth Care practice* (pp. 25–48). Washington, DC: Child Welfare League of America.

Maier, H. W. (1992). Rhythmicity-A powerful force for experiencing unity and personal connections. *Journal of Child and Youth Care Work, 8*, 7–13.

Maier, H. W. (2002). Learning overshadows teaching: Key issues in the preparation of care and social workers. *Child and Youth Care Forum, 31*(6), 439–443. doi: 10.1023/A:1021162401189

Maier, H. W. (2006). Primary care in secondary settings: Inherent strains. In L. C. Fulcher & F. Ainsworth (Eds.), *Group care practice with children and young people revisited* (pp. 87–116). New York: Haworth Press.

Mann-Feder, V. (2003). Relatedness and control. *Relational Child and Youth Care Practice, 16*(3), 10–14.

Martin, D., & Tennant, G. (2008). Child and youth care in the community centre. *Relational Child and Youth Care Practice, 20*(2), 20–26.

Mattingly, M. A. (1995a). Developing professional ethics for Child and Youth Care work: Assuming responsibility for the quality of care. *Child and Youth Care Forum, 24*(6), 379–391. doi: 10.1007/BF02128529

Mattingly, M. A. (1995b). Ethics of Child and Youth Care professionals: A code developed by the draft committee for the international leadership coalition for professional Child and Youth Care. *Child and Youth Care Forum, 24*(6), 371–378. Doi: 10.1007/BF02128528

Mattingly, M., Bean, J.A.., & Schaefer, A. (2012). Over sixteen million children in poverty in 2011. *The Carsey Institute at the Scholars' Repository* (Paper 176). Retrieved from http://scholars.unh.edu/carsey/176.

Mattingly, M., Stuart, C., & Vander Ven, K. (2003). Competencies for professional Child and Youth Care. *Journal of Child and Youth Care Work, 17,* 16–49.

May, L., Katzenstein., & Tonkin, R. (2004). *Healthy youth development: Highlights from the 2003 AHS.* Retrieved from http://mcs.bc.ca.

Mayer, M. F. (1958). *A guide for child-care workers.* New York: Child Welfare League of America.

McCammon, S. L. (2012). Systems of care as asset-building communities: Implementing strengths-based planning and positive youth development. *American Journal of Community Psychology, 49,* 556–565. doi: 10.1007/s10464-012-9514

McDermott, D. (1994). Editorial. *CYC Chronicle, 5*(1). (Available from Ontario Child and Youth Counsellors Association, RR #3, Harrowsmith, ON, Canada)

McMahon, L., & Ward, A. (1998). Helping and the personal response: Intuition is not enough. In A. Ward & L. McMahon (Eds.), *Intuition is not enough: Matching learning with practice in therapeutic child care* (pp. 28–39). London: Routledge.

McMillan, C., Stuart, C. & Vincent, J. (2012). Tell it like you see it: youth perceptions of child and youth care practitioner interventions and outcomes in an alternative school setting *International Journal of Child, Youth, and Family Studies 3*(2/3), 214-233. http://journals.uvic.ca/index.php/ijcyfs/article/view/10867

Merikangas, K., He, J. P., Rapoport, J., Vitiello, B., & Olfson, M. (2012). Medication use in US youth with mental disorders. *JAMA Pediatrics, 167*(2), 141–148. doi:10.1001/jamapediatrics.2013.431.

Mesch, G. S. (2012). Technology and youth. *New Directions for Youth Development, 135,* 97–105. doi: 10.1002/yd.20032

Meschke, L. L., Peter, C. R., & Bartholomae, S. (2012). Developmentally appropriate practice to promote healthy adolescent development: Integrating research and practice. *Child and Youth Care Forum, 41,* 89–108. doi: 10.1007/s10566-011-9153-7

Mezirow, J. (2000). *Learning as transformation: Critical perspectives on a theory in progress.* San Francisco: Jossey Bass.

Milan, A., Hou, F., & Wong, I. (2006). Learning disabilities and child altruism, anxiety, and aggression (Catalogue No. 11–008). *Canadian Social Trends, 81*, 16–22.

Moen, K., Little, J. N., & Burnett, M. (2004). *The Earth is dying.* Unpublished manuscript, University of Victoria, Victoria, BC.

Montgomery, H. (2009). *An introduction to childhood: An anthropological perspective on children's lives.* Malden, MA: Wiley-Blackwell.

Moody Jr., E. E., & Lupton-Smith, H. S. (1999). Interventions with juvenile offenders: Strategies to prevent acting out behavior. *Journal of Addictions and Offender Counseling, 20*(1), 2–14. doi: 10.1002/j.2161-1874.1999.tb00136.x

Morawska, A., Sanders, M. R., Goadby, E., Headley, C., Hodge, L., McAuliffe, C., et al. (2011). Is the Triple P-Positive Parenting Program acceptable to parents from culturally diverse backgrounds? *Journal of Child and Family Studies, 20*(5), 614–622. Doi: 10.1007/s10826-010-9436-x

Mordock, J. B. (2002a). A model of milieu treatment: Its implementation and factors contributing to "drift" from the model over a 30–year period part 1: Implementation of the model. *Residential Treatment for Children and Youth, 19*(3), 17–42. doi: 10.1300/J007v19n03_02

Mordock, J. B. (2002b). A model of milieu treatment: Its implementation and factors contributing to "drift" from the model over a 30–year period part 2: Outcome assessment, drift and planned changes. *Residential Treatment for Children and Youth, 19*(4), 39–60.

Munger, R. L. (1998). *The ecology of troubled children.* Cambridge, MA: Brookline Books.

National Alliance to End Homelessness. (2008). *Incidence and vulnerability of LBGTQ homeless youth* (Brief #2). Washington, DC: Author. Retrieved from www.endhomelessness.org/library/entry/incidence-and-vulnerability-of-lgbtq-homeless-youth.

Ness, A. E., & Mitchell, M. L. (1990). AIEJI: Creating a profession to work with troubled children and youth. *Child and Youth Care Quarterly, 19*(3), 199–207. doi: 10.1007/BF01088454

Nicolaou, A., & McCauley, K. (1991). Training the American educateur: An interagency approach. *Child and Youth Care Forum, 20*(4), 275–290. doi: 10.1007/BF00757284

Nunno, M., Holden, M. J., & Tollar, A. (2006). Learning from tragedy: A survey of child and adolescent restraint fatalities. *Child Abuse and Neglect, 30,* 1333–1342. DOI: 10.1016/j.chiabu.2006.02.015

O'Grady, B., Gaetz, S., & Buccieri, K. (2011). *Can I see your ID?: The policing of youth homelessness in Toronto.* Toronto: JFCY & Homeless Hub. Retrieved from www.homelesshub.ca/ResourceFiles/CanISeeYourID_nov9.pdf.

Ohio Association of Child and Youth Care Practitioners (OHIO). (2011). *Registration and certification package.* Retrieved from www.helpingohiokids.org/certification/certification.htm.

Ontario Association of Child and Youth Counsellors (OACYC). (2006). *Developmental milestones of the CYC profession and the OACYC.* Retrieved from www.oacyc.org.

Ontario Ministry of Training Colleges and Universities. (2002). *Child and youth worker program standard.* Retrieved from www.edu.gov.on.ca/eng/general/college/progstan/humserv/echildyt.html.

Oreopoulos, P. (2006). The compelling effects of compulsory schooling: Evidence from Canada. *Canadian Journal of Economics, 39*(1), 22–52. doi: 10.1111/j.0008-4085.2006.00337.x

Pacini-Ketchabaw, V. (2008). Perspectives on child and adolescent development: Challenges and possibilities for teaching. *Relational Child and Youth Care Practice, 21*(3), 39–42.

Pacini-KetchaBaw, V. (2011). Rethinking developmental theories in Child and Youth Care. In A. Pence & J. White (Eds.), *Child and Youth Care: Critical perspectives on pedagogy practice, and policy* (pp. 19–32). Vancouver: University of British Columbia Press.

Paglia-Boak, A., Adlaf, E. M., Hamilton, H. A., Beitchman, J. H., Wolfe, D., & Mann, R. E. (2012). *The mental health and well-being of Ontario students, 1991–2011: OSDUHS highlights* (CAMH Research Document Series No. 35). Toronto: Centre for Addiction and Mental Health. Retrieved from www.camh.ca/en/research/news_and_publications/ontario-student-drug-use-and-health-survey/Pages/default.aspx.

Paglia-Boak, A., Adlaf, E. M., & Mann, R. E. (2011). *Drug use among Ontario students, 1977–2011: OSDUHS highlights* (CAMH Research Document Series No. 33). Toronto: Centre for Addiction and Mental Health. Retrieved from www.camh.ca/en/research/news_and_publications/ontario-student-drug-use-and-health-survey/Pages/default.aspx.

Panitch, M. (2008). *Disability, mothers, and organization.* New York: Routledge.

Pence, A., & Marfo, K. (2008). Early childhood development in Africa: Interrogating constraints of prevailing knowledge bases. *International Journal of Psychology, 43*(2), 78–87. doi: 10.1080/00207590701859143

Pence, A. & White, J. (Eds.). (2011). *Child and Youth Care: Critical perspectives on pedagogy, practice, and policy.* Vancouver: University of British Columbia Press.

Perry, B., & Hambrick, E. (2008). An introduction to the neuro-sequential model of therapeutics. *Reclaiming Children and Youth, 17*(3), 38–43.

Peters, F. (2008). Introduction: Residential child care and its alternatives-professional approaches in a discursive field. In F. Peters (Ed.), *Residential child care and its alternatives: International perspectives* (pp. 1–20). Stoke on Trent, UK: Trentham Books in association with FICE.

Petrie, P. (2006). Care work in the nineteenth century. In J. Boddy, C. Cameron, & P. Moss (Eds.), *Care work: Present and future.* London: Routledge.

Phelan, M. (1988). The certification of Child and Youth Care workers. In G. Charles & P. Gabor (Eds.), *Issues in Child and Youth Care practice in Alberta* (pp. 128–134). Lethbridge, AB: Lethbridge Community College.

Phelan, J. (1990). Child care supervision: The neglected skill of evaluation. In J. Anglin, C. Denholm, & A. Pence (Eds.), *Perspectives in professional Child and Youth Care* (pp. 131–141). New York: Haworth Press.

Phelan, J. (2000, October). *A re-examination of the language and methodologies in Child and Youth Care work.* Paper presented at the International Child and Youth Care Conference, Cleveland, OH.

Phelan, J. (2001). Notes on using plain language in Child and Youth Care work. *CYC-Online, 34.* Retrieved from www.cyc-net.org/cyc-online/cycol-1101-phelan.html.

Phelan, J. (2003). The relationship boundaries that control programming. *Relational Child and Youth Care Practice, 16*(1), 51–55.

Phelan, J. (2008). Deciding to relax external controls: A Child and Youth Care framework. *Relational Child and Youth Care Practice, 21*(1), 38–41.

Powell, N. (1977). "A rose is a rose is a rose": The definition debate. *Child Care Quarterly, 6*(2), 147–149. doi: 10.1007/BF01554704

Preston, J., O'Neal, J. H., & Talaga, M. C. (2010). *Child and adolescent clinical psychopharmacology made simple* (2nd ed). Oakland, CA: New Harbinger.

Public Health Agency of Canada (PHAC). (2010). *Canadian Incidence Study of Reported Child Abuse and Neglect – 2008: Major Findings* (Catalogue No. HP5-1/2008E-PDF). Retrieved from www.phac-aspc.gc.ca/cm-vee/public-eng.php.

Quinn, M. M., Rutherford, R. B., Leone, P. E., Osher, D. M. & Poirier, J. M. (2005). Youth With Disabilities in Juvenile Corrections: A National Survey. *Exceptional Children, 71*(3), 339–345.

Rabinovitch, R. (1991). Fritz Redl and residential treatment at Hawthorn Center. In W. C. Morse (Ed.), *Crisis intervention in residential treatment: The clinical innovations of Fritz Redl* (pp. 73–82). New York: Haworth Press.

Rahikainen, M. (2004). *Centuries of child labour: European experiences from the seventeenth centruy to the twentieth century.* Burlington, UK: Ashgate.

Ranahan, P. (1999). Reaching beyond caring to loving in Child and Youth Care practice. *Journal of Child and Youth Care, 13*(4), 55–65.

Rasmussen, L., Haggith, K., Roberts, J. (2012). Transition to adulthood, moving needs into practice: A Canadian community partnership response to new adult service needs for individuals with disabilities. *Relational Child and Youth Care Practice, 25*(3), 29–38.

Ray, N. (2006). *Lesbian, gay, bisexual and transgender youth: An epidemic of homelessness.* New York: National Gay and Lesbian Task Force Policy Institute and the National Coalition for the Homeless. Retrieved from www.thetaskforce.org/downloads/reports/reports/HomelessYouth.pdf.

Redl, F. (1959). Strategy and technique of the life-space interview. *American Journal of Orthopsychiatry, 29,* 1–18.

Redl, F. (1966). *When we deal with children.* New York: Collier-MacMillan Canada.

Redl, F., & Wineman, D. (1951). *Children who hate: A sensitive analysis of the anti-social behaviour of children in their response to the adult world.* New York: Macmillan Canada.

Redl, F., & Wineman, D. (1952). *Controls from within: Techniques for the treatment of the aggressive child.* New York: Macmillan Canada.

Rhodes, J., & Lowe, S. R. (2008). Youth mentoring and resilience: Implications for practice. *Child Care in Practice, 14*(1), 9–17. doi: 10.1016/j.childyouth.2012.05.017

Richard, K. (2008). On the matter of cross-cultural aboriginal adoption. In I. Brown, F. Chaze, D. Fuchs, J. Lafrance, S. McKay. & S. Thomas-Prokop (Eds.), *Putting a human face on child welfare: Voices from the prairies* (pp. 189–202). Ottawa, ON: Prairie Child Welfare Consortium/Centre of Excellence for Child Welfare.

Richardson, K. B. (2011). *Access and Wait Times in Child and Youth Mental Health: A Background Paper.* Retrieved from: www.cihr-irsc.gc.ca/e/43055.html#s1

Ricks, F. (1989). Self-awareness for training and application in Child and Youth Care. *Journal of Child and Youth Care, 4*(1), 33–42.

Ricks, F. (1992). A feminist's view of caring. *Journal of Child and Youth Care 7*(2), 49–57.

Ricks, F. (2003). Relatedness in relationships: It's about being. *Relational Child and Youth Care Practice, 16*(3), 70–77.

Ricks, F., & Charlesworth, J. (2003). *Emergent Practice Planning.* New York: Kluwer Academic/Plenum Press. Doi: 10.1007/978-1-4615-0203-6

Roberts, M. W., & Alessi, N. E. (1999). Medication for the depressed child: Hope or harm? Reaching today's youth. *The Community Circle of Caring Journal, 4*(1), 1–10.

Rodgers, M. T. (1998). From the eyes of innocence and the mind of an adult. *Child Care in Practice, 4*(3), 211–220. doi:10.1080/13575279808413115

Rytterstrom, P., Cedersund, E., & Arman, M. (2009). Care and caring culture as experienced by nurses working in different care environments: A phenomenological–hermeneutic study. *International Journal of Nursing Studies, 46*(5), 689–698. doi: 10.1016/j.ijnurstu.2008.12.005

Saewyc, E., & Tonkin, R. (2008). Surveying adolescents: Focusing on positive development. *Paediatrics and Child Health, 13,* 43–47. Retrieved from www.ncbi.nlm.nih.gov/pmc/articles/PMC2528829/.

Salhani, D., & Grant, C. (2007). The dynamics of an inter-professional team: The interplay of Child and Youth Care with other professions within a residential treatment milieu. *Relational Child and Youth Care Practice, 20*(4), 12–21.

Sanders, M. R. (2003). Triple P-Positive Parenting Program: A population approach to promoting competent parenting. *Advances in Mental Health, 2*(3), 127–143. doi: 10.5172/jamh.2.3.127

Sanders, M. R. (2012). Development, evaluation, and multinational dissemination of the Triple P-Positive Parenting Program. *Annual Review of Clinical Psychology, 8,* 345–379. doi: 10.1146/annurev-clinpsy-032511-143104

Sanders, M. R., Turner, K. M., & Markie-Dadds, C. (2002). The development and dissemination of the Triple P—Positive Parenting Program: A multilevel, evidence-based system of parenting and family support. *Prevention Science, 3*(3), 173–189. doi:10.1023/A:1019942516231

Santrock, J., MacKenzie-Rivers, A., Leung, K. H., & Malcomson, T. (2011). *Life-span development* (4th Canadian Ed.). Toronto: McGraw-Hill Ryerson.

Sapin, K. (2009). *Essential skills for youth work practice*. London: Sage.

Savicki, V. (2002). *Burnout across thirteen cultures: Stress and coping in Child and Youth Care workers.* Westport, CT: Praeger.

Schon, D. A. (1987). *Educating the reflective practitioner: Toward a new design for teaching and learning in the professions*. San Francisco: Jossey-Bass.

Search Institute. (2012). *Developmental assets*. Retrieved from www.search-institute.org/developmental-assets.

Sesma, A., Mannes, M. Jr., & Scales, P. C. (2006). Positive adaptation, resilience, and the developmental asset framework. In S. Goldstein & R. B. Brooks (Eds.), *Handbook of resilience in children* (pp. 281–296). New York: Springer.

Shaw, K., & Garfat, T. (2003). From the front line to family home: A youth care approach to working with families. *Child and Youth Services, 25*(1–2), 39–53.

Skott-Myhre, H. A. (2004). Radical youth work: Creating a politics of mutual liberation for youth and adults. *Journal of Child and Youth Care Work, 19,* 89–94.

Skott-Myhre, H. A. (2007). *Youth and subculture as creative force: Creating new spaces for radical youth work*. Toronto: University of Toronto Press.

Skott-Myhre, H. A., & Skott-Myhre, K. S. G. (2007). Radical youth work: Love and community. *Relational Child and Youth Care Practice, 20*(3), 48–57.

Slade, A. (2012). *Taking a posthumanist stand in CYC ethics: An ethical-political experiment*. Master's thesis. Reteived from http://hdl.handle.net/1828/4162

Small, R. W., & Dodge, L. M. (1988). Roles, skills, and job tasks in professional child care: A review of the literature. *Child & Youth Care Quarterly, 17*(1), 6–23.

Smith, A., Stewart D., Peled, M., Poon, C., Saewyc, E. & the McCreary Centre Society. (2009). *A Picture of Health: Highlights from the 2008 BC Adolescent Health Survey.* Vancouver: McCreary Centre Society. Retrieved from http://www.mcs.bc.ca/ahs_reports

Smith, L., & Drower, S. J. (2008). Promoting resilience and coping in social workers: Learning from perceptions about resilieince and coping among South African social work students. In L. Liebenberg & M. Ungar (Eds.), *Resilience in action: Working with youth across cultures and contexts* (pp. 137–164). Toronto: University of Toronto Press. doi: 10.1007/BF01089398

Smith, M. (2006). Act justly, love tenderly, walk humbly. *Relational Child and Youth Care Practice, 19*(4), 5–16.

Smith, M. (2009). *Rethinking residential child care: Positive perspectives.* London: Polity Press.

Smith, M. (2011). Love and the Child and Youth Care relationship. *Relational Child and Youth Care Practice, 24*(1/2), 189–192.

Social Development Division (SDD). (2003). *Conflict negotiation skills for youth* (Ref. No. ST/ESCAP/2286). Retrieved from www.unescap.org/publications/detail.asp?id=789.

Sourander, A., Ellila, H., Valimaki, M., & Piha, J. (2002). Use of holding, restraints, seclusion and time-out in child and adolescent psychiatric in-patient treatment. *European Child and Adolescent Psychiatry, 11*(4), 162–167. doi: 10.1007/s00787-002-0274-2

Stacey, K., Webb, E., Hills, S., Lagzdins, N., Moulds, D., Phillips, T., et al. (2002). Relationships and power. *Youth Studies Australia, 21*(1), 44–51.

Statistics Canada. (2011). *Family Violence in Canada: A Statistical Profile* (Catalogue No. 85-224-X). Retrieved from www.statcan.gc.ca/pub/85-224-x/85-224-x2010000-eng.htm.

Stearns, P. N. (2005). *Growing up: The history of childhood in a global context.* Waco, TX: Baylor University Press.

Steckley, L. (2010). Containment and holding environments: Understanding and reducing physical restraint in residential child care. *Children and Youth Services Review, 32*(1), 120–128. doi: 10.1016/j.childyouth.2009.08.007

Steckley, L. (2012). Touch, physical restraint and therapeutic containment in residential child care. *British Journal of Social Work, 42*(3), 537–555. doi: 10.1093/bjsw/bcr069

Steinebach, C., & Steinebach, U. (2009). Positive peer culture with German youth. *Reclaiming Children and Youth, 18*(2), 27–33.

Stevens, I., & Furnivall, J. (2008). Therapeutic approaches in residential care. In A. Kendrick (Ed.), *Residential child care: Prospects and challenges* (pp. 196–209). London: Jessica Kingsley.

Stokes, J. (2011). *Mentoring the development of reflective practice in decision-making.* Victoria, BC: Research to Practice Network. Retrieved from www.fcssbc.ca/CoreBC/.

Storer, H. L., Barkan, S. F., Sherman, E. L., Haggerty, K. P., & Mattos, L. M. (2012). Promoting relationship building and connection: Adapting an evidence-based parenting program for families involved in the child welfare system. *Children and Youth Services Review, 34*(9), 1853–1861. doi: 10.1016/j.childyouth.2012.05.017

Stroul, B. A., & Friedman, R. M. (1986). *A system of care for severely emotionally disturbed children and youth* (No. ED330167). Washington, DC: CASSP Technical Assistance Center, Georgetown University Child Development Center.

Stuart, C. (2001). Professionalizing Child and Youth Care: Continuing the Canadian journey. *Journal of Child and Youth Work, 16,* 264–282.

Stuart, C. (2008). Shaping the rules: Child and youth care boundaries in the context of relationship. Bonsai! In G. Bellefeuille & F. Ricks (Eds.), *Standing on the precipice: Inquiry into the creative potential of Child and Youth Care practice* (pp. 135–168). Edmonton, AB: MacEwan Press.

Stuart, C. (in press). Developing the profession from adolescence into adulthood: Generativity vs. stagnation . In K. Gharabaghi, H. Skott-Myhre, & M. Krueger (Eds.), *Being with children and youth: Emerging theories, practices, and discussions in Child and Youth Care work.* Waterloo, ON: Wilfred Laurier Press.

Stuart, C., & Carty, W. (2006). *The role of competence in outcomes for children and youth: An approach for mental health.* Toronto: Ryerson University.

Stewart, S. L., Rick, J., Currie, M., & Rielly, N. (2009). *Collaborative problem-solving approach in clinically-referred children: A residential program evaluation.* Retrieved from www .thinkkids.org/docs/CPRI-CPS%20pdf.pdf.

Swanzen, R., & Marincowitz, L.G. (in press). Mimetic theory and the use of daily life events. *Relational Child and Youth Care Practice, 26*(2).

Taliaferro, L. A., & Borowsky, I. W. (2012). Beyond prevention: Promoting healthy youth development in primary care. *American Journal of Public Health, 102,* S317–S321. doi:10.2105/ AJPH.2011.300559

Taussig, H. N., & Culhane, S. E. (2010). Impact of a mentoring and skills group program on mental health outcomes for maltreated children in foster care. *Archives of Pediatrics & Adolescent Medicine, 164*(8), 739–746. doi: 10.1001/archpediatrics.2010.124

Taylor, E. W., Mezirow, J., & Associates. (2009). *Transformative learning in practice: Insights from community, workplace and higher education.* Hoboken, NJ: Jossey-Bass.

Thomas, D. (2004). Can a professional exist without a profession?: A response to Dunlop. *Journal of Child and Youth Work, 19,* 268–275.

Thompson, N. (2007). Using supervision. In R. Harrison, C. Benjamin, S. Curran, & R. Hunter (Eds.), *Leading work with young people* (pp. 156–176). London: Sage.

Thompson, S., & Thompson, N. (2008). *The critically reflective practitioner.* New York: Palgrave Macmillan.

Thumbadoo, Z. (2011). Isibindi: Love in caring with a Child and Youth Care approach. *Relational Child and Youth Care Practice, 24*(1/2), 193–198.

Tindall, T. A., & Black, D. (2008). *Peer programs: An in-depth look at peer programs-planning, implementation, and administration* (2nd ed.). New York: Routledge.

Tonmyr, L., Ouimet, C., & Ugnat, A-M. (2012). A review of findings from the Canadian Incidence Survey of Reported Child Abuse and Neglect (CIS). *Canadian Journal of Public Health, 103*(2), 103–112.

Traber, J. (1990). "Please draw me a sheep": My journey with child care. *Child and Youth Care Quarterly, 19*(2), 123–138. doi: 10.1007/BF01273354

Trieschman, A. E., Whittaker, J. K., & Brendtro, L. K. (Eds.). (1969). *The other 23 hours: Child care work with emotionally disturbed children in a therapeutic milieu.* New York: Aldine Publishing.

Tuckman, B. W. (2001). Developmental sequence in small groups. *Group Facilitation, 3,* 66–82. (Reprinted from Psychological Bulletin, 63(6), 384–399.)

UNESCO. (2003). *Conflict negotiation skills for youth.* Paris: Author.

Ungar, M. (2002). *Playing at being bad: The hidden resilience of troubled teens.* Toronto: University of Toronto Press.

Ungar, M. (2004). *Nurturing hidden resilience in troubled youth.* Toronto: University of Toronto Press.

Ungar, M. (2006). *Strengths-based counselling with at-risk youth.* Thousand Oaks, CA: Corwin Press.

Ungar, M. (2008). Putting resilience theory into action: Five principles. In L. Liebenberg & M. Ungar (Eds.), *Resilience in action: Working with youth across cultures and contexts* (pp. 17–36). Toronto: University of Toronto Press.

UNICEF. (n.d.). *The convention on the rights of the child.* Retrieved from www.unicef.org/crc/index_30177.html.

U.S. Department of Health and Human Services, Administration for Children and Families, Administration on Children, Youth and Families, Children's Bureau. (2011). *Child Maltreatment 2010.* Retrieved from www.acf.hhs.gov/programs/cb/stats_research/index.htm#can.

Vander Ven, K. (1990). From two years to two generations: Expanded career options in direct Child and Youth Care practice. In J. P. Anglin, C. J. Denholm, R. V. Ferguson, & A. R. Pence (Eds.), *Perspectives in professional Child and Youth Care* (pp. 331–345). Binghamton, NY: Haworth Press.

Vander Ven, K. (1991). How is Child and Youth Care work unique–and different–from other fields? *Journal of Child and Youth Care, 5*(1), 15–19.

Vander Ven, K. (1995). "Point and level systems": Another way to fail children and youth. *Child and Youth Care Forum, 24*(6), 345–367. doi: 10.1007/BF02128526

Vander Ven, K. (2003). Activity-oriented family-focused Child and Youth Work in group care: Integrating streams of thought into a river of progress. In T. Garfat (Ed.), *A Child and Youth Care approach to working with families* (pp. 131–147). New York: Haworth Press.

Vander Ven, K. (2004). Transforming the milieu and lives through the power of activity: Theory and practice. *Journal of Child and Youth Care, 19,* 103–108.

Vander Ven, K. (2006). Patterns of career development in Child and Youth Care. In L. C. Fulcher & F. Ainsworth (Eds.), *Group care practice with children and young people revisited* (pp. 231–255). Binghamton, NY: Haworth Press.

Veeran, V. (2011). Working towards a co-ordinated strategy for youth empowerment: The example of South Africa. *A Journal of Youth Work, 7,* 21–38. Retrieved from www.youthlinkscotland.org/Index.asp?MainID=9499.

Ward, A., & McMahon, L. (1998). *Intuition is not enough: Matching learning with practice in therapeutic child care.* London: Routledge.

Warner, J., & Griller, R. (2003). 'My Pappa is out, and my Mamma is asleep': Minors, their routine activities, and interpersonal violence in an early modern town, 1653–1781. *Journal of Social History, 36*(3), 561–585. doi: 10.1353/jsh.2003.0073

White, J. (2007). Knowing, doing and being in context: A praxis-oriented approach to Child and Youth Care. *Child and Youth Care Forum, 36*(5/6), 225–244. doi: 10.1007/s10566-007-9043-1

White, J. (2011). Re-storying professional ethics in Child and Youth Care: Toward more contextualized, reflexive, and generative practices. In A. Pence & J. White (Eds.), *Child and Youth Care: Critical perspectives on pedagogy, practice, and policy* (pp. 33–54). Vancouver: University of British Columbia Press.

Wood, M. M., & Long, N. (1991). *Life-space intervention: Talking with children and youth in crisis.* Austin, TX: Pro-Ed.

World Health Organization. (2009). *Violence prevention: The evidence. Preventing violence by developing life skills in children and adolescents.* Geneva: Author. Retrieved from whqlibdoc.who.int/publications/2009/9789241597838_eng.pdf.

Yates, S., Payne, M., & Dyson, S. (2009). Children and young people in hospitals: Doing youth work in medical settings. *Journal of Youth Studies, 12*(1), 77–92. doi: 10.1080/13676260802392965

INDEX